D0275199

ON THE ROAD
Reluctantly

ON THE ROAD
Reluctantly

Dream Catching in the Americas

Dyan Sheldon

LITTLE, BROWN AND COMPANY

The author would like to acknowledge her debt to
John Hemming's *Conquest of the Inca* for background information.

A *Little, Brown* Book

First published in Great Britain in 1995
by Little, Brown and Company

Copyright © Dyan Sheldon 1995

The moral right of the author has been asserted.

All rights reserved.
No part of this publication may be reproduced,
stored in a retrieval system or transmitted, in any
form or by any means, without the prior
permission in writing of the publisher, nor be
otherwise circulated in any form of binding or
cover other than that in which it is published and
without a similar condition including this
condition being imposed on the subsequent purchaser.

A CIP catalogue record for this book is
available from the British Library.

ISBN 0 316 91009 0

Typeset by M Rules
Printed and bound in Great Britain by
Clays Ltd, St. Ives plc

Little, Brown and Company (UK)
Brettenham House
Lancaster Place
London WC2E 7EN

For Riq

AUTHOR'S NOTE

Many things on this trip turned out to be other than imagined. Likewise, this book was supposed to be called *Dream Catching*, but it isn't.

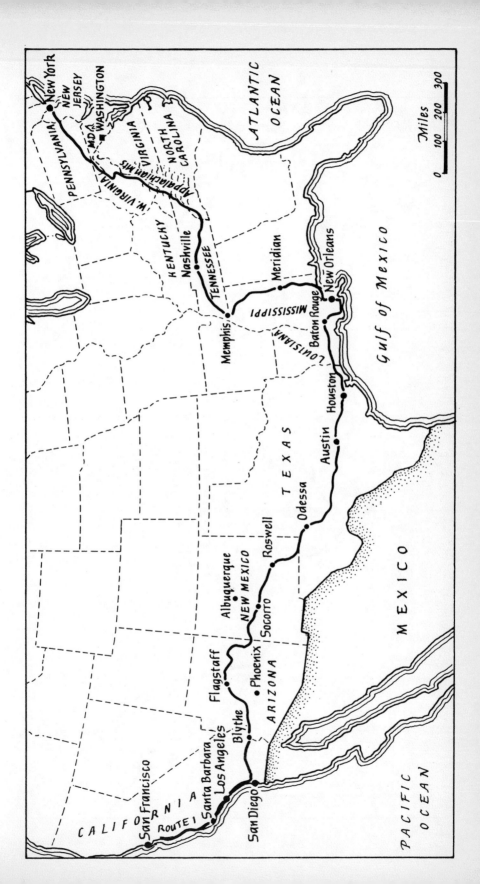

Caribbean Sea
Barranquilla
Cartagena
Mompós
PANAMA
VENEZUELA
Bucaramanga
Tunja
BOGOTA
COLOMBIA
Popayan
Pasto
Otavalo
QUITO
Tena
ECUADOR
Riobamba
Cuenca
P
Piura
Huancabamba
E
R
BRAZIL
Cajamarca
Trujillo
U
SOUTH
PACIFIC
OCEAN
LIMA
Cuzco
Pisco
Nazca
Puno
Lake
Titicaca
Arequipa
BOLIVIA

Miles
0   100   200   300   400   500

LAND OF DREAMERS

1

ARE THOSE ROCK-'N'-ROLL DREAMS IN YOUR EYES?

Some time in the heady years after the end of the Second World War, while the Soviet Union was making its plans and Europe was making its recovery, America invented paradise. The location of paradise was variable, but it was always white and electric, law-abiding and conservative, home to deserving families whose men were hardworking and steady, whose women were motherly and liked to bake, and whose children pledged their allegiance every morning and said their prayers before they went to sleep each night.

Paradise was where I was raised. It was green and leafy and located fifteen exits from New York City on the Long Island Expressway. Every house had a front lawn and a backyard, every garage had at least one car, every child had a bike, every family had a barbecue and a dog, the streets were safe and the schools were good. Saved from the filth, the violence and the squalor of the city, the people of paradise grew tomatoes, played cards, talked about crab grass and the Red Menace, and watched their children playing in the sun as though they were part of a margarine commercial.

What more could you want?

For most the answer was absolutely nothing. But even paradise had its discontents. Some of the sons and daughters of the pioneers of paradise didn't appreciate all the advantages they'd been given that their parents had never had. Instead of craving self-cleaning ovens and fridge-freezers, they craved romance and adventure. Instead of being happy playing bridge and spending their Saturdays washing the car, they wanted to sail down the Mississippi on a raft or work their way to Mexico. Instead of longing for magazine homes and sit-com families, they longed to take a steamer to Europe or a job in Hong Kong.

Sometimes even I thought about leaving paradise, though not with any real conviction. I was shy and unadventurous, and couldn't imagine a way out that didn't require a boldness and lack of fear that I always knew I didn't possess. I certainly never thought about trav-elling or setting off on my own for some unknown destination. Instead I stayed locked in my room, listening to the New York City stations on the radio, dreaming rock-'n'-roll dreams of fast cars and motorcycles screaming down endless highways under gigantic skies, and of young men in leather jackets who came from bad homes and died still innocent and wild.

And then we grew up.

I don't know how many of those suburban refugees ever got fur-ther than Miami or San Diego; how many did find themselves mysteriously transformed into their parents, washing the car on Saturdays or complaining about the price of chopped meat across the shopping carts, but I married a boy who didn't have a leather jacket, couldn't drive, and was as wild as a six-pack of Budweiser and a frozen Mexican dinner. Somehow, in leaving him, I'd wound up in London – and that was where I'd stayed.

The day I met Victor Ernesto David Sanchez was one of those uneventful, dank, dull, dreary winter days for which London is so justifiably renowned. A monochromatic day of grey rain falling on grey streets, and pale unsmiling people, hunched inside their rain-coats and under their umbrellas, hurrying to somewhere dry where they could grumble about the weather and have a cup of tea. The sort of day when, instead of working, you stare at the calendar of whale portraits that someone gave you for Christmas and imagine a small sailing ship crossing a jade-green ocean under a sky the colour of Colgate Gel, someone who might be you leaning into the wind, hair blowing. The sort of day when, instead of working, you tidy your desk three times, all the while thinking of the past with a vague and indeterminate feeling of regret. Maybe you should have taken that job in the Virgin Islands; gone on that blind date with the mer-cenary; moved to the stone cottage with no electricity or running water and a witch up the road. As another alternative to working, you go down to the basement and unpack a box that has been undis-turbed for the last two years, wondering how different things would have been if you'd been wilder and more reckless in your younger years, if you'd taken more chances, done more dares. You trim the brown tips off the spider plants, refill the sugar bowl, gaze into space, idly wondering what has happened to people you used to know, what happened to their dreams. England in February can make even the most tranquil soul a little restive.

Having run out of small chores, I go into the kitchen to make myself another cup of coffee, absentmindedly watching the people walking their Rottweilers and pitbulls on the estate behind my garden, dimly waiting for something to happen – dimly aware that I've been waiting for something to happen for quite a while.

The bell rings. I turn away from the window and towards the door. In a film or a novel, this would be that fateful something. In a film or a novel, the ring at the door would be an impossibly handsome and mysterious man with a bullet wound and somebody after him, or a psychopath with a bad attitude towards women, a sharp knife and an enormous, glad-to-see-you smile. Either way, my life would be radically changed. But I don't live in a film or a novel, I live in Camden. At the door is no renegade cop or serial killer; at the door is an alien and probably hostile visitor from a distant galaxy in ripped high strapped boots, torn leathers and a Darth Vader helmet, a radio attached to one shoulder like a mutant antenna. The courier who was on his way with my book proofs three hours before has arrived after all. I go to answer on the second ring.

'I'm having a bad day,' he tells me, in what I take to be an apology for the delay. Not only is it pissing down, he goes on, but the traffic is standing still. There were two security alerts, one in the West End and one in the City, and roads were blocked and the police out in force, a condition that makes him nervous. 'I hate cops,' says Victor. 'As much as this weather.' He had trouble finding his last job, and when he did find it, it turned out he'd been given the wrong packet and he'd had to go all the way back to Wapping for the right one. He came off the bike at Swiss Cottage and scraped his face. He's empty and will have to sit in the rain till another job comes up. As it's that sort of day, I invite him in for coffee and some TCP.

We sit in the kitchen. Victor studies the wall by the stove where the Do's and Don'ts for Foreigners notice someone sent me from Goa hangs. Don't tamper with your passport . . . Don't walk naked on the beach . . .

'Isn't that from India?' he asks.

I say that it is.

Victor has been to India. 'I saw this documentary,' he tells me. 'And after that I just had to go.' Victor is restless and unsure of what to do with his life. He loves to travel. Travel excites him, makes him feel free and alive. Victor thinks a lot about what winter in Ladahk is like or summer in Thailand. He wants to get on a train in some strange continent and get off whenever he feels like it, just to see what happens. He's going to South America in the autumn. Victor has wanted to walk the Inca trail to Machu Picchu since he was twelve.

I've never wanted to walk anywhere, never mind straight up a mountain on a pile of old rocks. I say that I know exactly what winter in Ladahk is like: pretty bloody cold. And I know what happens when you jump out of a train in the middle of the night, heading for some town whose name you can't pronounce: you're robbed; you get dysentery; strangers shoot at you or try to sell you drugs. I say that it seems to me that between the governments, the guerrillas and the drug wars, no one in their right mind would go to South America, not if they were fully committed to coming back.

Conversation shuffles awkwardly. I go to get him a towel.

When I come back, Victor is looking at the framed pictures on the far wall: Bruce Springsteen, Mick and Keith, Bob Dylan, Ray Davies, a Vincent Black Shadow, 1952 – the vestiges of my rock-'n'-roll dreams.

'Nice bike, that,' says Victor.

I admit to a small but inexplicably growing obsession with motorcycles. I'm not sure when it started or even how. The only time I've actually been on a motorcycle it wasn't a motorcycle but a scooter, and I fell off. Despite this bad start, motorcycles have begun to invade my consciousness. Pinned over my desk, besides the picture of the Vincent, there's a photograph of the Hell's Angels' headquarters, Manhattan Branch, that I don't remember taking. Motorcycles are also beginning to appear in my books, turning up where they might least be expected with what could almost be taken for regularity.

Victor says that if I want he'd be happy to take me for a ride on Monty the Maggot at the weekend. Monty's his CX500.

That, of course, is ridiculous.

'That's ridiculous,' I tell him. 'I'm well past the age when girls recklessly climb on behind some guy who does wheelies for fun.'

His expression is uncomprehending. 'Why else would you do wheelies?' he asks.

Part of my brain seems to think this a perfectly reasonable question and can't really find an answer – why would you? – but another
part doesn't consider it perfectly reasonable at all.

Victor smiles. 'Anyway, I promise no wheelies while you're on
the back.'

I don't answer. I'm too busy listening to that other part of my
brain. Remember Crazy Annie, Dyan? it is saying in a calm, sober,
toothpaste-ad voice. That's how she lost her leg.

'Really,' says Victor, misinterpreting my hesitation. 'I have nothing
else planned. Why don't you come?'

That's why Annie was crazy! the voice bangs on. Because she lost
her leg! She would've been all right if she'd stuck to cars. She would
have got married, had a family, lived a good life . . . It's shouting to
be heard, but at the same time it's growing fainter and fainter. In the
other part of my mind – the part that thinks it's perfectly reasonable
to do wheelies for fun – The Shangri-Las have begun to belt out
'Leader of the Pack'.

That's not why she was crazy, I inform the voice, aware that Victor
is still watching me, waiting for me to say yes. She was crazy because
she couldn't ride a bike any more.

The Shangri-Las step back and Richard Thompson picks up his
guitar and strikes the first chords of '1952 Vincent Black Lightning'.

You're not a kid any more, the voice is saying now. You're practically middle-aged. You ride your pushbike on the pavement.

All the home boys ride their bikes on the pavement, I argue. And
anyway, pushbikes are different.

Sure they are, it hisses. Pushbikes can't do 120.

But just at that moment Bruce Springsteen takes over from
Richard Thompson, suggesting that I strap my hands 'cross his
engine.

'Well?' prods Victor.

I open my mouth to say no.

'If you're sure it's okay,' I say, 'that'd be great.'

By the time Victor has decided that on his way to South America he
might as well ride a motorcycle from New York to California, Mr
Thompson, Mr Springsteen and The Shangri-Las have moved in
with me on a more or less permanent basis. Rrrmmm-Rrrmmm, I
join in as I mop out the flood in the basement. Baby, we were born
to run! I boom as I rub the cat hairs from the rug. And down to
Boxhill they did ride . . . I sing as I fight back the wistaria at the front

of the house. Every time a bike passes me on the street I turn to look. I find myself standing in newsagents', flipping through the biker magazines, trying to pick up the language. I buy a Sturgiss, South Dakota, T-shirt second hand in the market. I sign up for a motorcycle course. Somewhere along the line, I've changed my mind about Harley Davidsons, maybe they aren't so passé after all.

'Really?' I say. 'You're really going to drive across the States?' The old hippy dream.

'Sure,' says Victor with all the confidence of youth. 'Then go straight down through Mexico. It'll be excellent.'

A forgotten image of endless highways and a sky you could step into comes back to me. Springsteen is tuning up again. I block out the image and make Bruce shut up.

'I think you'd better watch *Easy Rider*,' I advise.

We watch *Easy Rider*. We both like it. The film is pretty boring and predictable, but the trip is great.

Victor glances over at me as Peter Fonda's bike rides into forever. 'You know, you could come with me,' he says slowly.

Am I already drunk? I put down my beer and turn to face him. 'Come where?'

'On the bike.' His voice is so normal and matter-of-fact that I think it's just that I didn't hear him right. He isn't suggesting that I ride across America on a motorcycle with him, he's suggesting that I go somewhere else with him – Brent Cross Shopping Centre, maybe, or to a film, or to a Mexican restaurant, or down the road to shoot some pool.

'On the bike?' I repeat.

'Sure,' he nods. 'You've never gone across the States, right?'

'Only in a plane.'

He grins. 'So come.'

Of course. You've never jumped from the roof of a forty-storey building? Hey, what are you waiting for? Grab hold of this hand.

'I can't do that,' I say, retrieving my drink. 'No, I really can't do that.'

'Why not?' he shrugs. 'What have you got to lose?'

Besides my life?

I stare back at him, young and rebellious, believing that life will keep all – or even some – of its promises, and looking, with his long hair, his nose ring, his tie-dyed T-shirt and his shredded jeans, like a government anti-drug poster, the telltale first signs.

'Because I can't,' I say. I don't live by myself in a squat, standing up for my ideals. I have a mortgage and a cat. I can't take off whenever I feel like it: I have commitments, responsibilities. I'm not a societal drop-out after all, I write children's books.

'But why not?' he persists. 'Because isn't a reason.' He takes my empty bottle from my hand. 'Maybe it'd be good for you. You know, bit of a change.'

A change, in my circles, is joining a gym or colouring your hair, not trying to cross the south-west on a 750 in a tornado.

I shake my head. 'No,' I say firmly. 'No, it's out of the question. I mean, it'd take weeks to get to California. And there's that desert, and Texas . . .' I give him a significant look. 'And your fondness for wheelies and certain controlled substances. Thanks for the offer, but I can't afford the time.'

'No drugs and no wheelies,' says Victor. 'I promise.' He gets up for two more beers. 'Think about it,' he says. 'Time runs away if you don't use it, you know.' He gives me a look over his shoulder. 'Think about going all the way to Peru.'

'You're out of your mind,' says my sister, Debbie. The connection to New Haven isn't a good one. She sounds as far away as she is, her voice unsteady and echoing, but there is no mistaking her tone. She sounds like my mother.

I answer calmly when the echo recedes. 'I didn't say I'd decided to go. All I said was I was thinking about it. You know, thinking about it. I'm allowed to think, aren't I?'

Apparently not.

'I told Jake I figured you'd finally gone completely mad,' my sister informs me. 'I said to Jake, "I don't know what's wrong with Dyan all of a sudden. She's talking about riding a motorcycle from America to Chile. Can you believe it? Chile! Do you think it's hormonal?"' There is a pause while she waits for the satellite to repeat this statement, distantly but indignantly.

'We wouldn't be going to Chile,' I explain patiently. 'I told you, we'd only be going as far as Peru.'

Her tone switches to one of exaggerated understanding. 'Oh, Peru, why didn't you say? That's different . . .' I can hear her smile. 'Peru's where they kill tourists, isn't it?'

'No,' I answer, still patient. 'That's Florida.'

'Ha ha,' says my sister. And then returns to her original theme. 'A motorcycle! A motorcycle to Peru! What the hell are you on? You haven't ridden a bicycle since you hit that bus.'

'That's not true,' I protest, keeping quiet about riding on the pavement. 'And anyway, I didn't hit the bus, the bus nearly hit me.' I'd signalled my turn and moved the front wheel and the handlebars left, as a good cyclist would, but instead of everything following as it should have done, my bike chose that moment to fold in two. It was a tricky situation. The bus braked sharply, there was a wailing of horns, a woman screamed. The bike and I walked home.

'Stop being so pedantic,' she orders. 'You know what I mean. How do you expect to travel for months on a motorcycle? A motorcycle isn't like riding in a car, you know. You're right out there, getting saddle-sores, inhaling toxic fumes, being soaked and frozen and run off the road and shot at by guys in pick-ups. And that's assuming, of course, that you don't wind up as highway pizza.'

'For Christ's sake . . .' I groan.

'James Dean,' says Debbie.

'That was a car.'

'Greg Allman,' she counters. 'Berry Oakley.'

'Lucille Ball,' I challenge. 'Doris Steuben.'

Doris Steuben catches her attention. 'Who the hell is Doris Steuben?'

'They found her sitting on the sofa in her council flat with a teacup still in her hand. She'd been dead for a week. Heart attack.'

'Stop trying to change the subject,' orders my sister. 'Do you have any idea how dangerous motorcycles are? Are you aware of the statistics? Jake's brother used to have a Harley and he nearly killed himself on it.'

And I'd nearly killed myself riding down the high street on a dark blue folding bike, City Sprite, lightweight, convenient, practical, ideal for town or country use.

'I'm not actually going to do the driving,' I tell her again. 'I'm just going to sit on the back and look at the scenery.'

'With flies up your nostrils,' says my sister. Something beeps. Her tone sharpens. 'You're not a kid any more,' she informs me. 'Nineteen-year-olds do road trips. Hippies. Gypsies. Guys with tattoos and earrings and switchblades in their boots. Not single, middle-class female novelists who live with a cat.' And then she adds, unnecessarily and pettily – another conversational technique she's learned from our mother – 'You're too old.'

'I'm not middle-class,' I answer coolly. 'I don't even own an electric kettle. I wear six earrings and a leather jacket.'

Two cynical laughs roll through the abyss that lies between

Connecticut and Camden. 'Jake thinks you're having a mid-life crisis,' announces my sister.

'Is he going to charge me for this diagnosis?'

I am about to go on to say that I don't really care what my brother-in-law thinks, that knowing him has done nothing to raise my opinion of psychoanalysts, but she cuts me off. 'So do I,' says my sister.

Echoes, beeps and static notwithstanding, her 'So do I' has the weight of a divine pronouncement. God peering over the clouds, leaning on one elbow. The Holy Spirit thinks you're hiding something, He says to Adam. And so do I.

'I'm doing a little travelling, not buying a Jaguar or shooting up McDonald's,' I remind her. 'Millions of people travel all the time. You and Dr Wisdom travel. I never go anywhere. Last year you guys went to Maine *and* Rome.'

'Not on a motorcycle,' says my sister. 'And anyway, we invited you to come with us to both places but, if you'll cast your mind back, you wouldn't come. Although you seem to have wiped this one little detail from your memory, you don't like to travel. You said wanting to travel was like having spiritual diarrhoea. You said you didn't like to get too close to nature. You said you couldn't stand tourists or churches.' She ploughs through the echo. 'You do realise that they speak Spanish in South America, don't you?' she asks.

'I speak Spanish,' I remind her.

'Being able to read the haemorrhoid ads on the New York subway isn't the same as speaking Spanish,' says my sister. 'And let's not forget the time you left Tampa early because of the heat and the lizards.' She raises her voice. 'They have heat and lizards in Peru, you know. And bananas.' Trust her to remember I hate bananas. She is talking so fast there seems to be two of her. 'Not to mention terrorists,' she finishes.

'We have terrorists in London,' I answer, feeling that at last I have right and reason on my side. 'The place is crawling with them.'

'In that case,' says my sister, 'you might as well stay home.'

I think some more about the trip. A lot of what my sister said was no more than the hysterical exaggeration of someone who has never forgiven you for killing her goldfish, but not everything. It is true that I don't care for travel. It is equally true that I have always preferred to keep nature at a distance, viewable but behaved and not too gooey or bloody. It is also true that I would rather stay in the kitchen for the rest of my life, scraping the limescale off the tap, than be a tourist; that I find looking at old churches less interesting than scraping the limescale off the tap. And it is true that if the discovery of the Americas had been left up to me, the Sioux would still be hunting the plains, the Aztecs would still be cutting out hearts, and the rivers would still be clean.

Only now I seem to be changing my mind.

I discuss this with Elvis, my cat.

'I guess I've just never really seen the point in travel before,' I confide. 'You know, people talk about lying awake, listening to passing trains, wondering where they're going, picturing their own faces pressed against the window as they hurtle through the night, but I never did.'

Elvis knows. He stretches across my lap and turns his head to be scratched. *Me neither.*

'I never see a plane overhead and wish I were on it,' I tell him. 'I'm not overcome with a dull longing every time I glimpse a ship out at sea.'

Elvis closes his eyes. He hides whenever his basket reappears from the basement. *I couldn't agree with you more.*

But. But there is no one who has never felt the pull of the unknown. The lure of what might be. The longing for free-fall.

'The important thing is that an opportunity like this isn't going to come along again, is it? I mean, the chances of another biker coming to the door and offering to travel from New York to Lima with me are pretty slim. Not impossible, maybe, but slim.'

One ear moves ever so slightly. *What's the difference if you don't want to go?*

'That's just the point,' I say warmly. 'Maybe, deep down, I do want to go.' I look around the room, untidily crammed with possessions and reassuringly familiar. Outside, the rain falls greyly. 'Not because I have this sudden desire to see the world,' I assure him. 'Good Lord, it's nothing like that. It's just that . . . well . . . I can't stop thinking about what will happen if I don't go.'

His tail hits my arm. *You mean besides living to see 1994?*

But it's a rhetorical question. In my heart, I know exactly what will happen if I don't go: nothing will happen. I'll finish another book, I'll watch some videos, I'll go out to dinner. On Friday nights I'll do my shopping, made happy by a three for one offer on sun-dried tomatoes or wholewheat pasta. On Saturdays I'll take the bottles down to the bottle bank and buy cheap vegetables on Seven Sisters Road.

Every couple of months an editor will invite me to lunch, and I'll go because it's a free meal. Some time during those months, someone might even invite me to a party, and I won't go because I hate parties. The clocks will go back. The dentist will send me a reminder that my six-month check-up is due. Hallowe'en will come. The holiday lights will go up around the city. Christmas will be over. A new year will arrive. Before I know it, it'll be February again. No, my life definitely isn't a film or a novel, it's a calendar.

Elvis rolls on his side. *Who needs things to happen?*

Unexpectedly – belatedly, even – it seems that I do.

'Let's look at it realistically, okay?' I suggest. 'If you really think about it, why shouldn't I go? I mean, Vic's right, I have nothing to lose. It's like buying a lottery ticket. Probably you won't win the jackpot, but maybe you will. Or maybe you'll win a little. Or maybe, on the way to buy the ticket, you'll save someone from being mugged or hit by a bus.' I pause, a little surprised that I feel like this and hadn't known it. 'I've always been steady and responsible,' I go on. 'I work hard. I'm reliable. I've never even bounced a cheque or had an adulterous affair. Other people do. Other people dance till dawn and drive their cars into swimming pools. But I've never done anything like that.'

Elvis twitches.

'After all, four months isn't forever, is it?' I inquire, not without passion. 'Four months is nothing. People go away for years. Four months is like not being away at all.'

Tiny claws, sharp as knives, grip my thigh. *But what about me?*

Victor says that Elvis will survive perfectly well without me. He says the flat and the plants and my agent will all survive, too. He says having to be around to pay the service contract on the gas heater isn't a valid reason for not seeing Cartagena. He says the council tax will wait for me, I don't have to wait for it. Victor says that if the worst does come to the worst, and the cat dies and the flat burns down and my agent dumps me, then I can keep on going and never come back.

'Maybe you are right,' I say to Elvis, thinking about never coming back. 'I mean, I've never been a sucker for romance and adventure, have I? I've never had a restless heart. Why start now when my life's finally got a little stability and security?'

He retracts his claws. *Why indeed?*

'Maybe my sister's right,' I muse. 'Maybe I am having a mid-life crisis.' I can hear a CX500 coming up the road. 'Maybe I'm trying to recapture my lost youth,' I say, not really listening to myself. Instead I'm remembering that most of my lost youth was spent in my room, walled in by suburban dreams. It hardly seems worth recapturing.

I turn to watch the bike pass in a cloud of rain.

My sister, whose phone calls to London are usually limited to my birthday and Christmas, rings me back. My mother is worried about me, says my sister. My mother thinks I've lost my mind.

'She can't understand why you're doing this,' says Debbie. My mother thinks that this is what happens when you never marry and settle down, when you have nothing.

'Nothing?' I snap. 'What does she mean "nothing"? I have a flat, I have a cat, if I pass my test I'll have a motorcycle.'

Flats and cats and motorcycles, however, are not on paradise's inventory.

Nothing. Just some crazy idea of gallivanting around the world on the back of a motorcycle.

'She says her heart fluttered when I told her what you were doing,' my sister continues. 'She said to tell you they have witches in Peru.'

'Tell her they have witches in Hastings.'

'She's more concerned about this man,' says my sister, sounding as though she probably is too. 'She says it never works out when unmarried couples travel together.'

'We're not a couple,' I remind her. 'We're friends.'

'But you don't really know anything about him, do you?' asks Debbie.

'I know I like him,' I answer evenly.

'That and a nickel will get you on the subway,' says my sister, which is exactly what my mother would say.

I try again. 'I know he's sane, intelligent and has a good sense of humour,' I say, trying to list the most important traits. 'He's not bossy or petty, he's kind and considerate, and I've never seen him be unfair or lose his temper.'

My sister laughs. 'Don't worry,' she says. 'You will.'

My mother, when it was explained to her that Victor was a motorcycle courier, thought that made him some sort of mailman. My friend Greg, however, doesn't think that being a motorcycle courier is anything like being a mailman. He thinks it's kind of like being a Hell's Angel, only wired for sound. And he should know, says Greg, running an advertising agency, he deals with them all the time. Usually from behind a raised chair, it would seem.

'With Hell's Angels?' I take a largish swig of wine.

He smiles sourly. 'Attitude,' says Greg. He eyes me sternly. 'That's what you get from couriers,' he informs me warmly. 'Attitude. Attitude and a hard time. Most of them aren't even house-broken.' He points a bread stick at me. 'Already he's changing you,' Greg warns. 'I can already see the first signs. Sarcasm. Defensiveness. Contempt for the Establishment. The blood's on the saddle and the grease stains are on the wall. He's going to turn you hard and cold.' He bites into the bread-stick. 'If by some miracle you do come back, your best friends won't even know you.'

I pour the rest of the bottle into my glass. 'I haven't said I'll go yet. I'm just thinking about it.'

'Well, stop,' says Greg. 'Put the whole thing out of your head right this minute.' He goes on opening my eyes about motorcycle despatch riders while I finish the Chianti. Couriers, according to Gregory Malanga, are tattooed hulks, dirty and ill-kempt, with lousy personalities and chips on their shoulders. The way they ride proves that they're morally irresponsible and pathologically careless about life as well as death. A courier, says Greg, is not the kind of person to whom you would willingly entrust your safety and wellbeing in countries where there's no one else to trust with those things.

'You're completely off the wall as usual,' I say when he finally runs down. 'Vic isn't anything like that. He's into t'ai chi and macro-biotic food and his hair is very well cared for.'

Greg's eyes take on a calculating, what's-the-hidden-agenda-here? look. 'How long?'

I touch the middle of my back.

He flinches. 'And curtain hooks in his ears?'

I shake my head. 'Just the nose ring.'

'Jesus,' groans Greg, 'it's worse than I thought. He's a hippy. You're going to Bolivia with some drug-crazed hippy none of your friends have ever met.' He picks up his wine glass, realises it's empty, and puts it back down.

'We're not going to Bolivia,' I say to the back of his head as he twists round in search of the waiter. 'We're only going as far as Peru.'

Greg waves one hand at me and one at the waiter. The one he waves at the waiter contains an empty wine bottle; the one he waves at me suggests that I don't know what I'm talking about. 'Bolivia . . . Peru . . . what's the difference? All those countries are exactly the same. Bad cops, bad roads, bad sanitation, bad fauna and bad food. If the Shining Path doesn't kill you, lunch probably will.'

'We're not just going to South America, you know,' I say a little loudly for the restrained ambience of Greg's favourite restaurant. 'If I go, we're doing the States, too.'

He turns back as the waiter begins to approach with a new bottle. 'I can't tell you what a relief that is to me,' says Greg. 'I was really worried, thinking you were only visiting the lawless, backward, life-is-cheap Third World. What a comfort to know that you'll be spending time in the lap of civilisation as well.' He leans back in his chair. 'We are talking about the same United States, aren't we?' he asks cheerfully. 'Birthplace of drive-by murders and snuff movies? The United States where everybody has a gun and half the youth is on drugs? The one whose woods are filled with Vietnam vets who can never rejoin society and where the ultra-right has secret bunkers of arms and ammunition to use against the blacks should they decide to take over? That United States?'

'Yes,' I say, wishing the waiter would hurry. 'That's the one.'

'Maybe you should plan a bigger trip,' says Greg. 'You don't want to miss anything really interesting, do you? What about Bosnia? Beirut? Somalia? Burma?'

'Next time I'll go the other way,' I promise.

Greg leans earnestly towards me over the single white carnation in the plain glass vase and the bread-stick debris. 'You can't do this,' he says, sounding serious. 'It's too dangerous. Even if you were going with someone reputable and responsible and not some drop-out with a bone through his nose, it would be dangerous. You're not up to it.' He grabs my hand. 'As one of your oldest and dearest friends, I'm forbidding you to do this.'

'I haven't said I am doing it yet,' I remind him again. 'I just said I'm thinking about it.'

'Think about something else,' advises Greg. 'Buying a time-share in Ibiza, for instance, or dyeing your hair.'

I can't think about anything else.

I walk into the bathroom, toilet-bowl cleaner on my mind, and then I suddenly stop in the doorway, staring at the spider crawling up the side of the tub, wondering just how big the lizards in South America really are. I'm working at the computer, my mind on plot and characterisation, and all at once I find myself trying to picture two months from now, and whether I'm still at my desk, wondering where Victor is, or whether someone else is sitting there, wondering about me. I stand at bus stops, trying to imagine the 134, colourful as a canal boat, with chickens on the roof. In the supermarket I buy coffee from Colombia, beans from Ecuador and rice from Peru. Not that thinking about it has brought me any closer to making up my mind. Whenever anyone mentions the foreseeable future – as in, 'Fancy doing some walking this autumn?' or 'Know what you're doing for Christmas yet?' – I leave the room or change the subject, afraid to find out what I'm going to say.

Just in case, though, I ask my friend Judy if she'd look after Elvis if I go away.

'Sure,' says Judy. 'And they can use my address when they ship your body back.'

I'm still thinking as I come home from the dentist on the number 27. There are no chickens on the roof, but upstairs a young man is standing at the front, lecturing on Jesus while he flips through a Bible and the other passengers pretend not to hear him. I'm downstairs, surrounded by tired-looking people in dark-coloured clothes. There's a little conversation about the weather, Marks & Spencer's ready-made meals, the recession, fitted cupboards and *Coronation Street*, but on the whole the downstairs is quiet, most of us dozing or reading the paper or wondering what to fix for supper.

The bus is passing Regent's Park, inching forward in the rush-hour traffic. Horns are honking on the Euston Road. There are a few grumbles about the slowness of the bus, and upstairs someone shouts at the young man with the Bible, 'Why don't you just fuck off, mate?' And then I hear it: RrrmmmRrrmmmRrrmmm. I glance to the right. There's a flash of colours as a CX500 comes out of Park Place on one wheel. It's Victor. I turn in my seat to watch him tear towards Baker Street.

The woman beside me follows my gaze. 'They're crazy, those couriers,' she informs me with assurance. 'Menaces. They don't retire, that lot, they all die young. Fancy anybody being mad enough to get on one of those things.'

She's right, it's madness. I think about my flat and deadlines and about being thirteen and believing that things will happen if only you wait long enough. I glance around at my fellow travellers, see-ing us all hunched in our seats, bored and worn out and looking as if we wished that everyone would fuck off. Couriers aren't the only ones who die young.

'They don't have the sense they were born with,' my companion elaborates. 'My husband says they should all be put in jail.'

I'm not really listening. Music is playing in my head. This time, though, it isn't Bruce, Richard or even The Shangri-Las. This time it's Canned Heat doing 'On the Road Again'.

2

TALKIN' NEW YORK CITY BLUES

We've had a bad day. New York may be a twenty-four-hour city, a place where you can get anything your heart desires, from stuffed artichokes to a masquerade orgy, but it isn't, it seems, a place where you can by a cheap second-hand motorcycle, helmets, a top box and saddlebags ready to travel to Peru.

Carefully stepping around the beggars with their open hands and empty cardboard coffee cups who are lined along the stairs, Victor and I make our way down into the subway.

Though it's nothing we've admitted to each other, discouragement has settled over us like soot. And at least one of us is starting to worry. In less than a week it'll be October, when the frost starts to appear on the compact cars and pumpkins of America – and on her roads and campgrounds, too. If we have to wait too long we'll miss our chance.

'We'll buy a bike in New York,' we'd told everyone, much as the Iroquois might once have said, 'We'll just wait till these white guys go back home.'

We'd thought buying a motorcycle and equipment would be as easy as buying a bagel or a scope-mount for your rifle, but so far we've been looking for four days and have come up with nothing. Nothing in the papers, nothing in the Yellow Pages, nothing on the streets. We ask in newsagents', we ask in garages, we ask the few bikers we come upon – we even ask Virgil, the guy who sells origami flowers on Seventh Avenue, to keep an eye out for us, but so far we've had no luck. In London old motorcycles are everywhere; in

New York the bikes are few, new and only come out on the weekends.

'I can't believe that wanker,' says Victor, pushing through the turnstile. He imitates the bored, condescending voice of the salesman in the store we've just marched out of with a certain amount of indignation. '"We don't sell anything that cheap . . . We don't carry top boxes . . . Buying a used helmet's like buying used underwear . . . And just how are you planning to get across the Rockies?"' He steps over an empty wine bottle in a brown paper bag. 'Jesus. We're going to walk them on our hands – what does he think?'

I tug him towards the downtown entrance. 'What I can't believe is the cops.' Every motorcycle store we went to today had a policeman in it. 'They're supposed to be in coffee shops eating donuts, not sitting around bullshitting about bikes.'

'See what I mean about cops?' says Victor. 'They're even unreliable.'

We come to a stop at the platform's edge. 'This is the station where that tourist was killed a couple of summers ago,' I tell him, taking up my position as guide.

See New York and die. He glances around. We're staying in Brooklyn with Tommi and Jack, my daughter and her boyfriend. There's a well-posted scenic overlook at our Brooklyn station, a six-foot Kodachrome photograph of a tree-covered mountain under God's blue sky, a reminder that the whole country isn't concrete and posters for movies and empty whisky bottles full of piss, but there's nothing like that here. The platform looks and smells like a very large urinal whose attendant died two months ago. It isn't the place you would necessarily choose to be your last sight of earth.

'That's why I'm glad I'm with you,' says Victor. 'You know all the really interesting spots.'

'I do try to concentrate on what's really important,' I admit modestly. 'I want visitors to see what makes New York New York.'

My tour of the city, though not recognised by the Department of Tourism, is a tour of love. We browse through the crammed shops of Chinatown, looking for Christmas cards in Cantonese. We battle through the packed sidewalks of Canal Street, steeling ourselves against the alluring array of goods on offer – crawling GI Joes, gold medallions big as a baby's fist, coloured electric tape and cheap tools, hot cassettes, batteries and telephones. We stroll across the Bowery and up Broadway to the best discount store in the universe, past the tables of jewellery, sunglasses and hats, past the food vendors selling sugared nuts, soft pretzels, sausages, and kebabs, the South American Indians selling sweaters, and the Black Muslims selling incense and oils. We explore the Lower East Side, take a spin around Little Ricky's, the original Elvis and God store, maybe have lunch at that great Jewish deli on Second or at my favourite restaurant on Spring Street, the only one in New York damaged in the LA riots. We visit the Village – Bleeker Street, full of out-of-towners being hip, and Washington Square, full of out-of-towners being hip and guys selling them drugs while the cops wind through the crowds on horses and motor scooters, the bird store where the cats sleep in the windows, the West Side docks, famous for sex and fireworks. We ignore the homeless and admire the ceiling in Grand Central Station, with more stars than the sky over Manhattan. We wander through Toys Я Us, getting lost in aisles of Barbie dolls and small arms, little girls crying for miniature prom gowns in Spanish and little boys mowing each other down. Uptown, it's the Sheep Meadow, where everyone too hip to buy drugs in Washington Square buys drugs, and the Fairway supermarket, so famous for its fresh vegetables and deli that people journey all the way from the East Side just to buy cheese and tomatoes and olives in oil, and the bar Castro frequented when he attended Columbia. If it's summer I usually include a Sunday afternoon in Riverside Park, just sitting on a bench, watching the Latino families drinking beer and playing cards and blasting their radios, and the white people in their designer sportswear jogging and running and walking their dogs, wondering what Peter Stuyvesant would make of it all.

I want to show Victor all the things I like best in New York – the Staten Island ferry, the clam house where Joey Gallo was hit, the Mosaic Mile in the East Village where a local resident has plastered the streetlamp-poles with broken glass and china, the way the lights at the top of the Empire State Building change on special occasions (red and green for Christmas, pink for Gay Pride Day, red, white and blue for the Fourth of July) – but we don't have the time for that now; we have our priorities.

I give him a nudge. A woman in a grey coat leans against a pillar further down the track, crying silently, almost casually, as though there is nothing else left to do. I know how she feels. So does Victor.

'I bet she's been trying to buy a motorcycle,' he says

We go back to staring at the puddles of urine and discarded wrappers between the rails.

'What'll we do if we don't find anything?' I ask finally.

'We will,' says Victor.

Just in case we don't, though, I have a suggestion. 'You know, we could get one of those deals where you drive somebody's car across and all you have to pay for is the gas.'

'We won't have to,' says Victor. 'We'll get a bike.'

The mice are scattering and the other passengers are closing in around us.

I have another suggestion. 'There's always Greyhound,' I go on. 'Everybody says the bus is a real experience.' Not a good one, necessarily, but not one you forget fast, either.

'So is a bike,' shouts Victor as the train pulls in.

I still get a pang whenever I see a subway train. It's true that now that they're graffiti-free, riding in them isn't as incidentally terrifying as it used to be when you couldn't see out of the windows because of all the paint and pilot marker covering the glass, but it's also true that they've lost quite a bit of their charm. Now the trains just look like trains. I'd give a lot to see one roll in with Dondi's Happy Birthday Mom! sprayed across the side.

'Don't worry,' Victor assures me with his usual confidence as the doors open in front of him, 'we'll get one,' and steps inside before I can say but what if we don't?

The subway car is full but not crowded. Crowded is when you aren't actively worried about being attacked because there isn't enough room for someone to wield a knife or snatch your bag. Full is when there are so many people in the car that were someone to stab you or grab your purse you wouldn't be able to get out of the way or give pursuit. We take the last two seats, near the door, the subway equivalent of the suicide seat; that's where the muggers get you as they're leaving the train.

Victor immediately starts reading the cardboard signs that run above the windows: ads for cosmetic surgery, credit for people who can't get credit, mortgages for people who can't get mortgages, and teeth for people who can't afford teeth, a story about a girl whose boyfriend won't use a condom, and a poem by Emily Dickinson, 'The Mob Within the Heart Police Cannot Suppress'. Only the poem is in English. I'm not sure if Victor's absorption in the deathless prose of the Metropolitan Transit Authority is because he's remembered the first rule of Metropolitan Transit travel – always have something to look at that isn't alive – or because he doesn't want to talk about not finding a bike before Texas is buried in snow. I study the flyer glued to the window in front of me, Tired of Losing? Sister Ashya Will Put

You in Touch with God and Your True Destiny, and for only ten bucks. For another ten, you can Learn Your Future, Control Your Life, and Find Out How to Make Money and Be a Success.

The woman across from us is eating a pint of Dutch ice-cream, made in New Jersey, with a white plastic spoon, but except for her and a group of very large schoolgirls with stiffened hair and over-sized gold earrings out of a conquistador's dream, all of the other passengers have their eyes closed, on a book or on the floor. No one is talking but the girls, who are having a loud discussion about someone named Marshalene who thinks her boyfriend's going to marry her when he gets out of the navy, but who, it would seem, has a bigger chance of waking up white.

The train stops at Fifty-ninth Street, where four Peruvian musicians in black hats and red ponchos are playing a lonesome song on the platform and a man in rags is going through the garbage. At Thirty-fourth Street the guy with the shopping cart full of flowers who got on at Columbus Circle gets off and is replaced by a man selling cheap wind-up toys. He gets off at Twenty-third and a tall, thin man, hunched inside his too-small clothes, passes through the car, dropping a hand-cut piece of pink paper on the lap of anyone not fast enough to stop him: I am a deaf mute, please help me, and hello, goodbye and the numbers one to ten in sign language. At Fourteenth Street he leaves and another man whose clothes don't fit him gets on, positioning himself in the centre of the car.

'Good afternoon, ladies and gentlemen,' he says in the voice of a lawyer addressing the jury. No one looks at him. 'My name is Bob and I'm a Vietnam vet.' The Vietnam vet on the train we took uptown earlier was Buddy, and he had AIDS.

Bob was proud to fight for his country. 'I volunteered when I was nineteen,' says Bob. 'Only things didn't turn out how I planned.' He doesn't look like the only one in the car who could say this, but he does seem to be the only one here at the moment who is homeless and on methadone. Bob doesn't want to turn to crime and violence to survive; he believes in the Lord and in human kindness. Not everything that happened to Bob is his fault. Bob is doing the best he can. 'What more can I do?' he wants to know. 'What more can any man do?' None of us has an answer to that. Bob would appreciate it if we could find it in our hearts to help him out. He thanks us for listening and asks God to bless us. There's still no one looking at him.

Bob and Victor and I all change at West Fourth.

Tommi lives in a landmark neighbourhood of rows of restored

Victorian townhouses on broad, tree-lined, gas-lit streets. Though small, it has four expensive gift shops, three frozen-yoghurt stores, two healthfood stores, a Japanese, three Mexican, six Italian and twelve Chinese restaurants, one fortune-teller over the largest of the ten Korean delis, six nail salons, and an almost all-black high school with a sign on its front door that warns that firearms are prohibited inside city buildings. In front of the toy store with the bubble-blowing bear outside is a streetlamp decorated with ribbons and flowers for the girl killed there one summer by a runaway car.

Surrounding Tommi's neighbourhood are less elegant neighbour-hoods – pockets of working-class Irish and Italians, slums and barrios where the cautious might hesitate before stopping for directions – but they seem far away. Even further away, Brooklyn becomes remorselessly suburban, home to people with statues of the Virgin wreathed in Christmas lights on their lawns and flags on their porches who would sooner go to Maine than into Manhattan, but where Tommi lives the inhabitants are sophisticated, middle-class New Yorkers who feel about their therapists the way the rest of the country feels about God, and who see those other Brooklyns only when they get lost on their way somewhere else.

'But it's so much cheaper,' I'm saying as we emerge from the train on Seventh Avenue. 'We save a dollar on the coffee alone.' We're discussing where to go for food, the supermarket down in the barrio or the one that's more expensive but closer to home. 'And they accept USDA food stamps.'

Victor leads the way up the stairs. 'We don't have USDA food stamps. And besides that it's miles away.'

'Three blocks.'

There are two transit cops standing in front of the scenic over-look, debating whether it's a photograph of Washington or Maine. One of them nods to Victor as we pass by.

'Three long blocks,' says Victor, nodding back. 'I'm too knackered to walk that far.'

At the far end of the station, Virgil sits on a folding chair next to his table of paper flowers. The police must have moved him off the street. 'Yo, England!' he calls when he spots us. 'Any luck with the bike?'

In London it's rare enough to speak to your neighbours, but in New York everyone who isn't actively trying to harm you is your friend.

Victor is optimistic. 'Not yet,' he says.

Virgil is optimistic, too. 'Don't you worry, man. There's a bike out there with your name on it. You'll find her.'

I am less optimistic. 'Maybe we won't.'

We rise out of the ground and into twilight on Seventh Avenue. If it were summer, whole families would be out on the sidewalks, sitting in folding chairs and drinking beer and Diet Coke while they listened to the radio, but now it's autumn and Brooklyn is preparing for All Hallows Eve. The air is cool and crisp, and pumpkins and apple cider have already appeared next to the dyed flowers and fruit on the stalls that extend from the Korean delis. There are skeletons and jack-o'-lanterns in every shop front window, and soon the lights on the Empire State Building will be orange. A large truck goes by, two boys on bikes holding on to either side, taking a ride.

'I wonder where we'll be for Hallowe'en,' muses Victor as we head towards the supermarket.

I don't say 'Here.'

At the church next to D'Agostino's, Johnno, the neighbourhood's favourite homeless vet, sits slumped in the doorway, his cup on its side at his feet, his eyes rolling back in his head, too gone tonight to remember 'Nam or to ask for money. In front of the supermarket itself, the other street guys are solemnly sorting out the cans and bottles they've collected for their refundable NY deposits, Budweiser in one bag, Miller in another, Pepsi and Coke as separate in death as they are in life. Only Johnno, Johnno's girlfriend, Rosie, and Johnno's buddy, the transvestite who dresses like Diana Ross, beg on this stretch of Seventh. Everyone has rules.

'I'll pay for the tortilla chips if you pay for the video,' says Victor as we stride through the automatic door.

It's that time of the evening when the peasants return from the fields – and the professionals from the offices of Manhattan. D'Agostino's is crowded. There's a queue of men in good suits and trenchcoats at the cash machine. They watch us like store detectives as we pick up a basket and a flyer of coupons and this week's specials. We buy little that isn't on sale.

'Jesus,' says Victor. 'I feel like I'm in an episode of LA Law.'

'No you don't,' I say, following his heels as I start tearing out coupons. 'If you were in an episode of LA Law you'd be in jail.'

There are more lawyers in Fresh Produce, where the greens and herbs are misted with water and kept on ice, and where the tomatoes are $2.99 a pound. 'Who needs a gun to commit robbery?' Victor wants to know. One of the lawyers looks over at him from behind a bunch of broccoli. 'Not this place,' he says.

We spend ten minutes selecting a loaf of bread – challah? sprouted wheat? wheat berry? pumpernickel with raisins? farmhouse white? sourdough? Bavarian rye? Latvian rye? black with walnuts? crusty Italian or soft? – and another ten searching for a coffee that isn't the flavour of a spice, a liquor or a nut. 'What is it with these people?' asks Victor. 'Whatever happened to just plain coffee?'

We move on to the deli counter, squeezing in between the weary-looking mothers whose children all carry Jurassic Park backpacks and have a preference for strawberry cream cheese and salmon pâté. Whatever happened to peanut butter and jelly?

'You pick,' Victor says when it's finally our turn. 'I'm exhausted from the bread.'

I pick cheddar. I'm exhausted, too.

'What about lentil soup?' I ask as we make our way past the musicians and teachers poking through the meat cases. 'It's two for a dollar with the coupon.'

He holds up the basket. 'Lead the way.'

I lead, but the way to Frozen Foods is blocked by a young couple standing in front of the snack section, each of them holding a bag of potato chips. He's large. His Christmas-red hair is spiked and he's dressed in a ragged flannel shirt, jeans and a torn leather jacket covered with safety pins, studs and chains, his ears edged with rings. He looks like a threat. She's small. Her hair is short as a marine's and dark blue and she's wearing black leggings and a black sweatshirt, her eyes rimmed with kohl. She looks like Peter Pan on drugs.

They turn as we approach.

'Hi,' says Tommi.

'Greetings,' says Jack.

'What's up?' asks Victor.

'Decisions,' says Tommi. She sighs. 'God should never have given us free will.'

'What do you think?' asks Jack. He points the bag in his hand at the bag in Tommi's. 'Kansas barbecue or sea salt and onion?'

Victor, the man who can't choose cheese, smiles. 'Depends what you like, doesn't it?'

Jack makes a face. 'I like them both.'

'It's Friday,' I say. 'Buy them both.'

Tommi whistles, causing several heads to swivel. 'A wild woman!' she shrieks, throwing an arm around my shoulder. She has never called me a wild woman before. She's always called me Mom. 'Go for it, girl!'

Jack is frowning. 'Then maybe we should get the mesquite instead of the sea salt'.

Eventually, the four of us and three bags of chips shuffle towards a register together.

'You guys are back late,' says Jack. 'Any luck?'

Victor starts telling Jack about our trouble finding a bike and Tommi starts telling me about their landlord, Hopeless Harry.

'It's because of the divorce,' Tommi says. She stops beside a man earnestly reading cereal boxes. 'Don't worry about it,' she advises him. 'They're all the same.' She starts walking again. 'Harry was fine till the court gave Mrs Harry the building,' she continues to me. 'It threw him into total denial. He holed up in that empty apartment on the top floor and Mrs Harry's boyfriend chased him out with a baseball bat.' She blows a green bubble. 'The cops came and everything.'

We get into the shortest queue. We're the only ones who don't have at least two litres of Diet Coke in their baskets.

Like sailors being lured to the rocks by the cries of sirens, my eyes are irresistibly drawn to the magazine racks by the checkout. TEN-YEAR-OLD GIRL GIVES BIRTH TO HER OWN GRANDMOTHER . . . EXCLUSIVE INTERVIEW WITH ELVIS: I COULD NEVER GO BACK TO MEMPHIS NOW . . . BURT REYNOLDS' SECRET SORROW . . . MICHAEL LANDERS SAVES LITTLE BOY'S LIFE . . . HOW YOU CAN TELL IF YOU'RE GOOD IN BED . . .

'What're you guys up to tonight?' asks Jack. 'Anything excitin'?'

By exciting I assume he means slam-dancing, casual vandalism or recreational drugs.

'Nah,' says Victor, 'We reckoned we'd get a video.'

Chains jangle when Jack shrugs. 'Us too.'

'Another victim of cultural inertia,' says Victor.

Tommi laughs. 'When in doubt, take it out.'

God knows where we are. One minute we were talking about going down to the corner for another six-pack and the next we were marching past the beggars lining the stairs at the Second Avenue station because Jack can't believe that Victor has been in New York for nearly a week and the only bar I've taken him to is the Irish pub on Seventh.

'Jesus,' said Jack. 'It's like going to Paris and only eating in McDonald's.'

We strolled past the homeless sleeping in cardboard boxes on Houston and the guys selling other people's garbage at Cooper Union and Third, and down the narrow lane of sidewalk on St Marks between the tables and stores full of books, socks, heavy metal T-shirts, smart-ass badges and cannabis earrings, death and Rasta jewellery, leather jackets, sunglasses and imitation Nepalese hats. We looped around and up again past the Indian restaurants shining like Christmas lights on Sixth. I think we're near the river now, but we've been in and out of so many bars tonight that I'm not totally sure which river – the East? the Hudson? the Potomac? Jack's soul is a restless one that can't stay anywhere for more than one beer, no matter how good the music or how free the pretzels.

Wherever we are, it is dark, crowded, noisy, smoky, and has a pool table, an electric train running around the bar, Guns 'n' Roses on the jukebox, and Larry Ramon on tap.

Victor is sitting on the stool next to Larry, and I'm on the stool next to Victor. Tommi and Jack are playing pool. Larry started talking to us after he heard Victor ask for two more Löwenbräus. 'I love your accent, man,' said Larry. 'Say something else.'

Larry is telling us his life story. We're just at the part where Larry saves his son from his first marriage by jumping out of a burning building with the baby in his arms.

Larry makes an empty gesture with both hands. 'So what could I do?' he asks Victor.

'That's right, nothin',' answers Larry before Victor can swallow his beer and answer for himself. Larry may love Victor's accent, but he doesn't give him much opportunity to use it. 'Fuckin' nothin', that's what. The whole place was in flames, man. Like Danny's inferno or somethin'. You wouldna believed it, Vic, I couldn't even see the door I came in through anymore an' I hadn't been in there more than a minute.'

'Jesus,' says Victor. His eyes wander towards the back of the room, where Jack has just fallen off the table trying to make a difficult corner shot and Tommi is talking to a girl dressed in plastic.

'Crazy bitch,' says Larry, 'passin' out like that.' He shakes his head sadly. 'I loved that woman,' he tells us, 'I really loved her. I'd a done anything for her, moved to California even, anything at all, and how did she repay me?' He shoves his glass towards the bartender, who starts filling it automatically. 'She throws me out, that's how she repays me. She throws me out and then she gets assholed and sets the fuckin' apartment on fire.' He points a finger at, of all people, me.

'Why are women like that?' he wants to know. 'I'm askin' y'as a friend. Why are they like that?'

I don't answer. The reason I don't answer is not because I don't know the answer – although I don't – but because Larry reminds me of Dean Martin. A Puerto Rican and much younger Dean Martin, but Dean Martin nonetheless. It's partly to do with his hair and partly to do with the way he smiles. And partly to do with how wrecked he is. Whatever it's due to, it has me mesmerised.

Larry isn't bothered by my lack of response; indeed it seems unlikely that he has noticed. He takes a cigarette out of his pocket and lights it, dragging heavily. 'So I jumped out of the window with the kid in my arms,' he continues, miraculously picking up where he left off, 'and that's how I fucked my back up so bad.' He snaps his fingers, speaking through a mouthful of smoke. 'Wham bam, the next thing you know I'm out of the navy.'

Victor and I both nod sympathetically. Larry loved the navy. He loved football more, but his temper had lost him his chance at the pros, and the navy had given him a second chance. It sent him to school, it showed him the world, it made him respect himself, it taught him a lot.

'Not that I'm complainin' or nothin' about bein' dumped,' says Larry, "cause I'm not. I never complain. That's one thing I've learned in my life, shit happens. You have to take it like a man and not whine. Don't never whine.' He chuckles, Dean Martin remembering how he got on the floor. 'Things could always be worse, right?' he asks, nudging Victor. 'I'm a lucky mother and I know it. I'm thirty-four, I've got a good woman, God bless her, let's hope she pulls through, and I like my job . . .'

Larry passes the cigarette to Victor, and for the first time I realise that it isn't a cigarette. This can't be legal, can it? I look around, but no one's so much as glancing our way. I try to catch Victor's eye, to remind him of his decision that drugs are out on this trip, but his eyes are half closed and blocked by smoke.

Presumably because we've already heard about his girlfriend's cancer and how much the hospital costs, Larry starts talking about his job coaching disadvantaged teenagers with attitude problems.

'I know how t'relate to them,' he tells Victor, "cause I was one myself.' He smiles at Victor, just like Dean Martin smiling as he explains that even though you would never guess it in a million years, he's actually just a little bit drunk. 'I was a real piece of work when I was a kid,' says Larry. 'That's why I don't take no shit from them now. I'm thirty-four, I tell 'em, I'm a survivor, I don't put up with nobody's crap.'

Victor, on automatic, passes me the cigarette, and even though I never break rules – certainly not so you'd notice – I take it.

Almost everyone I know smoked pot when they were younger, except for me. Even my accountant, who wears a Rolex and drives a grey BMW, smoked pot. I glance at Larry. What if he's an undercover cop? But if he's an undercover cop, this is entrapment. What's the standing of entrapment in New York? Surely it's illegal – after all, we're not in Peru. I hold the joint just below the bar and stare at it thoughtfully. Go on, the part of me that buys two bags of potato chips instead of one urges, just try it. This isn't Colombia. They're not going to entomb you for one little spliff. Tommi is dancing next to Jack, who is still trying to make his shot. I stare at the joint again. I'm a wild woman, aren't I? My actions are unpredictable and confined to no man's law. And anyway, if we do get a bike, I might soon be dead in Mexico, with yet another thing undone, so what the hell.

When I stop choking and the smoke clears, Victor's vanished and I'm sitting next to Larry.

Larry gently lifts the cigarette from my fingers. 'So you guys aren't a couple, huh?' he says.

A couple of what? The room's beginning to resemble a fading photograph, and one that's fading fast. I stare at him blankly, not quite sure what he means.

'I thought you was a couple,' says Larry. He moves a little closer.

Whatever Larry's drinking, there's rum in it. I'd move a little further away, but my bones have gone soft and I'm afraid of falling.

Larry's voice deepens, acquiring the consistency of slush. 'You know,' he drawls, 'you're a very attractive woman.'

Dean Martin. I'm sitting in a New York bar, drunk and stoned, and Dean Martin is telling me that I'm a very attractive woman. Maybe I'm dead.

And then he starts singing. R-E-S-P-E-C-T, that is what you mean to me . . . His voice isn't as croony as I remember it. He goes to put a hand on my knee. 'Now that I know you're not a couple . . .' he purrs, able to talk and sing at the same time.

I might have fallen off the stool after all if someone wasn't standing behind me.

'We've got to get out of here,' says Tommi, tugging on my arm. 'Jack's singing with Aretha. We have to get him air.'

*

There's plenty of air on the deck of the Staten Island ferry. Air, and wind and rain. It's late, and we're almost the only passengers on the last trip back to the city. The other two are inside, but the four of us are out, happy as ocean otters and just as wet. The boat dips and rolls. Jack, having sung 'R-E-S-P-E-C-T' at full tilt all the way to Richmond, is slumped on the bench against the wall, sound asleep. Tommi, Victor and I are at the rail, our hands over our plastic cups of beer, and our eyes are on Manhattan, huddled on the shore. Like a mythical kingdom of ancient dreams, it seems to rise from the water, its towers shimmering and glowing in a galaxy of lights. How could you not believe New York's promises? Not believe its streets are paved with gold?

Victor grins into the storm. 'This is brilliant,' he says. 'Really brilliant. Better than taking the underpass by the park at ninety.'

High praise indeed.

'Cheapest thrill in New York,' says Tommi.

'Jesus,' says a voice in the night.

'Jesus?'

Tommi, Victor and I turn to Jack. He's sitting up now. 'What's the matter, honey?' asks Tommi. 'You seein' things again?'

Jack doesn't answer her. He's looking at Victor. 'You said you wanna buy a bike, right?' He smiles, pleased with himself. 'Well, I think I know the dude who can help you.'

'Jesus?' asks Victor.

Jack shakes his head. 'Sean.'

3

BYE BYE NEW JERSEY, WE'VE BECOME AIRBORNE

'So?' asks Victor. 'What do you think?'

Prospect Motorcycles occupies a largish storefront on Coney Island Avenue. There are bikes parked out front, bikes in the garage at the back of the building, and bikes in a line the length of the shop. Its shelves are packed with parts and accessories, its walls lined with calendars and posters of shiny, well-equipped girls on shiny, well-equipped motorcycles. Dolores, the manager, has left Victor and me standing in front of a 1986 Honda Nighthawk that belongs to her son. The sticker on its windshield says I CAN REMEMBER WHEN SEX WAS SAFE AND MOTORCYCLES WERE DANGEROUS.

I am noncommittal, which, given my knowledge of motorcycles – they have two wheels, the clutch is on the handlebar, you have to watch them on gravel – is probably the best position to take. 'She looks all right.'

Which she does. She's black and red, 750ccs, no dents or rust, and though she doesn't seem to have our name on her anywhere that I can see, she does have HOMEY RACING glued to her windshield and a Tasmanian devil spray-painted on her tank.

Victor nods. 'They're good bikes, Nighthawks. Dependable.'

'Of course,' I say to the top of his head as he squats beside her, 'she is the first one we've seen. We'll have to look at a few more.'

Victor nods, yeah, yeah. 'She's exactly what we need.'

Mayo, husband of Dolores, father of Sean, and owner of Prospect Motorcycles, comes in from the garage, wiping his hands on a grease-black rag.

'Where'd Dolores say you guys say are goin'?' he asks.

Victor's still crouched beside the Honda, looking for something he's missed, so I answer. 'California, and then down to Peru.'

He drops the rag on the counter and walks towards us. 'Great trip,' he says. 'Crossing the States?' He shakes his head. 'Trip of a lifetime.' He stops beside me. 'And you've still got good weather if you don't leave it too long.'

'Have you done it?' I ask him. 'Have you made the trip?' I like Mayo. He's sane and responsible. I want to hear that he's been through Mexico without being robbed by bandits or killed by the cops.

'I could've,' he says, scratching his head. 'I've got friends who've done it, wanted me to go with them. Know a guy's got a Goldwing, took it all the way to Honduras, and another's got a Harley, drove it from Brooklyn to Brooklyn, said it was the best three months he ever had.' He smiles past me. 'One of these days,' says Mayo. 'One of these days, I'm going to shut the shop and do that ride myself.' He gives me a wink. 'Maybe me and Dolores should go with you.'

Still crouching, Victor moves towards the front of the Nighthawk.

'That's my son's bike, you know,' Mayo says, presumably to Victor, though Victor has yet to look at him. He turns to me. 'It's had the best of care,' he assures me. 'Never been thrashed.'

At the word 'thrashed' Victor looks over with new interest. Victor thrashes his pushbike. 'How about a ride?' he asks.

Having tried the other motorcycle shop on Coney Island Avenue and found nothing, Victor and I retire to a pizza and falafel place to discuss our situation.

The restaurant is long and narrow and has the atmosphere of a doctor's waiting room, albeit one that smells of cheese, pepperoni, fried onion and just a hint of coriander. There's a painting of a barn on the far wall and several out-of-date calendars of sunsets and kittens along the sides. We sit at the back.

Our situation is this: We've seen a bike we like for a price we can afford. We haven't looked at anything else. The pumpkins haven't started freezing on the vines yet, the anti-freeze hasn't been brought out, all the leaves haven't fallen from the trees. We still have time to shop around.

Victor eloquently makes the summarising speech. 'We can't just buy the first bike we look at,' he says. 'That would be mad.'

'You're right,' I say. 'That would be mad.'

He finishes his seltzer. 'Everybody'll think we've lost our minds completely.'

We certainly don't want that.

'So?' he asks as we get up to leave. 'What do you think?'

All of us have had the experience of hearing ourselves say we're going to do one thing while at the same time realising that we're actually about to do something entirely different, but this is the first time I've ever had it as a shared experience. I pick up my paper plate and throw it into the wastebasket. 'I think we should go back to Mayo and see if we get a discount for cash.'

Later we get a little lost as we're riding the Nighthawk back home. This could be because trying to figure out how to get gas out of the pump without a credit card has unnerved the driver, or because the co-pilot, her mind on the stars over the Smoky Mountains, wasn't paying enough attention at that roundabout by the park. Opinions differ, but the result is the same: we wind up in one of the several wrong parts of Flatbush, deciding direction while stopped at a light. A pack of boys dressed like violence in headscarves and leather struts past us at the intersection, not pretending not to stare. There are a few other white people around us, locked in their cars, but everyone else out in the open where the bush was once so flat is black. It's the sort of situation that can make you nervous. One of the boys, knowing that no one would be foolish enough to start moving before he's out of the way, comes to a stop in front of Victor. He makes eye contact. This could be the moment everyone's been warning us about, the moment when we finally understand why other people prefer to stay safe at home. Maybe it was a mistake not paying by cheque.

The boy raises his fist. 'That's a bad motherfucker you got there!' he shouts at Victor. 'You know that! A real bad motherfucker!'

Victor gives him the thumbs-up. 'I think we made the right decision,' he says.

Campmore is an over-large warehouse of a store where mountaineers brush shoulders with white-water rafters and skiers exchange smiles with men who shoot deer. There is nothing that might even just possibly come in handy out there in the open under God's blue sky, be it tent or lantern or freeze-dried goulash, that isn't available at Campmore, and with no New York sales tax.

We buy the smallest tent, the lightest camp stove, the most compressible sleeping bags, the cheapest liners, inflatable mattresses,

thermals, wets, and a flashlight the size of a large pen, both of us acting as though we know what we're doing and Victor carefully ticking
everything off on one of his lists. We're in sight of the checkout
when we remember knives.

'So where you guys going?' asks our salesperson, Barbarann.

Victor is checking out the Swiss army knives laid out on the
counter and doesn't look up, torn between the Huntsman and the
Fisherman.

'First to California,' I answer. 'And then down to South America.'

Barbarann's curls vibrate. 'Are you going to Ecuador?' she wants to
know. 'I spent a month at a biological reserve in the rainforest in
Ecuador last year.'

'You did?' Although it is obvious that all the salespeople in
Campmore are seriously committed to the outdoors, this still sur-
prises me. Blonde and bouncy, Barbarann is one of those bright-eyed,
fresh-faced American girls more commonly associated with football
games and beauty pageants than jungle adventures.

'Uh-huh.' She shakes her head, beaming as though her team just
made a goal. 'It was fantastic.' She sighs. 'Gosh, I'm envious. I wish
I was going with you.'

Victor pushes two knives across the counter. 'Where were you in
Ecuador?'

'Mishawally,' says Barbarann. 'It's kinda near Tena. You thinking of
going there?'

'Maybe,' says Victor.

Victor says 'maybe' with such confidence and assurance that
Barbarann is fooled into thinking he has some idea where Tena is.
She starts writing down names on a piece of lined paper: Tena,
Misahuallí, David Neil, Jatun Sacha, Barbarann.

'Say hi to David for me when you see him,' she says.

Victor takes the paper and puts it in his notebook. 'We will,' he
assures her.

Barbarann beams. She probably even thinks we own a map.

Despite my many and inventive attempts to dissuade them, my sister and brother-in-law have come all the way into the city to take us
out to dinner before we depart.

'I'm not checking up on you,' says my sister as she helps me get
the drinks. 'I'm your family. Have you thought how I'd feel if you get
killed? I'd never forgive myself for not saying goodbye.'

I hand her the wine. 'Please,' I beg, 'you're going to make me cry.'

She presses her lips together. 'I'm not the one who's going to make you cry.'

This means that she doesn't like Victor.

'I never said that,' says my sister. 'I only just met the guy, all he's said is hello and "I was raised in York" – how do I know if I like him or not?' She picks up the corkscrew and studies it to see if it is different from the one she has at home. 'But I will admit that he's not quite what I expected . . .'

I rip open the bag of tortilla chips and dump them in a bowl. 'Like what? Asterix on wheels?'

'At least Asterix would be some sort of protection.' She stares straight into my eyes. When did she start looking so like my mother? 'He's a hippy,' says Debbie.

I shove the bowl of chips into her free hand. 'That's not a punishable offence,' I remind her.

'It is in Mississippi and Mexico.'

'You were a hippy,' I further remind her. 'You used to wear a ring in your nose.'

'When I was eighteen,' says Mrs J. B. Wasser. 'You're supposed to be irresponsible when you're eighteen.' She shakes the bowl of tortilla chips. 'And then, once it's out of your system, you grow up.' She sighs. 'But you never got it out of your system, did you?'

I decide to ignore this change of attack. What does she do when she sees our mother, take notes? 'Vic's not irresponsible.' I remove two beers from the fridge. 'He's one of the most responsible men I've ever known.' I slam them on the counter. 'And the most grown up.'

'Um . . .' says Debbie.

She doesn't believe me.

'Of course I believe you. If that's what you think, then of course I believe you. But he isn't a man like Jake, is he?' Respectable, patriarchal, possessor of a gold American Express card and friends in high places. 'I mean, if something does happen . . . if you're arrested or something . . .' She gives me an exasperated look, my mother trying to understand exactly what it is that I have against marriage. 'I mean, face it, Dyan, he's not going to be much help if the sheriff's name is Bubba, is he?' Or Miguel, she might as well add.

'And a man like Jake wouldn't be much help when the clutch cable snaps.' I grab the beers and two wine glasses. 'If I remember correctly, he had to pay someone to put his new windshield wipers on.' I march towards the door.

Jake and Victor are in one corner of the living room, admiring our tent. Our tent is very small and very blue, and it took us four hours to figure out how to set it up, not including the fifteen minutes I spent on the phone to the tent company's troubleshooter, who had never come upon this problem before, but it does look like a real camper's tent.

The men stop talking about groundsheets and sit down on the sofa, side by side. Jake is wearing a linen suit, fashionably crumpled, and a tie painted to resemble a rainbow trout. Victor is wearing his vaguely patched jeans, his sweatshirt and a red bandanna. They look like two men thrown together by some fantastic twist of fate – a cosmic time warp, for instance, or a diabolically eccentric will.

'I didn't know you were into camping, Dy,' smiles Jake.

I've heard his informal lectures on psychoanalytical technique. I know that this is a leading question.

Debbie steps over the sleeping bags we've been practising rolling up and stuffing into their compression bags, and plonks the bottle and the chips in the middle of the coffee table.

'She isn't,' my sister answers for me. 'The only place she's ever been camping is in the backyard when she was twelve.'

'That's not true.' I pass Victor a beer. 'We went camping every summer in the Girl Scouts.' I pour out a glass of wine and hand it to my brother-in-law. 'In the woods.'

'Maple trails,' says my sister.

Victor is grinning. 'You were in the Girl Scouts?'

'My mother made me.' I pour a second glass of wine, which Debbie snatches from the table.

Jake leans back, the professional counsellor, let's all relax. 'Well,' he says, 'it certainly looks like you're ready to go.'

Victor nods. 'We're leaving first thing in the morning.' He looks at the stuff strategically stacked around the living room – the medical kit and the toilet bag, the tools and the food, the books and clothes and travel backgammon set. 'All we have to do is pack it all up.'

My sister smiles, my mother about to ask you if you've seen her good saucepan, already guessing that you buried it in the garden because you burned out the bottom making fudge. 'What route are you taking?' she wants to know. 'Jake thinks you're going to have trouble with the Rockies at this time of year. Show us how you're going.'

Displaying the mettle and resourcefulness necessary for long-distance travel, Victor doesn't blink. 'We're not into rigid planning like that,' he tells her. 'We're just going to go and see what happens.'

Debbie turns to me. 'This means you haven't bought a map yet, doesn't it?' she asks.

I'm beginning to have second thoughts. Maybe it's the artichoke pizza and the hot fries I had for supper, maybe it's the eight bottles of beer and the two shots of Cointreau, but after Debbie and Jake go back to Connecticut I lie in the dark, face-down on the pillow, while anxiety monsters larger than dinosaurs thrash around the room.

Dyan, they call, *Dyan, are you really ready for this? Sleeping in a tent? Pissing in the bushes? Cooking on a camp stove?* They laugh almost gleefully. *What happens when it rains?* they titter. *What happens if you hit snow?*

I roll over. I hadn't really thought about rain, much less snow.

Do you know how cold it can get in the mountains? coo the possibility-pushers of faceless fear, trampling over the bed. *Do you have any idea?*

I have no idea how cold it can get in the mountains. I haven't thought much about cold, either. I roll over the other way, burrowing into the blankets.

The cheerful cacodemons bounce up and down, shaking my ignorant confidence. *Where are you going to take a bath?* they want to know. *How are you going to wash your hair? Do your nails? Brush your teeth? What about your exercises? What happens when you run out of toilet paper?*

Toilet paper? When you run out of toilet paper you use tissues or paper towels. Or you buy more.

Not at the back end of the bayou, you don't! they shriek. *Not in the middle of the Peruvian desert!*

There are a few other things I haven't really thought about in any but the most casual, what-if-a-meteor-did-strike-the-house? sort of way, but now they come to me, too. Illness. Exhaustion. Snake bites. Dog bites. Accidents.

Familiarity breeds contempt, sing the sirens of doom . . .

Scenes and arguments . . .

Their sweet, discordant voices rise. *What if he meets someone in San Diego or Managua?* they query. *What if Victor falls in love?*'

Desertion and betrayal . . .

It's not too late to change your mind . . .

Maybe I should change my mind. I look at the shining blue hands of our travel clock. It's 2 am. We won't be leaving till ten or eleven. There's still enough time.

Time runs away when you're not using it . . .
But the voice which says that is no siren's. It's Victor's.
At 5 am I write a postcard to my cat. Dear Dude, We've looked at a map and are heading for the Appalachians in a couple of hours. Banjo music, pine trees and chitlins. We bought stars for the bike that glow in the dark . . .

Jack is sitting in the armchair, a beer in his hand and a look on his face that isn't easy to read, but it could very well be concern. Jack is watching Victor.

Victor is on the floor, hunched over the saddlebags, repacking for the absolute, not-one-more-bloody-thing last time. Around him is everything we aren't taking after all: the rubber pig masks for Hallowe'en, the extra chain for the bike, the extra lock, the emergency flasher and flares, the Walkman, the tapes, the rubber boots, most of my clothes. It's after one.

'You got a flask for water?' asks Jack.

Victor forces the zipper closed on saddlebag one. 'You can buy it in plastic bottles,' he grunts.

Jack shakes his hand as though he's burned his fingers and takes a slug of beer. 'What about plates?'

'We don't need plates.' Victor starts filling the other side. 'We've got the cooking pots.'

Jack belches. 'What about knives and forks and shit like that?'

Victor turns to me.

'I'll get them.'

'Two forks, two knives, two spoons,' Victor shouts after me. 'That's absolutely all.'

Rule of the Road number 1: Light is right.

When I come back with the knives and forks, he's holding my black and white cassette bag, eyeing it the way the Prime Minster might look at a letter suddenly slipped through the mail slot. 'What's this?' he demands.

Tommi, who has been sitting on the floor filling mini-zip-loc bags with herbs and spices, puts the last one aside and looks at him. Tommi thinks I'm brave – brave or stupid – to travel with a man. She and Jack once went away for the weekend and were back the same day they left because they couldn't agree on where to stay.

'Girls' stuff,' Tommi answers for me.

'Girls' stuff?' says Victor. 'What kind of girls' stuff?'

'You know,' say Tommi and I together. 'Girls' stuff.'

Victor doesn't know. He opens the bag and looks inside. He still doesn't know. He starts pulling things out. 'More shampoo?' He looks at me as if he's never seen me before. 'Why have you taken more shampoo? We've got shampoo.'

'It's not shampoo, it's conditioner.'

'Too bulky.' He tosses it aside. 'And this?'

'Emery boards.'

His eyes roll. 'We have a nail-clipper.' He throws the boards after the conditioner and reaches for the next thing in the bag, an over-sized pencil-sharpener. 'And what the hell is this?'

'It's for my eyeliner,' I explain, though pointlessly.

'Use your knife,' says Victor, and chucks it after the emery boards. After the pencil-sharpener he throws the body spray, the hair wax, the hand cream, the cleansing pads, the extra soap, the aroma-therapy oils Tommi gave me in case of stress or depression, and the multivitamins and the book of one hundred positive thoughts donated by my sister. He holds up two small squares of something wrapped in pink. 'And this? What's this?'

Jack starts to choke.

I start moving towards the kitchen. 'You do know what those are.'

'Oh, right,' says Victor.

Tommi whistles. She could make a fortune as a doorman if her hair weren't blue. 'Is that all you have with you?' she shrieks. 'Just two?'

I nod. I'm lucky to have that many, the way Wilderness Man has been dispensing with my things as unnecessary all morning. He probably thinks I should use dried grass. 'I'll get more when I need them.'

'You can say that in Spanish?' asks Tommi, clearly impressed.

'I'll point.'

She nods towards Victor. 'You know,' she says, 'he's kinda like Che, isn't he?'

Jack and I both look at Victor – tall, thin, long-haired, clean-shaven and blond, dressed in patched jeans and his West One sweatshirt – and then at each other. We have no idea what she's talking about.

'You mean because Che was half Spanish, half Irish?' Victor is half Spanish, half English. It's close.

Tommi starts gathering the tiny spice bags together. 'No. Because he couldn't stand to travel with anyone with luggage either.'

*

The afternoon of the 10 October 1993 is sunny and warm. Red and gold leaves litter the ground. By three o'clock the bike is loaded up like a pioneer's mule – saddlebags, tank bag, top box, tent, the old woven bag Victor found in a skip that used to belong to a guy named Roy, bulging with all the things we want to have handy, the wets rolled up in a black bin-liner, red and green cargo nets holding them down. Tommi, Jack and I stand on the pavement while Victor, wreathed in exhaust fumes, carefully pulls the Nighthawk out of the front yard and on to the sidewalk. Several of the neighbours are watching from their stoops and windows, their faces impassive but their stares intense.

'This is it,' says Tommi. She puts her arms around me. 'Just remember you're a free woman,' she whispers. 'If he acts like a jerk you can always come back.'

'I really wish we were going with you,' says Jack, who would, in truth, have joined us – if it weren't for the band, and Tommi's job, and the two cats, and the fact that he can't drive. 'What a trip.'

I climb on behind Victor, my legs straddling the saddlebags, my back against the tent.

'Ready?' asks Victor.

I put my arms around him. 'Ready.'

'Watch yourselves out there,' says Jack. 'They're all into God and guns.'

'Don't forget to send us postcards,' says Tommi.

'We'll bring you something special from South America,' I shout as we buck from the sidewalk.

'Drugs!' screams Jack, further intriguing the neighbours. 'Bring us drugs!'

'Wait!' screams Tommi, running beside us. She slips a blue plastic card into my hand.

'What's that?'

'It's an AT&T calling card. The PIN number's on the back.'

'What am I supposed to do with it?' I ask my little girl.

She rolls her eyes. 'Call me once a week.'

Victor toots the horn twice. We're on our way.

4

THE ROAD TO NOWHERE

The road is endless and the trees are thick and I'm singing a John Denver song as we cautiously move along. We might be in a photograph. One of those poster-sized pictures that decorate the 1-Hour Foto stores and camera departments in every shopping centre and mall across the States. It's the photograph of a peaceful country road on a perfect autumn day. The sky's a true blue, the dense green mountains are hazily streaked with the colours of flames. The photo of winter is nice, snow and a small child glowing in the lights of a Christmas tree, and the summer looks pleasant, sand and a happy family glowing in the sunlight reflected from a shining sea, and spring is all high skies and flowers, but this one is the best: Indian summer, vivid but mild, the last good days in the best place on earth. You can hear your feet scuffing through the fallen leaves.

I break off from my song. 'You know why it's called Indian summer?' I shout to Victor as our wheels crunch over the gravel road. 'It's because the clouds look like the smoke rising from Indian campfires.' And if you look really closely, my third-grade teacher told us, you can see braves in the cornstacks and hillocks of straw, sitting in a circle watching the birds vanish across a pink and purple sky.

'Shit,' says Victor. Reality is never as flawless as Kodachrome. The bike, already going as slowly as is possible without actually falling over, comes to yet another stop in front of yet another fork in the picturesque country road. He shoves up his visor. The visor falls to the ground. 'Jesus Christ,' Victor mutters, but he doesn't look down. The visor's always falling off. 'Take a picture.'

The strain of twenty miles of gravel has obviously gotten to him. 'You what?'

'Take a picture.' He hunches over the tank bag to study the state map we got from the tourist information centre. 'Take a picture of this bloody road. I'm going to put it up in the office when I get back.'

It is Day 6 – and Stop 12 in the last sixty minutes – so I know better than to ask him where we are. Or even where he thinks we might be. I pull out the camera from under my jacket and take a picture.

Victor straightens up with a sigh. 'Get the Rad,' he says. The Rad is our Rand McNally Atlas, bought in a hurry on our way out of Manhattan. 'This bloody thing is useless.'

I climb off the bike, graceful as a woolly mammoth in my layers of shirt, sweatshirt and leather jacket whose pockets are stuffed tight with miniature containers of milk and jam, envelopes of ketchup, mustard, salt, pepper, sugar and taco sauce, and wads of toilet paper.

Rule of the Road number 2: Take anything going.

Rule of the Road number 3: Always carry your own supply of toilet paper.

'Fuckin' gravel,' Victor's muttering as I start dragging the garbage bag that holds the atlas and the roll of tinfoil out from under the cargo net. 'Did you see we nearly lost it on that turn back there? It's like the bloody road to hell, this. It'll be a miracle if we don't get another puncture.'

He's worried about the tyre. We got our first puncture yesterday. But yesterday was Saturday, and we didn't see the puncture till two in the afternoon, by which time the only motorcycle shop for 200 miles was shut for the weekend. Now we're just praying that the sealant holds till we can get to a town big enough to get the inner tube repaired.

I'd start worrying about the tyre myself, but one of the primary responsibilities of the co-pilot is to keep up the pilot's morale. 'At least it's not raining,' I tell him.

Victor gets off to take a leak. 'Yeah, and there's no one shooting at us for a change,' he says over his shoulder. 'This must be our lucky day.'

'I'm sure they weren't really shooting at us,' I tell his back, with more confidence than I exhibited at the time. 'They were probably shooting at squirrels.' Or the road signs. More important than Indian summer, it's small-game season in West Virginia and the hills are full of attractive rodents gathering stores and overweight men in weatherproof jackets and bright baseball caps with shotguns and ice chests packed with cans of Bud. I've already collected several recipes for squirrel – goulash, roasted, stewed with dumplings, simmered in beer – from men met in diners. No one in an English café would suddenly start telling you how his mother, who had ten children, lived to be ninety-three and was never sick a day in her life, cooked squirrel, but in America it seems to be a more popular way of breaking the social ice than 'Please pass the sugar.'

'They might have missed.' He comes back to the bike. 'It'd be my dread hanging from some redneck's pick-up instead of some poor squirrel's tail.'

I've unrolled the Rand McNally and spread it out on the tank bag. We stand on either side of the Honda, gazing at it with expressions that might be mistaken for intent but are really just blank. We never seem to be anywhere that's actually marked on the map.

'So where do you think we are?' I finally ask.

'God knows,' says the pilot. He looks up, then down again, and points at a spot that looks to me pretty much like everything around it. 'We should be here.' He looks up again, then down, then at me. 'But we're not. We're nowhere as usual, and it isn't even paved.'

It's my turn to look up at the long blue-grey road that, God also knows, we may have come down before. It's sometimes hard to tell.

'You'd think there'd be some kind of signpost,' I say, reasonably.

But it's Day 6, and Victor knows better than to be beguiled by logic.

Rule of the Road number 4: Nothing you look for will ever be signposted.

Rule of the Road number 5: If what you're looking for is signposted, then when you get to it it won't be there.

Rule of the Road number 6: If what you seek is there, it'll be closed.

'No, I wouldn't.'

We both look up as a fountain of dust appears in the distance. Warily, we watch its approach. You can't say we haven't been warned. Every time we stop for a coffee, or to buy gas, or just to get out of the rain, someone will ask us where we're headed, and then they'll tell us why we shouldn't go there. Watch your bike. Watch the roads. You can get arrested just for having New York plates. Folk around here don't take kindly to strangers.

An old white pick-up, dents in the doors and rust on the fenders, the bumper held on by a length of washing line, emerges from the cloud. There are logs and a large dog in the back; two men and a boy in the cab. The truck stops beside us and the driver leans out of the window. 'Where you goin'?'

Victor takes the Rad over to the pick-up. 'We're trying to get to the national campgrounds at Big Bend,' he says. Not far from Petersburg there's a campsite by the river, one with water and showers.

The other man leans over to stare at the map with the driver. Trapped between them, the boy stares at Victor. 'Don't it hurt?' he asks.

The men, who have pretended not to notice the nose ring, don't look at Victor, but they're listening for his answer.

Victor winks at the boy. 'No, it doesn't hurt. It's just like an earring.'

You can tell how reassuring the men find this information by the quick glance they exchange. Just like an earring. The boy can't quite make sense of it. In New York even men who wear suits and carry attaché cases wear earrings, but not in West Virginia. He continues to stare.

The driver shakes his head. 'You can't get there from here,' he says simply.

The other man reaches out and puts his finger near to Victor's. 'You want to get back on the highway,' he says.

No we don't. We took 81 through Pennsylvania, fighting the wind and our new helmets, subtly designed to wrench back and choke you or disengage from their visors when you pick up too much speed, unable to see the scenery because of the tears in our eyes, and then we realised our mistake. The interstates are good roads, fast and direct, but they were intended for those for whom the only point of any journey is the destination. We don't want to get anywhere in particular. We want to see America, not just drive through it. Following the back roads is like following dreams you recognise immediately but didn't know you had; we follow them just to see where they go. Here they have led us through flat stretches of farmland and jerkwater towns too small to have names; past buildings that have seen too much weather and people who have seen too much nothing; past yard sales and flea markets, churches and billboards, churches and VFW halls, churches and churches; past houses with basketball hoops over garage doors and Hallowe'en decorations crowding their lawns; past houses with hand-made signs in the front windows (cuts and perms, roots and tips, piano and tap lessons, jams and honey, quilts, mechanics, cakes baked to order) and diners with lighted beer signs in the windows and movie marquees out front (Breakfast Special, Blueplate Special, home-made pie); past boys who stop their games to shoot at us with their fingers and little girls who stop theirs to wave from the safety of a porch. On the interstate the only signs of life are the beer and soda cans strewn along the shoulders and peeking through the roadside grass like hi-tech flowers.

'No we don't,' Victor explains. 'We're taking the scenic route.'

It's not quite a smile that the driver makes. He looks at the bike, which has now acquired a bag of groceries and several decorative chicken feathers. 'Not unless that thing can fly you do,' he says. 'Otherwise, you gotta get back on 221, 'cause this road here just goes in circles.'

'Where you from?' asks the other man, as though this might explain Victor's lack of realism.

'London,' Victor answers. And adds, just in case they think he means London, Connecticut, or London, Kentucky, or London, Ohio, 'England.'

'England? No kiddin'?' He whistles. 'You're a long way from home.'

A long way from home, and lost to boot.

The driver rests his arm on the window frame. 'My uncle was in England,' he says conversationally. 'In the war. Nearly got himself killed by a bomb. Said you couldn't get any oranges for love nor money. They used to steal fruit from the mess and give it to their gals instead of flowers.'

'That Leroy or Ed?' asks his friend.

'Leroy.'

He whistles again. 'Shit, no. Leroy? Leroy was in England?' He laughs. 'I ain't never seen Leroy go any further than the county line. And then he was drunker then a bridegroom with a shotgun at his back.'

The little boy's eyes haven't left Victor's face. 'How come you don't have oranges where you're from?' he asks.

'That was a long time ago,' Victor tells him. 'We have oranges now.'

'Yeah,' I say. 'But we still get bombed.'

Hope keeps us all going. Call us misguided, call us naive, but if it weren't for hope most of us would have given up and sat down by the roadside years ago, too depressed and discouraged to do anything but wait to be hit by a passing truck. Which, of course, would then never have come. Not that that would really matter. 'I sure hope that truck comes soon,' you'd be saying as the traffic sprayed you with mud and the blood of small mammals and aluminum cans bounced off your head. 'I hope it doesn't take too long.' The litter would be piling up around you, the raccoon innards looping you like party streamers, but still you'd sit there, hope as eternal as damnation, knowing your misery might soon be over, afraid to move in case the truck turned up two minutes after you left.

In hope, we wait for buses, for deliveries, for success, for love, for lucky breaks. In hope, I was waiting for the first time Victor and I set up camp in daylight.

Even when we were crawling through the gravel wondering where we were and how to get out of there, I'd believed that this time we'd find the campsite before the night birds started barking through the woods. When the men in the pick-up directed us back to the interstate, I no longer believed, I was absolutely sure. We'd lost time, it was true, but there was still plenty of sun left. The spot marked on the map by a tiny tent was no further away than the length of a match head or a small piece of gravel. We can make it, I told myself as we finally emerged on to the dark, hard pavement of Route 221 and started pushing the speed limit once again. We can be there while there's still enough light to see what we're doing.

We run a series of hills like a rollercoaster, the two of us singing 'Wheel of Death' as loudly as we can and the chicken feathers flapping from the windshield, but even then I am imagining our bright blue tent with sunlight on it, Victor starting up the Whisperlite while I chop the vegetables. I'm writing postcards while he stirs the soup mix into the pot, the two of us scuttling through the under-brush searching for kindling, singing 'The Night They Burned Old Dixie Down' as we haul the dead wood back to our camp.

We enter the sort of sleepy town often plagued by demons in hor-ror novels, and leave it two minutes later, my mind not on the colonial charm of its clapboard buildings or the fineness of our timing at that last light but on the image of Victor and me sipping tea by the roaring fire as the sun slowly melts over the party-dressed hills.

We stop for gas and even though Victor is bent over the map when I come out of the loo, that now-familiar brooding, searching-for-the-North-West Passage look on his face, I am thinking how nice it will be to see what we're eating for a change.

We'll be there soon, it's around that bend and over that river. We take the bend. We cross the river. Ten or twelve yards past the bridge, like a clock that's had its plug pulled, we come to a sudden stop.

You might think that it is here that hope jumps to the shoulder and heads for cover, but you'd be wrong. Hope, like evil, is tougher than that and much harder to lose. Hope starts to babble. *Maybe he dropped his visor again . . . Maybe he got a fly in his eye ... Maybe he wants to go back to town for something . . .*

'What's wrong?' I ask.

'It should've been there,' says Victor, waving behind us. 'It should've been just over the bridge.'

But hope, with its visions of a real fire you can get warm by and food you can see, has confused me. I have no bloody idea what he's talking about. 'What should've?'

Victor sighs. 'Westminster Abbey. What do you think?'

I pass him the Rad.

'See?' says Victor, stabbing at the map with a dirty finger.

Without my glasses, all I see is a blurred jumble of lines and blobs.

'Here's the river . . .'

We look back at the river.

'Here's the bridge . . .'

We look back at the bridge.

'And here's the campgrounds . . .'

We look over at the woods beside us, the perfect place to hide a tree, but it's unlikely that anyone's camped here since the Iroquois were run out of town.

'It must be in there somewhere,' I reason.

'Yeah,' says Victor. 'Only we can't get to it.'

But I am still hope's spokesperson. 'We must have missed the turning. It's probably on the other side of the bridge.'

On the other side of the bridge is a narrow dirt road that stretches past a field and a shack and half a rusting pick-up and into the fading mountains. We park the bike and stand side by side in the dirt and empty Budweiser cans, staring into the darkening distance, try-ing to decide if the road leads to the campgrounds, leads to someone's farm, or doesn't lead anywhere.

'What do you think?' asks Victor.

I think I'm going to cry. 'We're not going to get there by nightfall, are we?'

'I don't care about that,' says Victor, who doesn't. For him the excitement of pitching the tent in the dark with a flashlight between his teeth hasn't yet begun to wear off. 'I just don't want to ride around for hours trying to find the bloody camp.' He looks around again, just in case we missed the sign that points the way to Big Bend, but we didn't. He asks a rhetorical question. 'Why don't they ever mark anything in this country?' And then another. 'How do they expect you to find where you're going if nothing's ever marked?'

'Maybe we could just camp around here,' I suggest. After all, the pioneer spirit is what made this country great.

He shrugs. 'It's up to you. You're the one who gets raped by the locals, I just get beaten up.'

Well, maybe we shouldn't, then.

I'm mentally weighing up the advantages of putting up the tent where we are against the disadvantages of being raped by a bunch of guys with Bud on their breath when something ahead of us catches my attention. 'What's that?' I grab his arm. 'Look! Up there! Is that a car?'

It is a car, a dusty old blue Chevy with a God is Love bumper sticker and another that says I ♡ West Virginia, rattling and bumping its way down the trail.

Victor raises his hand to flag it down. 'You ask,' he says. 'American to American.' He's still pissed off that the attendant in the last gas station didn't understand him when he asked for the toilet. 'No,' he told Victor, and walked away. He speaks English, doesn't he? What did the attendant hear if he didn't hear 'toilet'? Do you have a room to let? Do you think it's too late? Do you sell tulips? Where are the toys?

The car stops. A large man and a very large woman are sitting in the front, two large children, one medium-sized dog and a smallish pig in the back. The woman has a watermelon on her lap. They're on their way to either a church supper or the filming of a Mountain Dew commercial.

The man leans out of the window. 'You folks in trouble?'

In my best American accent, I explain the trouble we're in while the wife, the girls, the dog and the pig all stare at Victor.

'Where you-all from?' he asks when I finish. 'Germany?'

'London.'

His eyebrows go up and his wife nods, smiling, giving the impression that she expected this.

He glances over his shoulder. 'You hear that?' he says to the group in the back seat, none of whom give him their overt attention. 'These folks here are from London, England.' He turns to me again. 'I'll tell ya one thing, you're a lot closer to Big Bend than you are to London, England.' He points in the direction he's just come. 'It's just back thereaways.'

The nearness of success makes Victor forget his vow of silence. 'So we follow this road . . .'

The black baseball cap shakes back and forth. 'No, no, you can't get there from here. You gotta go back on 221. 'Bout ten, fifteen minutes, you'll come to a big ol' suspension bridge. You want the road on the right.'

'Is there a sign?' asks Victor, no stranger to hope himself.

The man laughs. 'Nah, you don't need no sign, boy. That road'll take you straight down there. You can't miss it.' He reaches out of the window to shake Victor's hand. 'Welcome to America,' he says. 'You have yourselves a good time.'

'We've missed it,' Victor's shouting above the noise of the engine as we tortuously make our way down the steep and winding road that is gravel only where it isn't rocks, mud or gouged earth. We can probably stop worrying about the tyre now – there won't be anything left of it by the time we get to wherever it is we're going. 'We must have. This isn't leading anywhere.'

How would we know if it were leading anywhere? It's already too dark to see more than shapes and shadows. Ten, fifteen minutes in West Virginia doesn't mean what it means in London – ten to fifteen minutes. It means forty-five and then you lose the tarmac.

'But the man said it was straight down here,' I argue. I'm not arguing because I think I'm right, but because of that bastard hope again. I'm hoping I'm right. The night's turned cold and threatening, and we've been going straight down here for at least half an hour. I don't want to go back and start again, I want to crawl into my sleeping bag and forget how tired and hungry I am.

'And anyway,' I go on, 'we know it's by the river.' I point into the night. 'And there's the river.' Not, of course, that we can see the river.

Victor's body is tense as he tries to steer us clear of sharp stones and deep ruts and anything live in our path. 'Hell's by a river, too,' he says. 'And it's straight down.'

'Right at the suspension bridge,' I say just one more time. 'We went right at the suspension bridge. There wasn't any other road to take.'

'There wasn't any sign, either,' says Victor.

I tug his hair. 'What you talkin' 'bout, boy? You don't need no sign.'

Even as I'm saying this one of those coincidences that seem like divine intervention happens. My mother might even call it a miracle.

'There!' I shout, jabbing my hand over his shoulder. 'There's a sign!'

But it's not all good news. Suddenly the piny wood hills are filled with a stench so strong we both start to choke. Dead deer.

'What's it say?' gasps Victor. 'Fire and brimstone for sale?'

I bury my face against his back. 'Overnight camping straight ahead.'

'I told you we'd find it.' He pauses to choke some more. 'I don't know why you always worry so much.'

Unlike the state campgrounds, which feature not only paved roads but manned offices where you register and pay your fee, the national ones work on the honour system. There's a small wooden shelter at the entrance to overnight camping with several notices stapled to it, a pocket of envelopes, and a box for your payment. We drive right in.

'Let's get a spot first,' says Victor.

Campsite 1 is full of RVs, pick-up trucks and the unmistakable sound of human males having a bonding experience: hoots of laughter and the popping of beer tops. Several shadowy figures turn to watch us drive by. Too crowded for us.

We try Campsite 2. Campsite 2 is closed. Campsites 3 and 4 are closed too. We begin to suspect that we're out of season. We turn round, narrowly missing the drainage ditch that runs along the entrance to Campsite 4, and go back to Campsite 1, circling slowly, feeling observed.

Campsite 1 is like a mini-development on wheels. Lights shine in the curtained windows of the RVs, television voices and music drift into the night, campfires crackle like backyard barbecues. Some of the RVs have windsocks swaying from their awnings, patio lights strung along their sides, just like home. We can hear the sounds of suppers ending and card games beginning. More than anything at this moment, I long to be in one of those vehicles, warm and comfortable, eating something you need more than one pot to cook and drinking hot coffee while the tape machine blares. So strong is my longing that I can hear Willie Nelson singing.

I'm so immersed in this vision that I don't realise at first why I can hear Willie Nelson singing. The engine's stopped.

'What's wrong?'

'God knows,' says Victor. 'She's stalled.' He jerks his thumb behind us. 'I think there's a spot back there. You want to check it while I get her started?'

I check out the space as best I can given that visibility is what in the not-to-frighten-you terms of the British weatherman would be described as 'could be better'. I can't tell if it's infested with insects or dotted with snake holes, but it does have a fireplace, a tent pitch and a picnic table – if it had a sweeping staircase and a crystal chandelier you could have called it a palace. Victor, pushing the bike, comes up the road as I finish my inspection.

'I don't care if it's solid stone and full of anthills,' he's saying. 'We're taking it.'

We used to have standards. Two or three days ago. We chose our spot for beauty as well as function. We cleared the pitch of rubble and spiders before we put down the groundsheet. We were precise in our positioning of guidelines. We were careful in our hammering in of pegs. We were gentle with our sky-blue tent. But that was when we were still innocent and eager. Our tent is sky-blue now only if the sky is reflected in a dirty puddle, and our pegs are all bent. Standards have slipped. We no longer care how it goes up or even where as long as it doesn't fall down.

Dirty, tired, cold and hungry, we can't even be assed to dig in the saddlebag pockets for the torch. We stumble around in the dark, slapping down the groundsheet, wrenching the tent in place, feeling blindly for a rock large enough to bang the stakes into the unaccommodating earth, tripping over each other in our haste.

'Jesus!' says Victor, bumping into me for at least the third time. 'Why don't you sing or something so I know where you are?'

I'm about to burst into a heartfelt rendition of 'Mama Said There'd Be Days Like This' when Site 12 is suddenly flooded with light. We freeze. The high beams of the pick-up across the road are on us.

Victor asks another of his rhetorical questions. 'Now what?'

I can tell him. I've seen this movie – several times. The next sound you hear is a car door slamming shut and then a large man in a flannel shirt, down vest and a baseball cap steps out of the shadows, his smile sly and his gun pointing at you.

But I don't tell him. I don't tell him because a figure has just stepped out of the shadows, a large man in a flannel shirt, down vest and a baseball cap, walking towards us with a smile on his face and a lantern in his hands.

He doesn't speak, he drawls. 'Howdy doody,' he says. 'I thought maybe you folks could use a little help.'

'Mabel Marie Witherspoon, of 34 Sasqua Drive, died peacefully at her home on 12 October after a long illness. She's with her maker now . . .'

The hunters all pulled out at daybreak, leaving only three sites occupied. Across the dirt road Don and Jeannie, who work in a nuclear plant – 'They say there's no risk,' said Don, 'but what else would they say? And where else can you get a job?' – are listening to the local station for the weather report, which comes after the obituaries. It was Don who, at Jeannie's urging, turned his headlights on us last night so we could see to pitch the tent. In Site 12, Ron Castlewhite, dedicated fisherman, experienced camper, lifetime member of the Good Sam Club, and lender of lanterns, is having a conversation with Victor while Victor tries to get the stove going so we can make a morning cup of tea before it starts pissing down again.

'I was layin' in my trailer last night, listenin' to that storm kick up like a cornered bear,' Ron is saying, 'an' I thought to myself, I bet those two are gettin' pretty wet in that itty-bitty little tent of theirs.'

It wasn't exactly a long shot. The two of us were getting bloody wet in that itty-bitty tent; the two of us, our sleeping bags, our boots, our jeans, our air mattresses, Roy's bag, the two wholewheat rolls we were saving for breakfast and the postcard I'd started writing to my cat: Dear Elvis, You'd really like camping. Being in the tent is even cosier than curling up in a big brown bag.

Rule of the Road number 7: Don't let loved ones know what it's really like or they might start to worry.

'Least you had the lantern,' Ron is saying. 'Warm it up for you a bit. Colder than a witch's tits last night.'

Victor says, 'Um,' which is his way of admitting that the lantern would certainly have warmed it up for us a bit if it hadn't gone out and refused to relight, and that he now has a pretty good idea of just how cold a witch's tits might be. And I know how cold it can get in the mountains.

'My wife and I used to camp like you two,' says Ron. 'Little tent you couldn't kick a beetle around in. One of those damn stoves goes out soon as a bird breathes near it.' There's a nanosecond of silence. 'Had some great times,' Ron chuckles. 'Yeah, we had some great times, I'm not denyin' that, but I'm too old for that shit now.' He raises the mug of coffee he's holding and takes a sip. It's a Bart Simpson mug with the legend Underachiever and Proud of It printed along the bottom. 'I'm a fisherman, not a martyr. And since I hurt my back I've got enough pain without goin' lookin' for it.' Ron fell off a truck at work. The doctors thought he'd never walk again. He smiles over Bart's head. 'So I got me that trailer. Got a generator, stove, heater, toilet – even got me a shower . . .'

Which is considerably more than the hippies have. The little amenities at Big Bend like electricity in the toilet, hot water and showers were shut off for the winter the day we arrived. They must have known we were coming.

Ron shakes his head. 'Boys think I'm crazy, of course.' He watches Victor put another match to the stove. '"Dad," they say to me, "what you want to spend all your time out in the woods for? Sittin' around fishin' and you ain't even got no TV." But I love it. "What you want to stay cooped up in a house for?" I say to them. There's this whole big beautiful world out here.' He sighs. 'If their mom was still alive they'd be out here,' he says. 'She loved this life as much as me.'

The stove is burning with a fierce, orange light, which even I, the person who has never once managed to get the stove going, know is wrong. It should be a calm and steady blue.

'Maybe the wick needs to be cleaned,' says Ron.

Victor admits that he's already cleaned the wick three times. 'Maybe,' he says.

'Alaska,' says Ron. 'The last real wilderness.' He takes another sip of coffee. 'That's my dream. To see Alaska before I die.'

The flame on the stove pffts out. Some of us would just like one last cup of tea before we die.

'Already bought my plot,' says Ron. 'Next to my wife. All paid up. All the boys have to do is see that I get put in it.'

From what I've seen of Ron's sons – school photos of two hulking blonds with small blue eyes and superhero smiles – this might be more than enough to ask.

'But not till I've seen Alaska,' says Ron. 'I'm not goin' into no ground until I've seen that.'

'Shit,' says Victor as another match is extinguished by the Whisper Lite.

'You know, it only takes five minutes to boil up a pot of coffee on my Coleman,' says Ron.

Victor looks up. He is about to speak – presumably to say 'Cheers, mate' – but his attention is caught by Jeannie, who is coming across the road in her plaid shirt, jeans and canvas fisherman's cap decorated with flies. In each hand she holds a paper plate, circled in steam. 'I thought you two could use a hot breakfast,' she says.

'I've got a big ol' Harley back home,' Ron is saying. 'Turquoise blue. She's a beaut.'

The sun has finally broken through the clouds and is beginning to dry up the morning rains. Victor is wiping off the Nighthawk with toilet paper. 'We met a guy on an Indian,' he says. 'That was a nice bike.'

'Mine's a great bike,' says Ron. 'I told my eldest, you got yourself a car and if you want to use the pick-up, you can have it, but you keep your hands off my Harley. Nobody touches the Harley but me.'

The Honda now looking more like the victim of dew than of a monsoon, Victor puts the key in the ignition and gets on.

'Had a friend, Billy Warner, crazy guy – man, you wouldn't believe half the stuff Billy got up to,' says Ron. 'Billy, he was comin' down one of them little ruts between the trees we call roads around here one night on his Hog, and all of a sudden he slams into this thing – figured it must be a bear or a moose the way it didn't move when he hit it . . .' Ron starts chuckling. 'You know what he was sayin' when they found him? He was shoutin' out for whisky and fresh horses for his men. Man, he was somethin'.' Ron pushes his baseball cap back on his head. 'Wound up in hospital with his bike in pieces and a five-thousand-dollar bill from this farmer for killing his cow.'

'Jesus,' says Victor. 'Five thousand for a cow?' He turns on the ignition and pushes the starter.

'Shit, yeah,' says Ron. He slips one of his painkillers into his mouth, swallows it with a sip of coffee, then laughs. 'You gotta watch yourself on those roads, man. It ain't just the sheriff you gotta worry about. You hit somethin' that big and you ain't goin' nowhere for quite some little time.'

The engine catches, briefly, then thinks better of it. It doesn't look as though we're going nowhere for quite some little time anyway.

'Told Billy he shoulda kept the horns and tied them on the front of the bike like a trophy,' says Ron. 'Course, there wasn't that much to tie them on to, I guess.'

'Five thousand for a cow,' Victor says again as the engine almost catches a second time. He's thinking about our budget.

'You shoulda seen that Harley of Billy's,' says Ron. 'Customised the hell out of it.' He takes another swig of coffee. 'Course, I've never seen no sense in tryin' to improve on something that's already perfect, but even I have to admit that Hog was somethin' else.'

Victor's head is bent over the tank and his eyes are closed in fervent supplication. 'I'm begging you,' he's saying to the bike, 'in the spirit of Monty, start the fuck up.'

Talk all you want about Harleys, they don't have the soul of a Honda. She starts the fuck up. We finally have her name: Montoya.

'There you go,' says Ron. 'Maybe now you'll be able to get that itty-bitty stove of yours goin'.'

The itty-bitty stove is going, if reluctantly, and it and I are under the awning formed by the tarpaulin Jeannie and Don lent us to put over the tent. Victor's out in the rain trying to get the fire going while I chop vegetables with my Swiss army knife and try not to bleed on the carrots.

'Too bad you missed the big trail bike rally,' Ron is saying from the shelter of his parka. 'You'd've enjoyed it, Vic. I used to ride it myself, before I nearly got myself crippled for life, but now I just help out with the organisation and stuff. They got a course makes that road comes down here look like a four-lane highway.'

Victor, hunched on the ground building up the kindling, glances up at Ron. 'Really?'

'Shit, yes,' says Ron. 'There's guys come from all over the world for this. It's a real international event.'

Up until now it seemed possible that the only international event likely around here would be the passage of a flock of Canadian geese.

'How big's the race?' It hasn't escaped Victor's notice that Ron is a fisherman, either.

'Big!' Ron hoots. 'Shit, man, when I say big, I mean big. Twenty thousand people turned up to watch it last year. They haven't seen a party like that around here since we whopped you guys in the Revolutionary War.'

Victor, distracted from the task of creating heat by the seductive thought of speed and danger, sits back on his heels. 'Sounds all right.'

'Only had the one tragedy,' says Ron. He adjusts the hood of his parka around his baseball cap. 'Happened year before last.' He sighs the sigh of a man who knows human nature better than he'd like. 'Always people lined up all along the track, no matter how many times they're told to stay back. Anyway, this guy lost control and the bike went into the crowd like a dart thrown at a board. Killed a sixteen-year-old girl.' He snaps his fingers. 'Just like that.'

'Shit,' says Victor.

'Ain't the half of it,' says Ron. 'This was a real tragedy.'

'The rider died too?'

Ron shrugs. 'Eventually.'

Remembering what he was doing, Victor lights the kindling with his Zippo and starts fanning it.

'Girl's father was at the race,' Ron continues. 'Went to his truck, got his shotgun out from under the seat, went back to the track and shot the boy dead.'

'Shot him?' repeats Victor. 'Nobody tried to stop him?' He flicks the Zippo again.

'It's hard to stop a man with a shotgun unless you've had a few seconds to think about it,' says Ron.

'Christ,' I say. 'That's horrible. What about the cops? What happened to the father?'

Ron shrugs. 'Don't know.' He gazes over Victor's head at the dark shape of the wood in the gloaming. 'Too damp,' he says, changing the subject. 'You'll never get it started like that.'

Victor doesn't say anything; he's blowing on the smoking kindling.

'You just wait right here,' says Ron. 'I know an old Indian trick that'll get that fire goin' in a jiffy.'

'What do you think it is?' I say to Victor as Ron ambles off to his campsite in the rain.

'I don't care what it is,' says Victor. 'I'm just tired of being cold. I want to feel some real heat, even if it's in the rain.'

Ron returns with a five-gallon can of kerosene. He pours it over the wood and throws a match on top. It goes up like the bloody towering inferno.

He grins in the sudden light from the fire. 'You see?' he says. 'Damn clever, those Indians. Works every time.'

Ron has a string of coloured patio lights in the shape of fish across the width of his plastic porta-room. They were one of the last presents he got from his wife, a congratulations-on-starting-to-walk-again gift. In the darkness of the stormy night they make the porta-room seem homey.

'I know you're gonna find this hard to believe,' Ron is saying as he puts a pot of coffee on the stove, 'but I used to have hair as long as yours.'

I can't help myself. 'You were a hippy?' I had no trouble imagining him when he said he'd been a marine, but the image of Ron Castlewhite with his mountainman's moustache and thick glasses and hair to his waist defeats me.

Ron slowly returns to the table. 'Hell, no,' he grins. 'I wasn't no hippy, I was an undercover narc.'

Victor smiles one of his all-purpose smiles. 'You were a narc?'

'That's right,' says Ron. 'They needed young men, you know, you can't send some ol' boy with a crew cut and a beer belly out after the pushers, can you? Be like sendin' a bear down here to find out who the hunters are.' He smiles an all-purpose smile of his own. ' 'Sides, the pay was good and you got to know a lot of girls.'

Victor won't meet my eyes. I'm tempted to ask Ron if this was before or after he was in the marines, or before or after he was county sheriff, but it's a temptation I manage to resist.

'Shit, man,' says Ron, 'I'm tellin' you, you shoulda seen the set-up they gave me. Fancy apartment, expensive clothes, brand new Porsche . . .' He pops his after-dinner pill. 'Course, it had a few drawbacks. Nobody was allowed to know where I was. I couldn't even go home to see my folks.' He gives Victor a look. 'An', naturally, I wasn't the most popular fella in town, not drivin' around in a Porsche with hair halfway to my butt.' He gets up to check the coffee. 'Shit, I had just as much chance of bein' hanged by some drunken good ol' boys as I did of bein' shot by a drug dealer.'

'What's a good ol' boy?' asks Victor.

'You really do come from England, don't you?' says Ron. He puts a container of creamer and a jar of sugar on the table. 'A good ol' boy's a fella who's been in one place so long he thinks he owns it, and believe you me, he ain't the type to like any strangers comin' on his land.'

'Rednecks,' says Victor.

'Similar concept,' says Ron. 'Very, very similar.' He brings the pot and three mugs to the table and starts to pour. 'You're all right in West Virginia,' he says as he hands me a mug. 'Folks are poor, but they're good people – they ain't gonna give you any unprovoked trouble.' He passes a mug to Victor. 'You gotta watch your butt once you cross the border, though. There's guys out there'd take Christ down from the cross just to steal the nails. Mississippi, Louisiana, Tennessee – even in Virginia. Virginians aren't the same as us. You wanna watch out for those little hick towns where there's nothin' to do and the sheriff's name is Bubba.'

'We'll be careful,' Victor assures him. 'We're not taking any chances.'

'You don't hafta take no chances,' says Ron. 'You just hafta be there, that's all.'

'We're keeping the bubbas at bay,' I sing as I try to make my sleeping bag small enough to fit into its sack, 'down here it's the only way. They all have a gun, and they're lookin' for fun, so we're keeping the bubbas at bay.' I break off from this original composition to ask Victor a question. 'It doesn't seem odd to you?' I say. 'You breed the fish in one place and then you put them in the river so all these guys can fish them back out? Why not just sell them from the back of a truck and cut out the middle man?'

'Can't do that,' says Victor, effortlessly rolling his sleeping bag into a tight cylinder. 'It's not sportsmanlike. And anyway, there might be a shortage of empty Bud cans in the woods if they didn't encourage the fishermen.'

'Thank God we won't be here to see it.' I shriek slightly as my sleeping bag uncoils itself and pops into my arms. 'Thank God we won't have to roll these bloody things up again for one day.'

Although we're agreed that we really love camping and that our two days at Big Bend have been idyllic, if wintry, and that it's just as well we're poor so there's no chance we would ever become the type of people who always stay in hotels and miss all the fun, we've decided to push on to the next city to get the tyre repaired and spend the night in a motel. We're even thinking of buying a bigger top box before this one bursts under the strain.

Victor finishes shoving his sleeping bag into its compression bag and leans closer to me, sniffing. 'Good grief, woman! You expect me to take you into civilised society? You smell like a pit toilet.'

'That's you you're smelling.' I've got two hands on the stuff bag and my knee in its centre and can't take the chance of letting go and losing it all just to hit him.

He gives me a smug smile. 'No it's not. I have that rugged, real-man scent. But you . . .' He puts his face nearer my shoulder, sniffing hard. 'Maybe more a cesspool than a pit toilet . . .'

We haven't had a shower or done any laundry since we left New York. It's been too cold to wash without hot water, and proper brushing is hard in the dark. You can only imagine what the frontiersmen smelled like. No wonder they were reluctant to leave the woods.

'I'm not the one who stank the tent out last night with his farts,' I remind him. 'You're like a portable peat bog.' Lukewarm glop, our staple diet of vegetables and something with water (miso, dried soup, a packet of sauce mix), in cold rain could never be recommended as an aid to digestion.

'Oh, aren't you?' asks Victor. 'Just because yours are silent doesn't mean they're not deadly. Ron told me he could smell you from his trailer. He thought it was a skunk.'

'You mean he told you he could hear yours. You sound like a team of burros.' I jam the sleeping bag in the last inch and the stuff bag rips at the seam. 'Now look what you made me do!' Reflexes sharpened by getting back to nature, I wham him in the stomach with it.

'My wife hit me once with a fishing pole,' says Ron, suddenly materialising beside the bike. 'She was a little woman, but she sure could pack a wallop.' He watches Victor squeeze the sleeping bags into the saddlebags. 'Happy trails again, huh?'

Victor nods. 'We've still got a way to go.'

'Peru,' says Ron. 'I don't rightly know if I'd like to go that far, but I'll tell you one thing: if it wasn't trout season tomorrow I'd have half a mind to get my Harley and go with you as far as California, back or no back.'

'You should do it,' says Victor. He throws the saddlebags over the bike.

'Maybe next time,' says Ron. 'You never can tell, you know. It don't always help to have too many plans.' He pushes his cap back on his head and stares up at the mountains. 'If there's one thing I've learned in life,' he says, though so flatly he might be talking to himself, 'it's that we're all just passengers on this train. Ain't none of us drivin'.' He pulls his hat back in place and grins at Victor. 'Or maybe I'll run into you in Alaska,' he says with his usual heartiness. 'Hell, wouldn't that be somethin', seein' you two come ridin' through the snow on that Honda?'

I don't want to think about how cold riding a bike through Alaska might be. 'Let's hope we don't get that lost,' I say.

Ron jams his hands in his pockets. 'Still,' he says, 'West Virginia's not so bad, is it?'

You don't have to have visited Great Britain to know that its countryside is beautiful, you only have to have taken English in school. Shakespeare and his sceptr'd isle, Burns and his grasses, Wordsworth and his bloody daffodils. But we are far from the neat hedgerows of England now. The word beautiful isn't an adequate description of West Virginia, but what word is?

'It's great,' I say.

'It's fantastic,' says Victor.

Ron nods towards the iridescent mountains. 'It's funny, ain't it,' he says, suddenly in a reflective mood. 'Everybody comes down here gettin' all excited about the trees and the colours, but if you think about it, it's just a bunch of dead leaves.'

Victor and I look silently up to where the hazy mountains seem to touch the sky.

Death has never looked this good before.

5

I PITY THE POOR
IMMIGRANT

Rules of the Road numbers 8, 9 and 10 (What Gets Wet Gets Dry, What Gets Cold Gets Warm, What Gets Dirty Gets Clean) are in full operation. There are dead leaves and twigs scattered across the floor of the motel room, sleeping bags hanging from the curtain rod, one air mattress draped over the chair and another over the rail in the closet, wet clothes strung across the room on a piece of string and eye hooks, our two towels spread on the foot of the bed. MTV's on the set attached to the wall, but I'm not watching it. Unchilled and washed and smelling faintly of coconut shampoo instead of something rotting slowly, I'm looking at the map.

Henry . . . Gladys . . . Joel . . . Viola . . . Mike . . . Lester . . . Sarah . . . Helen . . . Jesse . . . Ethel . . . Sadie . . . Mary's Home . . . The town names remind me of a stack of old photographs found in a junk store, calling up questions without any answers. What happened to the couple on the sofa holding hands and smiling? To the three men in uniform in front of the fountain? To the little boy in his Sunday suit with the teddy bear in his hands?

Who were these Henrys, Sarahs, Joels and Violas? Where did they come from? Where had they been? Runaways, adventurers, prostitutes, railroad agents, mail-order brides, indentured servants, trappers, settlers, people with dreams or people with pasts – what were their lives like? Their deaths? Did they ever wish that they'd stayed at home?

Cucumber . . . Pickaway . . . Left Hand . . . Finger . . .

Sinksgrove . . . Furnace . . . Bud . . . Duck . . . Halfway . . .
Wolfcreek . . . Wolftown . . . Elk Garden . . . Eagleville . . . Forks of
Buffalo . . . Wolf Pen . . .

Things don't get named for no reason. I picture fields of cucum-
bers, groves of sinks, gardens thick with elk, trails black with
buffalo, whole villages of eagles, towns and creeks and pens of
wolves with shamans' eyes; struggling farmers scrabbling at the land
and gold-mad miners chipping at the mountains; severed hands and
digits lost in accidents and mayhem; a year of heat, a case of beer,
white-faced settlers crouched behind rocks, some poor half-starved
sod finally collapsing on a riverbed: I'm gonna stay here, it must be
halfway t'somethin'.

Independence . . . Temperance . . . Nicely . . . Liberty . . .
Improve . . . Enterprise . . . Prospect . . . Harmony . . . Justice . . .
Friendship . . . Pleasant . . . Good . . . Neversink . . . Hope . . . What
utopian dreams, what faith in the future, stopped them from being
called more apt names like Oppression, Drunk as a Cowboy,
Wholsale Slaughter, Land Scam, Watch Your Back, Shoot First, Drop
Like a Rock, or Pack It in Now?

Victor comes out of the bathroom, drying his hair with a white
towel that says Elkins Motel in green. He throws himself down on
the other bed and starts flicking through the channels with the
remote. Game show, game show, sitcom, talk show, sitcom, cops,
cops, home shopping, talk show, true crime, missing children, sitcom, sitcom, some geezer with an attitude but a pure heart who does
the cops' job better than the cops.

Victor groans. 'Jesus, what kind of country is this?' he wants to
know as the evening offerings flash by. 'You can't get an inner tube
repaired, you can't buy a top box, but they've got 500 bloody stations
and there's never anything on.'

Happy . . . Loving . . . Hometown . . . Darling . . . Felicity . . .
Friendly . . . Midnight . . . Sunrise . . . Defiance . . . Brandy
Station . . . Lone Bear . . . Lone Eagle . . . Lone Pine . . . Lonely . . .

I don't look up. 'You forgot to mention that they put sugar in
everything and they don't know how to make coffee.'

Bogota . . . Moscow . . . Athens . . . Birmingham . . .
Manchester . . . Norfolk . . . Lima . . . Ararat . . . Florence . . .
Verona . . . Dublin . . . Belfast . . . Hamburg . . .

Alone on the endless plains like a bottle on the ocean, stuck up a
mountain with no sense of time, sitting on the cabin porch waiting
for someone or something to come out of the wilderness – what

homesick moment of longing for smokestacks, steeples or a certain summer night gave these Podunk towns their names?

Victor puts MTV back on. The group singing now isn't the one that was singing before, but it might be. He throws down the remote and comes over to see what I'm doing.

'Beardstown,' he reads. 'You think the Indians named it because it was full of guys with beards?'

'Yeah, but I bet it must've been before the novelty wore off.'

'What about Cashpoint?' asks Victor. 'The first automatic teller in the new world?'

'Here's one.' I put my finger to the page. 'Only. What was that named for? Only hope? Only chance? This could only happen to me?'

'Oh, come on,' says Victor as Beavis and Butthead, the nation's most popular morons, replace the identikit band. 'That one's easy.' He drops the wet towel over my head. 'Only in America.'

'Incredible,' Victor mutters as we come back to 219. 'Totally bloody incredible.' In a land where a general store and a fuel pump are a town, Elkins is a city. It has a library, a movie house, motels, hotels, shopping centres, laundromats, bars, gas stations, a tourist information centre, several car dealers, and two motorcycle shops. What it doesn't have is a motorcycle shop that will patch up our inner tube or sell us a bigger top box, or a restaurant open after 8 pm.

'Let's go right,' I suggest. We haven't tried that yet.

He swings right. 'I just can't believe we have to buy a whole new tyre. A whole new tyre!' He kicks a Bud can out of our path. 'Nobody in London's going to believe this. They're going to think it's a joke.'

We pass a bar and both look in the window, thinking of food. Everyone in the darkened room behind the shining beer signs is male. If this were New York it would mean the bar was gay and that not only might it have food but the food would be good. That isn't what it means in West Virginia. We trudge on.

'Mayo must've known,' I say. 'If he hadn't put that sealant in the tyre we'd really be in trouble.'

'You mean we'd still be in Pennsylvania,' says Victor.

We pass a few more hamburger and submarine places.

'At least we got to watch the video.'

Al, the genial owner of Elkins' second motorcycle store and organiser of the annual big trail-bike rally, entertained us with videos of past races while we waited for the new tyre to be fitted. Dozens of young men in leathers covered with West Virginian mud, ploughing through the woods and streams while the onlookers drank beer, cheered and generally got in the way.

'Have any bad accidents?' asked Victor as the three of us stood in front of the television at the side of the shop, watching the Australian who sends Al a Christmas card every year side slide down a hill of rocks.

'Not a one,' said Al. 'Haven't lost a rider yet. Got the best safety record of any of the big meets.'

At the risk of giving the impression that I didn't believe him, I asked about the guy who killed the sixteen-year-old girl and was then shot by her father. Al looked at me as though I'd confirmed every suspicion he'd ever had about people from New York. If he'd been Tommi he would have said, 'What you on, girl?' Instead he said, 'Who told you that?'

I told him who told us.

'Never heard of him,' said Al. He put another tape in the set. 'Man's talking a crock a shit.'

At last, far along the highway where the gas stations and fast food chains began to thin out, we come upon a small white house by the roadside. Rosemary's Restaurant, Fine Foods. Victor holds open the aluminum door with the R in the centre and I sashay through. Victor walks into me, knocking me into the room. The reason he walks into me is because I have stopped deader than a cow hit by a Harley two feet inside the door. From what I can see, Rosemary's Restaurant isn't a restaurant, it is Rosemary's living room. There is a sofa and chairs and a coffee table covered with china figurines. There are pictures of roses and kittens on the walls. At the back of the room two plump women in flowered dresses and dark-framed glasses sit behind a folding table of old lamps and crockery. They look back at us expectantly, their red lips not quite smiling.

I can't speak. They remind me of my aunts, women who attacked life as though it were mildew, spraying everything that moved with deodorant or disinfectant and covering everything else in plastic. My aunts would never have let anyone who looked like me or Victor pump gas in their cars let alone enter their homes.

'Pardon me,' says the charming, well-mannered Englishman behind me, adjusting his bandanna, which slipped on the impact. 'We were looking for the restaurant.'

'Shucks, honey,' says the one with the pearls and the maple-leaf brooch. 'Restaurant's only open in the summer.'

She makes it sound as though it's something we should have known.

'Where you from?' asks the other one, her eyes on Victor. 'I just love your accent.'

'I love yours, too,' says Victor.

We missed the City of Brotherly Love, we missed Gettysburg, we missed the cranberry festival, the fiddle festival, the banjo competition, the blues bash and the catfish derby; we'll never see moonlight on the Chesapeake or have the bike stolen from under us at knifepoint in Washington, DC, but for the first time since we left New York, we have something we really want to see today. And, also for the first time since we left New York, we've actually found it.

White Sulphur Springs is not the thriving metropolis that Elkins is, but it has a prosperous, white middle-class air about it, and is several blocks and shopping centres long. We are not here for the shopping, however, we are here for the springs, warm pools deep in the woods where you can pretend that the continent hasn't yet been discovered while you soak off the dirt and grease of the road. But first we want food. We start at one end of town, pulling into every diner and café along the main street to check the menu, and wind up at the other, peering into the window of the Hong Kong Restaurant. This is not what I think of when I think of Southern cooking, but at least, says Victor, we know there'll be something we can eat, the Chinese think of vegetables as food not garnish. We're getting tired of the here's-another-fool smile that always follows the statement that we're vegetarians – no wonder you're so skinny, you mean not even chicken? Shit, what the hell do you eat? He opens the glass door with the announcement of a Saturday night square dance taped to it.

The Hong Kong Restaurant is a large, shabby storefront with a half-curtained window at the front and a painted screen at the back and country music playing from a radio on the kitchen hatch. The walls are stained and the ceiling's peeling. There are plastic flowers on the tables and a Chinese lantern and calendars of children, puppies and country roads hanging by the old-fashioned cash register. Victor says that according to William Least Heat Moon you can judge what the food will be like by the number of calendars in a place. There are five. Despite this, the only other people in the restaurant are the owners.

The wife, a small, chubby, smiling woman in rayon slacks and a yellow blouse, comes bustling towards us as soon as we step through the door, menus flapping. Here's someone else well acquainted with hope.

She grabs at chairs. 'Where would you like to sit? Here? Here?' Her gold tooth flashes. 'Sit where you want.'

'Spoiled for choice,' Victor mumbles as we head towards a table against the wall.

Her head bobs. 'You want Coca-Cola? You want Seven-Up?'

'Tea,' I say.

'Tea,' says Victor.

'Tea,' she bobs.

A small, bone-thin man in a white T-shirt and apron looks out at us from the even bleaker kitchen, a large spoon in his hand. He has the smile of a politically incorrect cartoon Chinaman on a bottle of soy sauce or a thirties movie poster.

This is the humble, nervous Chinese couple from a million films, but the only one, I'd venture, in White Sulphur Springs. How the hell did they end up here?

'Jesus,' whispers Victor. 'Have we walked into a Charlie Chan set or something?'

I pick up the menu of the Hong Kong Restaurant, Lee and May Teoh, proprietors. There's quite a bit of choice: vegetable chop suey or vegetable chow mein, both described in red print as 'very delicious'.

Victor tosses his menu aside. 'You order,' he says. 'Get me whatever you're not having and we'll split them. I've got to take a leak.'

The wife comes back with our tea. She's still smiling. 'You want to order now?' She's still bobbing, too.

I smile, but I'm not happy. Last night we eventually ate in one of the submarine sandwich places – the Vegetarian Special. Here to Serve You Maryann, who would clearly have preferred serving invading Russians to us, had slapped on the toppings with her naked hand. For breakfast we had a lot of the free coffee given by the motel and a bag of corn chips. I don't want chow mein. I want black-eyed peas and cornbread and home fries. 'One vegetable chow mein and one vegetable chop suey.'

'Luncheon Special?' She points to the hand-written sign attached to the menu with a paper clip: Lunchin Special. 'You have egg roll and soup. Very delicious.'

'No meat,' I say, starvation making me tetchy. 'Just vegetable chow mein and vegetable chop suey.'

She has, in fact, not one but two gold teeth. 'We have meat. We have beef. We have pork. Very delicious.'

'No,' I say, getting tetchier. 'We don't eat meat. Nothing with meat.'

'Chicken?' she asks. 'You like shrimp?'

Though a person who worries about how chickens are kept and cattle treated, I'm ready to slap her. 'No meat, no chicken, no shrimp. Just vegetables.'

'Fry rice? Fry rice very delicious.'

Or fry her, even. 'Plain,' I say, drowning out Merle Haggard. 'And soy sauce and chilli sauce.'

'No chilli,' she smiles, bobbing. 'Ketchup.'

I'm still grouchy after the food arrives. I hate white rice. I hate chow mein. I'm usually indifferent to chop suey, but today I hate that too. If I'd wanted to eat Chinese food I'd have gone to China, not West Virginia.

Victor doesn't give a shit. He shovels it in as though the only reason he came was to eat very delicious chop suey and drink weak tea. I'd like to slap him, too.

He sucks up the last grain of rice and glances at my plate. He gives me a thoughtful, suspicious look. You wouldn't think that two people with such divergent tastes in music and clothes as Victor Ernesto David Sanchez and my mother would have very much in common, but they do have this look – 'That all you're having?' – and a stubborn belief that I don't eat enough.

'I'm full.'

Thoughtfulness and suspicion are joined by scepticism. 'You're full?'

'Yes,' I repeat, 'I'm full.'

'If you don't eat it now it goes with us, you know,' he says. 'You'll get it tonight in the glop.'

But at least I won't be able to see it. 'Then I'll get it tonight in the glop,' I say, trying not to sound as though I'm talking to my mother. 'Right now I'm going to the loo.'

When I come back, my pockets stuffed with toilet paper, Victor and Mrs Teoh are deep in conversation.

'One year,' she's saying to Victor as I take my seat. 'One year here last June.' Her smile is like a sigh. 'Very quiet here,' she elaborates. 'Very different.'

Very different from what? Singapore? Canal Street? Hong Kong? Beijing? I want to ask her what apocalyptic mistake in map-reading landed them here, but I'm not sure how to phrase it. Did you come here on purpose? Did you get ripped off on your tickets? Are you working off a debt?

'Where were you before?' asks Victor.

'San Francisco.' Her smile becomes a smile again. 'You going to San Francisco?'

Victor answers, 'Yes,' with confidence, even though we're going to LA.

'Go to Chinatown,' she advises us. 'Chinatown is very nice,' and she lapses into silence, smiling at us but thinking, maybe, of somewhere else.

Victor asks her where the springs are.

'You going to the springs?' She seems half delighted, half surprised.

He is all surprised. 'You mean you haven't been?'

She shakes her head as though the question is ridiculous. 'No, no, we don't go, but you can go. You can see them. You're tourists.'

I look at Victor. There's a law?

From the opening to the kitchen, Mr Teoh nods. 'You're tourists,' he says. 'You can go.' He points behind him. 'Not far. Just up the road.'

The road we're on is an interstate.

'In the hotel,' says Mrs Teoh.

I look at Victor and Victor looks at me. In what hotel?

The guard made us leave Montoya in the employee car park with the pick-ups and Fords, where she looks vulnerable and alone. We pass through the formal entranceway and follow the frightfully immaculate landscaped sidewalk into the frightfully immaculate grounds on foot. I'm waiting for someone to stop us for trespassing. The White Sulphur Springs Hotel can't see a lot of ripped jeans, leather jackets and bandannas. It can't see a lot of people who shop at Walmart or Piggly Wiggly, either. Everyone we've passed so far looks like they stepped out of an ad in *Vogue*, with the exception of the groundskeepers, who wear uniforms. My sister must be right after all. I must be middle class, because, Lord, am I happy that for once we don't smell.

'You reckon that's the hotel?' asks Victor as we come around a graceful bend. On one side of the road is a massive, pillared mansion; on the other a stone bench where the lucky tourist can sit and admire the massive, pillared mansion at his or her leisure.

'It must be. It looks like the White House.'

White Sulphur Springs, we now know, is not some ancient tribal site but the well-appointed resort of presidents and the people presidents call friends – politicians, the heads of multinationals, movie stars, arms dealers. Enemy representatives were interred here during the war. It's a hell of a lot better than Auschwitz.

We follow the road, smooth as polished onyx, round the back. The setting is almost unreal, so perfect are the rolling lawns and markered trees and beds of flowers. Precise paved paths cut through the even grass to outbuildings and private cabins, but there is nothing that looks like a trail leading into secluded woodland sheltering a spring-fed pool. We continue past the wedding party having its photograph taken by a silver Rolls draped with white paper streamers and on to the tennis courts and outdoor café.

Victor stops two women dressed down for the afternoon in linen suits and silk shirts and Gucci sunglasses. The ad they're from is for a $1,000 watch, or maybe diamonds.

'You passed it,' says the blonde with a cocktail-party smile. She points behind us. 'It's over there.'

We look over there. Over there is a small pavilion.

Inside the pavilion is a two-inch hole in the concrete from which a tiny fountain of water dribbles. The fountain is marked. 'White Sulphur Springs,' I read.

Victor farts. 'Thank God we didn't miss this.'

On the way out of town we drive past the Hong Kong Restaurant, more quiet than the quiet afternoon. I hit Victor's shoulder. 'Look!' I shout. Mr Teoh is standing at the window, his head just above the net café curtain, staring out at the all-American street reflected in the glass. He smiles his dark smile and waves.

For once, Victor doesn't shout at me to take a picture. 'Christ,' he says. 'Now I wish I could put the loo paper back.'

It's a little after seven o'clock on a Saturday evening in Virginia. Sue and Johnny Wolfbaum are about to drive over the mountain in their new BMW and pick up their children from Johnny's parents.

Johnny is looking forward to the evening. He likes his mom's cooking. He likes sitting on the sofa, drinking beer and watching TV with his dad. He's been missing kissing his kids goodnight.

Sue is looking forward to the evening because it will make her feel normal. Life around here is as simple as a list of chores. People go to work, take care of the kids, watch TV, clean the house, get out videos, drink a few beers and have dinner with their folks once a week. Sue doesn't always feel like this, but tonight she wants to be like everybod else.

Johnny thumps around the trailer's living room, drinking from a can of Bud. His face is clean, his hair is combed, his leather jacket is on, the car keys are in his hand, and his mind is on supper. His stomach growls. He's been waiting to go since his first beer, and now he's on his third.

Sue is in the bathroom, staring at herself in the mirror. Her make-up's all right, but she has to do something with her hair. If they pass anyone she knows on the way to the Wolfbaums' – and how could they pass anyone she doesn't know, she's never lived anywhere else – she wants them to see her and think, well she's looking good. She tilts her head first left and then right. Maybe tie it back. She starts looking through the drawer above the cabinet for a scarf to match her blouse.

Johnny checks the clock on the microwave. If they don't get going he'll miss his favourite show. 'Ain't you ready yet?' he screams. 'What're you doin' in there? Havin' a face-lift?'

'I'll be ready in a minute,' Sue screams back.

Women, thinks Johnny. 'I'm gonna time you!' he threatens. 'Startin' now!' He figures there's a chance Sue might be on time for her own funeral, but only because someone else will be doing her make-up. 'Forty seconds to go!'

Sue closes her eyes and counts to three. One of the kids must have taken the scarf she wants. If she looks, she'll find it wrapped around a pink pony or a purple dinosaur. But she's not going to look. There's no sense getting Johnny all wound up for a scarf. She'll wear the blue one with the yellow hearts. 'Go start the car!' she shouts.

Johnny's finishing his beer when he hears a motorcycle pass by. There aren't that many bikes around here. If it were local he'd likely know who it was. He pulls the pink curtains aside, but he can't see it from the kitchen window – all he can see from there is the side of the garage. Suddenly he wishes they weren't going to pick up the kids after all. Suddenly he'd rather be taking the Harley for a spin than talking about football with his dad. He flips the can into the garbage. 'I'm gonna start the car now!' he bellows. Sue doesn't answer. Women. He doesn't understand them, and he never will.

The dog follows Johnny down the trailer stairs and into the rectangle of gravel in front of the garage. Sunbursts glint on the hood of the BMW. Johnny touches the warm metal – 0–90 in only ten seconds. But he'd still rather be on the Harley. He's just about to open the door when he hears the motorcycle again. He turns to the road as an old, overloaded Honda with New York plates rumbles by. He's still standing by the BMW, just gazing at the road, when he hears the Honda coming back. He steps towards the shoulder and waves his hand.

'Over there!' I scream, squeezing Victor's shoulder. 'That guy over there's flagging us down!'

Victor glances, Montoya slows, we make a sharp right into the driveway and stop in front of a large blue garage. There's a 3,000-more-payments to go BMW parked out front and a tricycle turned over on the grass by the steps to the trailer. The custom licence plate on the car says SUE YOU. The man who stopped us is maybe in his late twenties, large, stocky and fair. Chances are he used to play football. He's wearing a Harley jacket and a schoolboy grin.

'You guys lost?' he asks. 'I saw you go by before. What you lookin' for?'

As impossible as it might seem, given that we're more or less in the middle of a state park, we're looking for a place to camp. Higher than satellites, we came flying down the mountain through a fervent blur of colours, fucking with gravity and the speed limit of Virginia as we freewheeled blind round twists and bends and sudden turnings, blood stampeding. Talk about cheap thrills. But we're well down now. When we reached the bottom, the state park was closed. Till the spring. And the woman in the private RV site took one look at me with my red nose and eyeliner trails dried on my cheeks and asked $16 bucks for the night.

'We—' says Victor.

'Johnny.' He grabs Victor's hand and pumps.

'Victor,' Victor manages. 'And this is Dyan.'

But Johnny is already rolling towards the garage. Definitely a football player.

'Come on over here,' he's saying, gesturing as though he wants us to pass him. 'Just wait till you see what I got in here.'

It could be a horse, of course. Or a finished room that he wants to give us for nothing for as long as we like. But the chances are that it isn't. We exchange a look as we climb from Montoya.

'Vrrroom-vrrroom,' I whisper to Victor's back.

'There she is!' Johnny cries as the garage door rolls upwards and the light goes on automatically, revealing lawnmowers and baby buggies, a pile of wood and an old stove, stacked boxes and news-papers, tools and tyres, and there, in the middle, gleaming like a stallion that has just won the Derby, a 1993 Harley Davidson with fringed handlebars and more chrome than a '58 Caddy. The custom licence plate says ALL MAN. 'Whatta y'think of that?'

It's a big country, so generalities don't always hold, but it does to seem to me that nearly every man we've talked to either used to have a Harley or has one but it's somewhere else. This is the first one we've actually been close enough to spit on.

Victor whistles appreciatively, but his eyes dart to me. 'The legend lives.'

'Jesus,' I say, 'they really exist.'

Johnny hears only praise. 'Ain't she somethin'?' His face is so radi-ant with pride that if he turned off the garage light we'd still be able to see the cobwebs in the corners. He looks at Victor. 'I mean, man, my first bike was a Honda, too, so I ain't dissin' yours, but there just ain't nothin' like this here machine.' He pats the saddle. 'She's a fuckin' dream on wheels.' He looks over at Montoya. 'You goin' far?' he asks, clearly convinced that we'll never make it.

'Peru,' says Victor.

Johnny laughs.

'No, really,' says Victor. 'We're going to Peru.'

Johnny laughs some more. 'You're shittin' me, right? You two are goin' to Peru?'

'Not tonight,' I say. 'We reckoned we'd stay in Virginia tonight.'

'Peru,' howls Johnny. 'Are you guys serious?' He gives Montoya a second critical look. 'You're goin' to Peru on that?'

Maternal pride can be fiercer than Harley-owner pride and a lot uglier. I draw myself to my full height, just below Victor's shoulder, and raise my head. My visor falls off. Pronouncing every syllable as I stoop to retrieve the bloody visor, I confirm: 'Yes, we're going on her. She happens to be an excellent bike.' My voice is clear and res-onant. 'She happens to be the best bike in the country.'

Johnny doesn't hear me. He's telling Victor that he'd love to show him how the Harley runs; man, he should see the Harley come down that mountain, but he and his wife were just leaving to go to his folks' to pick up the kids. 'My wife's inside,' he explains to Victor, pointing towards the trailer. His grin goes conspiratorial. 'You know women, she's been gettin' ready for an hour. If I had t'take Sue to Peru I'd need three trucks and a portable toilet.'

It's just as well he isn't speaking to me.

'We've got to get going anyway,' says Victor. 'We like to camp before dark.'

I give him a look, but he doesn't accept it. He smiles at the heavy chrome mirrors on Johnny's bike, the Harley name elaborately engraved on the backs just in case he forgets the make.

'State ground's closed for the winter,' says Johnny. He grimaces, eyebrows drawn together. 'There's the RV park over the road. You try them?'

'She wants sixteen dollars,' says Victor. 'We're not paying sixteen dollars to pitch a tent.'

'Shit man,' he says. 'I don't know of anything else around here.'

'We're all right,' says Victor. 'There's bound to be something further on.' If not in Virginia, in Tennessee.

'Gonna be cold tonight,' says Johnny. His look of concentration deepens. He's either thinking or about to shit. 'You know, you could put up your tent in here, if you wanted,' he says at last, gesturing to the oil-stained concrete and the heaps of junk.

To my astonishment, not to say surprise, Victor looks tempted. 'Yeah?' he says, glancing at me. I stare back. Just how many drugs has he taken in the past?

'You don't think it might be a little difficult to get the stakes in the cement?' I ask them.

They're saved the trouble of grappling with this tricky question by the arrival of Johnny's wife. Sue's thirty-something, wearing jeans that are a little too tight, a pink mohair pullover, denim jacket and dangling gold earrings, a blue silk scarf decorated with yellow hearts tied in her hair. She looks bone-tired, despite her party make-up, but her smile is friendly. She stops next to me, taking us in. 'What's going on?'

Johnny explains what's going on.

'Peru?' she says, looking at me. 'You're goin' to Peru?'

'Dyan's a writer,' says Victor. 'She's going to write a book about our trip.' Victor has tried passing on this information before, because he's convinced people will find it interesting and that it will help the book if they know, but either no one has understood him or they all took one look at me and thought, he must be joking, if she's a published writer, I'm Secretary of State, and went straight on to what they were planning to say next. Until this moment.

Sue's eyes are suddenly bluer. She was interested in us before, but not as much as she is now. 'You're a writer?' Her ponytail swings. 'A real writer? Johnny, Dyan's a writer.'

Johnny gives her the sort of smile men give women when they start talking about cystitis. 'Yeah?'

Sue's not looking at him. 'You could write my life story,' she says excitedly. 'You won't believe the shit that's happened to me. It'd make an incredible book. Maybe even one of those mini-series.'

Johnny rocks back and forth on his heels. 'We better get goin',' he says. 'My mom'll be wonderin' what's happened to us.' He grins at Victor, not without a certain amount of manly pride. 'My mom hates the way I drive. You know what women are like.'

'Goin'?' Sue looks at him as though he's started speaking in tongues. 'We're not goin',' she says. 'We have company. I'll call your mom and tell her what's happened and we'll pick the kids up tomorrow after church. She won't mind.' Sue pats my arm. 'You two are stayin' here tonight. I won't hear any objections.' She glances at Montoya and the dirty blue tent showing through the holes in the garbage bag meant to keep it dry. 'I bet it'd do you two good to stay in a real home for a change.'

It depends, of course, on what you mean by a real home. Despite what the politicians and women's magazines may say about the importance of the nuclear family, reality teaches that many real homes are to insanity what a petri dish and agar-agar are to a bacteria culture. Don't get too close. And besides, one of the occupants of this particular real home obviously wants nothing more than to see our tail-light disappear around the next bend. On the other hand, the night is looking cold and the dark clouds are gathering. I'd just as soon spend the evening with the Borgias as drive four more hours to end up eating a carrot, a pepper and half an onion cooked in mushroom soup in the rain. I don't say anything, but my expression is open to suggestions.

Victor's manners are better than mine. 'We couldn't impose,' he says quickly.

'They wanna get goin',' says Johnny even more quickly. 'Vic wants to camp before dark, don't you, Vic? And besides my mom—'

'Your mom won't give a shit,' says Sue firmly. 'I'll just phone her while you help Vic bring their stuff inside.'

I look over at Johnny and Victor. Johnny's mouth is slightly open, waiting for his mind to catch up with events; Victor is smiling quietly, waiting to see what happens.

'But Sue,' protests Johnny. 'My mom's—'

'Not gonna give a good goddamn one way or the other,' says Sue, starting to move towards the trailer.

'But my dad . . .'

She stops and looks at her husband. 'You can talk about football with Vic,' she tells him simply. She turns to Victor. 'You have football in England, don't you?'

Victor's smile becomes a little louder. 'Yeah,' he says. 'We have football.'

'You see?' Sue says to Johnny. 'We're going to have a great time.'

'Johnny's never hit me,' Sue is saying as we pull into the parking lot. 'My first husband, he used to knock me around all the time.' She laughs. 'Even though I had all those muscles.' You might not think it to look at her now, Sue said, but she was State Female Bodybuilder two years running, came second in the nationals in '84. And she's right, you wouldn't think so to look at her now. To look at her now you'd think she'd spent her whole adult life worrying about her children's bowel movements and temperatures and organising Tupperware or underwear parties. 'You ever been beaten?' she wants to know.

I shake my head.

'You're lucky,' says Sue. 'My first husband, he was a real psycho.' She takes one hand from the wheel and holds her thumb and fore-finger so they're almost touching. 'I came about this close to death with that bastard. My daddy would've killed him if he'd known the truth.' She returns her hand to the wheel. 'But Johnny's not like that. He's never laid a finger on me, not once. And he loves the kids.' She takes one last sip of beer and puts the can in the drink holder. 'You and Victor married?'

'No.' I finish off my Bud. 'Victor and I are friends.'

She looks over at me, her hand on the door. 'You live together?'

I repeat myself. 'No, we're just friends. He lives in his apartment and I live in mine.'

'You mean you live by yourself?'

'I have a cat.'

'Shit, I can't even imagine what that's like, living by yourself.' She stares at me for a few seconds, trying to imagine it. 'Don't you get lonely?'

I stare back at her. Don't you?

'I have a lot of friends,' I say at last. 'I have a lot to do.'

Sue sighs. 'I guess that's the difference, livin' in a big city. Women don't live by themselves around here. You know, unless they're widows or old maids. People'd think you were weird.' She shrugs.

'Shit, I'm thirty-six and I've never lived by myself for more than a day. Even when Johnny was in the hospital all that time after he crashed his bike, I went home and stayed with my folks.'

We get out. She doesn't bother locking the car. 'Johnny's twenty-nine,' says Sue as we cross the lot.

He hides it well, I nearly answer, but catch myself in time. 'Really?'

'My daddy didn't approve of me marryin' Johnny,' Sue continues. 'My daddy's an important man round here and Johnny's family's practically hillbillies, but he wants me to be happy.' She doesn't quite laugh. 'Most of the time Johnny's more like twelve than twenty-nine, I guess, but he's not a bad man. He'd do anything for me and the kids.' She looks my way. 'You don't ever wish that you were married?'

'Not that I remember,' I answer as we enter the supermarket and I grab a cart. The supermarket is larger than an airline hangar, with an entire aisle for cereals, an entire aisle for snacks and cookies, an entire aisle for Coca-Cola, one shelf for health foods. It makes the Sainsbury's in Camden look like a corner shop. I follow Sue. If I lose her I may never get out.

Sue's surprised to learn that not only do Victor and I not eat meat, we don't eat fish or chicken either, but she rallies quickly. She tosses four baking potatoes, a packet of sliced mixed vegetables and a bag of salad into the cart. 'I'll make biscuits and gravy for Victor for breakfast,' she says, dropping four cylinders of pop-'n'-bake butter-milk biscuits on top of the steak. 'I bet he's never had real Southern home cookin' before.'

We get three family-sized bottles of diet Coke, a suitcase of Bud for the guys and a bottle of wine for us. 'Johnny doesn't drink wine,' says Sue, 'so I usually only buy it for Christmas or something like that. You know, special occasions.'

On the way home we stop in a second shopping centre to see Beauty and Beast, Sue's and Johnny's health and fitness centre. 'Johnny's in charge of the tanning rooms and the sauna,' Sue explains as she snaps on the lights. 'And I manage the business and run the aerobics classes.' On the wall over the reception desk is a life-size photograph of Sue on the Harley, looking wet and windblown in a leather jumpsuit. 'Johnny's friend took that,' says Sue. 'He's a photo-grapher. He wanted to use the bike in some magazine spread he was doing so we did him an exchange.

'Buying the business was my idea,' says Sue as she shows me the tiny tanning rooms. 'When Johnny got laid off I figured he wasn't going to get another job unless we moved to another state, so we took the pay-off they gave him and I borrowed some money from my daddy.' She makes a face. 'And anyway, if Johnny didn't have somethin' to do I figured he'd get into trouble.' She opens another door. 'This is the exercise room.' Two bikes, two rowing machines and a sound system. She makes another face. 'Course, he got into trouble anyway.'

We're climbing the steps to the trailer when Sue suddenly stops. 'There's just one thing I have to ask you before we go in,' she says, looking at me over her shoulder.

I shift the bags in my arms. It's got to be God, I think. She knows I'm not married, she knows I live on my own, she knows my mother drives me nuts. What else could it be?

'What?' I'm wary.

'Do you guys get high?'

'We'll be right back,' says Johnny, passing one of the cans of beer he's holding to Victor. 'Don't you girls get too drunk while we're gone.'

Sue looks up from the potatoes she's preparing for the microwave. 'You watch out for the cops!' she shouts as he opens the front door. 'I mean it, Johnny. You watch out! Don't drive too fast with Vic in the car.' The door bangs shut. 'And don't forget to get some aluminium foil from her!' Sue screams.

For a few seconds she just stands there, watching the space where Johnny was standing, and then she turns to me. 'I hope Vic don't mind driving fast,' she says. 'Johnny's a demon when he gets behind the wheel.'

'Vic doesn't mind going a little fast,' I assure her. 'He can take it.'

'Course they're not going to give it to Johnny,' says Sue. 'They' are Sue's friends Emmy and Barb who live on the other side of some mountain; 'it' is the nickel bag they've promised Sue. 'They don't trust him, 'specially after what happened.' She picks up her wine glass as the BMW leaves the driveway. 'You wanna hear what happened?' she asks.

I reckoned I had a pretty good idea of what kind of trouble Johnny had gotten into. Drunken driving. Speeding. Brawling in a bar. Over Victor's reminder that whatever I took I'd have to carry, I'd already bought a pair of Harley leather trousers for $25 from Johnny, a special deal because I'm the only person they know who's small enough to fit into them. If it wasn't drinking, speeding or fighting, it was probably petty theft.

Sue finishes her story. I've stopped opening the bag of salad and am staring at the housewife with the hearts on her scarf and the potato in her hand. Between the wine and Leonard Cohen being poetically meaningful on the tape machine I must have misheard her. 'How much grass did you say?'

'Seventeen pounds.'

'You can't be serious.' I glance around us. We're in the kitchen, which means we're more or less in the living room. After the living room is a bathroom and the kids' room. After the kitchen is the master bedroom and a bathroom. 'Where did he have it stashed?'

'In the bathtub off our room. It was just going to be overnight. I came home from the store with the kids and it was all just sittin' there.' She gazes at the potato as though it's a crystal ball. 'It was going to give us enough to start buildin' our house. It was for our future.' She takes a newspaper out of the work-table drawer. 'See,' she says, pointing. 'It's our names and everything. I've never been so shamed in my life . . . The whole town knows.'

I try to be comforting. 'At least it's not as bad as armed robbery . . .'

Sue isn't comforted. 'It is in Whyte County,' she says. 'You don't know what these people are like. They're as bad as West Virginians with their attitudes and airs. Everybody knows everybody else's business round here. They're all just waitin' to see you fall. Especially me, because of my daddy. They think I've got a high opinion of myself.' She puts the paper back where it was. 'And because of Johnny. You know, 'cause he's a little wild.' She laughs. 'You don't think they're already talkin' about the hippies stayin' with us, you've got another think comin',' says Sue. 'They've spotted those New York plates. They probably think you've brought us drugs. I'm surprised they ain't drivin' past the trailer tryin' to catch a look at you two.'

With a little bit of luck we might even get busted. I look at the bag of salad, wondering what I'm supposed to be doing with it, then back at Sue. 'So who set you up?'

She pours us more wine. 'This guy Johnny used to hang out with when he was single. I told him the minute Buddy turned up all interested in the Harley and acting like they was long-lost friends not to trust him. "Don't you say nothin' to Buddy about nothin'," I told him. "Buddy's bad news."' Her scowl is resigned. 'But would Johnny listen? Everybody knew Buddy musta done a deal to get off so light, but Johnny's like a kid. He trusts everybody.'

Seventeen pounds of marijuana in the bathtub and you tell some guy who got parole after serving six months for heavy dealing what you're up to. Trusting might not be the most accurate word.

'Jesus,' I say. 'When's the trial?'

'January,' says Sue.

'And then what?' Five-ten in the state pen, the future secure at last.

'I have a lot of faith in God,' says Sue. 'If I didn't have faith in God I probably wouldn't be alive right now. I probably would've given up a long time ago.' She takes a set of silver candlesticks from one of the cabinets and puts them on the counter. 'I've been praying since it happened,' she says. 'I know God will look after us all right.'

I don't say that I reckon God's got his work cut out for him; I pour more wine.

Sue puts blue candles in the holders. When she speaks again her voice is a whisper close to crying. 'I'm thirty-six. Thirty-six. What happened to my life?'

Now there's a question. I hand her her glass.

Later, after Johnny and Victor return with that 90-round-a-hairpin buzz in their eyes, but no grass and no aluminium foil from Emmy and Barb, and Sue and I have gone next door to borrow foil and have a pre-dinner shot of bourbon with her neighbours, who have already had several, and we finish radiating the meal, and Johnny has accepted the fact that he can't watch *Beavis and Butthead* while he eats, he has to sit at the table with the rest of us, and Victor, over Johnny's protests about giving Sue ideas, has laid the table, we sit around it holding hands in the candlelight. Sue bows her head and closes her eyes. Johnny bows his head and closes his eyes. Victor and I stare at the bowl of salad.

'Thank you, God, for all you do for us,' says Sue. 'We really appreciate it. We know you're looking after us. And thank you for bringing these nice people to our door. Amen.'

'Amen,' says Johnny. He opens his eyes. 'I don't know why we have to have these damn candles,' he says, reaching for the largest piece of meat. 'How's a man expected to see what he's eating?'

'We have company,' says Sue. 'It's nice to have candles when there's company.'

Johnny reaches for a few slices of bread. 'It's a good thing we don't have company too often, then,' he laughs.

Kimberley and Matthew Wolfbaum's room is small, colourful and crowded with things. Bright plastic baskets of toys are stacked in the corners, string bags of toys hang from the bunk beds, posters of animals and cartoon characters cover the walls. There are munchkin baseball caps hanging from plastic hooks on the door and munchkin trainers and party shoes and bedroom slippers that look like Mickey Mouse lined up at the bottom of the closet.

Victor is already tucked into the upper bunk under the Batman sheets when I stumble into the room, trying to get to the bed without stepping on something that will squeak or snap in two. The men went to bed at midnight, leaving me and Sue on the sofa listening to Neil Young while Sue talked about the life she might have had if things weren't the way they were but some other way – if anything ever turned out the way you planned.

'Turn on the light,' Victor whispers. 'I'm awake.'

I trip over a plastic pull toy and turn on the light.

Victor sits up. 'How is she?'

'Not so good. She was getting a little weepy,' I whisper back. I've tried so hard, Sue kept telling me and God. All my life, I've tried so hard . . . Johnny's dream is black and chrome and has fringe hanging from the handlebars, but Sue's has no shape or name, hovers between Johnny's open road and her daddy's three-bedroomed house. How can you work so hard to win and still lose? Sue wanted to know. Neither God nor I had an immediate answer, and then Johnny came out, rubbing his eyes, wanting to know why Sue hadn't come to bed yet, didn't women ever stop talking?

'She says she wishes they didn't have the kids so they could just pack up and come with us. She thinks he's going to jail.'

'She's right,' says Victor. 'He is going to jail.' He adjusts his Batman pillow. 'Johnny says he'd come, too, if it didn't mean jumping bail.'

I pull something pink out from under the covers on the bottom bunk and check under the pillow: two My Little Ponies, a white patent-leather handbag on a strap, and half an Oreo.

'What's he think's going to happen?' I get into the bottom bunk. My sheets aren't Batman, they're Barbie. 'Is he worried?'

'How do I know?' asks Victor.

What does he mean, how do I know? They were talking together all night. 'Oh, come on, I saw you two mumbling and grunting together man to man when we were getting supper. What was that about?'

Victor leans over the side. 'It wasn't about the bust. He wanted to know if you were scared on the bike. He said Sue doesn't like him going too fast. And then he was warning me about grizzlies. Says they'll just come into the road and stop the bike and there won't be anything I can do about it.'

'Grizzlies?' I'm not good on bears, and I can't remember where Grizzly Adams lived. Was that Virginia? What about Davy Crockett? He killed a bear when he was three. But that wasn't Virginia, that was Tennessee.

Victor grins. 'He wanted to know if I was carrying a piece.'

'A piece of what?'

Victor whacks me with a stuffed giraffe. 'Are you drunk again, woman?' he demands. 'A piece of what?'

'Leave me alone,' I plead. 'It's been a long day.' I switch off the light and get into bed. 'Sue was worried about you driving with Johnny,' I say into the dark. 'I told her you don't mind dicing with death.'

'He's a good driver,' says Victor. 'I felt safe with him, even when we were taking those mountains at 95 and he was knocking back his Bud and telling me how to outmanoeuvre the cops. And anyway, I knew nothing would happen. This trip's too important for me to die on some back road in Virginia.'

'Christ,' I say. 'What would have happened if you had been killed?'

The mattress sags over my head as Victor rolls over. 'Then I'd never have the chance to know what it's like to be attacked by a grizzly.'

6

GRACELAND

It's not true that there is no specific thing we want to see in the Americas. We want to see, if even for just the wingbeat of a hummingbird, what the earth was like before men began to recreate it. To glimpse it as a planet of magic and miracles, of reckless beauty and antemundane soul – a planet where even man fitted in. In most of the world, even the memory of that planet has vanished, but in the Americas it lingers still. We want to see wilderness and jungle, deserts like lunar landscapes and mountains of whispered legends. We want to see the Grand Canyon at sunset and Machu Picchu at dawn. We want to see one of our last living links with our unimaginable past. We want to see Indians.

In search of Indians, we spent one wet night in North Carolina on the Cherokee Reservation, land of mystery and excitement, according to the postcard I sent to my cat. 'Bury my heart at Wounded Knee,' said Victor as we splashed down the main drag past the pancake houses and the Holiday Inn, McDonald's and KFC, souvenir shops, Santa's World and Cherokee Bingo. Outside one of the souvenir shops was a bear in a cage, outside another an Indian in presumably full Cherokee war regalia. It was $5 to have your picture taken with either of them. The only Indian we actually talked to in Cherokee was the man who ran the RV park, who had been in England during the war. 'I brought an orange from the ship to the pub one night,' he told us, 'and instead of eating it they just passed it around.' Going deeper into Indian territory, today we've crossed the border to Tennessee.

Tennessee Tourist Information is as busy as a shopping centre on a Saturday afternoon. With all the toing and froing, the long shining lines of parked vehicles and the noticeable presence of black people, you might even think it was a shopping centre if it weren't for the fact that none of the black people are pushing the white people's grocery carts to their cars. I sit back on the grass, humming a Chuck Berry tune and watching everyone come and go as I sip my lemon-flavoured iced tea from a can and, next to me, Victor studies the map for a route through Tennessee. There's not an Indian in sight. The women all have perms and red lips, dressed for comfort in bright cotton slacks sets and costume jewellery that winks in the sun. The men are in jeans or Walmart work pants and short-sleeved shirts, notebooks and maps sticking out of the pockets. The children wear advertising: Barbie, Batman, Ninja Turtles, Bart, Homer, Jurassic Park. I watch them get out of their clean, comfortable cars and RVs and go into the information centre, coming out again with pamphlets for pumpkin harvest festivals and homecoming fish fries, marbles championships and inter-tribal pow-wows, discount tickets for historic tours, hotels with pools and restaurants with special menus for kids. The ones who aren't bickering among themselves wear satisfied smiles. They buy cans of Coke and Seven-Up and packets of snack foods from the machines outside the restrooms and sit on wooden benches in the sunshine, dropping wrappers on the lawn. They gather in front of the welcome sign, taking pictures of themselves in Tennessee. Still humming, I pursue my newest hobby, checking out the names of the well-equipped, good-as-home RVs. Pioneer. Prowler. Scamper. Renegade. Wanderer. Nomad. Wilderness. Lynx. But no Last Chance, no Now What?, no Running on Empty.

'People!' a nearby voice suddenly booms. 'Real people!'

We both look up. Stopped in front of us is a battered white van, and grinning from the driver's window are a grizzled black dog wearing a blue bandanna and a thin, wiry, weather-beaten man in his late fifties with excited, not to say lunatic, blue eyes.

'Where you guys from?' he demands. 'You ain't from around here.'

'We started in New York,' says Victor, 'but we come from London.'

The grin deepens. 'Shit!' he hoots. 'A Limey!' He points a finger at Victor. 'You stay right there!' he orders. 'We'll be right back.'

John Carley and Isaac park the van across the road and come right back. John kneels between us; Isaac wanders off, sniffing at the grass. John and Isaac have been in Washington DC on a Vietnam vets demonstration, but they're on their way home to Texas now, thank God. John shows us the bruises on his legs and arms. Fuckin' rednecks jumped him when he was sleeping in the van last night by the side of the road, took his radio and his camera – would've killed him if they could've.

John shakes his head. 'Shit,' he says. 'I ain't seen any real people since I left Texas.' He waves a hand. 'Just these robots with their TV minds. Shit, imagine meetin' real people in Tennessee.' He winks at Victor. 'I got some pot in the van, Vic, you wanna smoke?' It's eleven in the morning, not a good time to be arrested in Tennessee. He tries again. 'How about a shot of bourbon?' Victor holds up his can of iced tea. We're fine. 'You two just stay where you are,' says John, jumping to his feet. 'I got some stuff I want to show you.'

John Carley was a helicopter gunner, a hero. He enlisted in the United States Army in 1968, when he was nineteen. I check my figures: that makes him forty-four, not fifty-nine. John was gung-ho. He shows us the photograph of a handsome young soldier in sharp creases and boots like mirrors receiving a medal from General Haig. It's a proud moment; the young soldier's smile is full of teeth and free of guile. 'It's a weird feeling the first time you kill a man,' says John. 'It's a little like being God, and a little like killing yourself. After that, lots of things don't matter any more.' John spent two years as a prisoner of war, but all he'll tell us about it is that he soon enough gave up and ate the rice the guards always pissed on; he soon enough learned that survival often means compromise. He takes out his false teeth, impersonating Popeye, and waggles a finger near his head. 'It was pretty crazy,' he says. Something so crazy, so out of mind, that over twenty years later you can't sit in the sun surrounded by people as wholesome as pie and give it a name. John stares over our heads, not grinning for the first time. 'Shit,' he says. 'What did I know? I was nineteen, fighting for my country. I had no idea what it was going to be like.'

It's the outraged, baffled refrain of the Vietnam vet. Nobody told us what it was going to be like, nobody told us it was going to change us, nobody told us that we wouldn't be the same as the people who stayed home and mowed their lawns, and paid their mortgages, and watched the game on Sunday after dinner; nobody told us we were going to be diving back into the dark.

Victor gives me a look. What had John thought it was going to be like? Hadn't he ever seen a war movie, watched a documentary, read *Catch-22*? How is it possible that so many men could have been so surprised to reach south-east Asia and discover that war was brutal, dehumanising, uncivilised, that it made you go against everything you thought you believed? You'd think no one had ever fought a war before. America may have given us Coca-Cola and the CIA, but we can't blame it for that.

John shows us the letters his mother received from the State Department, missing in action, and President Johnson, praise for her son who acted above and beyond the call of duty. 'Shit, man,' says John, grinning again. 'And that's all the thanks you get.' Victor digs the duct tape out of the saddlebags and helps John put up a MIA poster in the back window of the van, Don't Forget Them, while Isaac sniffs at the tyres of an RV with a picture of a litter of kittens with red ribbons around their necks in its window.

John shows us a yellowed newspaper clipping about him and his friend, Bob, land-sailing from Texas to California. John says we won't have any trouble in Texas, Texas is cool.

'That's not what everybody else says.' What everybody else says – 200 miles without a house or a gas station or another car, drive-by shootings, land big enough that you'll never be missed – has made even Victor a little nervous.

'Everybody else is lying,' says John. He hoots with laughter. 'I may bullshit, but I never lie.'

One head in a Vietnam vet baseball cap and one head in a red bandanna bend over the map. One large black paw rests on the legend that runs along the top. 'This here's where they marched the Cherokee to Oklahoma,' John is saying. 'Tsa-la-gia, the Trail of Tears. Now there's a whole reburial movement to bring the Cherokee remains back to Tennessee.' He moves his grubby finger eastward. 'And this here is the Cherokee National Forest.' He stabs at a patch of green on the map. 'You should see this, Vic,' says John. 'Right there at the entrance there's an Indian's got his teepee pitched and he ain't movin' till the government buries the Cherokees back on their land.'

'We stayed on the reservation in North Carolina,' says Victor warily. 'Cherokee.'

'More bullshit,' says John. 'Ain't the same thing at all. You don't want to waste your time with all that tourist crap.' He takes another piece of paper from his black attaché case. 'I don't usually show this to white men, but you're different.'

It's a Sioux prayer. He gives Victor a copy of the prayer in Lakota and a handwritten translation.

'White man came along and fucked everything up,' says John.

Isaac, sniffing again, stops behind me. I swing round. 'What are you doing?' Isaac licks my face. I turn to Victor. 'I think he just pissed on me. Did he piss on me?'

Victor smiles, slow.

'That means he likes you,' says John. 'He doesn't take to everyone, you know.'

As we stand on the pavement, John and Isaac waving goodbye, Victor says, 'What do you think?'

I give up trying to smell the back of my leg. 'I think he bullshits, but he doesn't lie.'

'Born on a mountaintop in Tennessee, greenest state in the land of the free . . .'

'Can't you go back to the Chuck Berry?' shouts Victor as we inch along. 'You know, the one about Memphis.'

Eight, maybe nine hours into Tennessee and we're already talking about Memphis. In Memphis we'll find a decent motorcycle shop where we can buy a replacement for the now busted top box and see to our jamming gear selector. In Memphis we'll find a healthfood store where we can stock up on couscous and miso. In Memphis we'll find people who don't look like they're married to their cousins and hate outsiders. In Memphis lies the land of grace. Eight, maybe nine hours into Tennessee, and already we want to get away from its yards of rusting cars and kitchen appliances, its 'missing' posters taped to the doors of grocery stores and gas stations, its bumper stickers for Jesus and America, its pick-up trucks with guns on the roofs and dogs in the back and nobody smiling, its heavy-set men with hard eyes and sexless women with fixed expressions watching us pass, its churches like warnings: After Death: Judgement. Don't Be Afraid Of Tomorrow: God is Already There.

It's not tomorrow we're afraid of, it's tonight. We're somewhere in the Cherokee National Forest, where we plan to camp for a couple of nights, but the Cherokee National Forest looks as though it's been ravaged by an incensed giant – trees broken and uprooted, campsites abandoned, the dirt track rutted and blocked by rubble. Every sound in the preternatural stillness is as sharp as a gunshot, every movement as quick as a threat. We might have been riding through the enchanted forest of a fairy tale for the last hour, the shadows deep and dark and keeping secrets. We've passed no cars, heard no human noise, seen no colours but the reds and golds and browns of death since we left the main road. Who knows what hides behind those trees, within those shadows; what watches and what waits – what wild animals, wild spirits, or wild men. Across the road the river is low, its banks strewn with trees. We're either in an enchanted forest or an out-take from *Deliverance*.

We bump cautiously on. The sun is fading, the evening is chilling, and the clutch continues to slip. The driver curses under his breath.

I rest my chin on his shoulder. 'That looks like another campsite over there.'

'It'll be closed,' says Victor, slowing down even more. The last sign was at least forty minutes behind us, an equivocal 'Cherokee National Forest', that said nothing of the hurricane that must have torn it apart. 'Why the fuck did we ever come here?'

At least it's a question that has an answer.

'Tellicoe Plains,' said John. 'That's where you want to go.' We wanted to go to Tellicoe Plains, John said, because Tanasi, the capital of the Cherokee nation, was near there. Because there were still Indians living the old way at Tellicoe Plains. Because there, at the edge of the National Forest, we'd find the man who won't move his teepee till the Cherokee remains in Oklahoma are brought back home to rest.

Victor pulls into the campsite and we climb off Montoya. The campground is officially closed. It says so on the notice board.

'What do you think?' asks Victor. 'Go on? Go back?' He looks around. 'Or we could stay here. At least we wouldn't have to pay.'

Not that we pay if we don't have to. Ron gave us the score on economic camping. If you have a choice, always go to a national park since there's more of a chance there'll be no one on duty. If you have to go to a state park, go after dark when the office is likely to be closed. If there is no ranger on duty or the office is closed, take your envelope, fill out your envelope, even place the money in your envelope, but don't do anything foolish like put it in the box until you're actually asked.

I look around, too. 'You don't think there are any bears around here, do you?'

'I wouldn't worry about bears,' says Victor, hunger and exhaustion making him a little snappy. 'This is Tennessee.' Don't fuck up here, the guy filling his Harley at the last gas station told us, you're in the real South now. 'I'd worry about the geezers in the boots and baseball caps. You're the one who'll get raped, not me.'

There's something about the way Victor says 'You're the one who'll

get raped' that always makes it sound to me as though this is somehow my fault.

'Oh, you might get lucky,' I snap back, a little hungry and tired
myself. 'The guys down here are really into sheep, they might be
willing to stretch to a Limey hippy.'

It's almost dusk when we come back to the highway, now on our
way to Tellicoe Plains. We pass more woods, more dirt roads, more
trucks and cows, a small wooden building with a Bud sign in the
window and an aluminium screen door, a family sitting on a sofa and
armchairs on their front lawn, a paved road that stops two feet past
a house, more silent stares. I think of John's van door wrenched
open in the night and hands grabbing for him. I think of a knife cutting through the blue nylon of our tent. I think of *Deliverance*.

'Shit,' shouts Victor as we slip on gravel coming up to the fork. He
stops the bike at the mouth of the road where there are no signs
suggesting where we are or where we might be going. 'Now which
way?'

We climb off and spread the Rad across the seat, leaning forward
side by side. Montoya falls over, and we fall with her. The battered
blue pick-up about to turn past us screeches to a halt.

'Great,' mutters Victor. 'Now we get shot.'

Two large, blondeish women who might be related look over at
us. The driver leans out of the window. 'You two all right?' she asks.
'You need some help?'

George, the new owner of Camp Cherokee, is a Native American,
but of Irish persuasion. He comes back to talk to us and sneak a cigarette out of sight of his wife while I pitch the tent in a shelter of
trees and Victor cajoles the stove. There is no one else here. The two
neat rows of RV lots with picnic tables and hook-ups face each other
silently over the gravel path that runs through the camp. It must be
as attractive as a suburban development when it's full, every one
right on top of each other, but empty it is a clearing in a pine wood
that Davy Crockett would have loved. Talking about the storm that
did so much damage to the forests of Tellicoe Plains, George brings
us firewood and turns on a light. Victor takes the torch out of his
mouth and puts it on the table; I find the missing stake.

George has been in Tennessee for eighteen months. His in-laws
live just a few miles down the road. George comes from Detroit,
where he worked for twenty years in a Nissan plant. 'I've reached the
age when my friends are beginning to die like bees,' says George.

'When that happens you start looking around and you say to yourself, "What am I doing here? Is this my life?"'

'I know what you mean,' says Victor as the stove goes out again.

'So I decided to quit the job and come down here, do something I liked for a change.'

George likes camping; he likes Tennessee; he likes being able to sit on his porch at night and just watch the sky. 'We're not making much yet,' he says, 'but we're getting by.'

Victor asks him if he's ever heard of the man whose teepee is pitched in protest at the very start of the Trail of Tears.

'Around here?' asks George.

There's the most famous cavern east of Carlsbad not too far away; there's the Sequoia Museum and the park; there's a lot of beautiful forest and deer, bear, raccoons, possums, all kinds of birds, and even some mountain cat; there's a guy who breeds llamas and, of course, there's the village of Tanasi, now under water, but no guy in a teepee warring with the government. 'No . . .' George shakes his head. 'I never heard of anything like that.'

The community hall of the Cedars of Lebanon State Park is new. There's a stage at the front, curtained windows all along each side and solid doors at the back. The hall is half filled with rows of folding chairs, most of which are taken. In one corner, on two folding tables covered with paper cloths, several women who look like the grandmother in an AT&T commercial – the grandmother who's so happy to hear from you – pour out cups of coffee, tea and orange punch and explain which cookies have the nuts and which the raisins. 'Try those little cheese things,' the one all in pink and rhinestones urges me. 'Look at how skinny you are, honey, you look like you could use something to eat.' In America, skinny is pretty much the same as not overweight.

I fill a plate with little cheese things, Louella's chocolate raisin fingers and something made with Rice Krispies, take two cups of watery coffee and go to find Victor. It isn't that hard. Most of the men are over fifty, short-cropped hair and ironed cowboy shirts, dark-rimmed glasses and string ties.

'Looks like it's going to start soon,' says Victor as I sit down. 'Two guitars, a fiddle and a mandolin just went backstage.'

It's Thursday, Bluegrass Night in Cedars of Lebanon, when the local bands all play for free. We're hoping this will make up for our morning excursion to Nashville, which was not the sort of side trip of which memories are made. Highway going, highway coming, and in between just another sprawling, dirty city – easily distinguishable from others by its leering billboards of Dolly and Waylon – a quick buzz past the Conway Twitty Museum and the Country Hall of Fame, and half an hour lost among warehouses and sleazy side streets, trying to find the way back out.

Victor, helps himself to a little cheese thing. 'At last we're going to hear some real country music,' he says happily.

I bite into a raisin finger as the MC introduces the first band. Just don't be too country, I silently beg. I love Willie, and I love Merle, and I have a warm spot for Lyle singing 'Stand by Your Man', but Victor doesn't share these feelings. The audience only stops applauding when the first chords are struck.

It's real country. It's really, really real country: a little gospel, a little bluegrass, a little traditional folk, a Bob Dylan song about Jesus, a lot of hoke. By the time the third band is playing, everyone who isn't dancing at the foot of the stage is tapping or clapping in their seats.

'I wish I was drunk,' says Victor, no dancing man when sober.

'I wish you were, too.'

The teenage girl in front of us in the pleated skirt and sweatshirt hands her can of Coke to her father and stands up. With a determined, if nervous, expression she walks down the aisle and stands for a few seconds at the edge of the dancers, just watching. She's concentrating so hard that it almost looks as though she's trying not to vomit. The lead guitarist gives her a wink and the music picks up tempo. The girl starts to dance by herself. Her first steps are slow and self-conscious, but then she is off, not just lost in the music but part of it, an instrument without sound. The other dancers all fall back except one white-haired man. Across the room, he matches her step for step.

Time has fallen back, too. The dance the young girl and the elderly man are doing, though not, perhaps, quite as old as the hills, is older than the rusted horseshoes and hand-made nails left behind by the first settlers that decorate the wall of the park's office, and older, too, than the arrowheads and trinkets in the Sequoia Museum. We are no longer sitting among contented, silent-majority Americans eating cereal cookies and drinking Diet Coke in the Cedars of Lebanon community hall in 1993, but among homesick Scots and Irish at a barn-raising on hostile land, dancing away the demons of uncertainty, the unknown and bad luck.

'It's a jig,' I whisper. 'It's some sort of jig.'

Victor starts clapping louder. 'It reminds me of the duelling banjos.'

Night in our corner of the Cedars of Lebanon is bright and peaceful and far away from fears. On the other side of the woods, the music goes on, a fiddle wailing through the night like a long-distance train. Instead of reading *Zen and the Art of Motorcycle Maintenance*, our book for this part of the road, we lie with our heads sticking out of the tent, counting shooting stars.

'So, are you sorry you didn't listen to your sister?' asks Victor. 'Do you wish you'd stayed at home?'

'Eight!' I point to the right of Orion, where a tiny bright light streaks through the sky. 'Not yet.'

'Nine,' says Victor, his arm stretching into the air. 'Me neither.'

The four-lane highway leading into Memphis is so busy you'd think Elvis, despite his recent public refusal ever to set foot in the city again, had been spotted downtown, buying two litres of Coke and a family-sized bottle of ketchup. But we're not letting the heavy traffic delay us; on this warm and hazy morning beside the treacherous Mississippi we're the Honda from hell. Victor is hunched forward, tense, concentrated, the image of the spectre that haunts the roadways of London and casts rage and terror into the hearts of its mobile citizens: the despatch rider on a mission. Up ahead, two serious Harleys cut through cars, filtering lanes, flirting with fenders and bumpers, and we cut, filter and flirt right behind them. 'You hold on tight,' the woman at the Teddy Bear Café whose husband had been stationed in Germany for two years of longing for cornbread and Ed Sullivan had advised me earlier. I hold on tight as we wind like the river. It's clear from the faces of the other motorists that they're not used to this kind of riding in Memphis, and that they don't want to be. I'm not used to this kind of riding, either. Not in traffic. And I don't feel it's something I've missed. A red foil balloon shaped like a heart brushes my knee as we squeeze through the crawling cars. I pull my knees in. Drivers are tapping their steering wheels and running their fingers through their hair, tracking the passage of time. We pick up a little speed. The next thing that gets a bit too close is a wing mirror. The traffic lights go yellow. We pick up a little more speed. The other bikes glide through the signal. Victor hits the brakes.

'Okay,' I shout as we manage to come to a stop. 'I give up.' I gesture over his shoulder to the Harley stopped at the next light. 'Why are we chasing those cops?' It's an historic event, this, Victor Sanchez in pursuit of the police – as significant in its way as the dismantling of the Berlin Wall – but it's one I wouldn't have minded missing. What happens when we catch them?

I can't hear him, because of all the traffic noise, but I know Victor is sighing. With forbearance. 'Why are we here?' he shouts back like a third-grade teacher.

He's testing my lineal thinking. I pull my toes in a little more and think lineally. 'A camping place.' To have the stove checked before someone ends up throwing it in the Mississippi because of another supper of half-cooked glop or crackers and nuts.

This is not the first occasion my travelling companion has shown impatience with my lack of mental dexterity. But it may be the last.

'And . . .?' This time I can hear his sigh, more long-suffering than forbearing.

'And to find a decent healthfood store.' Before we starve.

'And?' asks Victor as he slams the gears into first.

And 'A motor—' We steam through the green light before any of the cars have moved and the rest of my sentence, '—cycle shop', is lost in the wind.

'If you're looking for a motorcycle shop,' shouts Victor, already happier now that he's gaining on the Harleys, 'then the best person to ask is someone with a bike.'

God knows why I hadn't thought of that.

'You can't imagine what it's like,' Priscilla is saying. 'I mean, really, have you ever thought about it?'

I have to admit that I haven't ever really thought about it. I have given some serious consideration to what the day of the apocalypse, moonlight in the jungle, taking a skid at 90 across a wet highway, getting drunk with Che Guevara or William Shakespeare and living with an insurance salesman, three kids and a salamander in a split-level outside of Michigan might be like, but not this.

Priscilla shakes her pretty head sadly. The cascade of ribbons attached to her hair clip shivers. 'No one has.' Her voice is resigned. 'Everybody thinks it's all glamour and romance, you know? Like I live in this big, twenty-four-hour-a-day party.' She adjusts the barrette. 'But it isn't. If you want to know the truth, it's a kind of hell.'

On the other side of the parking lot, in front of the motorcycle shop we were directed to by the Memphis patrolmen – one of whom used to have a Nighthawk, great bike – Victor and the mechanic listen intently as the mechanic runs through Montoya's gears. Hell, like most things, has many faces.

'It must be hard,' I mumble, though it is difficult to give Priscilla all the sympathy she deserves when you're as worried as I am about the clutch. One of the other things to which I've given some serious thought is the possibility of breaking down in the boondocks of Mississippi and what that's likely to mean: hound dogs, water proof flashlights, men who ride around in pick-ups shooting people who don't count, just for fun.

'Everywhere you go, they're after him,' Priscilla goes on. 'You can never rest, not for a second.' She smiles in much the way Che might have smiled those last days of losing and running in Bolivia. 'I can't even let him go to the deli for a six-pack by himself. One time he went for a six-pack and a couple of bags of chips and salsa and I didn't see him for two days.'

'Gee,' I say. The mechanic is shaking his head. Victor's nodding. It doesn't look good.

'He might come back with his clothes in shreds. He might come back with a gang of them on his heels.' She shrugs – Che thinking of the future as he neared the Yuro Ravine. 'He might not come back at all.'

Now Victor and the mechanic are kneeling by the side of the Honda, staring at some small spot covered in dirt and grease.

'I guess it's my fate,' says Priscilla. 'It's like my mother always says, you buy your ticket and you take your chances.'

'Bruce Springsteen said it too,' I say.

'You just can't expect the life of the girlfriend of an Elvis imper-sonator to be easy,' says Priscilla. 'It's not the way it is.'

Not everyone comes to Memphis for equipment refurbishing and couscous. Businessmen come on business, students to study, lawyers and politicians to make money, musicians to entertain. In fact, according to the rumour going round, Bob Dylan is in town to see Booker T. and the MGs. But most people come because of Him. Wives abandon husbands, mothers desert children, waiters, gas-station attendants and short-order cooks walk out of their jobs, sons climb out of windows, fathers slip from their beds and tiptoe to the car. They come to Memphis to be near Elvis – to see the carpet his feet walked over, the bathroom where he cleaned his teeth, the bed where he dreamed. They come, in part, because they think he's them. Them, or their husband.

That was why Priscilla Mulhooney, beautician and nail specialist from Oklahoma, and Denny Patricio, television repairman from Pennsylvania, came to Memphis two summers ago. 'I just had this feeling,' Priscilla explained. 'This feeling that Elvis wanted to talk to me, you know? I mean, everybody says that – you wouldn't believe the number of women I've met who talk to Elvis all the time – but this was different. I knew he wanted me to be here.' Denny, too, had this feeling that he had to see Graceland. 'He knew he'd never be the greatest Elvis impersonator if he didn't come,' said Priscilla. I suggested that this was similar to being called. 'He wasn't just called,' said Priscilla. 'Denny was chosen.'

It was 16 August 1991. Priscilla was sitting on a bench at Graceland, drinking a Diet Coke and crying, and Denny, dressed as the Elvis of the Jailhouse Rock era, sat down beside her and started singing 'I Can Help'. 'I just couldn't believe it,' said Priscilla. 'First I hear his voice, and then I look up and there he is, holding out his two strong hands to me. I couldn't stop crying. He was wearing this red shirt, kind of like Mickey's shorts? You wouldn't believe how great he looked.' Elvis was always beautiful, of course, but less so during the decline and fall. Denny had chosen his era well. Denny was in love with Priscilla even before he found out her name. Fate. Kismet. Brought together by the King.

'You been to Graceland yet?' asks Priscilla.

'Not yet,' I say, though I am looking forward to buying my own copy of the book of Elvis's favourite recipes written by his favourite cook, and of taking a picture of Graceland for my cat.

Victor and the mechanic are shaking hands. I've seen this handshake before. He can't fix the bike.

'You gotta see Graceland,' says Priscilla. 'It's like Vegas, a not-to-be-missed.'

The traffic hurtles past in the changing light as the sun, as tired as I am, drops behind the rooftops of Memphis. The changing crowd that has been watching Tom and Victor for most of the afternoon, stopping to ask where we're going and where we're from, to chat about camping at high altitudes and kerosene stoves, is down to two: Robbie, the kid with the long hair and the Grateful Dead T-shirt who works at Outdoor World when he isn't being a rock guitarist, and me. Robbie is telling me about his musical influences as we sit side by side on the steps, while Tom and Victor talk about the Inca Trail and Tom shakes the last drops of kerosene from the stove. Tom would like to go to Peru, but not on a bike – he's a trekker. Robbie nearly bought a Harley last summer.

Tom turns to Robbie. 'Go in the back and get me a bottle of white gas.'

Robbie, his mind more on Elmore James than camping equipment, just stares back at him. 'White gas?'

'Yeah,' says Tom. 'In the storeroom.' He looks over at Victor. 'So you guys staying in Memphis awhile?' he asks.

'No,' says Victor. 'We want to get to Mississippi before dark.'

This is news to me. 'What about Graceland?'

'We'll still have time to buzz Graceland,' says Victor.

'Where are you headed?' asks Tom. 'Chewella Lake?'

Victor nods.

Tom shakes his head. 'That's at least a hundred miles,' he says as Robbie appears in the doorway with the gas.

I wonder if there's anywhere nearby where I could get just a postcard of Graceland to send to my cat.

'That's not so bad,' says Victor. 'We did 225 getting here.'

This is news to me, too. 'Really? It didn't seem that far.'

'That's because we were going so fast,' says Victor.

Tom takes the gas from Robbie and slowly pours it into the stove. 'You'd be much better off with white gas than kerosene,' Tom says to Victor. 'If you can't get that, use gasoline.'

'What octane?' asks Victor.

'High,' says Tom. 'Ninety-two. No less than ninety.' He closes the tank of the stove and explains again about pumping as he demonstrates. Victor nods. Tom lights a match. In a few seconds, the Whisper Lite is burning a deep, clear blue.

'You see?' says Tom. 'Great stove.' He sits back and smiles at Victor. 'It's the nature of kerosene not to burn clean,' he says. 'That's all that was wrong.'

7

DRUGSTORE
TRUCK-DRIVIN' MAN

'My wife comes from the city, too,' Marshall, the wily host camper who spotted us coasting through the camp with our lights off, hoping to avoid him, is saying. 'When I told her this was my dream, to live in Holly Springs when I retired, she thought I was crazy. But I told her, "Trust me, Anne. You haven't lived till you've seen the moon over Chewella Lake."' He waves his flashlight across the wall of trees and up into the night. 'You just haven't lived.'

Victor pounds the last peg into the ground. 'And what does she think now?'

Marshall smiles at the unnecessary question. 'She loves it. She never saw anything like this in her life.'

Victor stands up. 'It's a beautiful country,' he says, not committing himself to any position on Chewella Lake. We're too tired to look for the lake tonight, and tomorrow morning the moon will be as gone as we. 'Except for all the litter.'

'People are stupid,' says Marshall with the finality of a philosopher who has given the question of human nature several decades of thought and can see no way out of his conclusions. 'You give them a little unspoiled beauty and right away they have to spoil it.' He lights a cigarette and pockets the match. 'I spend half my time picking up cigarette butts and cans. Doesn't matter how many signs we put up, doesn't matter how many trash cans we put around. Where an animal will shit a man will throw his garbage.'

'People don't have the sense they're born with,' comments Victor.

'Either that or they're not born with much,' says Marshall.

I concentrate on filling out the camping permit with one hand while I hold the mini maglite with the other, trying to remember what day it is and the number on Montoya's licence plate, and thinking about Mississippi. When I think of Mississippi I think of lazy grace and the sunlight shimmering on the blacktop and on an old black woman with a black umbrella patiently standing at the side of the road waiting for the traffic to pass. I think of heat as an ocean, mansions like spectres, of long-dead voices rustling through the Spanish moss. I think of grey wooden shacks and shoeless shoeshine boys, of blind harmonica-players, of silence like a threat, and hopelessness like air. Of slowness: slow days, slow movements, slowly being watched and noted; violence as sudden and predictable as the afternoon storms. I think of an unresolved past and a hidden present; of secrets; of fear; of a place where it's easy as sipping water to be disappeared. I think of men riding through the dark with shotguns on their laps, of swollen bodies swinging from trees, of burning crosses and hooded smiles.

Victor thinks I'm mad. 'I don't know what you're so nervous about,' he said when we stopped over the border for gas. 'Mississippi's just another place, it's no different to any other place we've been.' Maybe not. But the surfaces of places, as of people, show only what they want to be seen, only themselves as they'd like to be. As far as I'm concerned Victor's words are something you might have written in the last letter you sent before you vanished in Germany or Chile; the greeting you scrawled on the postcard you mailed from Iran or Mexico before Amnesty International became aware of your name. 'You're letting your imagination run away with you again,' said Victor. Maybe so. He climbed back on Montoya. 'And for God's sake, stop singing that song about being run out of town.'

I put the pen and the flashlight in my pocket and look around me. It's a cool, clear, night, fragrant and timeless, owls crying, the underbrush crackling and the stars drawn across the sky like a map. Shaking off the memory of a boy I once knew, dead in a ditch in the State of Magnolias, blood black and eyes opened, killed, perhaps, on a night just like this, I get up and go over to give Marshall the registration and the fee. Marshall and Victor are still talking about litter.

'There were these college kids in California I read about in the paper,' Marshall is saying. 'Paid for their entire education by spending the summer collecting beer and soda cans. They had a system. Up one side of the highway and down the other. At night they'd go through the rich neighbourhoods, where no one ever bothers taking their deposit bottles back, and they'd pick 'em clean.'

'You could do it,' says Victor, sounding thoughtful – he glances at me – 'if you had a pick-up.'

If we had a pick-up we wouldn't have to worry about crossing the Rockies. We could see Colorado. We could take one of the stray dogs who hang around the camps begging food with us. We could sleep in the truck when the tent was wet from last night's rain and we couldn't be assed to fight it up.

'Easiest thing in the world,' agrees Marshall. He taps out his cigarette on the sole of his shoe, grinds out the ashes and pockets it with the match. 'That's what I'd do if I were you two,' he nods. 'You could go all over the country, finance the entire trip . . .'

Even in the fragile light I can see that Victor is calculating: 2,000 cans a day is $100, 4,000 is $200 . . . you could go forever as long as you avoided the states without returnable cans.

'Sounds good,' I say. I hand Marshall the form and the money. 'Maybe next time.'

He gives me a piece of paper with a number written on it. 'I lock the main gate at ten,' he explains. 'Try to keep the troublemakers out.' He points to the paper I'm holding. 'That's the combination.' He turns and points his flashlight across the road and through the trees. 'I'm right over there in that trailer if you have any trouble.'

I say, 'Trouble?'

Victor says, 'We won't have any trouble.'

'This is Mississippi,' says Marshall. 'Trouble might just have you.'

We're sitting in the City Café, waiting to order.

Outside the front door is a cigar-store Indian, and inside it is wood panelled and decorated with old photographs of Crawford, Mississippi, in the days before there were paved roads or electricity or integration – though not all of these modernisations are as obvious as others. The tables are covered with red and white checked cloths and the cash register is the old-fashioned kind that makes it useful to be able to count. The waitress's name is Sara. I know this is her name not because it's written on the tag she wears above the pocket on her white blouse but because the woman sitting at the round table in the centre of the room with a group of good ol' boys in cowboy shirts and string ties discussing law and order in loud, own-the-world voices, the heavily made-up blonde who was probably Crawford Homecoming Queen in 1962, keeps calling her by it.

'Sara, where's those pancakes?' 'Sara, did you give table three their refill?' 'Sara, does this toast look done to you?' It seems likely that besides having once reigned over the big game of the autumn, the blonde owns the café. There's no one else in the room but a husband and wife and elderly mother at one of the booths towards the back, fussing over their order, and a couple sitting across from us, solemnly laminating their stacks of pancakes with syrup.

'It's the damn government,' the man with the diamond pinky ring is saying. 'If you leave it to them they don't do diddly squat, and if you do it yourself they try to slap you in jail.'

'Soft,' says the man beside him. 'They're all as soft as tar in summer.'

Bracelets jangle. 'It's like my daddy always said,' says the blonde. 'If you want something done you gotta do it yourself.'

We're sitting in the City Café, waiting to order, and I'm staring out of the window while Victor reads the menu. In the centre of Crawford is an immaculately tended, iron-fenced square, and around that square the four equal blocks of the main street. There's a large old oak tree, the town hall and a Civil War monument in the square, and the buildings of the town are awned and bordered by a raised wooden walkway, making it look like a cross between Dodge City and Thrush Green. There's a bird picking through the grass at the foot of the memorial and a man on horseback waiting for the light to change, and I'm wondering if that oak was a lynching tree.

'Stop it,' says Victor from behind his menu. His voice is low but not without power. 'Stop singing that bloody song.'

I wasn't aware that I was singing that bloody song, the one about the head of the Ku Klux Klan. I look over at him. The light coming through the gingham café curtains is shadowing him with red.

'I wasn't aware that I was singing that bloody song,' I say coolly. 'And anyway I happen to like it.'

He puts down the menu. 'Well, I don't like it. You're driving me mad with it. If you have to sing about Mississippi, can't you sing that one about the mud instead?'

'This place doesn't inspire me to sing about dipping my feet in the Mississippi mud,' I hiss back. 'It makes me think of tar and feathers.'

Victor ducks behind his menu again. 'Maybe you should have juice instead of coffee.'

But it doesn't look as though I'm going to have anything. Sara, finally on her way to us with two glasses of water and her pad, is waylaid by the snap of fingers. 'What happened to those extra grits, Sara?' asks the blonde. Sara hurries back to the kitchen.

We're sitting in the City Café, still waiting to order. Beyond the gold lettering on the window, a tall, dark man in riding breeches and a cowboy hat has just parked his horse beside our bike.

'I'd just like to see somebody try and take my gun from me,' one of the men at the centre table is saying to a rumble of agreement. 'It'd be the last time that son-of-a-bitch ever put his hand on anything.'

'A man has certain rights.' The blonde picks up her water glass, rings clinking. 'It's like my daddy always said, nobody touches my gun or my woman but me.'

At last Sara appears beside us, slapping down the water glasses and taking out her order book. She could be as old as twenty-five, thin and fair with pale skin and the look of an animal not born in captivity but captive now. 'What'll it be?'

I'm not very good at this sort of thing, but her accent's definitely northern. Maybe Newcastle.

I pass her my menu. 'I'll just have coffee.'

Victor glares at me. Over the weeks together it has become obvious not only that our appetites are dramatically different, but that beneath Victor's visage of rebellious youth lurks the heart and soul of a Spanish mother. 'You should eat something.'

'I just want coffee.'

'You're from England!' cries Sara excitedly, interrupting what could have turned into an ugly scene. 'I'm from Leeds. Where are you from?'

'York,' says Victor, 'but I live in London.'

'I lived in London for a while.' Sara sighs. 'I hated it because it's so cold and grey and wet all the time, and everybody always seems so depressed. I couldn't wait to get to America.' She presses her pad against her stomach. 'I never thought I'd say this, but, Jesus, I wish I were in London right now.'

Church bells are ringing. The green is glowing, the monument and the clock tower of the town hall glint gold. A designer jeep passes on the sleepy street, a white boy rides by on a BMX and waves at the window, the horse shakes his head. It's a picture of perfection, like an ad for life insurance. I have an image of Camden, dark, dull and dirty, shadowed with fumes: the winos, bruised and red-faced, huddled together drinking beer; the junkies and drop-outs in front of the tube station and Sainsbury's with their dogs and their homeless-and-hungry signs, people shoving past, hard expressions, heads down in the rain. I'm not completely sure I don't agree with her.

'How long have you been here?' asks Victor.

'Nine bloody months.'

He whistles. 'Nine months . . .'

If I could whistle, I would, though I'm not sure which surprises me more: that Sara's been in Crawford so long or that she's in Crawford at all. 'So how did you wind up here?'

'I guess it was a combination of things,' says Sara. 'I guess I always thought America was so exciting and all, you know, not like England . . . that you could make more of yourself here.' She makes a face. 'And then I fell in love.' Sara's a new-age GI bride, lured across the ocean not by oranges and stockings but by dreams of a you-can-have-anything world and an airman with an accent as sweet as Tupelo honey and a break-your-heart smile. 'Till death do us part,' says Sara. 'Death or Mississippi.' She glances over her shoulder and lowers her already low voice. 'What about you two?' she demands. 'What the hell are you doing here?'

Victor is more than happy to explain. He tells her how we bought the bike in Brooklyn, how we're riding first to California then down to Peru, though God knows what we'll do with it when we walk to Machu Picchu – we can't take Montoya on the Inca Trail.

Sara isn't interested in the Inca Trail's unsuitability for motorcycle travel. 'But why have you come to Mississippi?' she wants to know. 'Why come here?'

Victor shrugs. 'It's on the way.'

'No it isn't,' says Sara, her excitement gone. 'It isn't on the way to anywhere. It's the cesspool of the universe. If I were you I'd just keep driving till I got the hell out.'

Bracelets jangle behind us. 'Sara!' calls the voice that once made a shiver run through every boy in the senior class at Crawford High, and that clearly causes a few shivers still. 'Sara, are you almost done there?'

'This place is sick,' Sara mutters, but she doesn't look around. 'Really sick. If I were you, I'd just get away from here while I can.' She puts her pencil to her pad and gives Victor a smile. 'So what'll it be?'

Victor smiles back. 'I guess I'll have coffee, toast and a couple of grenades.'

It's my fault we're not going to do another 150 miles tonight. It's my fault we tested the radar equipment of the Mississippi State Police to get here before total darkness. And it's my fault the second visor was run over by a pick-up because I thought the third guy in the cab, the one in the middle, looked like a psychopath and wouldn't let Victor flag them down before they hit it. The third guy in the cab was a Labrador.

Despite all this, Victor is in a good mood – excited even – as we finish unloading the bike. 'All this and heaven, too,' he says, gesturing at the empty campsite. The RV owners are all huddled together in the campsite further down the road, starting up their barbecues and turning on their garden lights. It's as good as being alone. 'Now, let's get started,' he says. 'If we're quick we could check out that bar we passed after supper.'

'Oh, great.' I sigh. His good mood is not totally shared by his travelling companion. 'Do you think we should bring some blunt, heavy instruments with us, or do you think the guys in the bar will already have their own?'

Victor is walking towards the tent. 'Don't start,' he advises. 'You're being totally irrational.'

'I'm not irrational,' I shout after him. 'Everything I'm saying makes perfect sense.'

As much as we'd all like to believe that there must more to the world than what we see, it is easy to scoff at the new-age ethos of the nineties. At least, I've always found it easy. In the new-age nineties, we embrace high technology and technocratic medicine – and then hang crystals in our windows and take oil of basil for bronchitis, camomile for earache, sage for fear, patchouli for depression, and lavender for burns. We talk over dinner about space travel and genetic engineering, and then wear amulets, check our horoscopes every morning, still knock on wood when we think we're tempting fate. In the new age of the nineties, psychotherapists and policemen consult psychics, presidents don't make a move without their astrologers, businessmen and physicists have gurus, and everyone searches their lives for signs. But now, as it turns out, I'm finding it more difficult to scoff.

'For Christ's sake,' says Victor. 'Will you give it a rest?' He stops halfway into the tent to point towards the sky. 'Look,' he says. 'There's still some daylight . . .' He points to the right. 'There's a ranger on duty . . . We've been waiting for this for weeks.' He motions me forward. 'Now come on, nothing's going to happen.'

As though no one's ever said that before.

'I can't give it a rest,' I answer as I slowly crawl in after him. 'Maybe it is just a coincidence—'

'It is just a coincidence.' He leans across me to pin the flap closed. The zipper went weeks ago.

I ignore his interruption. 'But it is a pretty big one, if it is,' I persist. 'I mean, you have to admit that. We've only been here two days and we've had two warnings already. Two warnings, Vic. One might be meaningless, but you have to pay attention to two.'

'No I don't.' Victor starts taking off his clothes. 'They weren't warnings, Dyan,' he grunts as he tugs on his jeans. 'They were just statements.'

'"Get out while you still can?"' I almost laugh. 'You consider that a statement?'

'Yes,' says Victor. 'I consider it a statement.' He throws his jeans at me. 'What do you consider it?'

An oracle. A prophecy. A harbinger of impending doom. Angels and magicians in the form of retired insurance salesmen and waitresses in exile trying to protect us from choosing the wrong destiny. Get out of Mississippi . . . you shouldn't be here . . . get away . . . this may be something you won't live to regret . . .

The last light of the evening shimmers bluely inside the tent.

'I told you, a warning.'

'Sure you do,' says Victor. He gives me a look. 'Just remember, *The Omen*'s the name of a film. And we're not in a film. We're just in an ordinary place where a lot of ordinary people live.' He throws his leggings my way. 'Now stop stalling and get everything off.'

'Everything?'

'Yeah, everything. We might not have another chance like this till California.'

I look at my socks. I've only been wearing them for two days – as with all our clothes, two twenty-four-hour-long days, it is true, but only two days nonetheless.

'Them too,' says Victor. He rolls his eyes. 'They smell like you pissed on them.'

The educational benefits of travel cannot be overstated. Already I've discovered at least one reason why it is usually men who do road trips and not women: men can take a leak anywhere. Not only can a man just turn his back at the side of the road without having to scrabble down gulches and fight his way through the underbrush, but he rarely has to worry about pissing on his shoes.

'I was sure I missed them.'

'Well, you didn't,' says Victor. He pulls some clean things from the saddlebags and tosses them to me. 'Now let's get going while the laundry room's still free.'

I start pulling off my dirty clothes. 'At least I know if we get shot tonight, my underwear will be clean when they bring us into Emergency.'

'Doesn't matter,' says Victor, stuffing the laundry into a plastic bag. 'If they shoot us, there's no one around here who will bring us in.'

Shenandoah Burns, twenty-one but looking older, dressed in faded jeans and a faded flannel, is sitting on the one chair in the small and dingy laundry room, most of her washing meticulously folded on top of the dryer beside her while she waits for the towels and jeans to be done. 'You could write a book about my life, sure enough,' she is saying to me.

Judging from what Shenandoah's told us so far – that she was separated from her family at four and a half, raised by foster parents until she ran away at fifteen and went in search of her real folks, and that by the time she found her real folks her twin sister, Shannon, was dead and her mother had gone on the drink, and then she met Whitney Burns, who saved her soul and won her heart, and now they travel around the country with the German Shepherd they found on a campsite in California and the cat they found on a campsite in Texas, working at whatever they can get and writing and performing songs about the Lord in their spare time – this is probably true. At least one.

'Um,' I say, slightly distracted. Shasta, the German Shepherd, thinking there might be food involved, is sitting on my feet, waiting for something to drop, while I try to figure out how to work the detergent dispenser. The instructions say 'turn handle', but I can't find the handle to turn.

Encouraged by my enthusiasm, Shenandoah goes on. 'See, what happened in the first place was my mama had me and Shannon when she was only fourteen – it's that little handle on the side, Dyan – and then in the next place, our daddy, he ran away to the army before we was born, and my mother married Sturgis Manger, and then she got pregnant with Amory, and then Parker, and then Sturgis lost his job, and he decided they couldn't afford to keep both me and Shannon around any more, and so in the last place my mama gave me away through the Church.'

I thought that churches just gave away clothes and canned goods at Christmas. Through what church, I wonder, but decide not to ask. The box of detergent falls from its slot with a thud. Shasta jumps up, knocking it out of my hand.

'Fourteen, that's pretty young,' says Victor, showing the national flair for understatement as he loads the best washing machine, the one Shenandoah recommended.

'It just about broke her heart to give away one of her own little daughters,' says Shenandoah, 'but what else could she do? She wasn't but eighteen by then and Sturgis wouldn't give her any peace.'

'Eighteen . . .' Victor stands up and holds out his hand for the soap powder. 'It must've been rough for her.'

Shenandoah's nod is matter-of-fact. 'They never had much money, and gettin' rid of me didn't solve any of their problems. Sturgis never did get a real job again, and then little Amory fell off the roof, and in the end both Sturgis and my mother were drinking all the time, and fighting, and all that kind of thing. That's why Shannon drowned herself like that.'

I can't respond. Listening to Shenandoah is like watching daytime TV, and watching daytime TV is like falling through the rabbit hole, the world you thought you knew turned inside out and upside down. On the afternoon talk shows, thousands of Americans reveal their selves and deepest secrets to millions of other Americans. Transvestites, sex-changers, female impersonators, wife-beaters, beaten wives, women with weight problems, women with daughters with weight problems, women who've had their bodies remodelled, men who remodelled their own wives' bodies, women who stole their daughters' boyfriends, men who kidnapped their children, school bullies, the victims of school bullies – they're all there, sitting in comfortable chairs, conversing with the world at large about the most intimate details of their lives. Today we're discussing teenage mothers . . . Today Andrew and Jim are going to tell us why they decided to get married . . . Today we're going to talk about incest . . . Today Shenandoah Burns is going to tell us how being given away as a small child helped her find the Lord.

'This is a great dog,' says Victor, giving Shasta a playful shove. Shasta jumps into his arms, knocking the two of them back against the machines.

'You just give him a slap when he gets too rough,' advises Shenandoah. 'He's just a puppy yet, he don't know his own strength.' She opens the dryer and feels her wash. 'And then Sturgis and my mama had one of their fights and he shot her as she was tryin' to leave, and that's when I found out Sturgis wasn't really my daddy. So I went lookin' for him.'

I force myself to say something. 'He shot her?'

'I don't think he meant to,' says Shenandoah, pulling clothes from the dryer, 'he was just blind crazy on the drink.'

Victor is trying to gently slap Shasta away, but the dog thinks he's still playing.

'Shasta!' Shenandoah claps her hands and Shasta falls on the floor in a pretty convincing impersonation of a bearskin rug. 'He's the reason it's so hard to get a real place to live and a job,' says Shenandoah. 'Folks don't wanna rent to you when they know you've got a dog.'

'What about your real father?'

'I found him in California.' Shenandoah shakes out a towel and begins to fold it perfectly. 'He works at the Budweiser plant. I think he's a foreman or somethin' like that.' She shakes out another towel. 'We didn't like each other.'

'You didn't?'

She turns to me with the ironic, God-isn't-done-with-me-yet smile I always pictured Jesus wearing when he was talking to the disciples. 'You think you're supposed to, don't you? After all that happened, you'd think I deserved that much. I thought so. I thought that, what with all the trouble I'd had with my mama and Sturgis, and my foster parents bein' so strict with me and everything, and poor Shannon walkin' into the gulf with every record she owned in her arms, when I met my real dad everything would be all perfect.'

The real American dream: having everything all perfect – the breasts you want but didn't get, the sex you want to be but aren't, the baby you want but can't have, the father who was supposed to love you.

'And then I met Whitney,' says Shenandoah, stacking her laundry in a cardboard box. 'And he made me see the plan the Lord had for me and how good life could be.'

Victor and I watch from the doorway as Shenandoah and Shasta get back into the beat-up old Ford with the Jesus Loves You sticker on the bumper. There are more cardboard boxes stacked on the back seat and the cat is asleep on the dash.

'You take care of yourself,' I shout as she starts the engine.

Shenandoah leans over to the passenger window. 'You guys, too,' she says. 'Remember we've got some crazy people here in Mississippi.'

*

As far as I can tell, even if Victor weren't the sort of man who responds to the words 'No', 'You can't' and 'Don't' the way other men respond to the words 'Yes', 'You can' and 'Do' we still couldn't get the hell out of Mississippi. Sara, it seems, was right about one thing. Mississippi isn't on the way to anywhere. Not so you'd notice. Not so we'd notice, anyway. The Rand McNally map for Mississippi is webbed with roads marked 'other' and 'paved' and we seem to be hitting every one of them.

'Where are we?' shouts Victor suddenly, both hands up in the air. 'I don't know where we are.'

Rule of the Road number 11: Always have a destination, even if it's only the next Taco Bell. Having a destination helps to keep you from getting totally lost, because at least if you have a destination you know where you *were* going.

I lean closer. 'Bob Jones Road!' I shout back. 'We're on Bob Jones Road!'

'Where?'

'Bob Jones Road.' I saw the sign just a few miles back, when the gunshots first went off.

'But where the hell is that?'

I gesture around us. 'It's the middle of nowhere.' In case you ever wondered what it was like.

There are people in New York who think that the middle of nowhere is anything above Fourteenth Street, and people in England who think it's anywhere you can't get a decent cup of tea. But it's not. With no particular place to go, and no particular place to be, the middle of nowhere is where we are. Nowhere itself is three hours behind us, back along the old two-lane highway cutting south, where the monotony of the usual roadside attractions was occasionally broken by a pawnbroker or fortune-teller. I counted over 1,000 beer and soda cans before we left the main road, $50 dollars in less than an hour, but in the middle of nowhere even they have petered out. The countryside is almost flat now, the colours muted. Everything looks poor and struggling, or simply forgotten; the cotton fields and dull brushland, the small farms and weathered, windowless wooden shacks, the shabby houses and lawns ornamented with rusting cars and kitchen appliances, the people sitting on their porches, staring out at the road as though watching TV. But the middle of nowhere has its charms. The afternoon is silent in a dreamy way – so far from somewhere that it is happy enough just to sit back and watch the world go by – the sky is high and a vivid blue, and there are cows tentatively dipping their feet in a small stream. Despite the gunshots that announced our passage a few miles back, my fear has gone. Three ragged young boys who should be working are laughing in the grass nearby. All of them wave as the bike flies past. We both wave back. I could ride through this dreaminess like this, dreamy myself, for hours and hours, with time like something you lose yourself in, not to.

But not so all of us. Some of us want lunch.

Montoya screeches to a stop at the end of the road. Left or right? The State Department of Roads either has a sense of humour, or doesn't feel that clues are necessary.

'No signs!' yells Victor. 'Why the hell don't they ever put up any bloody signs?'

Probably because nobody around here could read them, I think. I look back to where the cows are now sitting by the stream and the boys are chasing each other through the grass. On the other hand, why should they bother?

Victor pulls the bike into the no-parking zone in front of Piggly Wiggly and shuts off the engine. I heave myself off the back, dislodging the map and the box of aluminium foil it's wrapped around. I force them back under the cargo net.

'Don't take hours like you usually do,' says Victor. 'I'm starving.'

It's my turn to shop for lunch. 'I don't take hours.' I hand him my helmet. 'I don't take any longer than you.'

'Yes you do.' He hands me the list he's made of the things we need. 'For once, just get what you went in for and come straight out. Don't go wandering up and down the aisles as usual.'

'I will,' I say. 'I don't.' I march off.

I bloody well wish I didn't. But the truth is that I do. I go in for cheese, a couple of salads from the deli, a loaf of bread, two apples and a jar of salsa, and half an hour later I'm still there, watching the overweight families in their bargain clothes fill their shopping carts, listening to their conversations, reading the labels on the dressings to see what the difference between Ranch and Ranch Lite, Zesty Italian and Italian Vinaigrette might possibly be.

I admit it. I'm fascinated; mesmerised; transfixed. For me, the lure of the super-foodstore is not unlike the centripetal pull of disaster. There you are, on your way to an important date, and you find yourself passing a four-car pile-up or some poor bastard teetering on the edge of a roof. You glance over. Jesus, you think. I wonder what happened. I wonder what he'll do. You know what happened, you know what he'll do, but still your footsteps falter. You don't want to watch. You don't like seeing blood pooled on the blacktop, you don't like seeing bodies shovelled into plastic bags, you've never been that interested in seeing someone die. You watch anyway. Your mind is saying 'Let's go,' but your feet don't move. You're staring at the way the ambulance light winks across the shattered windshield; you're watching the poor bastard's face, wondering what happened to get him on that roof. 'Now!' shrieks your mind. 'Let's go now!' You check the time, you're already late. You still don't move. And nor do I.

This is where life in America begins. Here, in buildings bigger than a Cherokee village, bigger than a frontier town, large enough to easily accommodate a suburban block. Whole lives unfold between the fresh produce and the frozen foods – births, deaths, marriages, divorces, fallings in love and fallings out of love, hatreds and friendships, break-ups and reconciliations, rivalries and treacherous betrayals – and all the while the temperature never changes, the light never shifts, the plastic grass under the vegetables never wilts, and the soporific electronic ballads blend in with the air. No wonder I'm hooked. I'm like an astrophysicist trying to understand the nature of the cosmos through studying a black hole.

This is where life in America is revealed. Brightly coloured, brightly packaged, music in the background and always a television on somewhere, it's a life of infinite choice and variety. Life has meaning, has something to offer. Ten different kinds of cornflakes and twenty different breads. Half an aisle of fruit drinks and cake mixes, half an aisle of cookies and crackers, half an aisle of snack foods and detergents, two aisles of frozen foods, one just for soda and beer.

The force that drives the universe to constantly recreate itself, change and diversify; that drives life to strive harder, move higher, ameliorate itself, pulsates here in new sodas, different toothpastes, better dish detergents, plastic-wrapped chickens that have been improved.

If there are fifty-seven channels and nothing on, there are dozens of ice-creams, cereals, detergents and soaps and they're all the same.

If this is the pinnacle of man's civilisation, then what was it like down there in the cellar? Exactly how scared were we, deep in the dark?

I stare at the rows of salad dressings, pickles, sauces and relishes, neatly grouped and clearly priced, trying to choose something to go with our lunch, while robots play an old Beatles song and the women beside me discuss Elizabeth Taylor.

Reality, say the mystics and physicists, is only an illusion. Here in Piggly Wiggly that is certainly true. The illusion of choice, of purpose, of sense. The illusion that something is going on.

'I never thought she'd marry again,' says the woman in the purple stretch pants. 'I'd'a thought she'd had enough.'

'She'll never love anyone like she loved Richard,' says her friend. 'Everybody knows that.'

Life is experience, say the physicists and mystics. Life means what it means. Under the fluorescent glow of Piggly Wiggly life means *more* – and it comes with directions. Open here. Shake well. Remove from container before heating. Do not leave within the reach of children.

'She doesn't look as good as Joan Collins,' says the friend.

'She must be sexed like a bull,' says the one in the purple stretch pants.

The mystics believe in an intricate design that includes every drop of water and grain of sand, and the physicists argue that God plays dice. But here in Piggly Wiggly there is a plan. It's a plan that includes microwave popcorn, a chance to win a new car or $1 million or save 25¢ on a jar of peanut butter, instant meals and instant soup. It's a plan in which repetition is the same as motion, busyness the same as purpose, miracles found in a tube of shampoo.

The woman in the stretch pants holds up a bottle of blue cheese salad dressing, New! With Chunks of Real Cheese. 'You ever try this?' she asks.

Her friend squeals in horror. 'Oh, no, not me. That kinda cheese gives me indigestion.'

And what about time? The mystics and the physicists say that time is not, it doesn't exist. Past, present, future are all as one. In Piggly Wiggly, however, time not only exists, it can be counted and saved. Oatmeal is three minutes, soup is five, the brown-and-serve sausages ten to fifteen. Forty-five minutes saved on the mashed potatoes, four hours saved on the vegetable soup, two hours on the barbecued chicken, seventy-six on the frozen sauerbraten dinner – saved so there are a few more hours in which to shop, a few more years to watch TV, enough time to afford that vacation in Hawaii.

And the time that's lost in saving – the time that you would have spent making a soup or preparing a big dinner, reflecting while you peeled and chopped, humming as you stirred the pot – what happens to that? I finally decide on a jar of Woody's Barbecue Sauce, because it's the cheapest.

The skinny kid doing the packing gives me a look as I start to help him. 'That your bike out there?' he wants to know. I have a little trouble understanding his accent, but he nods behind him to where Montoya, the squirrel tail tied to her back rack blowing in a breeze, sits by herself on the yellow lines.

I tell him she is.

'Whereyall from?'

'London.' I pick up the bag. 'London. England. But we started in New York.'

'New York.' He nods slowly, thinking about it. New York, the moon. 'Whereyall goin'?'

'California,' I say. 'But we're taking the long route.'

He smiles. 'Ah see,' he says. 'You're just watchin' the world go by.'

When I emerge from the Piggly Wiggly, Victor is sitting on the kerb with an old man in a shiny black suit, a bright white shirt, a thin red tie and a straw hat that's probably older than Victor. They're deep in conversation. Twenty years ago, a white hippy and an aged black man might have been shot for sitting together like this, watching the world go by and talking in the sun. Now people only eye them as Victor rises and the two shake hands. Maybe time can only be measured in change. In which case at least two days must have passed since we climbed down from the trees.

A string orchestra is playing 'Raindrops Keep Falling on My Head', but I'm humming 'You Can Look But You Better Not Touch' as I carefully make my way through the tomb-still department store, all at once conscious of my filthy jeans and leather jacket and the fact that I smell like the inside of a pretty crowded teepee. Out on the planet, for which time, indeed, does not exist, I'm just another traveller passing through, no more important than a red bird or a possum, and no less, but in here I'm a threat: I'm either going to steal something or break it. I jam my hands in my pockets and glance down to see how much dirt I'm leaving on the polished floor. Enough to mark my passing. The aisles are empty except for a few white women immaculately dressed and co-ordinated, their make-up perfect and their hair short and curled, lazily looking through the torturously perfect displays of gold jewellery and perfumes named after drugs and dependencies, shopping with no real need or desire.

I come out into the glass-roofed mall, where no raindrops fall, and stop to get my bearings. The storefronts are open, the temperature is comfortable, the music is soft, there's a fountain, benches and plants so perfect they might not be real. I might be in Long Island, New Jersey, Pennsylvania or California. I might even be in England. But I'm not. There isn't any directory. I'm still in Mississippi.

I try to look past the green and white café on the corner and down the row of shops for some sign of the healthfood store mentioned at the entrance to the mall. I'm vaguely aware that the small boy sweeping the floor in front of the café has thrown down his broom and is hurling himself across the plaza, shouting excitedly and waving his hands, but it isn't until he's practically on my boots that I realise he's talking to me.

He's about nine years old, small, thin, blue-eyed and brown-skinned, his hair shorn, and dressed in the clothes of some charitable organisation. He's still shouting, quickly and with genuine emotion, but a white Mississippi accent is enough of a challenge for me. At the speed he's speaking, I can't make out more than an occasional word, and most of them are conjunctions. This close, though, I can see that the genuine emotion in his voice is concern; concern tinged with terror.

Who the hell does he think I am? 'Excuse me?' I say. 'What?'

My lack of understanding makes him almost hysterical. He starts jumping up and down, urgently pointing to my neck.

'You have to talk a little slower.'

He tries to talk a little slower. I make out the words 'bandanna' and 'kill'.

I touch the blue bandanna I've pulled off my face to lessen the impression that I'm wanted by the law. 'The bandanna? What's wrong with my bandanna?'

He makes an effort to hold himself still and tells me again.

Necessity mothers more than invention. If you really have to, you often can. The question at the moment is whether necessity's other child is comprehension or imagination. I understand what he's saying, but what he's saying still makes no sense.

I smile. 'No one's going to shoot me because I'm wearing this bandanna,' I tell him, hoping I did understand him and am not making it up. 'It's just a scarf.'

I did understand him. It's not just a scarf. It's a blue bandanna, the bandanna of a gang. The Bloods are their enemies. The Bloods will shoot me on sight. I just manage not to laugh. They'd have to be on enough drugs to make everyone in Europe see God to mistake me for a member of a rival gang. Instead, I try distraction. I ask him where the healthfood store is.

'I'll take you.' He turns back towards the café to shout to the boy behind the counter that he's going to show this lady where the healthfood store is. The older boy nods. My saviour leads me by the hand, past shoe stores and record shops and the first health food-store, which only sells pills. When we finally reach the second healthfood store he doesn't give me a chance to speak, but himself explains to the rather stiff young white man dusting off the shelves of vitamins that I'm looking for healthy food.

I hold out my hand to thank him.

He shakes it, but all the time his eyes are on me and still worried. 'Please,' he says, though what I hear is 'police'. 'Please don't wear it.'

If this request had come from someone else – my mother, for instance – I would have tied the bandanna around my head in true warrior fashion and marched away. I look at the small boy in his shabby clothes and his blue eyes so sincere. I take off the bandanna and stuff it in my pocket.

'Maybe everybody thinks we're members of rival gangs,' says Victor when I tell him what happened. 'You know, we're madly in love and we're running away from them to try and make a new life together.' He takes another handful of raisins. The stiff young man in the healthfood store didn't know what couscous was, but he did know raisins. 'Like in *West Side Story*.'

Tony and Maria, fleeing the Jets and the Sharks on a Nighthawk 750.

'Only our gangs won't let us go,' Victor continues his story. 'They chase us from state to state, always just a few gas stations behind.'

Romeo and Juliet trying to get out of town before the pick-ups full of Capulets and Montagues arrive.

'They'll leave our bodies in a ditch if they ever find us,' concludes Victor.

I give a tug to his red bandanna. 'No they won't,' I say. 'You they'll kill, me they'll rape.'

The town itself is another postcard from the past. Clean, quiet streets, a square of buildings with gleaming plate-glass windows, a well-tended green with a war monument and wooden benches. If you arrive here early in the morning, the air still fresh from a heavy rain and the sunlight soft and cloudy, when the shopkeepers are unlocking their doors and extending their awnings, chatting to each other about the weather and the government and this week's shocking crime while they work, and there's a brown dog in a hurry coming down the sidewalk and a white cat sleeping in the window of the Blue Fish Café, this is the kind of town that almost makes you wish you could stay. Stay and become part of this pattern of living, get to know the names of the postmistress and the men who hang around the barber's shop on drowsy afternoons; get to know which children belong to whom, when the town clerk goes to lunch and how often the sheriff's car circles the square; get so you can tell the time just by noticing who's walking by. Stay and grow old slowly and imperceptibly, noticing that time's moved on only when they put up a new supermarket or someone dies. A woman and a small child stop to admire the cat; the boy washing the window of the gift and card shop waves to someone in a passing car. A plastic bag flutters from the branches of the tree beside the tribute to the dead of two world wars. Here you can find safety and order, certainty and tranquillity.

'Left or right?' shouts Victor.

'Left.'

But you can't find coffee, not this early. For that you have to go to a fast-food chain.

There's always a Hardees on the edge of town.

'That your bike out front?'

The Hardees is decorated in yellow, brown and orange, like the hills of West Virginia, the windows posted with special offers and missing posters: Bobbie Jo Powell, age five and a half . . . Misty Cortelou, age fourteen . . . Kimberly Amster, seven years of age . . .

Although the take-away trade is brisk at this hour, mainly men stopping to pick up something on their way to work, at the moment there are only four people in the dining section. Victor and I are two of them. The third is a thin, bearded man of around forty, in jeans, a blue flannel and a red baseball cap, eating the breakfast special while he reads his paper. The fourth is also around forty, a stocky, smiling, muscular guy in filthy fatigues and a black T-shirt advertising a drug-free California who managed to talk the girl behind the counter into giving him honey for his coffee because he can't stand sugar. I know it's him speaking and I don't want it to be. The other guy looks like a labourer, either farm or construction, but this one looks like a Vietnam vet. It's too early in the morning for a Vietnam vet. As with reading a book or having a lobotomy, talking to a Vietnam vet is something you have to be in the mood for. And I'm not. I lay awake most of the night, listening to the futile barking of the birds, suddenly too vividly aware of why most people prefer the seven-day cruise over rolling like a stone.

I don't look up from the postcard I'm writing to Tommi: I'm beginning to understand how the package tour got started. Because man, unlike the universe, wants things to stay the same while seeming to change.

Victor stops talking to himself through the steam rising from his coffee and does look up. 'Yeah, she's ours.' And then, as though Montoya's listening and might be offended if he doesn't mention it, adds, 'She's a great bike.'

I can hear the paper of the man in the baseball cap rustle as he turns a page and the other man pulling off the tops of the tiny tubs of honey and pouring them into his coffee.

'Where you guys headin'?'

'California,' says Victor. 'Then down to Peru.'

When you travel with a group, you have certainty. You not only know where you'll be at 8.15 tomorrow evening, what you'll see on Wednesday, why you should see it, and where you'll have lunch, you know all the time exactly where you are.

'Shit, man,' he laughs, 'and I thought I was coverin' ground.' He picks up his coffee and his backpack and moves to the table across from us. He smells worse than we do.

When you travel with a group you know what you'll come back with: some photographs you'll never look at, a hand-made shirt you'll never wear, a few facts the tour guide told you that you'll soon forget, and you. You, just as you were, just as you would have been if you'd never set one foot out of the door.

'So where you goin' from here? New Orleans?'

Victor says yes with enthusiasm. We're going to sleep in a motel, drink beer and eat hot fries in a bar with live Cajun music, and get the bike fixed.

'Nice city.' He stirs his coffee. 'What route you taking? You oughta go down—'

The paper rustles behind me again. 'Eighty-one's best.'

He picks up his cup. 'Yeah,' he says. 'Eighty-one's okay.'

When you travel with a group, though you may acquire a new taste for olives or fermented corn liquor, you never confront the real nature of travel: which is not to contain, but to open up; not to conserve, but to rip apart.

We all introduce ourselves and the men start to talk about roads. Which one is fastest, which one is safest, which one goes through the nicest country.

Travelling like a stone means facing the fears we make nations, tribes, sects, cities, towns and families to forget.

Al rests one leg on his backpack and says we have to be careful from now on. 'You got a gun?' he asks Victor. He leans down and taps the pocket of his pack. 'I've got a gun.' Careful in Texas, careful in Louisiana. In Louisiana, they drop water-bombs from the fly-overs. 'You know how heavy that is when it hits you?' he asks. 'Killed a guy in a refrigerator truck, that's how heavy.'

Glen laughs. 'I've been all over and I've seen a lot of things,' he says, 'but I ain't never heard of that.'

The fear that you are unprotected in a hostile environment.

The men start talking about where they have been. Glen lived in California, used to hitch across the country when it wasn't like now, when it was safe, worked in Montana and Texas and Las Vegas, hated Vegas, and now he's here, settled down. 'I've got a job, a little house, a girlfriend, I'm doin' okay.'

That there is nothing to hold on to.

Al's been walking the roads for the last ten years, sleeping rough, working in carnivals and fields and gas stations. Al was in Vietnam, on a kind of package tour. Al was a Green Beret.

That there is nothing certain but uncertainty.

Al starts telling the story of his life. Glen and Victor sit back, sipping their coffees. Despite my mood, I put down my pen.

Al joined up when he was eighteen, after his older brother was killed in action. His voice is matter-of-fact as he talks about the war, so he sounds like one of the girls serving the coffee and the breakfast specials talking about last year's Hallowe'en dance. There were streamers and there were orange lights, there was a girl who came as Madonna and was sent straight home, one of the boys threw up on the vice principal's shoes. There was death and there was torture, there was a guy who tried to swim home one night, just another body never found, there was no one you could trust, not even a child. I glance at the picture of five-and-a-half-year-old Bobbie Jo Powell taped to the glass beside me, and back at Al. 'Shoot,' he's laughing, 'you couldn't even trust a dog.' Sunlight falls on him like a shadow. 'But I'm a survivor,' says Al. You learn not to be careless, not to be sentimental. 'Maybe they got my brother, but I was damned if they were going to get me.' He finishes his coffee with a smile. 'I know more ways of killing someone than you guys can imagine,' says Al.

The fear that you are all alone.

Al finishes describing the device he designed for a NASA space shuttle for which they never gave him any credit. 'You can go to Washington and check the patent,' he says. 'It's mine.'

Victor glances at Glen. I glance at Glen. Glen rolls his eyes. He picks up his tray. 'I gotta go,' he announces. 'Gotta get to work.' He wishes us luck.

Al starts talking about the carnival, about setting up the ride and cracking it down. For the first time there's some emotion in his voice as he describes how the whole thing folds back into the truck, boom boom boom. 'Fuckin' beautiful,' says Al. 'A perfect design.' He takes a paperback book on calligraphy out of his backpack. 'I'm teachin' myself,' he says, passing the book to Victor. 'Next I want to learn glass painting, make some money doin' signs.'

Glen gets into an old stationwagon with a pile of tools in the back and a large black dog in the passenger seat. I watch him pull into the road, the dog pushing his face into the wind. The traffic's getting heavier, a gaggle of kids cut through the parking lot, loud and laughing, going to school.

Alone is not the same as by yourself; not the same as lonely. Alone is alone. Alone with your thoughts and nothing to fill them – no dates, no times, no duties, no responsibilities, no hundreds of things to be done or complained about. And that's the fear. That once you step outside the world where you are known and named, where you belong, you will discover that you don't belong anywhere. The things that used to matter to you – which paper you read, what food you ate, where you lived, your job, your friends, the team you supported, whether or not your bills were paid on time and the bathroom window was always open one inch – don't matter any more. You stop identifying yourself as Jeremy Fishbone who lives in Duluth, votes Republican, sells insurance and likes Pink Floyd, who has a house and three kids and a mortgage and a grey stationwagon that's always breaking down, connected to hundreds of others you believe to be just like you because they, too, live in Duluth, or vote Republican, or sell insurance, or like Pink Floyd, or drive a car that's always breaking down, and become just another stone, rolling towards oblivion, just another fragment of some long-gone planet speeding through space.

'FBI killed my sister,' says Al.

I turn back to the room.

'FBI?' Victor's smiling a wary smile, unsure of what to ask next. But he doesn't have to be. Al is a self-starter when it comes to conversation.

Al nods. 'Up in Oregon.' His voice raises slightly. 'Eugene, Oregon. 1988. You can check the papers. She was eight months' pregnant. Killed her, my brother-in-law Eddie Ridgewood, and his friend Lawrence Rivers. Shot them all right in front of the house.'

I ask the question that someone always winds up asking in the end. 'Why?'

'Bullshit,' says Al. 'Government crap.'

The FBI raided the home of Kathleen Stanton and Eddie Ridgewood because, they claimed, they were running arms. They thought they were going to find an arsenal in the cellar. Acted like they were storming Saigon. Shot down a pregnant woman and two unarmed men. Fuckin' heroes.

'Did they think they were somebody else?' asks Victor.

'No,' says Al. He's no longer speaking without emotion. It's only now I notice how blue his eyes are, bright as glass. 'They knew who they were.'

Like Al Stanton himself, Eddie Ridgewood, Kathleen Stanton and Lawrence Rivers all belonged to the American Patriots.

'We're not racists,' says Al, slapping the table. The girl emptying the wastebins pauses for a nanosecond. Only the customers in Hardees aren't black. 'We're white separatists. I'm not against black people, they just don't belong with us, that's all. We oughta give them their own country where they can do what they want. We're not supposed to live together, it isn't right.'

Victor and I exchange a look, but neither of us says anything. There are times when you argue because it would serve some purpose, and times when you don't because it would be like trying to dance with a man who is dying. This is one of the times when you don't want a corpse pissing over your shoes.

'Don't matter that they were born here,' says Al. 'They're just not the same.' He's talking more quickly than he was before, his non-chalance replaced by something like passion, defining American ideals, American values, American dreams, the differences between whites and blacks. 'If the government wants to be soft it's their business, they're just a bunch of corrupt bastards anyway. But a man's gotta fight for what he knows is right.'

Most of us don't ever want to admit that we're alone.

Victor gets up to go to the loo.

'You know, Vic, I like you,' says Al with his laser smile. 'You know why I like you?'

I can see Victor thinking, because you think I'm a psycho-racist too, but he shakes his head.

Al waves a hand. 'Turn around,' he orders.

Victor turns his head.

Al points at Victor's ear. 'Because you don't wear no earring, that's why I like you.'

Victor smiles. 'You mean besides the one in my nose?'

8

HIGHWAY 61

Victor hangs up the phone with a shrug that is becoming more and more philosophical as the days go by. You can't travel without learning to wait.

'Here's a surprise. It'll take them maybe a week, maybe two weeks to order the part.'

This announcement doesn't cause me even to pause in hanging my laundry on the line we've strung across the room. 'It's a good thing it isn't anything major, or we'd be carrying her to California.' I'm becoming more and more philosophical, too.

'Um . . .' says Victor. He lays back on the sleeping bag airing across the bed, absentmindedly picking up a stray twig caught in the nylon.

'At least that means we don't have to run around getting things done all afternoon,' I go on. 'Maybe we can actually see something of New Orleans.' I don't add, 'For a change.'

But Victor hears it anyway. 'I knew it!' He flicks the twig at me. 'You're still pissed off about Graceland, aren't you?'

'No, I'm not still pissed off about Graceland.' And I'm not. So we missed Graceland and all of Memphis except for a couple of gas stations and a camping store – so what? We didn't come all this way to look at buildings. We can look at buildings back home. But I am showing signs of that fundamental human emotion, the fear that everyone else is at a better party. Whole economies are based on tourism, whole lives planned around six weeks in Europe or the exotic east. Surely there must be more to this tourist thing than itemised itineraries and regular meals. 'I'd just like to see what everybody else is seeing for once, that's all.' I squeeze the last sock on to the line. 'So I know what we're not missing.'

'You know what we're not missing,' says my travelling companion. 'We're missing nothing. We're seeing it all.'

Thus speaks a biker. Bikers agree that travelling on a motorcycle is different from travelling in a car. In a car, you're an observer, eating and listening to the radio as the highway falls behind you, more involved in the conversation you're having about your best friend's problems with her husband or the book you're reading to utilise all the wasted time of getting from A to B than in what lies beyond the windows of your car. On a bike, you are part of the scenery, part of the whole.

But, just for a bit, I don't want to be part of the whole. I want to be in the picture of the five-for-a-dollar postcards sold in every café, souvenir shop and service station. And for that you have to be on foot.

Victor leans over and gives the sleeping bag I've sat down on a yank that nearly rolls me to the floor. 'Admit it,' he says. 'You are still pissed off about Memphis.'

Tulane Avenue runs right by our motel and into the centre of town. It's a typical, busy, sprawling-American-city road, hot and bleak in the afternoon sun, lined not with trees but with cheap motels, dingy storefronts and shabby wooden houses with lawns of crab grass and garbage and late-model cars parked out front, gas stations and used car lots, twenty-four-hour bail bondsmen, fast-food chains, pawnbrokers, junk stores and fortune-tellers. We step over puddles of glass and empty cans, the only people on the sidewalk who aren't either waiting for a bus or simply hanging out. The only white people not in a car. We're not in the postcard yet. This is not the picturesque New Orleans of song and legend, sad-eyed whores watching the streets from latticed balconies and manic musicians leading the dance to another grave, but nonetheless I can almost imagine Buddy Bolden staggering out of the pawn shop across the street and into the bright blue house next door to have his fortune read.

I'm not totally impervious to the attractions of dingy grocers and bail bondsmen, but it's the fortune-tellers that command my attention. Here we are stumbling around at the entrance to the twenty-first century, cordless phones jammed in our pockets and computers in our arms, and there they are, reading whole lives in cards, crystals and stars, unacknowledged keepers of the instruction manual. Does it make sense?

We pass another woman wearing a faded cotton dress and a plastic shower cap.

'Jesus,' says Victor. 'Do you think that means it's going to rain?'

You would, of course, expect fortune-tellers in a neighbourhood like this, poor and low on hope, but there are fortune-tellers everywhere in America from Manhattan on. We like to say that it doesn't matter if you're white or black, rich or poor, but this is one of the few areas where that is really true. Why?

I imagine Buddy Bolden sitting in the small, close room behind the window curtained with coloured beads. He takes a pint of rot-gut whisky from his pocket and finishes the last inch in the bottle, unfolds some crumpled bills and lays them on the table. His hand shakes. 'Tell me what's going to happen to me,' he says. The fortune-teller looks at the cards she's laid out on the dull, scarred wood and then she looks at Buddy, half dead already and his back against the wall. Does he really want to know how close he is to a pauper's grave, his dreams all dust? Does she tell him? If she does tell him, what does he do then?

We stop at a major intersection, waiting beside a row of fruit and flower stands for the light to change.

'We must be getting close,' says Victor. He nods across the four-lane road divided by an island of trees. 'I see white people over there.'

Two of the boys selling by the roadside are practising dance steps while they wait for customers, the radio up loud. They're laughing and making faces, so strong in the moment that it is impossible to imagine a time when they won't be young with the sun shining and the smell of hot-house roses in the air.

If you really thought someone could tell you your future, would you ask? If you did ask, would that mean that you really wanted to know? What do you want to know? That you'll be run over by a drunken teenager two weeks from now? That you'll contract MS before you reach thirty? That that pain in your back isn't a wrenched disc but death pounding on your door? That you're never going to find true love? That you're never going to get out of debt? That your friends will leave you, your spouse will betray you, your children will never visit? That you'll have love and money, but will never be happy? That you'll have love and money but will still spend the last years of your life in a wheelchair by the window, waiting for the nurse's aid to come round with the library trolley?

'Why do you think so many people go to fortune-tellers?' I ask Victor as the light changes and we start across the road. 'Is it because we hate uncertainty? Because we fear the unknown more than the known?'

Victor puts his arm out to stop me from walking into a car coming round the corner. 'Nah,' he says. 'I think it's just because everybody likes to talk about himself.'

By the standards used to judge this kind of thing, it's the postcard of a place interesting enough to deserve a visit.

And it's not a bad postcard, as postcards go. *New Orleans's colorful and lively French Quarter*, says the blurb on the back, *famous for its food, music and legendary past.*

The sky is blue over narrow, cobbled streets and palely painted buildings, their shutters closed against the sun. You know, just by the way the light falls across the pavement, that a slow, muddy blues is drifting like smoke from an opened window, that behind heavy doors there are shady courtyards and flowers still in bloom and someone singing a song about love, that the ghosts of young women in white silk dresses and velvet ribbons still stand on those ornate balconies, whispering secrets while their eyes follow the backs of men in long black coats with unknown pasts and uncertain futures. It couldn't have any more old-world charm if there were still people being sold on the block.

Victor and I are there, right in the corner of the photograph, huddled together under a street light trying to read our pocket map as night falls and a noisy drove of sightseers spills past us and into the road. Cameras strapped around their necks, guidebooks open, they eat ice cream and sip cocktails in plastic cups as they shuffle along. Their faces bright with gee-whizz smiles, they wander in and out of shops; linger in front of window displays of T-shirts and crafts; read with interest the historic markers on the sides of buildings; take pictures of each other under signposts and balconies, standing next to horse-drawn carriages, posing with a parrot or a python for just a few bucks.

Victor brushes back his hair. 'Shit,' he mutters. 'Now what?'

Now what indeed. For a change we know exactly where we are. We're on Bourbon Street. What we don't know is where we'd like to be.

Though larger than the one street of colonial Singapore not razed to the ground, the French Quarter isn't as big as, for instance, East LA, and we've been walking around it for quite some time now, up one quaint street and alleyway, down another, once around the block and back to the beginning again. We've been in the voodoo shop, the poster shop and the trendy gift stores with their peace-symbol neck-laces and marijuana-leaf earrings. We've checked out the crafts stores and the postcard places, and we've ignored the shops selling soft-porn tat and dodged the hawkers outside the bars – 'Live music . . . New Orleans jazz . . . real Dixieland . . . come on in.' We've seen the park with its energetic buskers and toe-tapping onlookers and the fortune-teller dressed up like a nineteenth-century madam all in blue – blue gown, blue picture hat, a trailing boa of bright blue feathers – sitting at a table beneath a yellow umbrella. What there is to see here, what atmosphere to soak up, we've seen and soaked up.

'Is it me?' he asks. 'Or do you think we're in *The Twilight Zone*?'

In some ways, it's beginning to seem to me, most cities resemble one another in the way that most carrots resemble one another. See one and you have a pretty good idea of what the rest of them are like. A shopping district is a shopping district, a business centre a busi-ness centre, a traffic jam in New York or Memphis essentially the same as one in Birmingham or London, one street of sex shops and porn shows strikingly similar to the next. What distinguishes one city from another for the casual visitor is usually the area that has the best bars and the worst reputation. 'Colourful', the guidebooks will tell you. 'Bohemian . . . arty . . . streetwise . . . interesting . . . full of character . . . keep an eye on your things . . . be prepared for sur-prises . . .' In New York this area is the Village or Soho; in London it's Camden or Soho. In New Orleans they seem to make do with this, the eccentric centre as conceived by aliens or a set designer.

I step out of the way of a bunch of guys in baseball caps carrying cups of beer and talking loudly about Batman and whether or not the movies are true to the books.

'It's either *The Twilight Zone* or this is what they mean by virtual reality.'

'Stressing the virtual and not the reality,' says Victor. His eyes fol-low the Batman fans as they lurch across the street. 'Beer,' he bleats. 'It's time for a beer. At least that's real.'

This is the postcard of a good time.

People are crammed together at round, polished tables, eating and drinking, talking loudly, throwing their heads back and howling with laughter, playfully hurling food, straws and balled-up napkins at one another when the mood takes them, clapping and whistling whenever they recognise a song.

The room itself is large and high-ceilinged, panelled in wood and mirrors and decorated with posters for events that happened decades ago, yellowed as though they're old. Behind the brass-railed bar, three young men in striped shirts and snappy bow ties good-humouredly pour out drinks. Dance-hall girls with scrubbed faces swish between the tables carrying trays of food. From the look of it, you'd think that everything here had stayed the same for at least a hundred years – excluding, of course, the four screens of football and the $5 price on a bottle of Bud.

'I knew we should have gone somewhere else,' screams Victor.

A peanut lands on our table and I flick it at him. 'Where?' I shout back.

Not only can we not find the Cajun music and hot fries we could have found in New York, but the bars around here are as similar as plastic alligators.

Victor shrugs. 'Baton Rouge?'

On stage, squeezed into a corner near the toilets, the Dixieland Duellists spar against the din from the televisions and the audience with session-man enthusiasm and enough skill not to be immediately pierced through the heart.

Victor takes a cautious sip of beer. 'It is real,' he screams. 'It tastes just like regular Bud.'

One of the men at the table next to ours, the one in the floral shirt and the slave-driver's hat, staggers up beside the trumpet player and starts to sing along. His friends all cheer, his wife is laughing and shaking her head.

'Yo, Chuck!' shouts the guy in the T-shirt that says 'When Better Women Are Made, I'll Be the Man to Make Them'. 'Show 'em how we do it back home!'

Back home, they close their eyes and clutch the mike when they sing the blues. They quiver with emotion. Their faces contort with inner pain. They sway into the trumpet player and back into the drums.

Feet begin to tap and hands to clap – except for ours. Our feet remain flat on the floor, our hands stay close to the bottle.

'This is your fault,' yells Victor. 'It was your idea to act like a tourist.'

Tourists are what everyone but the staff, the Duellists, the guy asleep with his head in an aspidistra and the LSU students watching the game are acting like. It's not so much the way they're dressed – like people in a disaster movie that takes place in Hawaii – as the way they're enjoying themselves. Uninhibitedly. Unreservedly. With abandon approaching frenzy. The men are knocking back the beer and bourbon and the women are draining small goldfish bowls of pastel drinks with crushed ice, cherries and paper parasols. Their faces say that they like everything. They like the band, they like the bar, they like the decor of the bar, they love New Orleans. They talk about the trolley and the cemetery, the riverboat ride, the plantation visit, the tour through the swamp and the souvenirs they bought; they argue about which was better, the jambalaya, the blackened cat-fish, the creole okra, or the crawfish pie. They are having, exactly, the time they came to have.

But just as not everybody can be a professional dancer, or an accomplished surgeon, or a stupendous stewardess, not everybody can be a good tourist. It takes a certain temperament and person-ality, a certain frame of mind. You can't, for example, be squeamish, self-conscious or easily bored. You should be outgoing and sociable, game for a laugh. It helps if you're pretty immune to tedium and don't mind being ripped off. It helps even more if you don't mind getting so drunk that you have to close one eye to be able to see. It's a temperament, personality and frame of mind that we don't possess.

'I feel like we're in Blackpool,' says my travelling companion in such a way that not even someone from Ethiopia who had never heard of Blackpool could mistake this for good news. 'Or Majorca.'

'You can't feel like you're in Majorca.' I duck out of the path of another peanut. 'You're the only Englishman here and you're not complaining about the lager or throwing up by the door.'

We sip our Buds and glance over towards the toilets. In some weird way, it's actually less like being in Majorca among a busload of Englishmen bemoaning the lack of Newcastle Brown and bangers and mash than it is like watching daytime TV. I half expect an explanatory sign to flash on the screen beneath the singer as he sprays saliva across the audience and gives it all he's got. *This is Chuck. He always wanted to be a black bluesman who's known hard times and shares them with the world through his music, and now he's having his chance.* The band finishes the song, but Chuck starts another. There's a nanosecond of instrumental silence and then the piano comes in and the rest all follow. Chuck gives the piano player the thumbs-up.

Chuck, in his real life, might easily be a dentist, a lawyer or an accountant. A man people go to for advice. A man people trust. Clerks and tellers call him 'sir'. He is quiet and responsible, upright and conservative, a believer in traditional values and a rule-making God. Society rests on men like Chuck. The neighbours can never understand the doctor who beat and starved his children, or the builder who buried twelve bodies under the stairs, or that nice couple across the road who turned out to be running a child prostitution ring, but I find this no less baffling. The tourist's is a temperament, personality and frame of mind that permits a person to do all the things in someone else's city or country that he would never do in his own without feeling either embarrassed or guilty – or possibly both.

Chuck kicks over the bottle of beer next to one of the amps. Catcalls and hoots echo through the bar. Someone throws a hamburger roll at the stage. It bounces off the mike. Several objects that look rather like fried potatoes land at the feet of the Dixieland Duellists.

'Take your beer,' orders Victor.

I'm torn between looking at him and looking at the handful of salad that just hit one of the dance-hall girls on the back.

'Take your beer!'

Barbecue ribs soar overhead, splashing participants and non-participants with sauce; hunks of cornbread explode against a wall. More than one woman starts screaming. The Dixieland Duellists, accustomed to a lack of attention from their audience, play on, but Chuck slips on a smashed slice of mud pie and brings down the mike.

Victor grabs his beer with one hand and me with the other and pulls us to the floor and under the table.

I'd always reckoned – as one does – that I'd pretty much seen everything a person who had missed the Holocaust, Operation Rolling Thunder and a party given by the Khmer Rouge was likely to see, human behaviour-wise. I've been in blackouts, hurricanes, stalled, unlighted subway cars, minor riots and the January sales, but I've never been in a food fight before. It makes you wonder.

I hunch next to Victor. 'Do you think that on other planets this is what they consider fun?' I ask.

Victor raises his bottle to his lips. Half a hamburger slaps into the sawdust beside us. 'It's what's considered fun on this planet that worries me,' he says.

It's one of those typical, almost humdrum, human stories of injustice, degradation and oppression. Early in the seventeenth century, French colonists settled an area along the Bay of Fundy in Canada, and called it Arcadie. While they farmed and fished and raised their families, control of the region was taken by the British, who at the start of the French and Indian War deported the possibly treacherous Arcadians and left their lands and homes in flames. The deportations took place over thirty years, another trail of tears that sent some Arcadians to Britain as prisoners of war, some back to France as impoverished refugees, and left others scattered across the Americas and Caribbean like ocean debris. In 1785, to get rid of them once and for all, 1,600 Arcadians were packed out of France on seven ships bound for Louisiana.

Louisiana is Cajun country. Swampland and bayou, fiddles and accordians, pirogues, alligators and crawfish, accents from another place, living from a different time.

Having reached Baton Rouge without finding the new Arcadie, we doubled back and are now moving west again along Highway 61, as on the way to Lake Charles. Highway 61 runs from Minnesota to Louisiana, drawing a line that connects nowheres the way a rosary string connects beads. It's the kind of road that can be considered either the way out or the way in.

The way out of Podunk towns and back-of-beyond communities where everyone not only knows each other but is related to everyone else or soon will be. The way out of sameness and stagnation, out of days that repeat themselves like sunsets and nights that could well be the same night, naturally allowing for changes in the weather and our movement through the stars. If you were born with a hungry heart in a place not levelled by the blades of time – a place too small for dreaming – it's at the side of a road like Highway 61 that you stand, staring into the horizon, aware that you can't even imagine what marvels, what breathtakers, what blood-pumping dangers might lie at the other end, and are perhaps too scared to try.

The way into the centre, where people live as they have always lived, sure of where they come from and where they want to go; knowing what to do because it's all been done before, because the rules were lodged so long ago they seem like the voice of God. The way into the core, where it's so easy to forget that we've ever been before. If you were born with a restless soul in a place recreated by time – a place too new for memories – you follow a road like Highway 61, trying to find what you don't remember having lost

At the moment, however, we know what we've lost. We've lost Arcadie.

Well, maybe not lost it exactly but we certainly haven't found it. We've been riding all day, past fields of sugar cane and elaborate cemeteries built above the marshy ground, down past Houma to Timbalier Bay, had coffee in a marina that might have been in Maryland or Cornwall, ate our lunch among the litter at the side of a canal, rode round Houma for two hours before we found the way out, and now here we are at Alligator Annie's on Highway 61, deciding what to do next.

Alligator Annie's is a barn-sized room with Venetian blinds at the windows, divided in two by a low partition covered with plastic bricks down which plastic ivy trails. On our side of the partition, Annie's is a diner by day – grits, eggs, fried ham and black-eyed peas on the menu, black and white checked tiles on the floor, booths against the wall, formica tables topped with bottles of ketchup and bowls of creamer and artificial sweetener. On the other side, it's the local hot spot – black and white checked floor, formica tables covered with floral plastic cloths, arcade games that you have to be eighteen to play, a mike and an amp, a jukebox, a large photograph of what could be Holland and a poster for Alligator Annie's Bayou Tour. The walls are dingy white and battleship grey, the lighting dim, the kitchen empty. If it weren't for the red light glowing on the coffee-maker and the two large, middle-aged women in housedresses and Nancy Reagan hairdos smoking cigarettes and watching a talk show on the oversized television in one corner of the diner, you might think the place was closed for the winter. The woman in the blue dress and chilli-pepper earrings is Peg; the one in pink with the rebel flag apron tied around her waist is Alligator Annie herself. Neither of them thinks we should go to California, because California is full of blacks and Chicanos.

I look over to try to catch Annie's attention, and without taking her eyes from the screen she says, 'You-all just help yourselves if you want more coffee, honey. The milk's there on the counter.'

I get up from the booth by the door to help ourselves, glancing at the set as I pour out two cups of what passes for the ancient drink of the infidels here in America. Today's subject under discussion is teenage girls who have babies for their mothers. Victor bends his head over the Rad, pretending to be unaware of Cathy, eighteen, and her mother Letitia, thirty-two, explaining how they inseminated Cathy with a tube of semen borrowed from Letitia's new husband.

The hostess asks Letitia how she got Robert's semen without telling him what was going on. Letitia smiles. It's the smile of someone explaining why they have to skin you alive.

'I'd like to've seen that one,' says Annie.

'You'd think he'd'a noticed it was missin',' says Peg.

Annie lights another Salem. 'He was probably asleep.'

'You didn't think this was a lot to ask of your daughter?' the interviewer inquires in a flat, reasonable voice.

Letitia smiles her Charles Manson smile. 'No,' she says. 'I know she loves me.'

'We could be in Texas tonight,' says Victor as I sit back down. He seems to think this is good news.

'Texas?' I didn't know that was where we wanted to be. I push his cup towards him and lean over the map. Even I can find Texas. It's way over there to the left. 'Have they moved Lake Charles again?'

But Victor isn't in a joking mood. Last night was a bad night, and today has been a less than great day. We wanted preternatural swamps through whose blackened, huddled trees the cautious ghosts of Choctaw warriors and runaway slaves still slip, but what we got instead were roads littered with dead owls and broken stalks, darkling bogs and half-harvested fields of sugar cane under a sky partly blocked by the smoke from the refineries and marked by flames that burn suspended above their chimneys, like the Holy Spirit that hovered over the head of Christ in the portrait that hung in Sister Mary Jean's catechism class.

'You remember Mary Shinnie's cousin?' Peg digs at her back teeth with a toothpick. 'The one who moved to Mobile? She tried that artificial insemination when she couldn't have any more kids.'

No wonder Annie's a famous alligator hunter – she rarely seems to blink. 'The Good Lord blessed me with only one child,' she says, 'and that was enough for me.'

'But it didn't work,' says Peg.

'Today's just been another wild-goose chase,' says Victor. 'All we've done is go in a bloody circle.' He stops tracing a bloody circle in the middle of Louisiana and instead traces a line from where we may be now, past Lake Charles and across the border, stopping his finger by the green tree and tent that mark a state park. 'We should make up some time.'

I try to gauge how far it is to Texas by the legend. Not as far as we've done today, but farther than I'd like it to be, especially since the afternoon is already losing light. 'But it'll take hours. Why don't we find something around here?'

'Because everything around here is private,' says Victor, 'and I'm not spending another twenty dollars to camp in a field of RVs.' On gravel, he might add. With a few trees dotted among the campsites and no firewood on the ground, stringing owl feathers together to cover Montoya's windscreen instead of eating supper because the stove has given up halfway through cooking the glop, he might also add. Awake most of the night, with the cold and the wind which threatens to blow the tent over the restrooms and the vending machines, with someone who thinks she can hear wild dogs prowling through the garbage.

We sip our coffee in silence while the interviewer introduces Ellen, her mother, Darlene and their daughter Shawn. Ellen has had sex only once, thirteen years ago, with a man she didn't like and never saw again, because Darlene said he was the right one. Ellen wanted to give her mother a baby to replace the one killed in a car crash on her first birthday. It was her idea. She was fifteen. Shawn, scrawny, blonde hair in a ponytail and braces on her teeth, stares at the floor while this is explained, ready to run.

The interviewer can always take up 'gator-hunting if this job fails. 'How did you know this was the man you wanted to father your child?' she asks Ellen.

'Because my mother said he was.' Ellen folds and unfolds her hands. '"That's the one," she told me. "He's got the right colouring."'

The interviewer presses on. 'But tell us, Ellen, you never had second thoughts before you went through with it?'

'My mother was depressed for years,' explains Ellen. 'I couldn't stand to see her so unhappy. It was awful.'

Darlene, so short and fat she looks almost square, her eyes as blank as those of the owl we took the feathers from, has been sniffling since the cameras turned on her. If this is Darlene happy, her depression must have been demonic.

Peg stubs out her cigarette. 'That's what family's all about,' she says. 'Sticking together.'

'My Terry would never've offered to have no baby for me,' says Annie. 'It was all I could do to get her to clear the table once a week.'

'What about Lake Charles?' I ask at last, as neutral as the

interviewer asking Shawn if she's happy being her grandmother's child. 'There's camping there.'

Shawn says she loves Mama Darlene, but she'd rather live with Ellen Mom.

Victor says, 'We could try Lake Charles.' He raises his cup. 'Let's see what sort of time we make.'

When I go over to pay, Annie waves me away with a swirl of smoke. 'No charge, honey,' she tells me. 'You got a long ways to go yet.'

I glance back at Victor, rolling up the Rad and wrapping it in its garbage bag like a man who isn't planning to check it again until well into Texas, if at all. How does she know?

In the starless, moonless night, driving on the interstate is as close as some of us would like to get to driving through space. There's nothing to hold on to. Nothing behind us, nothing in front of us, nothing at the sides that tells you where you are but the exit signs and billboards advertising lodging, food and gas. When I was a kid, Texas was the Wild West. I thought that every movie and television show with a cowboy or an Indian in it was automatically set here. Texas was wagon trains and small wooden towns with sheriffs and saloons, wild ponies and stampeding cattle, herds of bison kicking up the dust into towering clouds, rough men in Stetsons and hand-tooled boots with spurs that jingled and jangled and Colt 45s at their hips, quiet men with searching eyes, braids down their backs and feathers in their hair, able to vanish into the hills like ghosts. It was certainly nothing like this. We could be anywhere in the universe where there are trees and hills and litter along the roadsides. Anywhere the wind is cold and against you and the most comforting sight you've seen in four hours is the shimmering blue light from a television screen shining through a distant window like a campfire in the wilderness.

I thump Victor's shoulder as a small sign with a tent and the words Next Exit drawn on it suddenly materialises out of the shadows. 'That's it!'

Having left any fears about the intrepidity of the state police at least a hundred miles behind us when he abandoned all attempts to stay within range of the speed limit, Victor makes a sharp right, going so fast we might be heading for the deep, dark sky.

I don't give a shit where we're heading, so long as we get there very quickly. And when we do get there, I'm not going to insist on a cup of tea or a late supper of the cheese and Fig Newtons left over from lunch. I'm not going to lumber through the dark to find the wash-room, for one night I can piss in the woods and let my teeth rot like a real pioneer. I'm not even going to mention the fact that we hadn't actually agreed to go on to Texas. All I want is to go to sleep. It's all I've been able to think of for the past hour and a half. *No night, no matter how bad, can last forever . . . soon you can go to sleep . . . soon you can go to sleep . . . you can go to sleep very soon . . .* I lean my head against Victor's shoulder. But preferably not on the bike.

We hurl past a strip of gas stations, stores and fast-food chains, cutting left up an unlit road that passes several houses with jack-o'-lanterns on the front stoop and ghosts hanging from the eaves before it gives way to woods.

'Isn't this better than staying in Louisiana?' asks Victor as we hover at a crossroads, guessing left or right. 'Now we can get a really fresh start in the morning.'

I'm too tired to be as positive as he. 'What if the park's closed?'

We take the left again, gravel spitting behind us. 'It won't be closed.'

'It's gone ten o'clock.'

'It's a state park, it won't be closed.'

'But what if it is?'

'It won't be!'

The entrance to the park lies in a strip of electric light that makes the woods around it look even darker. We stop at the barrier. The park is closed

'Look on the bright side,' says Victor. 'At least we won't have to pay.'

We climb off Montoya and start searching along the sides of the road for enough of a gap to push the bike through. There isn't one. There's a ditch on one side and too many trees on the other. Back in London, Victor always slides the cycle around the barrier to the supermarket parking lot, but you wouldn't get a pushbike through this.

The moment is ripe for an ugly, emotional scene between the two travellers. This is the point in the story when Tonto tells the Lone Ranger just what Kimosabe means. 'You and your bloody silver bullets,' Tonto rages. 'You and your "Hi-ho Silver!" I'm sick of it. If you'd listened to me we could be warming ourselves by the fire reading *Zen and the Art of Motorcycle Maintenance* right now instead of standing here in the freezing cold with nowhere to go!' This is the part where Pancho tells the Cisco Kid that he didn't leave his home and his cat just to wander aimlessly around looking for trouble. That he's pretty damn sick of being dragged all over the territory on Cisco's whims – let's head north, let's head south, why don't we see if we can find a store around here that sells brown pasta – that they could at least have stopped at a Taco Bell for a couple of burritos if they were going to get stuck on the wrong side of the border. This is where Dale Evans stops singing, cracks Roy Rogers over the head with a cast iron pan, and bursts into tears.

All of these events are just about to happen when Victor grabs my arm. 'Look!' he says, pointing behind me. 'The cavalry.'

I turn round. A convoy of jeeps full of grey-haired couples in plaid shirts and quilted vests has pulled up behind us. The driver of the first car leans out his window. 'Left-right-left-right,' he says. '2791.'

Victor dials the combination on the lock. 'You see?' he says as he opens the barrier. 'There was nothing to get upset about.'

'Um,' I say. I put out my hand to feel the second drop of rain.

9

RIDER IN THE RAIN

The rain comes down like judgement. Inflexible. Relentless. Taking no hostages. We managed to set up the tent in the depthless dark before it broke, diving in with our boots on, scrabbling in the dimming torchlight for more safety pins to hold the flap closed while we discussed who it was that forgot to buy more batteries, but we almost needn't have bothered. In a storm like this, there really isn't an enormous amount of difference between being hunkered under a tree and being hunkered under a tree with a bit of blue nylon over your head. All night long the rain slams against the tent, soaking it through on every side, burrowing under and over the groundsheet, forcing its way through the gaps in the zip, touching everything that isn't taped up in plastic. Not taped up in plastic, I wake every hour or so, too cold and damp to sleep, listening to the tumult around us and to a lonely, longing cry nearby, as familiar as a heartbeat and as foreign as the sound of footsteps on the moon. On a night like this, so wild and furious, so near to Hallowe'en and the cracking of the doors, it might be the call of a wicka or a demon trapped in a twisted cypress, looking for its own – or something a little hungrier and less romantic looking for those soggy Fig Newtons.

The wind tears the top cloth free and shakes the tent as though it might lift it into the sky. The bottom of my sleeping bag is wet. There are times in life when it is impossible to understand why anyone would want to be part of that two-headed monster the couple. All the compromise and bickering, the disappointment and resignation, the insanity and doubt. And then there are times when you do understand why. The difficulty of travelling with a man who isn't your husband or lover that my mother failed to mention was the simple fact that there is no one to hug on nights like this when everything seems frightening and inherently wrong. I pull my feet up another few inches and yank the hood around my head, wishing, as my sister said I would, that I were back in London, watching the sky shake with lightning from behind a closed window with a cup of coffee in my hand. A cup of coffee and a tempeh sandwich with fried onions, avocado, tomato and hot sauce. And maybe a brownie. The cat would curl up beside me, and I might call Judy to see what the storm was like south of the river. Thunder would rumble over the rooftops and the sky would pale to puce and I'd say to Judy, 'I really love it when it's like this', and she'd say, 'It's a bit like that old line in the films, isn't it, when the hero says to the heroine, "I love it when you're angry"? We love it when nature's enraged.' So long as it's on the other side of the wall and she's pissed off at somebody else.

Another cry stitches through the night, obliterating the very concept of walls. No walls, no doors, no windows, no rules, no protection as we spin through space. The wish to be in London where there are nothing but walls and rules and protections passes. Cities may be where we are now, but a cry out of chaos is where we have been. Beside me, Victor mumbles 'Bloody clutch' and turns over in his sleep. I try to pull the hood tighter and break the cord.

Man is nature's greatest challenge. Every other animal, vegetable, mineral and sub-atomic particle in the universe cheerfully allows nature to get on with her show, but not so man. If life really were a stage, man's the guy who would want to be the director. Not a stage-hand, not an understudy, not even the star, but the chap who's in charge, the one with the pensive expression and the gold pen in his pocket and a million things to do. 'Move that to the left . . . change that line . . . turn off that bloody light . . .' Desperate to organise the unorganisable, make tractable the intractable, contain what can't be held, man has to clamber up on the stage, waving the script he's written, kicking the props he doesn't like out of his way. 'I believe in You,' man says to God, 'I really do. But I don't like the way You're running things.' I don't want death or disease or natural disasters. I don't want uncertainty or danger. I think this life thing should come with a guarantee. Look at me!' orders man. 'I can bake a potato in fifteen minutes. I can paint a landscape that looks so real you can smell the cut grass. I can irrigate the desert and illuminate the night, but I might as well be a cactus or a hummingbird or a bloody grain of sand the way You treat me.'

I huddle in my sleeping bag, disappointed in the day, unhappy about our flight to Texas, feeling somehow that something's missing, listening, waiting for nothing, wondering what that night cry longs for, wondering how it can be that I suddenly long for it myself.

But I dream about double-fudge brownies. I dream about double-fudge brownies, and wake when Victor treads on my hair as he tries to get out of the tent. He hunches in the doorway for a second, staring at the wash-house that has materialised across from us in the foggy, rainy dawn. We can hear someone on the outside telephone. 'What you doin'?' he shouts. 'Gettin' dressed? We're gettin' a few days off here 'count of the weather so I'll be home tomorrow.'

'Jesus,' says Victor. 'Does that mean this is normal?' and then he disappears. Five minutes, I think. I can stay here with my eyes closed for at least five more minutes.

But apparently I can't.

'Come out here!' Victor's voice is urgent but not loud. 'Dyan, come here!'

Reluctantly, I open my eyes. 'What is it?'

'Come here!'

This had better be good, I think as I scrabble out of my sleeping bag and reach for my wet boots. The bike had better be gone, or the cops waiting to arrest us, or a snack van parked on the road with hot coffee and English muffins that aren't raw and served with Taco Bell taco sauce, the way we usually eat them, but toasted and served with blueberry jam.

'Hurry up!'

I open my mouth to tell him that I am hurrying up, what's so important at six o'clock on a rainy morning in the middle of bleedin' nowhere, but at that instant I emerge from the tent and I can't say anything.

We're camped by a cypress swamp. In the diaphanous light, blurred by mizzle, the water is jade-green, the trees bent like bodies, phantasmic in their colours. Cranes and herons, geese and ducks silently skim across the water or watch us from the shore. A young otter slips away from the nearest islet and swims past us as though we're not there.

I'm not aware that the phone call is over and that there are footsteps behind us. 'Nice bike you got there.'

Reluctantly, we both turn.

'What you folks doin'?' asks the telephone caller. 'Just bummin'
around?'

Victor picks a green feather from the ground and hands it to me,
glancing back towards the water, where the shadow of a crane is
darkening the jade. 'Yeah,' he says. 'We're just bummin' around.'

It's a cold, dark day in God's country. Under a remorseless rain, the
plains stretch emptily away from the pitted tarmac, the line to forever broken by the occasional gas station or clump of stores,
a scattering of oil pumps nodding up and down like mediaeval
wind-up toys, an iron gate and miles behind it a building or two, a
fenced-in range and one lonely bison staring out through the bushes
as though wondering where everyone's gone, gaggles of trailers and
cheap houses bunched together among the scraggy pines and scrub,
billboards promising happiness and pleasure, the occasional dead
armadillo by the side of the road. The land is as flat and enormous
as silence. There might be nothing else in the world but this – the
smudgy handprints of civilisation grasping at whatever it can. A
moving spray of water appears on the horizon, small at first but
growing as it nears. Two riders are approaching, dressed in green
plastic trousers and hooded jackets and long, blue rubber gloves,
hunched low. A diesel truck howls past. The bike swerves, then
slows down, pulling over to the shoulder and coming to a stop.

'Fuckin' cowboy,' screams Victor. 'We're not having enough
trouble staying on the road, we have to have some asshole like that
nearly knock us off.' He looks back at me. 'You all right?'

I pull my hood out of my mouth and nod, too numb with cold
and exhaustion to be assed forming sentences. The only way I can
stop myself from counting every second of every minute of every
hour as we struggle across the Lone Star State is by telling myself
stories of the way things used to be – or of the way they never were.
'Umph,' I say.

'Let's go and get some gas,' says Victor. He gives me a wary but
friendly, almost fatherly smile. I haven't actually burst into tears in
front of him yet – even I can appreciate that crossing the continent
on a motorcycle is a hell of a lot better than in a Conostoga wagon –
but I can tell that he's aware it could happen. I've been showing signs
of stress. Señora Sanchez's youngest son, however, is not a man
impressed by tears. 'Grab a coffee. Warm up a bit.'

Maybe we aren't in Texas after all. Maybe we're in ancient Judea
around the time of one of Jehovah's really bad moods.

'Umph,' I say. I'm sure it never rained on the Lone Ranger. Never once in all those episodes do I recall the Masked Man wrapping a plastic bag over his hat or reaching into his saddlebags for a white umbrella. But it's been raining on us for two long days. We stop for gas every chance we get, terrified of running out on that 200-mile stretch of nothing everyone has warned us about that we haven't yet found. We stop for a coffee and a packet of biscuits just to have ten warm, dry minutes in which to remember what life was like when you lived indoors and didn't have to eat fast because it was so cold and the rain was turning your dinner to soup. And every time we stop, we hear the same comments – even from the guys on the Harleys and Goldwings who nod to us when we pass each other at tourist information centres or while circling through campgrounds looking for a space away from them and the RVs. 'Must be pretty cold on that bike.' 'Must be pretty wet.' 'Bet you wish you had a truck.'

'I'm singing in the rain,' sings Victor as we crawl along the shoulder to the next exit, 'just singing in the rain . . .'

Still singing, we pull into the gas station. I can't see the usual two or three tables crowded against the window between the snack foods and the auto supplies, so coffee is out. Normally, I don't consider the absence of a styrofoam cup of hot water that's been filtered through a few stale coffee beans a major disappointment or defeat, but this afternoon it strikes me as just a little less devastating than losing a wheel while crossing the Rio Grande. Victor stops with his hand on the hose to give me an is-this-it? look.

'I'll go pay,' I say, and march across the lot.

The guy behind the counter, whose pocket seems to suggest that his name is Jobo, glances out at Victor filling up Montoya in the downpour and then smiles at me. He opens his mouth.

I don't smile back. 'Yes,' I say. 'Yes, it's cold and it's wet, and I'd much rather be in a truck right now.'

He blinks. 'What kinda bike is that?' he asks. 'I use t'have a Harley.'

Al, owner and chef of La Cantina, Real Tex-Mex Home Cookin', a free Margarita for the ladies on Thursday nights and a scrapbook-worthy view of a busy intersection on the interstate in a torrential downpour, rushes back and forth between the kitchen and the dining room, talking to himself. He isn't used to waiting on tables. He forgets the napkins and has to go back. Forgets the cutlery and has to go back. Has to go back for Tabasco sauce and water. 'It's this weather,' he apologises when he has to go back for the menu as well. 'My waitress is late.' He looks out of the window. 'The weather.'

We apologise for dripping on his floor.

'It doesn't usually rain like this,' says Al. Nine inches a year, according to the Rad. 'But it's Texas. What can you do?'

I can look at the Rad and try to determine how much further we have to go today before we can stop. Victor studies the menu. 'Why do you think they use the same symbol for historic sites, wildlife refuges, points of interest, Indian reservations and military installations?' I ask him. 'Do you think it's because they think military installations are culturally significant or because Indians are like eagles – first we kill them off and then we feel bad about it?'

Al brings us a complimentary basket of chips and a bowl of salsa. 'It must be pretty cold on that bike,' says Al. Al is Indian. The Wild West at last. Except for us, he's the only other person in the restaurant. He rushes off to get a pad and pencil.

'I think it's because they want us to think military installations are something to be proud of,' says Victor. He hits my hand. 'Hey, look at this! They have hot fries.'

'Get two.' I close the map. The nearest campsite is too far away to be a comfort. 'And nachos.'

Carol, the waitress, comes in as Al is running back to the kitchen for milk.

'You lunatics riding that bike in this weather?' she asks as she hangs her raincoat on a hook by the door.

'Not at the moment,' says Victor.

She looks over at Al, trying to deal with the nachos and the fries and point her to her apron at the same time. 'Look at him,' she says. 'Rushed off his feet.' She strolls back to the kitchen for the food and the apron and comes back to chat.

Carol comes originally from Pennsylvania. She ran away when she was seventeen with Duane, a man she met while she was working as a waitress in a diner. He had eyes the colour of one of those tropical lagoons they use in rum commercials. Duane ordered two breakfast specials and asked her if she'd ever been to Texas, he was so sure he'd seen her before. She laughed at him. The only time Carol had been out of Pennsylvania was when her family went to New Jersey for her grandmother's funeral. It looked just like Pennsylvania. Duane said he was a rodeo rider. It turned out what he meant was that he *wanted to be* a rodeo rider – what he was was AWOL from the

United States Army. Though Carol didn't find that out till later, after Duane went out for a six-pack and a bag of barbecue potato chips in Albuquerque and never came back. Barbecue were Carol's favourite. Duane was pretty good to her in a lot of ways.

Victor scoops up some salsa with a tortilla chip. 'So how'd you wind up here?' he asks.

Carol leans against the window ledge and shrugs. Diesel trucks as big as houses inch up the road behind her. From this distance, you can't see the naked-women, come-and-get-me mudguards or bumper stickers, and there's something about their lights that reminds me, momentarily, of Christmas, of a nice place to be.

'Oh you know what life's like,' she says. 'One thing kinda leads to another.'

Victor and I fight for the hot fries and nachos and pickled jalapeños while Carol tells us about living in New Mexico, Vegas and California, and how she eventually came to Texas. With Guy. Guy's workin' in California now – jobs aren't so easy to get that you can be fussy about where they are – but he's hopin' to be back by Christmas.

'It's hard without him,' says Carol. She nods towards the kitchen where Al, the owner, chef and part-time waiter of La Cantina, is putting a fresh filter in the coffee machine with an earnest expression on his face. 'I gotta work nights a lot 'cause a *him*,' she says, 'so it means my kid's alone a lot. But I make sure he calls me every hour so I know where he is and that he's okay.'

We finish off the salad and the second free basket of chips and salsa while Carol tells us what she thinks of Texas. Not that much. There's lotsa drugs around here, says Carol. Lotsa violence, lotsa trouble. A few people have money and everyone else has shit. And then there's all these niggers ridin' round in their Cadillacs like they own the world, thinkin' they're better than everyone else, showin' off.

'They're everywhere,' says Carol. It makes people mad.

'Really?' Victor looks at her over a forkful of salad. 'I haven't seen all that many.' He turns to me. 'Have you?'

Not the gentleman my travelling companion is, I take the last hot fry and bite it in half. I shake my head. 'No,' I answer. 'Surprisingly few.' I chew slowly. 'Given the vast numbers.'

'You two should watch yourselves in Texas,' says Carol. 'Lookin' the way you do.'

Al raps on the hatch. 'Carol!' he calls. 'Carol, don't you have something to do?'

Carol makes a face and waves an arm at the large and empty dining room with its chilli pepper Christmas lights, brightly coloured serapes and prints of men sleeping behind sombreros that decorate the walls. 'It's not like the place is packed,' she shouts back. 'You'll be lucky if anyone else comes in the rest of the day with this rain.' She rolls her eyes and makes a face that only we can see. 'Fuckin' Indians,' she says, lowering her voice. 'I hate workin' for Indians. Money, money, money, that's all he ever thinks about.' She makes another face. 'What does he know about runnin' a Mexican restaurant?' she asks us. 'He doesn't eat this shit. He eats curries.' She rolls her eyes again. 'I mean, can you believe it? His wife even wears one of those things, whattayacallit?'

Victor pushes his plate away. 'A sari.'

Carol snaps her fingers. 'That's it, a sari. I never can remember what you call them.' She straightens up and starts picking up dishes. 'You guys relax,' she says. 'I'll be right back with some fresh coffee.'

Maybe we're not going to see Dallas, the Alamo or Galveston, Fort Worth, the islands off the gulf, or the Budweiser plant that offers a tour and complimentary beers and snacks, but at least we are seeing Houston – if from afar and through a haze of exhaust fumes. I adjust my bandanna across my face and absently gaze at the traffic. 'Practise Random Acts of Beauty and Kindness', says the bumper sticker on the old white van beside us. 'Dream On . . .', says the one on the black Cherokee.

We begin dreaming. Everything's possible; everything's new. Young and high on hopes and hormones, we each set out to win the world. We have courage, we have strength; we know our lives will be different from the lives of others. Some special destiny will be ours. Our steps are sure as we stride across lush fields towards those distant mountains where all the promises lie. Not everyone makes it. Some drop behind, or fall off a cliff, or get lost and wind up in a ranch house with a long mortgage, but some go on. We go on, even though the road gets rough and what was once green grass turns soon to sand and the mountains, when we reach them, are steep grey rocks with few toe-holes, no shelter and poisonous snakes. We go on, because we're looking straight ahead. Straight ahead at the golden light that marks our prize. And when we finally lurch to the top, ready to claim our beautiful reward, what do we find? We find that what we thought was gold was just another sunset giving way to yet another night. We find ourselves exhausted, strength and

courage gone, dreaming sadly of moments in the past. We find ourselves up a great bloody mountain with no idea of how we even got
there – or what we might have missed on the way.

It's sunset now. The sky, still overcast but dry, is tinged with pink
and crimson, brushed with gold. Ahead of us, behind us and on
either side are lines of motionless cars, bumpers almost touching.
Beyond them is a smoggy sprawl of buildings, peaked like frosting,
shimmering in the sleepy sun. Sunset over Houston, and I'm thinking of dreaming.

People came here with dreams – with dreams and hope and little
else. This was their one opportunity for something more. Ten,
twenty, fifty years before, they wouldn't have had even this. Most of
them would have died where they were born – where and as –
trapped in a life they got by chance, with no possibility of change.
Here – proof of miracles – there were possibilities. The old rules
didn't matter; you could do what you could do.

People were here with dreams, but then the future happened too
fast. Fragile piece by fragile piece, they watched their dreams ground
to dust by the dreams of others, gone not just from today but from
memory, too. Until they became just another lost tribe on the ragged
earth, abandoned by God, now dreaming only of redemption.

Around 1870, a prophet appeared to the Paiute in Nevada. His
son, Wovoka, would later say that his father wasn't a preacher but a
'dreamer' with supernatural gifts. Wovoka, however, was a preacher.
Wovoka went up to heaven and saw God and all the Indian dead.
God gave him a message to bring to his people. God gave him a
dance. By 1890 the Ghost Dance religion had spread across the West,
practised by the Paiute, Shoshoni, Cheyenne, Arapaho, Kiowa,
Caddo, Wichita, Walapai, Ute and unyielding Sioux.

The Ghost Dance religion promised that the time of salvation
was near. The earth would be replenished and renewed, and all
Indians, living and dead, would be reunited to live in happiness forever, free of any misery – and of any white men as well.

It didn't work.

The traffic slips forward a few inches and we slip with it.
Someone's listening to the classical station, someone else to old rock,
the man on our left is singing along to the Pogues. The woman in
the van lights a cigarette, while the girl in the yellow convertible
starts putting on her make-up, lifting herself in the driver's seat so
she can see herself in the rear-view mirror. A small plastic ghost
sways slightly from the rear-view mirror of the Cherokee.

Victor looks over his shoulder, pulling down his mask. 'Jesus,' he says. 'Fancy coming all this way to be stuck in traffic.'

Victor thinks I'm being unreasonable. 'What's wrong?' he demands. 'Why don't you like it?'

I stand on the other side of Montoya in the near-dead light, leaning against the chain-link fence that encircles the Alley Oop Trailer Park, my hands tucked into my armpits for warmth. I know my feet are there because I can see my dirty Docs at the end of my jeans, but I can't actually feel them. The next campgrounds shown on the state map are three hours away. Three *more* hours away. There are six gravel campsites, each with its own small tree and water tap, on either side of the faded pink building with the faded green dinosaur on its roof and the broken swings and slide that divide the park in half. All of the campsites are empty and covered with dark droppings. Now I know what deer shit looks like. It's the Day of the Dead, and instead of spending it in Mexico, as we'd once thought we might be, we're going to spend it in the trailer park at the end of the universe.

'Why don't I like it?' I look over at him, just to make sure that he isn't joking. You can't always tell with Englishmen. 'You mean besides the fact that it's in the town park?'

'It's next to the town park, not in it,' he corrects me.

Which, to be honest, is strictly true. The town park is to our left across the narrow road lined with Bud bottles and young trees. Each tree is marked by a small stone plaque. In Memory of Wire Line Jack Larsh 1878–1954, Mack and Jane McKee . . . In Memory of George Bivins 1900–1971, By the Mildred Parker Garden Club . . . Clyde Everett Teal Jr 1934–1952, Mr and Mrs Clyde Teal . . . In Memory of John W. Brewer 1894–1950, Monica and Daughters . . . In Memory of Mrs Doris Sims 1919–1971, By the Mildred Parker Garden Club . . . In Memory of Mrs Rose Sims 1870–1961, By the Mildred Parker Garden Club . . . In Memory of U. T. Noelke 1874–1940, Mr and Mrs Leo Richardson . . . In Memory of Sammy Shaw 1948–1965, The Junior Class of 1964–65 . . . Chris Carrusca 1972–1989, Killed by a drunken driver, Mom and Dad . . . If we're in anything, we're in the parking lot of the factory to the right – and not that far from the highway behind it.

'There isn't any washroom.'

'Sure there is,' says Victor. He jerks a finger towards the park. 'There's one right there.'

This, too, is true. It's a small, windowless stone building with a broken green door and used condoms in the bushes.

'There isn't any water, or lights, or a lock.' I want a hot shower. I want a place where no one is likely to jump us while we sleep. I want a campgrounds with a candy machine.

'So?' Victor thinks I'm getting soft. He thinks he should have listened to my sister and taken a companion who wasn't going to fall apart every time things weren't perfect. 'That's no problem. I'll go with you.'

'And while we're there, bored, drug-crazed teenagers who have watched too many violent videos will steal our things and trash the bike.'

'That could happen anywhere,' says Victor, but he's climbing back on Montoya. He turns on the ignition.

'Now what are you doing?' Not wanting to stay isn't the same as wanting to go. All I want is for things to be different.

'I'm starting the engine, what does it look like I'm doing?'

'Why?'

'Why?' He gives me the look usually reserved for difficult receptionists. Sleep deprivation, exposure, and lack of protein aren't bringing out the best in either of us. 'Because we're going on.'

'But I thought we were staying here.'

If he had a packet in his hands he'd probably have thrown it at me. 'You said you didn't like it here.'

'I don't,' I say. 'But I can live with it.' I hope.

'Whatever you say.' He turns off the engine. 'You're the one who gets raped.'

It's a quiet night in our little campsite by the side of the motorway. A few birds bleat in the trees of the park. The traffic swishes past just behind the factory. Something hums. We set up in silence. We cook in silence. We eat in silence. We walk across memorial lane by torchlight in silence. Victor stands outside, silent, while I grope around in the dark, and then we cross back, our footsteps loud and my teeth chattering. He doesn't say, as he usually would, 'Don't tell me you're cold?' Each of us is wondering what we're doing here, in the shadow of a plaster dinosaur whose smile has been chipped away and eyes bleached white. Is this freedom and adventure? Is this a pit stop on the trail of dreams? We pin up the tent flap in silence. We get into our sleeping bags in silence. In silence, Victor falls asleep.

It's the night of the Day of the Dead. In Mexico there would be fiestas, laughter and music, chocolates shaped into skulls. We'd be drinking tequila and waiting for the sunrise. Here in Texas there is only that soft electronic whisper and the whoosh of wheels going somewhere fast. The living aren't celebrating on the streets, but locked inside their houses, expecting rain or watching cable TV.

But the dead do walk here, too.

Light footsteps fall outside the tent. I lie awake and listen to them crossing the gravel and the grass. I can see a thin, bony man with a stubbled face and broken teeth, limping slightly as he walks around the rusted dinosaur slide. He looks a little like John Carley without his dentures. It's Wire Line Larsh, looking for his old shack and that dog he had with the one chewed ear and a fondness for jerky. There's a pasty young man in a cheap suit, his tie too tight, going back and forth beneath the row of trees. George Bivins, nervously pacing, getting up his courage to propose to the girl who worked in the dry-goods store, not knowing, in this moment, that she will accept only because she can see nothing else when she stares across the plains. A fair, stocky boy in dirty jeans and a plaid shirt trots beside his father, wanting to know when he'll be old enough to have a gun. Clyde Jr, in a hurry to grow up. A corpulent man wearing a white Stetson and Navajo rings, marches purposefully across the mown lawn, watched by a woman who doesn't wave goodbye. John Brewers is heading for the pick-up, glancing at his watch – he doesn't want to be late. Two smiling, overweight women, who might be twenty or forty, in floral housedresses and dime-store jewellery, hurry across the lot with dozens of flowers in their arms. Doris Sims and Rose Sims, going to their first exhibit at the Mildred Parker Garden Club autumn show. A dark, spotty young man in a white sports coat with a pink carnation in the buttonhole is turning round and round in front of the broken door of the toilet. Sammy Shaw is getting ready for the prom. A small child suddenly jumps out from the bushes. It's Chris Carrusca chasing fireflies across the road.

There are other footsteps, softer, more cautious – more faint. A woman running with an infant in her arms. An old man gathering wood for his fire. Young boys tumbling between the broken swings. Dancers with their eyes on the stars.

They're all gone now – they and their dreams – gone but still going. Dreams go on without the dreamer. And dreamers must sometimes go on without the dream.

Victor rolls over. 'Why are you still awake?'

'Ghosts,' I tell him. 'They're all over the place.'

'Deer,' mumbles Victor, and falls back to sleep.

10

TAKE IT EASY

'I knew we should never have stopped for that picture,' Victor is muttering, his head bent towards the ground as he pushes Montoya up the narrow, broken road towards the huddle of featureless buildings far in the distance. 'If we hadn't stopped for that picture this would never have happened.'

It had been our last chance to get the photo he wanted of a Texas state highway sign, shot full of bullet holes, and so we'd taken it.

I walk beside him, carrying the helmets. 'Sure it would've.' I am certain of this much at least. 'It just wouldn't have happened then.'

This isn't the first time Montoya has thrown a sudden wobbly. She has been pushed across some of the best parking lots and major intersections in the country, down some of its worst dirt trails, and up one or two of its less travelled hills. Usually she starts after one or two tries, but today she's being difficult.

'We didn't even get the bloody picture.' The feathers on Montoya's windscreen quiver as Victor shoves her through a rut with no sign of his usual affection, but we all know whose fault it is that we didn't even get the bloody picture.

'I said I was sorry,' I say again. 'He surprised me.' Jumping out of nowhere with a knife in his hand and two large dogs running behind him.

'You'd think it was his sign the way he carried on,' says Victor.

Rule of the Road number 12: It's all just on loan. In this life, no matter how many things we may accumulate and hold, and no matter how much you wanted them or how much they cost, none of us owns anything. The most we can hope for is a short-term rental. The car, the house, the clothes, the collection of teapots, the $2,000-dollar coffee table, the closet full of shoes – none of it is really yours. When you're dead the things you called yours will go to someone else, and the things that no one wants will be sold for cash or packed in plastic bags and given to some charity. We all know that, but we have a hard time really coming to grips with what it means.

'It was his fence.'

Victor gives me a look. 'So is that this afternoon's song?' he asks, having finally forgiven me enough for dropping the camera to pick up our regular game. '"Don't Fence Me In"?'

D. H. Lawrence lived in New Mexico. Georgia O'Keefe lived in New Mexico. It was in New Mexico that Oppenheimer sat around playing cards and drinking beer and designing the atomic bomb. The Anastasi, the Navajo, the Hopi, the Zuni and the Apache have all lived in New Mexico, too, of course, but then they had less of a choice. In the distance, the black rocks and red hills press against the sky, but it isn't literature, art, annihilation or even ancient cultures that they bring to mind. It's the absence of man.

'No,' I say without thinking. 'It's "The Shifting, Whispering Sands".'

He glances at the landscape. The sands aren't exactly shifting and whispering, but the land surrounding us is flat and ruddy and unstopping, covered with dark brush and cacti and cut by wire fences, some of which bend to the ground. There are no houses or stores or gas stations to be seen, and there haven't been for over ten miles. Thank God we're not still in Texas, or we might be worried. He gives me a look. It's wary. 'What's this song about?'

'It's about an old miner who gets lost on the desert and dies and his bones are covered by the shifting, whispering sands and there's nothing left to say he ever lived.' It was my favourite record when I was maybe nine or ten. My mother broke it into several pieces one night – quite suddenly, as I remember – because, she later explained, it was driving her crazy.

'I knew I shouldn't've asked.'

We're close enough now to see the town clearly. Two boarded-up stores, one boarded-up gas station and a house half fallen down. A beer can blows across the lot of the gas station.

'Well, here's a new thing to experience,' I say. 'A ghost town.'

'You and your shifting, whispering sands,' says Victor.

*

Creatures of habit. Every morning the alarm rings at the same time and we turn it off in the same way. We get ready for the day in a sequence close to ritual, always putting on our socks before we brush our teeth, always having orange juice and coffee, always picking up a paper before we get on the train. We go to work and do the same things we did the day before. We come home from work. We eat. We watch TV. We go to bed. In the morning the alarm rings and we turn it off with our left hand and our eyes still shut. We need order. Even free-spirit wanderers with bad maps have their routines. Even bats.

'Christ,' I said. 'I didn't realise bats were so organised.'

Not so fresh from a night under the clouds – one of us muttering about oil leaks in his sleep and the other checking every hour or so to make sure her Swiss army knife was still under the pillow made from her jeans in case of visits by snakes or coyotes or dead prospectors – Victor and I stood outside the White City gift store this morning, staring at the announcement of bat flight times.

'Everything's organised,' said Victor. 'But we're the only ones who make money out of it.'

I have to admit that I'd had a different image of the bats of Carlsbad in my mind. It was the one thing I'd known I wanted to see, the bats leaving their caverns at sunset. I think I'd imagined that you rode into the hills, scrabbled among the rocks till you found a good spot, and waited for the blue to bleed to purple to pink and the bats to emerge, close together, drawing a dark pattern in the blankness of the sky. I'd imagined that in that moment you would hear nothing but the beating of their wings. I hadn't imagined that they charged admission. Or that what you would actually hear would be the amusing anecdotes on bat behaviour that spice the guide's set speech. That your thoughts would be distracted by the tourists fussily setting up their cameras and videos while they discussed what to do with the rest of the evening and their bored children sulked in the car. From that viewpoint, it was probably just as well that the bats were gone, headed south and out of the cold.

Victor sighed. 'Now all we have to do is figure out where we're going.'

We sat outside the hotel, which, with the single quaint and rustic old-West street of shops and the gas station, makes up White City, drinking coffee from the restaurant and eating raw English muffins with our last two tubs of strawberry jam while we worked out where to go next.

Although there are already reports of snow and ice further north, everyone we've talked to has assured us that we'll be all right if we go straight into Arizona. No problem. The guy in the diner who used to have a Harley said so. The guy in the gas station who wants to go to Bolivia said so. The cowboy with the pet pygmy pig said so. So did the postmistress who once visited Germany and the barmaid who'd had a stroke. Despite all this advice, in the end we decided to follow the example of the bats and stay south. We'll take 60 into Arizona and won't go up to Albuquerque or Santa Fe after all. Missing them isn't as disappointing as the truth about the bats. Albuquerque, despite a great blues bar and a good Mexican diner, is just another city and Santa Fe is just another gruesomely picturesque set decoration in the middle of miles of nuclear waste. Better to save our time for things worth seeing, the Petrified Forest or the meteor crater outside Winslow.

'There,' Victor had said, pointing to a blue and green spot on the map with a name that spins stories. 'That's where we'll go. Arrive before dark.'

According to the map, the place we seek is on Route 409, just out of Dexter. The sky is still blue and the fields of chilli peppers are still catching pools of light when we finally find Dexter. We take a left on 409 and drive on past farms and wooden houses, the flatness of the land broken here and there by small huddles of trees. We go on. The houses become more frequent, the trees closer to the road. There's a sign for a new shopping centre straight up ahead. We stop. We consult the map.

'We've missed it,' says Victor. 'How could we miss it?'

A tricky question. I have no idea how we could have missed it. It's like taking 40 into Albuquerque and coming out the other side still wondering when you're going to arrive. It's right there, well behind us now on Route 409, as clearly marked on the map as Fort Bliss or the Horn of Death.

'Why don't we ask back in Dexter?' I suggest. 'At that gas station on the crossroads?'

Victor considers this briefly. 'Because they won't know.' Travelling is making him a little pessimistic.

We go back. We climb off the bike and go inside to join the queue of men in flannels, denims and cowboy hats buying six-packs of beer and loaves of bread on their way back home. 'Where?' asks the girl behind the counter.

'Bottomless Lake,' I repeat.

'Bottomless Lake State Park,' says Victor.

She gives him her full attention. '*Where?*'

'Bottomless Lake State Park,' explains the man next to Victor. He gives him a smile. 'You ain't from around here, are you?'

'Never heard of it,' says the cashier.

The man next to me puts a can of stew and a box of doughnuts on the counter. 'Sure you have,' he tells her. He turns to Victor. 'You just take that road out there and it'll lead you right to it.' He pays for his things. '190,' he says. 'You just follow it straight through.'

We take 190. There are signs for tractor repairs and fertiliser and fresh eggs, but nothing that suggests either a lake or a park. We follow it straight through.

The few houses that have been keeping up with us give up and we are all alone on the desert, mountains in the distance, the sun red and ducking behind purple clouds.

Victor guns the engine. 'Here we go again,' he says. 'Another wild-bat chase.'

'Hell,' says Franz, pointing to the vegetables and bag of pasta on the picnic table. 'Are you telling me that's all you're having for supper?'

Victor stops blowing soot from the stove. 'We're vegetarians.'

Franz, like others before him, finds this amusing. 'Shit,' he says. 'I've been all around the world on everything from a sailboat to a Harley, but I'm sure as hell glad I never travelled with you two. I'd'a starved.'

Sheba, Franz's fat old dog, sniffs at the pepper I'm chopping. She'd'a starved, too.

'And that's the only light you got, right?' he asks, pointing to the torch propped on top of a beer can we found in the rubbish.

'It's enough,' says Victor. 'There's not much room on the bike.'

Franz points at me. 'You just hold everything,' he orders. 'I'll be right back before you cut off your fingers.'

Franz is a large, bearded man close to sixty with long hair and wire-rimmed glasses. He lives with his second wife, who is taking her accountancy exams tonight, and Sheba in the small trailer with the dirt bikes parked under the awning, one campsite over.

When he comes back he's carrying an old Coleman lantern, shining white. He sets it on the table and sits back down. While I fix the vegetables and Victor fusses with the stove, and Sheba whimpers for something to eat, Franz talks.

He tells us about first coming to America when he was still a boy.

He tells us how he left home at seventeen, and didn't see his mother for twenty years, until she saw his picture in a newspaper receiving an award for something he'd invented. He rode with the Angels, cut lumber in Canada, earned and lost two fortunes in less than five years. His marriage broke up because he spent more time designing and testing sailing boats than at home. He never sees his kids. They're not like him. they want straight lives, like their mother. After the divorce he took his hand-made catamaran around southeast Asia with a ninety-six-pound girl as crew.

We're happy enough to cook and listen.

'You want to hear a story?' asks Franz.

It's a night for stories. The air is sharp and frosty, the sky is high and star-cut, the moon's a smile. The desert spreads around us, phantasmic and remote, dark hills and figures of trees. The lake is only yards away, lying as still as polished stone. This is a place where things end. Doomed hopes, doomed loves, doomed lives. End with no interference, no excuses, no doubt. Peace at last.

'What's it about?' asks Victor. He glances towards the lake. 'About something that happened here?'

Franz shakes his head. 'No,' he says. 'This story started in Germany, before the war.'

'My mother's name was Hannah,' Franz begins. 'She was an orphan and was adopted by strict Lutheran farmers whose own daughter had died from smallpox. They thought the outside world was full of devils and infidels.' The lantern, its flame jumping in the wind, is reflected in his glasses. 'They wouldn't let her go to school, never mind a dance or a party. She had to sneak away at night to learn to read and write.' He rubs Sheba's head, which is resting on the tabletop. 'My father was a lawyer who came from a wealthy family in Düsseldorf. He was sophisticated, political and free-thinking.' Sheba looks up as I start chopping a carrot. 'He thought man was the devil.'

Victor stops fussing with the stove and gives Franz a smile. 'You mean he isn't?'

Franz smiles back but is not about to be sidetracked into a different conversation. 'And then one day my father's car broke down outside the farm and my mother brought him water.' He shrugs. 'She was very charismatic.' He smiles again. 'And very beautiful.'

Hannah ran away with the stranger in the silver sports car. They were married and lived in the family penthouse in Düsseldorf, happy among the antique furniture and china vases full of flowers. Franz's mother had first a daughter and then a son, while Franz's father helped the first refugees to get away. When the war came he refused the commission offered him by the Nazis. They took him anyway. Franz's father spent the war in a prison camp; his mother, his sister and he spent most of it in the beautiful old apartment, once the scene of the best dinners and parties in the city, able to tell, in the end, whose planes were flying overhead by the sounds of the engines.

'And then the Gestapo came,' says Franz. 'Germany was losing now. There was no money, no food, no gas, no hope. Düsseldorf was being levelled. So my mother decided it was time to get out.'

The man downstairs was a friend of Franz's father who had promised to look after the family. When the Gestapo came he was ready. He had a precious can of gasoline hidden under his bed. He stole an abandoned car from the street.

'That's how we got on the train,' says Franz. 'We were the last ones on.'

It wasn't the train to hell or from it, it was hell itself. Hundreds of starving, homeless refugees, with little left to lose, crammed into a few filthy cars going nowhere. There was nowhere to go. The cities were in ruins, the countryside devastated. They were allowed to stop, to barter their last possessions for meagre supplies, but nowhere they stopped were they allowed to get out of the train. There wasn't enough left to share with strangers. No room for more desperate people. They kept on going, from one month to the next, battling farmers for cabbage and potatoes, dodging the bombs and the military police.

I finish with the vegetables, and Victor puts the pot on the stove.

'My mother had a teenage girl and a young boy to look after,' Franz says, 'and still she cared for the ill and the wounded.' I can see Victor reflected in his glasses now. 'I used to wonder why she never cried.'

And then one day the train picked up a Russian soldier, half dead from starvation and exhaustion.

'He'd walked all the way from the Russian lines.' Franz rests a hand on Sheba's head. 'Christ knows how he made it without being shot.'

The soldier's name was André. André was a philosopher, a poet, a scientist and a professor of linguistics. He'd been arrested in Moscow for his anti-party views and aristocratic past. They released him from the prison camp to fight the Germans.

'My mother nursed him. She saved his life.'

Hannah shared her family's food with André, stayed up with him when he was delirious, dressed him in her own clothes. André was an old woman hunched in the corner when the soldiers came on board. Hannah talked to them herself, showing them some dead woman's papers, saying, 'This is my aunt. She's very, very ill.'

Franz shakes his head, more wistful than sad. 'And then they fell in love.'

It was passionate and mutual – and never to be consummated. Not even later, after the war, when the four of them lived in a room in a cellar. André made a crystal set to remind them there was a world outside. At night they would all sit around the table, Hannah and the girl sewing, André teaching Franz physics and electronics and entertaining them with stories from a better time and place.

'And then we got the letter that my father was being sent home.'

Blind and crippled, home to die.

'André disappeared,' says Franz.

At last he saw his mother cry.

'After my father died, she married Martin and we came here.' His voice takes on an edge. 'All they did after that was work. They had to have everything they saw in the ads. The two of them never stopped talking about the war.'

'Jesus,' says Victor, suddenly aware that the glop is boiling too hard. 'What a story.'

'What about André?' I want to know. 'You mean you never saw him again?

'I talked to him once,' says Franz. 'I heard he was teaching at Columbia and I called him on my way back to California from my mother's funeral.'

'What did he say?'

Franz looks past us. 'He said, "Hi."'

The penultimate thing that Franz said to Victor was, 'I'd recommend stopping in the first mall you come to and buyin' yourself one of those little radios the truckers use that receives the weather and road station. Only costs fifty bucks or so. It could save you a heap of time.'

Victor said, 'Thanks, we'll think about it.'

Franz studied him silently for a second, and then made his final statement. 'Just don't go any higher than this, all right? And go straight into Arizona. You'll be fine.'

We aren't going higher. We're going straight into Arizona as fast as we can. We are fine in the sense that we're still moving.

'Jesus,' says Victor, as we peel ourselves off the bike, shaking our feet and flexing our fingers to see if they still function. 'Can you believe it? Snow.'

I can believe it. What I can't believe is that there isn't more snow and ice, that the bike hasn't broken down on top of one of these pine-covered mountains, that we haven't skidded over a cliff or into a wall of stone. What I can't believe is that all these men wander aimlessly across the country on their pilgrimages for truth and knowledge, and instead of being consumed with the tedium, repetition and futility of it all – and losing it in the diner because the hash browns are frozen and cold and there isn't any Tabasco sauce – they think about God and man and life all the time, work out convoluted philosophical systems and have Buddhist revelations.

My reply is simple. 'I'm going to the loo,' I say, and march off towards the small wooden building behind the gas pumps.

I'm not speaking to Victor. Unofficially. I know he can't really be held responsible for the weather, but I'm holding him responsible anyway. I'm holding him responsible for everything. Was it my idea to come on this bloody trip? No it was not my idea. It was his.

I march through the door. Seventy years ago, there would have been a circle of grizzled men gathered around the pot belly stove in the corner, a barrel of cheese and a barrel of pickles in front of the counter, flour, salt, sugar, tins of meat and jars of home-made jams on the shelves that line the back of the store, but today there is a dog sleeping by the stove and a woman watching a soap opera on a personal TV behind the counter, and the usual mix of snack foods, auto supplies and cheap videos on display.

She looks up at the ring of the old bell over the door. 'Must be cold on that bike,' she says. Before I can exhibit my bad mood she adds, 'Bathroom's back there on the left.'

The bathroom, which has no bath, is yellow. Around the sink is a home-made cotton skirt of daisy print material that matches the curtain at the window and the cover on the toilet bowl brush and the box of tissues. There's a bar of pink soap in a plastic dish that looks like a Victorian tub and a jar of dead petals on the sink, two yellow towels hanging from a rack on the wall beneath a picture of a tropical sunset printed over with the Lord's Prayer, the Protestant version.

I stare at myself in the mirror. My face is red, my nose is redder. There's a slightly wild look in my eyes. Why am I here?

'Why are any of us here?'

I turn around, half-expecting to see Victor.

A large, rough man in a pea jacket and blue knit hat is sitting on the closed toilet seat, Indian-style. It's Jack Kerouac. I'd recognise him anywhere. He's drunk.

'You know,' he goes on, 'this reminds me of my mother's bathroom.'

'Really?' You can travel the world and never leave home. 'Is that why *you're* here?'

'Ignorance is a virtue,' says Jack. He belches. 'You have to take life the way a child takes it.'

In this country, children take life by the label. Adidas trainers, Simpson T-shirts, Batman cereal bowls, notebooks covered with photographs of this week's most popular group.

Trying to get the last drop from the bottle, he loses his balance and sways into the wall. 'That's what it's all about.' He straightens up, wipes his arm across his mouth. 'Innocence and bare beauty.'

'No it's not,' I snap. It's about getting from one day to the next. It's about having a reason for getting from one day to the next. It's about always looking straight ahead. 'It's about doom.'

The empty half-bottle of whisky falls to the floor. 'My mother was a wonderful woman,' says Jack. 'Nobody ever really appreciated her, but she was a wonderful woman.' He starts to cry. 'I should've listened to her more.'

Victor is standing with his back to the pot belly stove and his hands flat behind him. He looks tired and cold and about ready to pick a fight with the first motorist who cuts him off, but he's trying not to show it. Instead he's smiling and nodding at a blonde woman with two small boys. The boys are American, but she comes from Leeds. She's been here ten years. 'Ten years,' she says. 'I never thought I'd make it through the first one. I cried all the time.' She misses fish and chips. She misses the weather. She misses *Coronation Street*. But she's gotten used to it. It's better here for the kids. The kids stare silently at Victor, visitor from their mother's home planet. She puts a hand on the tallest one's head. 'More opportunities.' And now they've almost finished building the house. She invites us back for hot dogs with her and the kids. Dan works late on Thursdays. Even with the snow. 'It's not too warm because the windows aren't in yet,' she says, 'but it's got to be better than being on that bike.'

Victor looks at me. Maybe yes and maybe no.

*

The night is as cold as the tits of several witches and probably an ice queen or two, but the stars and moon overhead belong to Arizona. And have done for the past two hours.

We can't find the campgrounds. We have stopped and asked. We have stopped and looked at the map. We have stopped for a piss at the side of the road and discussed the possibility of changing our itinerary and simply driving on until we hit Mexico. There's a chance that we drove through it, in at one end and out the other without actually noticing, of course – we have done it before – but there's also a chance that it's closed for the winter.

We're coming down a hill we have already come down twice. But this time Victor cuts the engine, and instead of being desperate and lost on a mountain road we are freewheeling on a strip of moonlight. An owl slips out of the trees, wind-gliding over the road.

Think about how you know what you know. About the world. About God. About yourself. How you know what will make you happy. How you know what to expect, what to believe in, what to want.

We coast to a stop as the moon-strip levels.

Victor leans back his head and looks up at the night. I look up, too.

And you could never leave home and travel ten worlds.

'This is better, isn't it?' asks Victor.

It's warm and sunny and we're sitting at the side of the road, eating the lunch we bought at the gourmet deli of the healthfood store in Sedona, the last sort of place we expected to find hidden in the mountains, not so much a town as an artistic community full of Indian crafts and wealthy white people. Ecologically sound cardboard containers of tabouleh, houmous, pasta salad and marinated vegetables sit among the rocks and wild flowers. Montoya's new Dream Catcher hangs from her handlebar. The Indians hung dream catchers over the beds of their children to protect them from the night. The bad dreams, not knowing the way, would get caught in the web to be burned off by the morning sun. The dream catcher stirred slightly in the breeze, good dreams passing surely through its centre. Our helmets are strapped under the cargo net, where there going to stay till we steam into California – Arizona has no helmet law.

A person in a bad mood – myself, for instance – might give him a look and ask, 'Better than what?' Better than being pulled for speeding by the cops in the Petrified Forest? Better than riding for three hours trying to find the bloody meteor crater, and then leaving in disgust because they wanted more to see it than even the bats were charging? Better than trying every restaurant in Flagstaff, searching for one that would let you have a cigarette with your morning coffee? Better than going up to the Grand Canyon and camping in snow?

I look at the mountains around us, one of which we've just come down – thick green pines, red rocks like totems, a steep, narrow road twisting with the river. You couldn't ride through this and be in a bad mood. It'd be like buzzing Jupiter and complaining about what you'd had for breakfast.

'Yeah,' I say. 'It's better.' I grab the last piece of cheese. 'It's better than better.'

He snatches the last olive. 'Is that better than better as in best?' he wants to know.

But before I can answer a dented, rusted old Ford full of kids tears around the curve, dust flapping around it like wings. One of the kids leans out of the window. 'Bitchin'!' he screams. 'Really bitchin'!'

Victor frowns. 'What did he say? Did he call you a bitch?'

'No, he said it was better than better as in best.'

All we did was turn a corner. One second we were climbing up the rock face, straight towards the summit, and the next we're in the middle of a town of ramshackle houses growing up against the mountain like moss. We turn a second corner and come on to Main Street. There's a bar at the intersection, all its doors wide open, red chilli pepper Christmas tree lights strung across the room, a rock band cooking in the middle of the floor. The guy selling hot dogs from the snack wagon dances along. 'Get a picture!' screams Victor. 'Get a picture!' I can't get a picture. I'm too busy being in the moment: the turn-of-the-century Main Street, the brightly painted houses staggering up the mountainside, a woman and a child standing in the middle of the road while music pours out of the bar and the traffic light seems to swing in time. I'm still looking back at Jerome as we reach the top and come down the other side doing 80, flying into the valley formed by black mountains. Something to the left catches my eye. It's a glider, coming in for a landing, so close that it's almost beside us, keeping level with the bike as the hill falls behind us.

Victor glances over his shoulder. 'Did you get a picture?' he screams. 'Did you get a picture?'

It's almost touching that he even bothers to ask.

*

The sun bleeds over the desert. All along the roadside are stores and stalls selling rocks and the equipment you would presumably need if you wanted to dig up some rocks of your own. Behind them, as far as you can see, are fields of well-equipped RVs, shining in the dying light.

Victor takes the right directed by the kid at the last campsite we were turned away from. 'Tent?' he kept repeating. 'You wanna camp with a *tent*?' On one side the land is flat and empty except for the usual assortment of beer cans; on the other it is covered with rows of RVs. Sunnyside Trailer Park. Peaceful Valley Trailer Park. Rock On RV Grounds, season rates.

Victor slows the bike. 'Where are we?' he shouts.

Assuming that the question is a geographic one, the answer is obvious. We're in the rock and RV capital of Arizona. Assuming that it isn't, we're likely to be in the Twilight Zone.

'I'm afraid to ask,' I shout back.

Victor points to a hand-painted sign that says 'Big Moon Trailer Park'. 'Let's check that one out,' he says, as though we don't already know what we'll find.

Almost all of the RVs are state-of-the art; clean and undented, windows gleaming, awnings stretching out from their roofs, patio lights strung under them, barbecues and garden chairs and tables ready for an evening of chicken and bridge. Some of them have the owner's names carved on a piece of wood that hangs on the door; other have small gardens out front, plastic picket fences, plaster garden gnomes. You could go anywhere in one of these – comfortable, self-sufficient, as secure as you can be in anything with windows and a door. You could roam through the mountains, wander across the desert, catch the most perfect sunrise in the last million years. But these vehicles are going nowhere. Tract housing on wheels.

We are watched as we crawl through the camp, white and grey heads appearing among the café curtains. We're used to being watched, but usually it is by people sitting on their porches or behind their front windows, staring at the road as though it's a film, now and then wondering what would happen if they froze the frame and climbed into the scene. The people here aren't watching the road. They're settled, fixed; already arrived at where they want to be.

'Let's try the next one,' says Victor. 'There's no place for us here.'

You never know what you've forgotten.

There's something in the way the shadows fall across the road, something about the six-o'clock sounds of plates being laid out and glasses being filled and television voices slipping into the evening that reminds me of a summer in the Poconos. I'm not sure which one. My mother and my aunt are inside, getting supper ready while they talk about what things have changed here since the summer before and whether next year they should rent the same cabin or try for one near the stream. 'Better not,' says my aunt. 'Water carries germs.'

'Isn't this better than going to someplace like Europe?' says my mother. 'This is what I call a real vacation.'

You never know what moment you missed.

The Desert Dog Trailer Park is bordered not by hedges or collapsing fences as the other parks are, but by plaster dogs, most of them smiling and all of them unrealistically painted. Victor turns in at the entrance. 'Here we go again.'

Two small, long-haired brown dogs with large yellow bows around their necks come running out from behind the office, barking hysterically. Victor cuts the engine. Three more beribboned dogs bang through the screen door, bumping into each other in their rush to get to the courtyard.

'Jesus,' says Victor as all five of them circle us, jumping off the ground in excitement. 'Are we at war again or something?'

A sandy-haired man in his fifties, dressed in old green work pants and a flannel shirt, comes on to the porch, a cup in his hands. 'Cut it out!' he screams at the dogs. 'Stop making such a racket.' He smiles at me and Victor. 'You'll have to excuse them,' he says. 'It's their birthday. That's why they're wearing the ribbons.' He takes a sip from his cup. 'They're celebrating.'

It's like camping in someone's backyard. Or several people's backyard. We're out in the lot that has yet to be provided with any amenities, the tent pitched behind the only bush, the only light coming from the windows of the RVs around us. There's no toilet, no fireplace, no water. We can't find the stove-cleaner in the dark, so we take turns sneaking into the bush to take a piss and then crawl into our sleeping bags without any supper.

'At least he's not charging us,' says Victor as he pins up the flap.

On the other side of the small ravine, the birthday dogs are barking at someone passing on the road. At least we're safe.

'California tomorrow,' says Victor. 'Then two or three days to get what we need and we're off.'

We made it. No shootings, no arrests, no rapes. No more trouble than we would have had if we'd stayed at home – maybe less. We fall asleep talking about mosquito nets and malaria tablets, maybe building our own raft to go into the jungle, finding witches in the mountains of Peru.

I wake in the night, not knowing where I am. Something howls in the distance, bringing the night so full of stars into the tent.

'What's that?' I whisper.

'Coyotes,' says Victor, still sound asleep.

LAND OF DREAMS

11

ACROSS THE BORDERLINE

It divides, controls and separates, yet it is invisible. It imprisons, yet it is arbitrary. It causes wars that last for centuries, contributes generously to homelessness, famine and wholesale oppression, and yet it doesn't, in fact, exist. Described to a dog, a dolphin or a visitor from Alpha Centuri, said dog, dolphin or unwary tourist would be hard put to know what the hell you were talking about. Unseen, despotic, powerful enough to destroy millions of lives without question, but it isn't really there? Still thinking about it, the dog falls asleep, the dolphin drifts away, the bloke from Alpha Centuri gets back into his ship. What can it be?

A border. Cross it and enter the land of your hopes and dreams and promised glories. Cross it and reach the land of your nightmares and deepest despairs. One step is all it takes.

The small town is quiet in the hot and languid afternoon. Sunlight spills across the tin roofs and whitewashed buildings; spatters patterns over the late-fifties Buicks and Chevrolets parked in the dirt. A dog barks, a rooster crows, someone coughs in the dust of a passing truck, twelve people packed in the back with a dog, a pig and a cask of honey.

There's a chicken sitting on the roof of the wooden shack with the peeling paint and broken shutters and the sign that suggests that this, indeed, is the Office of Passport Control. Two barefoot children in someone else's old clothes sit on the steps, throwing stones at a skinny dog with scabs along its back.

Inside the shack, the once-white walls are cracked and dirty, decorated with a calendar and a gold crucifix. The calendar is for the year before. The room isn't crowded. There are no long queues of anxious immigrants, fingers crossed, waiting for that fateful stamp. This is a country more people want to get out of than into.

Three men and a woman are gathered around the desk in the centre of the room, the contents of a top box, a tank bag and two saddlebags spread out between them. On the floor are unrolled sleeping bags and a tent to which leaves and twigs still cling.

Two of the men are dark-skinned and black-haired, dressed in fatigues and combat boots. The older one, the one leaning back in his chair, is smiling and shaking his head. He holds out his hands in an expression of helplessness. '*Qué puedo hacer?*' he asks. He would help if he could. '*Qué puedo hacer?*' But he can't.

The second soldier isn't smiling. He picks up the two passports that are lying on a pile of dirty boxer shorts and begins to flip through them slowly – as though he can read English; as though he hasn't flipped through them before. He starts talking about insurance and laws and special stamps. He looks at the third man, the fair-skinned one in the jeans and leather jacket, his eyes as blank as a puddle. You have to understand, he says. You're not in your country now. Things are different down here. He wouldn't help if he were God.

'*Entiende?*' he asks, turning to the woman. '*Hay problemas.*'

He doesn't have to itemise just what problemas there are. I do understand. Problemas that might mean they have to keep our bike. Problemas that might mean they have to keep our passports. Problemas that might mean they have to keep us.

'Jesus,' whispers Victor. 'Welcome to hungry Mexico.'

That, as an account of our arrival, wouldn't have surprised me. It makes sense. It's what I expected. A memorable entry, an event that would have become incredibly funny by the time we were back in London, safe and sound and sitting in the Prince of Wales, entertaining friends and strangers with our travellers' tales.

What I didn't expect was to have no idea of when we took that one momentous step across the border. It could have been when they were serving the drinks. It could have been while I was in the loo. But it doesn't matter. Planes don't really cross borders, they simply fly over them.

'And this is for my little grandson.' Señora Herrera, sitting on my right, lifts a Bart Simpson backpack from the shopping bag between her feet.

Or it could have been while she and I were discussing the red silk roses that she bought for her sister.

'For going to school,' she explains.

Señora Herrera is returning to Costa Rica after a week of Christmas shopping in LA. I admire the backpack as I have admired the roses, the toaster oven for her mother, the Barbie doll and Barbie clothes and accessories for her little granddaughter, and the Elvis tie for her son. 'I'm sure he'll like it,' I think I say. My Spanish is proving a little rustier than I'd rather fervently hoped it would be.

She starts putting her presents back in their bag. If what I actually said was 'He's sure that I like it', which is what I may have said, she doesn't let on. 'There are so many more things in Los Angeles,' she says. 'And so cheap.'

So cheap? This isn't something I was expecting, either. Everyone knows that one of the principal reasons for travelling in the Third World – aside from the opportunities for broadening the cultural horizons and widening the cosmic vision that it offers – is to shop. The Third World's cheap. Cheaper than LA.

I glance over at Victor to see if he heard Mrs Herrera. He's asleep.

Señora Herrera looks over too. '*Qué pasó?*' she asks. What happened?

I smile blankly. What happened to what?

She points across me. '*Su mano,*' she says. 'What happened to his hand?'

It isn't easy to explain in Spanish what happened to Victor's hand. At least it easy isn't for me. I'm all right when it comes to things like getting a bottle of beer or a plate of rice, and finding the location of the bathroom, but the complexities of the explanation for the cast on Victor's right hand are a little advanced for my vocabulary. How to explain the ride up Highway 1 after a night of rain and mountain-lion warnings? The excitement of finally reaching LA? The ill-spent evening in the karaoke bar drinking domestic beer? The way fate twists when you're least expecting it?

I manage a sentence that contains the words 'motorcycle', 'New York to California and then down to Mexico', and stop.

Mrs Herrera is nodding. She understands. '*Motos,*' she says, '*son tan peligrosos.*'

I agree that motorcycles are dangerous. People drive so crazy. Roads can be so bad. And they are pretty *muy rápido*.

'*Pobrecito*,' says Mrs Herrera. 'It's lucky he wasn't hurt more.'

'Oh, no,' I say quickly. 'No, he didn't—' I punch my hand into my fist, Castilian for crash '—the bike.'

'No?' she looks at me expectantly.

No.

There are things beyond plans and control. This was something – like being blown away in McDonald's or sideswiped by a lorry – that could have happened to anyone. It's just unfortunate that it happened to us.

We were a little drunk. Very a little drunk. The victorious army celebrating the first battle won. As Bobby, the orthodontist, and Lara, the paralegal, sang a heartfelt rendition of 'Stand By Me' to Ted's Tavern, Victor and I staggered out of the door and into the electric night. We waved at police cars. We laughed. We belted out the refrain to 'Hotel California' and danced across the street. When we got back to my friend's apartment we had a nightcap – an undomestic beer – and tossed for the sleeping accommodation. Heads. I got the sofa. Victor got the platform. Worried about leaving Montoya by herself on the mean streets of LA, Victor dreamed that she was being carried away in the back of a pick-up by a bunch of guys wearing red bandanas. He woke in an alcohol-induced panic, convinced that he had to go out and check the bike, no matter what time it was, no matter how malignant the night.

The answer the Señora is waiting for forms itself, perfectly and effortlessly, in my mind. *Cayó de la cama.*

Victor turns in his seat. He doesn't open his eyes as he says, 'Don't you dare tell her I fell out of the bloody bed.'

My mother said that there is only one reason anybody goes to Colombia. Because it's the setting of *One Hundred Years of Solitude*? Because it's the only country on the continent with both an Atlantic and a Pacific coast? Because it's the gateway to South America? Because of its natural beauty? Blend of cultures? Exotic creole and native cuisine?

Because, forced to abandon your Honda because of a broken hand which would delay you too long and eat up your money, you decided to think laterally: skip Central America and wander aimlessly down from Colombia to Peru by whatever means you can instead? Che and Granados were also forced to abandon the motorcycle they had started with on their tour of South America, and they'd had a good time.

The only reason anyone goes to Colombia, said my mother, is for drugs. It's common knowledge. When my mother told her friend, Teresa, that we'd changed our plans and were flying straight into Barranquilla from LA, that's what Teresa told her. She saw it on TV.

'Are you saying you think I'm a drug smuggler?' I asked her.

'I'm not saying anything,' said my mother. 'I'm just telling you what Teresa said.'

The guidebook is pretty clear about the way to approach Colombia. An army would help, but failing an army caution is necessary. Don't stop to talk to anyone. Don't stop to pick up anything that has fallen on the ground. If someone dumps a load of shit on you don't stop to wipe it off. Don't let anyone help you wipe it off. Watch out for false policemen. Watch out for real policemen. Watch out for strangers who are too friendly. Don't relax your guard just because the stranger in question only comes up to your waist. Be courteous but firm with officials. Take a cab from the airport. Keep your luggage with you at all times. Act as though you know both where you're going and what you're doing.

We arrive in Barranquilla at ten at night after nearly thirty-two hours of buses and planes, and no food or sleep worth mentioning. We are neatly turned out in cleanish jeans and plain T-shirts, carrying our new backpacks, which have side straps so they can be carried as regular suitcases, thus impressing officials that we are serious tourists and not hippy gypsies. We are cautious, not to say wary. As we trudge through the spare and dingy terminal, following the gaggle of crumpled travellers headed for the uniformed twelve-year-olds at passport control, drugs don't strike me as such a bad idea. But there are no dark men with slow smiles hissing, 'Psst, gringo, over here.' There are just the boys with their small arms and official stamps and solemn expressions.

'*Americano?*' asks the one with Victor's passport in his hand.

'*Inglés*,' says Victor.

He stares at the open page. '*Número del pasaporte?*' he says, pointing to Victor's date of birth.

'No,' corrects Victor. 'That's the passport number.'

He points it out to the boy, who writes it down on the official form. 'And what is the purpose of your visit to Colombia?' Thank

God my mother isn't with us. 'Why do you think they're here?' she'd be saying. 'Drugs! Why else would anyone come here?'

'*Viajero*,' says Victor.

'*Turismo*,' says the boy, and gives him his stamps.

I hand him my blue passport with the gold eagle on the front.

He scrutinises it. '*Inglés?*' he says.

We march into the warm and noisy night, just as though we know what we're doing, where we're going, and how to get there. Just as though we have Colombian money on us, which we don't. You can't buy pesos at LA Airport.

Landing in a strange country late at night with no money is the kind of thing that makes me nervous, but Victor isn't bothered about this lack of means. The American dollar is taken everywhere, he assures me. Like nuggets of gold. He says that the cab driver will take American money. The hotel will take American money. We can even use it to buy water on the way to the hotel, says Victor. No problem. He leads the way to the jumble of taxis with me close behind, wishing we weren't quite so conspicuous; that Victor were shorter, or I were darker, or our backpacks weren't so green and new.

Through the veins of my travelling companion pounds the blood of hidalgos and conquistadors. He does them proud as he negotiates the cab fare. Not ten, he says, as though he has made the journey from the airport into town at least a dozen times before. Six.

The driver waves his hands in exasperation but opens the boot. 'Put your bags in here,' he orders.

Victor says no, we'll keep the bags with us.

Despite his un-Spanish Spanish and the rapidity with which he speaks it, I have no trouble understanding that the driver is telling us to think again. There's no way on earth we're keeping the bags with us, he says loudly, we're putting them in the back as we're supposed to. He grabs hold of mine.

There is no doubt in my mind that if I were alone I would already be in the boot of the cab with my luggage, tearing out of the airport headed for some deep ravine outside Barranquilla. Within days I'd be a cautionary tale told by one traveller to another over bottles of beer. 'Did you hear about the American woman? Thirty people watched her tossed into the boot of a cab and no one did a thing. God knows what happened to her. No one's going to notice another body around here.' But I'm not alone. I'm with a man whose ancestors would have sent back the coffee or shot the chap blocking their way with the same casual authority. I hold on tight. 'No,' I say, pulling backwards. 'I'm keeping it with me.'

The driver holds on tight as well. 'No,' he says, pulling it towards him. 'It goes in the trunk.'

'No it doesn't.' Victor yanks me so hard that the three of us stumble into a pillar.

The driver is screaming in earnest now. Based on my experience with irate New York and London cabbies, I'd say that he's giving us a lesson in idiomatic street slang that might come in handy in the future, but there's no chance now to take notes. Victor has already flagged down another car and is hauling me to it. 'Do you know the Hotel Zhivago, Plaza Bolivar?' he shouts into the window. '*Seis dólares Americanos,*' he goes on when the cabbie nods, and before he can get out Victor has opened the door and shoved me and the bags inside.

Our new driver leans across the front seat and shouts out to our old driver, what's going on?

The other man rattles off an explanation in which I can make out only two words. Crazy gringos. It seems likely he's talking about us.

We pitch and bounce into darkest Barranquilla. In London, it takes some knowhow to buy a pint of milk after ten o'clock at night, but in Barranquilla the shops are open and the pavements thick with vendors selling drinks and snacks and cups of ice covered with flavoured syrup. In London, people conduct their lives quietly, privately and indoors. But not in Barranquilla. Most of the town must be out, milling in front of the cafés and food stalls, hanging out in doorways, standing on corners and in traffic, discussing their lives in raised voices with a lot of gestures. Shadowy and indistinct in the feeble electric lights and the gas lanterns of the vendors, the city has a fantastic, almost carnival air.

'Jesus,' mutters Victor as the cab cuts in front of two packed buses, first to leap for that sudden gap to the right. 'They all drive like couriers.'

This seems to be true. Either that or there simply aren't any traffic regulations in Colombia. There are signs and signals here and there, but they seem to function only as suggestions. If you'd like to, you can stop at this corner, but if you'd rather go for that gap between the van with the dog and the bed on the roof and the doorless bus covered with Christmas lights, by all means do. If you feel so inclined you might consider applying your brakes just about now, but if not just blow your horn. Directions are for decoration and lanes are arbitrary. The tendency seems to be to drive on the right, but if the right lane is jammed and the left lane is clear, the left lane will do.

'Here!' shouts Victor suddenly. 'Stop over here!'

If you want to stop, stop. We stop. More horns sound behind us.

'Over there,' says Victor, indicating an open-fronted store on the other side of the crammed and blaring road. 'You can get water in there.' It has been agreed that if one of us has to stay behind with our bags, that one is not going to be me, the rapee.

I look across the street. The store looks pretty crowded. If I have to ask the price of a litre of water in American money, I'd much prefer to do it without an audience. Maybe I should take my chances in the cab after all.

'What are you waiting for?' Victor gives me a shove. 'Go on!'

I go on, rehearsing as I wade through the traffic, dodging bumpers and potholes and anything in the road that looks as though it might once have lived. *Se vende botellas de agua? Se vende botellas de agua? Hay agua en botellas aquí?*

When I did Spanish in high school, the family in our textbook was the Lopez family: Señor Roberto, Señora Maria, Juan and Luísa. The first time Luísa was sent to the shops on her own, she couldn't find the list her mother had given her and couldn't remember what had been on it. Luísa stood in the middle of the modern grocery store with its well-stocked shelves, overwhelmed by the choice. The shopkeeper was patient and helpful. Ham? he asked. Sausage? Rice? Potatoes? Onions? Beans? The other customers were patient and helpful, too. Señora Mendoza suggested that Luísa's mother might have asked for milk or eggs; Señora Alvarez that Señora Lopez might have wanted cheese. None of them suggested a bottle of water.

As no one is suggesting it now.

'Qué?' asks the girl at the counter for the third time. She is not nearly as patient as the Lopezes' grocer. 'Coca-Cola?'

Everyone is looking at me. Though not expectantly. They know I don't speak Spanish, and that even if I could they wouldn't understand me. They're looking at me as though they're amazed I can speak at all.

'Agua,' I repeat in what even I can hear is a heavy Brooklyn accent. '*Una botella de agua.*'

'*Qué?*' she asks again. '*Una botella de qué?*'

If I shared the English passion for after-dinner games of charades

I might not have a problem now. I'd be able to mime 'bottle of water' so swiftly and surely that even the shoeshine boy hovering near the entrance, his eyes on my dirty Docs, would be jumping up and down shouting, '*Botella de agua! Botella de agua!*' But I don't, and I can't point it out because though there are several shelves of soft drinks and liquor behind her, there is nothing that looks like a bottle of water.

'*Agua!*' There are only two syllables in the bloody word. How can she not understand them? '*Agua!*'

'*Agua mineral*,' says a voice to my left.

I look over. It's Señora Alvarez with her curly dark hair and her flowered dress and her net shopping bag, straight out of *Let's Speak Spanish, Book 2*. She was helpful to Luísa; I should have known she wouldn't let me down.

'*Sí!*' I cry. I have to stop myself from embracing her. '*Agua mineral!*'

We both turn to the assistant. '*Agua mineral!*'

She shakes her head. '*No hay.*'

Our disappointment – not to say depression – at having to abandon Montoya has been tempered by thoughts of the new luxuries promised by this change in means of travel. Except for the nights when we're camping, we won't be in constant battle with the elements. We won't have to fight the bloody stove every night, but will have our meals cooked by someone else. We'll sleep indoors, in safety and comfort; in beds. We've been quite looking forward to sleeping in beds.

The Hotel Zhivago is recommended by the handbook. It is basic, says the book, but it is cheap, clean, sometimes has hot water, and the owners are friendly and helpful. I'm usually a little sceptical about recommendations, even ones in print, but I trust the guide-book. The cab noses to a stop at a pile of rubbish by the kerb. Victor and I look at the hotel and then at each other. This was not the time to suspend suspicion. Except for 'cheap', none of the information in the guidebook is something you could have gathered from outside. Outside, the Hotel Zhivago is a squalid wreck of a building that was once painted blue. The front door is open – or possibly just missing – and there is no light in the foyer that can be seen from the street.

'Hotel Zhivago, Paseo Bolivar,' says the driver.

Not Plaza Bolivar. It's the wrong hotel. I feel nothing but relief. We may not have money and we may not have water, but at least we won't have to throw away the handbook on the first day. My relief is short-lived.

'It'll do,' says Victor, already stepping on to the pavement. Tomorrow we will get money, get water, be on our way to Cartagena. 'It's just for one night.'

'So was the sinking of the *Titanic*,' I remind him, but I'm quick to follow him out of the cab.

Inside, the Hotel Zhivago lives up to its first impression of age and squalor. There are chunks out of the ceiling, chunks out of the floor. Mildewed strips of faded paper still cling to its walls, and there's something about the staircase that makes me instantly uncurious about what lies at its upper end. At the back of the ground floor, illuminated by what must be at least a 10-watt bulb, is an old wooden counter, behind which two boys and a girl drink soda and listen to the radio. We follow the oldest of the boys up the dark, creaking staircase to the first floor. I'm afraid of losing my footing in the dark, but I'm more afraid to touch the dank wall or the tilted banister. I take each step slowly, trying to imagine the Hotel Zhivago when its floors were tiled and its walls stencilled in pale patterns, when it was, perhaps, the place to stay. 'You're going to Barranquilla? Oh, you *must* stay at the Hotel Zhivago. You won't believe the views.'

'It reminds me of a squat,' says Victor as the three of us make our way down the narrow hall to room 12. He might add, 'One that's been trashed,' but doesn't. He's not a man to waste words.

The boy struggles with the lock for a few seconds. '*Esto es*,' he says, and pushes open the cracked wooden door. He turns on the light, creating gloom. We step cautiously in.

It's unlikely that no one has ever died here. And badly.

Room 12 is painted in something close to green, and divided from the room behind by a partition that stops two feet short of the ceiling. There is no view, because there is no window. The light is on on the other side of the partition, but there are no sounds. Room 12 has two single beds that were thrown out when the local prison was refurbished in 1963 for a UN inspection, and a small sink in one corner. The sink is filled with dirty water. I poke my head in the doorway beside the sink. It's the size of a closet, but instead of a clothes rail it has a stub of piping sticking out from the wall.

'*La ducha*,' says the boy. '*Privada*.'

The private shower.

After the boy goes, Victor takes the change we got from paying for the room and goes out to search for water. I continue standing where I am, beneath the dim bare bulb, Roy's bag in my arms and my backpack at my feet. As tired as I am, I'm afraid to sit down on the bed without my sleeping bag over it. The sheets are filthy. The mattresses are filthy. I put Roy's bag down on the burn-scarred coffee table between the two beds. Gingerly. The bag is hand-made from a piece of woven cloth, with a drawstring to close it and woven bands as shoulder straps, mended in places with odd bits of material. I stand there just looking at it for a few seconds, imagining Roy sitting on the rusted metal bed in the room beyond the partition, stitching on the patches beneath that dull, bare bulb. The reason we brought the bag with us was because it has been here before. Not in the Hotel Zhivago, perhaps, but in Colombia.

When Victor comes back he puts the lock we brought with us on the door while I put up my mosquito net. Bumping into each other with fatigue, we unroll the sleeping bags. I don't remember getting into bed, or saying goodnight, or closing my eyes, but when I wake up the room is darker and Victor is sound asleep with his mosquito net wrapped around him, like a chicken in clingfilm.

I lie awake in the gloom, Roy's bag beside me, black as a buzzard, thinking about deaths. Sad deaths in sad rooms alone and far from home. When Victor found it in the skip, Roy's bag was empty except for a few old Biros and matches, a ticket stub for a bus from Santa Marta and a suicide note. Roy was in Bogotá. He was staying in a brothel that doubled as a hotel, broke and alone, ill with the clap, hallucinating monsters in the water stains on the ceiling and the scuttling of the cockroaches from hunger and exhaustion – and probably clinical depression. 'I'm twenty-eight and look at me,' wrote Roy. 'Is this what it's all about? Is that what it's all for?'

The single tap drips into the full sink.

Yes, it is saying. Yesyesyes.

Until this moment, it hadn't occurred to me that Roy might have been using the same guidebook as we.

Welcome to the Hotel Zhivago.

Most things really do look better in the morning. You lie with your eyes bolted opened at 3 am, listening to the birds of the apocalypse braying in the branches or the leaking tap dripping into the abyss, and you worry about that parking ticket you forgot to pay, or the bump behind your ear that you've been ignoring, or the young man who wanted to kill himself in a city named after a Chibcha chief. But when the sun returns and the coffee is brewing you can no longer remember what you were so worried about. You can still pay the ticket, the bump is just a bump, the young man didn't die.

Of all the things that look better in the morning, however, neither the Hotel Zhivago nor Barranquilla are among them.

In daylight, the Zhivago loses most of its charm. It's hard now to imagine a time when its rooms were elegant and cooled by ceiling fans; when wealthy European holidaymakers sat in the lobby in their tropical suits and large-brimmed hats, sipping rum and playing cribbage while sunlight fell between the slats of the shutters and striped the patterns of the tiles. The doors along the hallway are opened to let in some of the sunshine squeezing through the dirt that covers the skylight, revealing smaller and smaller, shabbier and shabbier rooms, a towel or a shirt thrown across a broken bedstead, a hairbrush and some keys, maybe a watch or a small photo on a table, a worn pair of shoes on the floor, blankly wary faces looking back.

We step out on to Paseo Bolivar. Carefully, aware of our backpacks, hoping to give the impression that we haven't just stepped off the plane.

Barranquilla, too, is not as picturesque now that we can see it. Now that we can see it, cloudy with exhaust fumes, it is clear what Barranquilla is. You are on your way somewhere. It's a long, tedious journey. The road is bad, the car is acting up, you don't pass anywhere where you could stop for as much as a cup of tea. After twelve gruelling hours your head is pounding and it's begun to rain. Four hours later, the rain now a downpour, you realise that you've lost the route and are hopelessly lost. You keep on going. The car breaks down. The place where the car breaks down is Barranquilla.

I stand close to Victor, looking alert and on guard while he checks the guidebook for the location of the bus depot and money exchanges.

'We're in luck,' he says. 'The station's just down the road.'

Thank God for that. We've only gone a few metres, and already the backpack feels as if everything in it has turned to steel.

'There'll probably be some sort of exchange there.'

I nod. This seems so reasonable that it doesn't occur to me to ask why. Why would there be an exchange at the bus depot when there isn't at any other bus depot this side of Mars?

'And breakfast.' Victor sticks the book back into Roy's bag. 'There's bound to be somewhere to eat.'

This, too, sounds reasonable. Of course there'll be somewhere to eat, and by then we'll have money with which to buy it.

We adjust our backpacks. It's day one. As confident of where we're going as Dorothy setting out for home before the storm breaks, we stride across Paseo Bolivar.

12

SEÑOR

The bus started out full, its roof loaded with bags, boxes and pieces of a bed, its aisle piled with more bags and boxes and a chicken in a sack. Now that we are a mile or two from the station, near the wall with Bart Simpson painted on it, the bus can be considered crowded. We're squashed into the two front seats by the door that separates the driver from the passengers, our feet up on our backpacks – Rule of the Road number 13: Never let your luggage out of your sight – a basket of fritters pressed against the side of my head and a small child leaning against my legs. The woman behind me is singing along with the radio; the conductor, who is all of eleven, is forcing his way up the aisle, demanding tickets. The decal Christ staring back at us sadly from the door looks a lot older than thirty. He's been on this bus too long. All of the other passengers are eating. Unlike America, where the traveller not particularly fond of snack foods and cookies faces the possibility of starvation, in Colombia every time the bus slows a gaggle of boys jumps on selling fruit, breads, *empanadas*, fritters, ices and juice drinks. Also unlike America, where the use of gloves or implements is often optional when serving food – and almost touching given the general level of sanitation – the hawkers here all use tongs or napkins.

Only Victor and I aren't eating. Don't drink anything made with water or milk, warns the guidebook. Be careful what food you buy on the street. Peel all fruit. Stay away from raw vegetables. Avoid salads. If you're not concerned about your stomach at least consider your bowels. But that isn't why we're not eating. We're not eating

because we still have no money. We're not eating because the bus
depot had moved from where it was last year and we used the little
change we had to get to the new one. There was no *caja de cambio* at
the station. There was no one selling anything who was willing to
take American money. Victor says there's nothing to worry about. We
can change money when we get to Cartagena. Look on the bright
side, says Victor. We've already learned one new word. *Propio*. Tip.
Which is what the man who led us to the bus going to the new depot
wanted for his help, hanging in the doorway as it moved forward,
complaining about us to the driver, stingy gringos.

We come to another military checkpoint. More vendors squeeze
on. '*Yupi! Yupi!*' '*Helados! Helados!*' 'Coca-Cola!' The driver gets off
and, after showing his papers, stands with the conductor, staring
solemnly at the right front tyre. If we get to Cartagena.

Victor, immersed in the handbook, doesn't look up. I lean right as
the kid selling ice-cream pushes his way to the back of the bus and
the basket of fritters presses into my head, and go back to thinking
about the treasure city of the Spanish Main.

Cartagena. A name once whispered in dark rooms and heartless
nights. A name reverently repeated in the lighted courts of European
kings. Cartagena, city of dreams. City of adventure. City of rebellion.
City of doom.

Perched like a heron at the edge of the Caribbean, guarded by
twenty-nine stone forts and surrounded by a coral wall, Cartagena
was where the Spaniards kept the gems and minerals brought down
the Magdalena to be shipped back across the ocean for the coffers of
home. The pirates followed. Their ships shadowed the blue-green
harbour, their guns aimed at that wall of coral, their flags waved a
greeting to the stalwart citizens – 'Honey, I'm home.' Three times
sacked, besieged by the British, besieged by the Spanish, devastated
by famine, war and disease, Cartagena was constantly defeated but
never really beaten. It was at Cartagena that Bolivar, who would
later feel that he'd done no more than plough the sea, ploughed
rich fields of hope and glory. It was at Cartagena that Joan Wilder
and Jack T. Colter spun together on a plaza decked with party lights
and caught their first glimpse of love.

Victor passes the guidebook to me, careful not to hit the head of
the little boy now more or less sitting on my knees. 'See which hotel
you think we should go to.'

I think we should go to a hotel overlooking that carousel plaza. I
say this to Victor.

'First of all,' says Victor, 'that movie was filmed in Mexico, not Colombia. And second of all, that wasn't Cartagena. Cartagena was where they were captured by the police and nearly killed. Remember?'

I sort of remember. So not overlooking the plaza, overlooking the harbour, where at night we can sit at the window and glimpse the ghosts of galleons in the play of light across the water. Or one that looks out on the siren sea.

'Stick to the hotels graded G,' advises Victor. 'They're the cheapest.'

El dueño of the Hotel Monterrey sits behind the wooden counter, his chair tilted back as he reads his evening paper, his feet resting on a spiral notepad that says 'Jean Book', presumably because it has been made to look like a pair of Levis. '*Pero in este momento . . .*' he is saying into the telephone held between his neck and his chin. '*En este momento . . .*'

None of the guests sitting on the plastic-covered sofa in front of the TV seem to notice that this is a sentence *el dueño* says quite often but never finishes. Nor does his wife. She's busy. We didn't have to register at the Zhivago, but we do here.

'*Nombres y apellidos?*' she asks, her pen poised on the page.

'Victor Ernesto David Sanchez,' I answer.

Much to my surprise, she understands me. She nods and writes down Victor Sanchez.

'*Número del pasaporte?*'

On a roll, I read Victor's passport number off to her, one digit at a time, and she copies them down exactly.

'*Qué trabajo?*'

I stare at her lips. What work does he do?

The roll has ended, smashed against a solid stone wall. '*Moto*—' I begin, and freeze. As far as jobs go, I can say professor, waiter, seamstress, driver and farmer in Spanish. But I can't say motorcycle courier.

Her lips are smiling. '*Moto?*' she inquires politely. She glances at her husband, but he is muttering, '*En este momento . . . pero en este momento . . .*' and waving one hand in the air, his eyes on the sports page. She looks back at me. '*Moto?*' she says again. Your companion is a motorcycle?

'*Conductor*,' I try. Driver. '*Conductor de un moto.*'

She's still smiling, but shaking her head. 'No, no,' she explains. '*Qué trabajo? Qué occupación?*'

I glance at the register and the list of travellers before us. All of them were students. Sounds all right to me. '*Estudiente*,' I say quite clearly.

She's as relieved as I am that the confusion is over. She moves her pen to the next line. '*Y usted?*'

We glide through my name and my passport number and then crash once more into the wall of occupation. There is no way she's going to believe that I'm a student. If I say I'm a student she'll know instantly that my mother is right and I'm only in Colombia for the drugs. She'll call the police. The police will come and plant drugs on me. Then they'll arrest me. Then my mother, seeing my arrest on the news, will know she was right. If my mother knows, her friend Teresa and everyone in King Kullen and the church will know. She'll put me on the prayer chain. The word '*escritora*' flashes through my brain. '*Escritora*,' I blurt out. She smiles at me blankly.

My linguistic confidence is a fragile thing and now it's gone. She doesn't understand *escritora*. And then I realise, of course she doesn't understand *escritora*. *Escritora* doesn't mean writer. It means desk. My hostess is still smiling uncomprehendingly. Jesus Christ, if it's not *escritora*, what is it? Clinging all these years to some unused synapse, another word surfaces. *Autor*. Pray God it doesn't mean car.

'*Autor!*' I cry.

'*Autor?*' she asks patiently.

I pretend to write. '*Escribo novelas.*'

'*Autora*,' she corrects, but doesn't start moving her pen. There is something about the way she pronounces *autor* and *autora* that suggests the words carry a certain weight and solemnity not borne out by my appearance. I am not an *autora*. But la Señora is a kind woman. '*Ponemos escritora*,' she says.

Ponemos escritora? I smile enthusiastically to hide my confusion. What the hell. Let's put down desk.

The Hotel Monterrey overlooks the stalls and cram of people on La Calle Media Luna. The Hotel Monterrey is graded G.

It doesn't take more than a second or two to realise that this is not the area of Cartagena where Bolivar stayed. If Joan and Jack had stayed in Cartagena, it wouldn't have been here either. It is not in this neighbourhood that busloads of tourists are brought to buy over-priced souvenirs in renovated dungeons or driven in a horse and cart down cobbled streets to view the historic sites. This is where the whores throw kisses in the dark and men with fast movements offer to change your dollars or sell you drugs. As Victor, recipient of quite a few thrown kisses and offers of controlled substances, says, it's a very friendly part of town. The guidebook recommends care, 'This is not a very safe neighbourhood.'

'Don't forget your flip-flops in the shower,' says Victor. 'You don't want to touch the floor with your feet.' He is lying on the bed nearest the window – the hole in the wall filled with a block of concrete in a Moorish design – making notes from the handbook.

Just the word 'shower' improves my mood. It's been five days now since it had any significance other than as a description of weather.

'I haven't forgotten them,' I say, and hold them up to prove this is true.

'And watch where you put the soap.'

'I'll watch where I put the soap.' I take our toilet bag and our towel from my backpack and lay them on top of my clean clothes on the third bed, the one we're using as a wardrobe.

'And remember, don't put any toilet paper in the toilet.'

This is something I couldn't remember, since I've never known it. Maybe I should read the handbook in a little more detail myself. 'Why not?'

Victor sighs. He thinks I should read the handbook in more detail, too. 'Because it fucks up the plumbing.'

Fucks up what plumbing? is the question that occurs to me as I shut the door of the bathroom behind me and, with some difficulty given the fact that my hands are full, loop the wire attached to it over the nail in the wall. There's a toilet bowl without a seat in one corner, beside a basket of used toilet paper drowning in water, a drain in the mildly flooded floor, and the stub of a rusted pipe coming out of the wall. There's one tap. I take a wild guess that it's probably cold. The sink is outside in the hallway, presumably for reasons of hygiene.

This isn't going to be as easy as I'd thought. One can't help but notice that the male guests think nothing of wandering into and out of the *baño* with just a towel wrapped around them, but this is not something that I'm about to try. Which means that I not only have to keep dry the towel, the toilet bag and the clothes I'm wearing while I shower, but the clothes I'd like to wear afterwards as well. The question is how?

My eyes go around the minute chamber for a fourth time. There are no ledges, no hooks, no toilet tank, no toilet-seat cover, no nails in the door. It is true that the door, an obvious afterthought, is only a partial one, so things can be hung over it, but not everything can be put there.

I stuff my underwear into the pockets of my jeans – clean in the right, dirty in the left – put the shampoo bottle and the soap box on the floor and very, very carefully balance the toilet bag on the narrow rim of the bowl. I turn on the tap just as someone knocks on the door.

'*Ocupado!*' I shout quickly. It wouldn't take an Arnold Schwarzenegger to get in here. '*Está ocupado!*' Lassie could do it just by throwing herself against the door.

A hand appears over the top of the door, waving a wad of toilet paper. 'You forgot this,' says Victor.

I take the paper from his hand and stuff it up the leg of my jeans.

'And one other thing.'

'What?'

'Keep your mouth shut in the shower.'

Rule of the Road number 14.

If the conquerors of South America had been not the Spanish with their Mediterranean temperament and fondness for coffee, but the British with their state-of-siege island mentality and devotion to tea, Cartagena wouldn't confuse us into thinking we're in Spain.

Assuming the British hadn't been totally successful in the casual policy of genocide they employed in North America, you would still be able to buy woven bags from the Indians of Santa Marta on the Plaza Bolivar and *molas* and hammocks in the tourist shops along the wall of the old prison or take a boat trip to the islands (lunch included) and see the aquarium in the sea for another dollar. But Cartagena as it is would not exist.

The saints' names would vanish from the narrow cobbled streets, taking the whitewashed buildings, their balconies and tiled roofs with them. There would be no tranquil inner courtyards, plants and caged birds hanging in the sunshine, no *tinto* sellers with their thermoses of thick, silty coffee and their tiny plastic cups circling the plazas, no small boys in American T-shirts and sneakers peddling cigarettes and sweets. The fresh fruit-juice stands would go from the riverfront. The uniformed children who exercise in the courtyard by the old city gate in the evenings would be home watching videos. The crowds that jam the pavements of the shopping district wouldn't be buying fried plantain, potato cakes, roasted corn, *arepas*, *empanadas* or paper cups of ices from the stalls along the kerb but fish and chips and kebabs from too bright shops. The dim and dingy six-tables-and-a-magazine-photograph-of-a-bowl-of-fruit-or-a-wind-mill bars, where friends and couples go to share a large bottle of soda and pimps and bachelors dine on the menu of the day and workmen drink beer and play dominos and cards would be tea shops and pubs instead. There would be an orderly high street with Marks & Spencer and Our Price records and a British Home Stores, and an amusement arcade along the fortress wall. No carts and horses, no whole families packed on a rusted motorcycle, no open-backed lorries filled with passengers. The brightly coloured buses decorated with stars and decals and fairylights that belch through the streets with a devil-may-care spirit – defying the laws of physics, defying common sense, scaring the shit out of the unwary traveller – would be sombre double-deckers driven by men who favour the use of directions and brakes, and there'd be no jumping on and off when-ever you felt like it, no hanging out of the door talking to the chap hanging out of the door of the bus beside yours.

No Cartagena, jewel of the Caribbean, just Hastings by the sea.

'Come on, *amigo*,' pleads Wilson, 'I've had a bad day. Buy a pack, not just two. I'm giving you a good deal.' Wilson has a winning smile.

'No you're not,' says Victor, who also has a winning smile. 'And anyway, I don't want a pack. I only want two.'

Wilson, it's clear, has seen it all – from tourists who buy every-thing he has in a spontaneous gesture of rum and magnanimity to tourists so afraid that he might rob or infect them that they chase him away – and has learned his lessons well. In a competitive field such as his, understanding human nature is part of the job.

Wilson shrugs expressively. 'But, *amigo* . . .'

Victor holds up two fingers. '*Dos*,' he repeats, and hands Wilson the coins.

Wilson Horacio Antonio Hernandez Salcedo is eleven. He wears a shabby Lakers T-shirt, jeans that are still too big for him and cheap sandals. Every afternoon we come to the café for beer and a game of backgammon, and Wilson sells Victor two cigarettes. Every evening we come back to the café for beer, backgammon and the customised *plato corriente* because Cartagena's two vegetarian restaurants – the Govinda, with its walls decorated with pictures of a young, blue and playful Krishna, incense and the *Baghavad Gita* in Spanish and German for sale; and the one earnestly dedicated to healthful eating, the one that sells tarot cards and books on biorhythms and astrology, and has a picture of Christ over the till – are only open for lunch, and Wilson sells Victor two cigarettes, sometimes three.

Wilson lights Victor's cigarette but instead of moving on, leans against a pillar, watching Victor as he passes the guidebook to me with a mumbled 'You see what you think.' 'No game tonight?' he asks.

Wilson is perplexed by our lack of interest in the church that is now a movie house, the convent that is now a police station, the multitude of monasteries, the statue of Columbus, the balcony from which San Pedro Claver, Slave of the Slaves, watched for the arrival of those sorrow-filled ships, his work cut out for him, and the canoe ride round San Fernando, but he likes to watch the backgammon – even though he'd prefer it if we played chess.

'No,' says Victor. 'Not tonight.' He leans back in his seat, blowing smoke over the heads of the celebratory crowd sitting on the pavement. It's summer-holiday time and Cartagena is packed with Colombian tourists, who could, by the looks of them, be American or English or German tourists except that their Spanish is better. 'We're leaving tomorrow, we have to get ready.

'*Sí?*' says Wilson. '*A dónde van?*'

Now there's a good question.

A band is playing enthusiastically from the back of a truck parked on one side of the Plaza Bolivar. Once this was the plaza of the Inquisition, a place, I assume, most people visited less out of choice than under duress, and not the spot for a pleasant evening stroll, but now the seats around the central statue of the Liberator and the benches that line the paths that cross the square are filled with people drinking *tinto* or playing chess as the last light drips into the sea. A middle-aged couple dance on the grass. I'm reading through the guidebook. Once more.

Heading for Bogotá, we have talked about going to Mompós first, the town where Bolivar claimed his 'glory was born'. Mompós, says the guidebook, has retained its original character more completely than any other Colombian town. It talks of cobbled streets and whitewashed houses, of time standing still. It also says that malaria is endemic in the surrounding area. We're a little uneasy about endemic malaria. Seeing no reason not to wait till we got to California to buy our malaria pills, it wasn't until California that we discovered why we should have got the medicine in London: $300. So we didn't get them. We got homeopathic pills instead. But for all our distrust of modern technocratic medicine with its cures for symptoms and disregard for the illness, we're both a little nervous of the ability of those tiny chichonella pills to deal with mosquitos that can bite through clothes.

The idea of going to Mompós has paled.

'What about Quibdo?' I finally suggest.

'Where is it?' asks Victor.

I can answer this confidently. 'In Choco Department.' It says so in the guidebook. 'It's a friendly jungle town and Indians come to the Sunday market in their canoes.' The guidebook says this, too.

Victor holds out his hand. Indians in canoes interest him more than Spanish towns. 'Where is it?' turning to the map.

Quibdo isn't on the map.

'Maybe not Quibdo,' says Victor. 'What about Sincelejo?'

But the only notable thing about Sincelejo is that it was near there that the security forces killed the drug king José Gacha in 1989.

'Montería?' I try.

Victor vetos Montería on the grounds that even the guidebook finds it uninteresting.

A faraway look comes over Victor's face. 'Christ,' he says. 'I wish we had the bike.'

The guidebook heavily advises against speaking to strangers. Interspersed with the lists of cathedrals, churches, convents and historic sites of death and mayhem it recommends you see are cautionary tales of vanished traveller's cheques and passports and waking up in an empty lot, lucky to still have your fillings in your teeth. I reckon that the guidebook would frown on stopping to talk to someone in a half-deserted plaza, dark now that most of the shops around it are shut, just because he shouted out, 'Hey, English! English! How do you do?' as you were walking past him discussing where you might be going in the morning, but we stop anyway.

Henry's voice is thick and gritty, and he speaks so quickly that bits are lost in gulps of air, but I can understand most of the words he is saying, even the ones in English. What I can't do is fit them into continuous sentences that make any sense. I think he said that he was in the merchant navy for fifty years, but Victor thinks that what he said was he was in the merchant navy fifty years ago. Victor thinks that Henry said he worked for the UN – for some agency like WHO or UNESCO – but I think he was asking if we worked for the UN. I think that Henry's daughter was born while he was in Norway and that his wife left him while he was in Japan, but Victor understood him to say that his daughter was born in Norway and his wife ran away to Tokyo. Foreign languages are tricky like that.

Henry puts the little plastic *tinto* cup from which he's been drinking down on the stone seat beside him and smiles. 'I am what you call in English a rolling rock,' he says. 'I have been everywhere – England, Canada, the United States, Europe, the Orient . . .'

And now he's here, a short, thick-set man in his sixties in well-worn trousers and a Giants T-shirt, sitting under the feet of Simon Bolivar.

'And did you enjoy it?' asks Victor.

Henry stares at something on the toe of his trainer for a second, then looks up and smiles. 'Sometimes,' he says.

We make a move to leave. 'We have to get back to the hotel,' explains Victor. 'We're going in the morning.'

'Where to?' asks Henry.

We admit that we haven't quite decided that yet. He's not the only rolling rock in this group.

Henry waves us back down beside him. He's concerned that we see the best of Colombia. He thinks we should go back to Santa Marta. He can arrange a ride to the national park for us.

'No,' says Victor. 'We don't want to go to Santa Marta. Too many tourists.'

Then, says Henry, we should go to Turbo. He has a friend who has a boat that takes rice and concrete to Turbo, he can get us a lift with him.

Victor gives me a look. Even he knows how the guidebook would feel about getting a lift on a cargo boat to Turbo because some stranger you met on the street knows the owner. You might as well hand over your cheques, your passport and your camera now and leave out the middle men.

'We'll think about it,' says Victor.

'What about Mompós?' asks Henry. 'Mompós is very nice.'

Mompós catches my interest. 'Is it nicer than Quibdo?'

Henry nods. 'Much nicer.' Surprisingly enough, Henry has a friend who drives a *colectivo* to Marangue. If you want to go to Mompós, you have first to go to Marangue. Henry's friend leaves at 8.30 in the morning from la Calle Media Luna. 'I'll meet you at your hotel at eight and take you to him,' offers Henry.

I wait for Victor to politely refuse. He politely accepts, and makes a face at me. 'What the hell?' he wants to know.

*

What the hell, indeed. I am restless all night long in our blue room with our basketball boots hanging from a nail on the wall to discourage scorpions and poisonous spiders from using them as crash pads, thinking of Henry and his many friends. Their faces appear in the shadows, rough men descended from rapists and pillagers and guys who didn't mind a little human sacrifice from time to time. Men who scrape together a living any way they can. Including kidnapping gullible tourists in stolen vans and dumping their bodies in the Magdalena. The faces in the shadows laugh grimly.

I'm still worried in the morning, but Victor's more worried about our luggage. We have too much. He packs his backpack twice, sighing heavily and mumbling to himself, wondering why we brought such a large towel and six pairs of socks.

'But what do you think?' I insist. Do you think there'll be other people in this *colectivo*? Do you think it's really going to Marangue? Do you think they haven't been sitting up all night deciding where to jump us? Do you think we should take the bus?

'I think we're going to have to get rid of some of this stuff,' says Victor. 'We don't need all this gear.' He kicks the tent. 'We have to be realistic,' he says. 'How much camping are we really going to do?'

'Let's be realistic about this ride to Marangue first,' I counter. 'Do you really think we can trust Henry?'

'I don't think you can trust anyone.' He picks up the tent and starts strapping it to his pack. 'Why don't we just wait till we meet this guy and then if you still have a bad feeling about it, we won't go.'

'We won't?'

'You're the one who gets raped,' says Victor. 'The decision's up to you.'

At 7.45 we lug our bags downstairs to wait for Henry. The street is already packed with traffic and vendors, the air grey with fumes.

'I wouldn't mind a coffee right now,' says Victor.

I sit down on my pack. 'Me neither.' But we can't. We can't because of the homeopathic medicine. Coffee is top of the Never Take With list.

At eight o'clock, having thoroughly discussed our bowel movements for the past two days and found them satisfactory, we decide to risk a *lulu* juice and a *mayaguana* made with tap water and served in glasses probably washed in the river.

'What the hell,' says Victor. 'We have to start building up our immunity.'

At 8.15, when there is still no sign of Henry, we start up Media Luna on our own to search for the *colectivo* going to Marangue.

'I can't believe, after all that, that he doesn't even bother to turn up,' I complain as we trudge up the block.

'I should've thought you'd be relieved,' says Victor.

But I'm not relieved, I'm annoyed. Now that he hasn't shown, it's clear his intentions were benign after all. He probably didn't want to rob us, he just wanted a tip.

At 8.30, having found no *colectivo* loading up for Marangue, we reach the road that leads to the bus terminal.

'We might as well just keep going,' says Victor.

I shift my pack so that some other part of my back will ache for awhile. Such is the nature of human beings that I'm not annoyed any more. Now that I know there's no chance we'll be kidnapped by desperados and left to die in the vibrant green countryside, I'm disappointed.

'We should have taken that lift to Turbo,' I say to Victor.

Victor says, 'I know.'

13

ROLLING ON THE RIVER

It isn't that easy to get to Mompós. First you take a bus to Marangue, and from there you take a launch, a *chulupa*, downriver, where, if you're lucky and quick, you get a jeep.

We weren't quick, but we were lucky, and managed to get on the second jeep. I'm sitting at the back with a large packet wrapped in newspaper on my knees. Victor is up on the roof. To my right are two girls in bright make-up with a considerable amount of shopping and a tyre; to my left a small woman all in black with a birdcage on her lap and two large plants squeezed between her legs who was on the *chulupa* from Marangue with us. The packet I'm holding belongs to her. There was nowhere else to put it. Four large men are jammed into the seat across from us, and there are two more up front with the driver. It is impossible to move even half an inch without causing everyone else to move, but despite this we all bounce out of our seats each time we hit a rut. The way to Mompós – empty except for the occasional makeshift house with a chicken in the doorway or someone leading a burdened horse – is nothing but ruts.

The man opposite me is reading a newspaper; the girl beside me starts to sing.

EXTRA! says the headline of the paper. MUERTO DE UNA LEYENDA . . . LOS ULTIMAS HORAS DE PABLO ESCOBAR. The girl is singing a song about love.

The murder of Escobar was all that there was on the news on the bus; tours of his house, views of the death room, scenes of weeping women and angry men, troops guarding the casket and the streets of

Medellín, a dark woman in glasses reading Pablo's horoscope – he should have known. I squint through the dust that fills the jeep to read about the final hours of a legend.

'I love you, I love you, that's all that I know,' sings the girl.

Difficult as it is to read when your head is constantly hitting the ceiling, from what I can gather, Good, in the interesting form of the Colombian government, has triumphed over Bad, in the less interesting form of a powerful drug lord. But there is also the sense that something has been lost.

A small child walking a pig on a rope stops to wave to the jeep. The girl who is singing waves back. 'Why don't you love me, too?'

You see what a good job we're doing? say the satisfied faces of the officials. You see how serious we are about law and order? About conquering crime? – much as they must have said in 1989 when they killed Gacha. But the tear-stained faces of the pilgrims who have come to see the last few hours of Pablo Escobar are mourning a hero. Not a hero quite in the mould of Che, perhaps – like politicians, drug dealers are seldom overburdened with impossible ideals – but still a carrier of dreams. Dreams that you can live outside the system, that you can break the rules and sometimes win. Dreams of escape.

'Why don't you love me? Why don't you love me? When I care so much about you.'

The driver looks over his shoulder at me as we pass a few dilapidated buildings and a statue of the Virgin, flowers strewn around her feet. 'Mompós,' he says.

This isn't quite the step back in time described in the guidebook. It doesn't even look as nice as Henry made it sound. A straggle of shabby houses, chickens in the yards, pigs in the bushes, dogs in the dust. Given that this is not the most accessible town on the continent, why would Bolivar come here? Why would we?

It's not until we get closer to the centre that the answer becomes clear. We're in a colonial outpost, blocks of pastel houses, tree-lined squares, mission-bell churches and bats weaving like phantoms in the sultry dusk. We might be in Macondo, place of possibilities and doom. There's where the gypsies brought their tricks and trinkets, there's the courtyard where Aureliano Buendía stood before the firing squad, there's the tree where the chained José Segundo talked with Melquíades's ghost. We come to a stop in the plaza near the river. And here's where the men from the banana company disembarked, greed sounding like progress on their smiling lips.

Victor, leaves in his hair and generously dusted with dirt, jumps down from the roof, grinning like a courier who's just gone four London miles without once stopping for a light.

'What a ride,' he says. 'Wasn't that great?'

It isn't any easier getting out of Mompós than it is getting in. Though the hour is still too early for the sun, the riverside dock is crowded. The *dueño* of our *residencia* warned that if we wanted a seat on the 6 am *chulupa* to El Banco we'd better get there early, and he was right. Besides all the people waiting for the boat with their boxes and bags around them and their tickets in their hands, there are at least a dozen men just hanging around, buying bread and *tinto* from barefoot children and making each other laugh.

In the fading dark you can't tell that the Magdalena is the colour of yesterday's coffee. Wide and swaying gracefully through the jungle, it looks as though it must be deep, dark blue. A solitary heron stands at the opposite shore, still and luminous as a soap carving.

'That can't be the *chulupa* to Banco,' says Victor. 'It's too small.'

I've been squinting at the plastic sacks of rubbish dumped by the kerb, trying to determine if they're really moving or not, but now, as dawn's bloody fingers tear at the sky over Mompós, I see that they are moving – and why. 'Good grief,' I say, 'there are turkeys in those bags.'

Victor isn't listening. 'Even if you could get everyone and their luggage on it,' he's saying, 'where would they fit all the bikes?'

I look over. Several metres away a brightly painted *chulupa* bobs gently on the water. The *chulupa* in question is no larger than the launch that took us from Marangue: half a dozen narrow benches, a space at the back for the man in charge of the motor, a seat up front for the driver and two passengers. Where would the turkeys go? 'You're right,' I say. 'That can't be the boat. It's much too small.'

But more people than you'd think can fit on one thin wooden bench; more bikes and baggage can be lashed to the roof of an aged *chulupa*.

The driver and the motorman hand out lifejackets, a safety precaution I hadn't expected. Up at the front, jammed in between three other men and the driver, Victor nonchalantly waves the offer of a jacket away, but I glance nervously at the other passengers. These people shower with their mouths open. They wash in the river. They drink the water and eat unpeeled fruit. They've probably never seen a malaria pill in their lives. How dangerous is the river to make them even think about lifejackets? How many cadavers must be caught in the weeds at the bottom of the Magdalena if they actually hand them out?

The woman beside me passes me the last jacket. There aren't enough to go round, a slightly cheering detail. There can't be that many corpses down below if there aren't enough to go around. I hold it on my lap, contemplatively. Though it is yellow, it isn't the compact, inflatable jacket available on planes for falling into the sea. It's large and bulky. Wearing it, I decide, would be like wearing a hooped skirt on a London bus. I sit on it instead. It's uncomfortable, but not as uncomfortable as the bench.

The *chulupa* to El Banco is the local. The thirty or so kilometres take nearly three hours, not just because the shallow, twisting river is mined with surface eddies, submerged rocks, plants and debris, but because we stop at every village along its banks. Just when you think there is no one for miles, the boat will cut to one side, slowing down, and an old white church, a saintly statue and an official name sign will suddenly appear in the seamless vegetation. There's always a gathering at the quay, one or two people meeting someone or hoping – usually futilely – to get on; men and boys who have nothing else to do standing around, waiting for a chance to help pull the launch in and find out if anything's happening somewhere else.

Aside from the children, and, every so often, one of the turkeys, most of our fellow passengers are quiet on the journey, their eyes gazing straight ahead. No one points out anything on this trip. The driver, mercifully, is absorbed in avoiding destruction and the motorman in keeping the blades of the outboard from becoming choked with weeds. No one talks about Quesada searching for El Dorado behind the banks of the Magdalena. No one explains the mosque just visible through the thick vegetation. No one comments on the statue-like herons or the shimmering lizards, lazy in the sun. No one indicates the women washing their clothes in the river, the boys drawing water in buckets, the fishermen in their dugout canoes, saying, 'Here people carry on the way of life of their ancestors. You can take a picture if you want.' Nor does anyone mention the men whose flesh and dreams were eaten by the muddy Magdalena, who found in this jungle lonely death rather than a city of gold, looking at the light breaking through the canopy but seeing themselves talking to their brother in the kitchen back home. Blue in the distance, the mountain range rises higher than Babel towards heaven, its peaks caught with clouds.

At El Banco we have a fifteen-minute wait for the *chulupa* that will take us to Barranca. Victor goes for cold drinks while I buy the tickets and hold a place for us, sitting on our bags on the dock, reading up on our destination.

Victor comes back with two warm sodas, a cigarette and a cassette he bought from some kid on the street.

'What do you think?' He hands me the tape.

Los Betos, two chubby men in black and white striped jackets, black and white striped shirts, and, as far as I can tell, black and white striped ties, smile back at me over glasses of either urine or champagne.

But I have a question, too. 'Did you know the book says we should ask about conditions at Barranca before stopping because of recent violence?'

Victor sits down beside me. 'That was last year,' he says.

'*Ay, Dios mío!*' cries Nieves. She clutches my knee with one hand and crosses herself with the other as we tilt sharply and more of the Magdalena pours into the boat. 'Oh, my God, please let us live.' The child on her lap continues eating his orange.

The woman on Victor's left, a seasoned *chulupa* traveller, takes a towel from her bag and dries herself off.

We snake around more floating branches in a spray of water. Nieves's hand tightens on my knee. 'It's all right,' I assure her. I point to the back of the man at the wheel. 'He's good,' I say. And he is good. He drives like Victor.

Though she has never ridden behind Victor on a Honda steaming down a mountain, this doesn't console her. '*Madre de Dios!*' she cries as we cut right around a paddle boat carrying cargo, and blesses herself again.

Too close to the cargo boat, we get caught in her current. The right side of the boat, the side Nieves and I are on, suddenly smashes into the water. Everyone but Victor and I scream. I don't scream because I'm too surprised, and too distracted by what amounts to the arrival of Nieves and her son on my lap.

'Christ!' says Victor, unable to stop grinning. 'That was close!'

We recover and take off again. Things settle down. Victor passes our peanuts along the row and Nieves passes her fruit. The children fall asleep.

Time is in no hurry here. A pair of small birds, red as berries against the vibrating green of the land and the unending blue sky, follows the *chulupa* past a village of thatched huts, its dirt road strung with tinsel and its bushes splotched with flowers, and a young girl riding her bicycle home. Time is in no hurry here, and has no face. It might be yesterday, it might be tomorrow, it might be thousands of yesterdays ago. I watch white birds with black-banded tails glide above us, necks in so that they look as though they're flying backwards, while Nieves dozes with her head on her boy and Victor explains to the woman beside him that in England we celebrate Christmas, too.

We stop for petrol, a tricky affair involving a rubber tube and a bucket. The man selling *arepas* sits on the pier watching while he smokes.

It's late when we finally reach a large town. *Dios mío*, we're back in Texas. The same black and yellow oil pumps, the same high towers with the same orange flames, the same black smoke crowding out the clouds.

'Barranca?' Victor asks his neighbour. '*Es Barranca?*'

'*Sí*,' she says. She puts her towel back in her bag.

Another *chulupa* pulls out from the small landing, passing us as we pull in.

'This can't be it,' I say to Victor. 'There's nothing here.' Just two flimsy huts and a handful of young men in camouflage fatigues.

'*Sí*,' says Nieves. '*Es Barranca.*' We bump into the pier and she squeezes my hand. '*Gracias a Dios.*'

A soldier with a large silver crucifix around his neck peers in through the front of the boat, his eyes moving backwards through the passengers until they come to us. Victor smiles. He doesn't smile back.

Without a word being spoken, the rest of the passengers start to get off the *chulupa*, leaving their bags and their children behind.

'Don't move until they tell us to,' says Victor.

With none of the formality and politeness cited by the handbook as typical of Latin Americans, a second soldier crouches down at the front of the boat and tells us to move.

We move.

The men are standing in a group to one side of the soldier sitting at the small wooden table, the women in a group behind it. No one is talking. The women look bored in the way that women do when their children ask for just one more minute of play. The men look at the river. We don't join either group, but stop together near the table. It has never actually occurred to me before, but if there is anything more frightening than men with guns, it is boys with guns.

A combat-ready sixteen-year-old shifts his rifle and holds his hand out to us. '*Documentos*,' he says.

My documents are in my body belt, which is under my shirt and my jeans. Victor has no trouble pulling out his passport, but it takes a certain amount of agility as well as time for me to extract mine. The men have stopped staring at the river now.

Another soldier is going through Roy's bag. He pulls out the backgammon set.

'*Es un juego*,' says Victor.

The soldier shakes it, opens it, closes it, and puts it down. He lifts out a small pink and blue bag covered with silver stars and moons and tied with a lavender ribbon, and holds it up so that everyone else can see it, too. The women no longer seem that bored.

'*Qué es?*' he demands of Victor.

Victor's face wears exactly the right expression of respect and solemnity necessary when dealing with children who can put you in jail and forget that there's a key. 'Homeopathic medicine,' he says. 'For malaria.'

The others start back to the boat, anxious to reach the public dock a short distance further down.

From the roof of the *chulupa* the soldier wearing the crucifix shouts out, 'Which are your bags?'

My instincts honed by weeks on the road, I immediately know that he's talking to us.

'The green ones!' I shout back.

'No, not that,' yells Victor. 'The two the same.'

The two the same are at the bottom of the heap. He pulls at the rope, pokes at the bags, then climbs back to land.

The first soldier, having glanced through them the wrong way round, hands back the passports. 'All right,' he says. 'You can go.'

We're the last ones back on the boat. Everyone is sympathetic. '*Es siempre así*,' they assure us. '*Es normal*.'

I'm so relieved not to have my bag opened and my dirty clothes scattered over the shore that it isn't until later that I realise that this means it will happen again.

14

STOP MAKING SENSE

It's the landscape from a primal dream, deep mountains dense with jungle rising blue and jagged through the clouds. We have nothing to do most of the time but look out of the window of the bus and lose ourselves in it as the grey streets and houses of home fade into memories and we no longer bother to keep track of the days.

As any creature hurtling through space all on its lonesome in a malignly indifferent universe where it can never be sure what will happen next might, we need things to make sense. We explain the things we can never know nor imagine – creation, for example, death for another, life itself – and make reasons for the things we never mean to change – war, for example, poverty for another, duplicity and greed. As long as logic and reason can interpret we are happy enough to meet each day, believing that there are rules to be followed, things we can do to protect and secure us, a way we have to be.

The present makes sense for most of us because we think we know what we're doing. Our eyes on the future if we're young, on the past if we're not, we keep busy and wait to be rewarded for doing as we're told, filling our diaries, making our schedules, ticking off the days with a felt tip pen, too busy in the present to ever stop and think.

Unless you step out of your life. If you step from your life, you can see that the present is all that you have – this moment, this day, this week, this now – and that you haven't a clue what's going on. Out of your life, there are no more assumptions, no more certainties, you can't even read the bloody rules. You don't know where you are, you don't know what you're doing, you no longer know what to expect. You don't get up at eight every morning, you don't have a breakfast of toast and jam, you don't start work at 9.30 or eat lunch at noon. Fridays aren't for shopping, Saturdays for chores, Sundays for taking a walk on the heath. You're too busy worrying about the next ten minutes to give any thought to the future or the past. If anything can happen, then nothing makes sense.

Yours might be the first eyes ever to see them. Older than the genes locked in your cells, the Andes rise towards heaven, the sky blankly blue around them, deep and dense and quivering green in the hard, high sun. Except for the occasional flash of a wing, everything is still. Still and hazy and out of focus, peering through clouds. The mountains look untouched, but you know they're full of secrets. You try to read them like a deck of cards. What lies hidden in those mountains? What sleeps in that darkness? What waits in those depths? You imagine a tribe still dreaming in the jungle, lost to the world of glass and plastic and cellular phones. Imagine cities made forgotten and invisible by time. Picture the disciples of Che, hunkered in the undergrowth on ancient stones, talking about the future as they count their ammunition. And then, far off, you see a movement in the leaves. Something white or palest beige glints between the long, broad fronds. Slowly, like an image materialising on a developing print, a figure emerges from the forest. From his bearing you can tell that he is a strong, quiet man, a man who knows who he is, where he is and why he's there. He walks along the thin dirt trail that snakes steeply down the slope without effort or fear. The man stops in a clearing, raising his hand to his eyes as he searches the distance. Is this the leader of a prehistoric tribe, the last son of a city once as great as Tenochtitlan, the force that will at last bring Texaco to its knees? Sweet female voices start to sing softly. Although you can't see the singers, you somehow know that their lips are glistening red, their eyes dark with promises, their skin dusky and smooth. You know that they're smiling and that there are flowers in their hair. A laden mule comes up behind the man. The voices grow louder. Coffee of Colombia, they sing. Coffee of Co-lom-bi-a. Now it's clear who the man is. It's Juan Valdes, the man from the coffee commercials.

I wake up as we pass a family eating dinner at a table outside their wooden shack, the radio on, the boy straddling his chair, a red

baseball cap worn backwards on his head. The shack has been decorated for Christmas with a string of tinsel and a dead branch,
decorated with bows made out of old plastic bags, stuck in the dirt
by the door. I stare out of the window of the bus, thinking about the
Chibcha, revolution and the lack of coffee bars in Colombia as we
twist through the Andes.

Victor's thinking about San Gil, where the handbook says there's
a good vegetarian restaurant. 'I think I'll order two meals tonight,' he
says conversationally. 'Make up for Barranca.'

He gives me a sideways look. 'We both could use some bunging
up.'

It took us two hours of walking deeper and deeper into the streets
of few lights and many bars filled with men who looked like the guys
who stand at the back of the crowd in cowboy movies and shout out,
'That's right, lynch 'em!' to discover why the handbook failed to recommend any restaurant in Barranca. In Barranca, there are billiard
parlours every block or so, and soldiers on almost every corner, but
there aren't any restaurants. Not ones that serve anything not made
with meat, anyway.

I pull out the zip-loc bag of peanuts and an orange – our only
food for the past two days – and hand the nuts to Victor. 'It'd take
more than a plate of steamed vegetables to make up for Barranca.'
Except for the taxi cabs, their aerials festively wrapped with lights
and tinsel and plastic bells, the hysterical laughter of the girls in the
market when Victor bought a red towelling elastic band for his ponytail, the pigeons in the roof, and a slightly seedy sense of danger, the
charms of Barranca were pretty thin on the ground. A couple of
weeks in Camelot would still come short of making up for it.

'That's what I said,' says Victor. 'Two plates of steamed vegetables.
And hot rice.'

Hot rice . . . hot water . . . hot anything . . . In the hotels we frequent there is only one tap, and in the restaurants there isn't a menu,
there's just a meal, and that meal is cooked just the once, early in the
day, and left to meet the temperature of the room. If you want hot
rice you'd better be there when the pot comes off the stove. I peel the
orange and pass Victor half.

'Jesus,' he says, pointing out of the window. 'Eight at one go. It
must have been a van.'

There are eight wooden crosses, painted white, stuck into the
earth at the edge of the cliff. 'If it was a van, that means twenty
people must have lived,' I say.

The mountain road is marked with boulders painted with political slogans and ads for chicken stock, and with crosses like these, some dated and named, 1969 . . . 1972 . . . 1977 . . . 1984 . . . 1987 . . . 1989 . . . Hiuelgos . . . Fernandez . . . Guzman . . . Boliche . . . the spot where Jaime Mendoza bought the farm. I stare down into the valley far below. A goldfish would have no trouble imagining the plummet down these dense green mountains through trees hung with fruit like Christmas ornaments and flowers more vivid than the dyed daisies of the Korean shops on Seventh Avenue – or how easy it would be to take it.

My doctor's suggestion that the bus drivers of South America, as well as not getting enough sleep and having a tendency to drink on the job, all drive as though the Terminator is in pursuit and gaining, is not borne out by the bus drivers of Colombia. They are captains of their ships, concentrated, sober, taking the steep and narrow roads with caution and skill, navigating the ruts and rubble with sureness and care when there aren't any roads, which is most of the time. It isn't roads that the government spends its money on. If the guerrillas are up in the mountains as everyone says, then it's probably because they can't get down.

I doze again, waking as the bus slows to a stop between red hills. I look out of the window at what the government does spend its money on. In Barranca we saw a building with the earnest face of the young Guevara in his beatific phase painted on it in black, and another urging the youth of Colombia to rise up in revolt against their oppressors, but the evidence suggests that most of the youth of Colombia is too busy milling around the towns and countryside dressed in combat fatigues, heavily armed with the guns of their oppressors, to worry about the revolution.

'Jesus,' I say. 'They're in warpaint.' At least I now have no regrets about missing Vietnam.

Victor closes the Quechua phrasebook he's been studying and leans over my shoulder. One of the faces smeared with the colours of a swamp looks back at him impassively.

'Thank God,' he says. 'At least we can get out in the air for a few minutes.'

Though all the windows are now open, the smell of infantile diarrhoea from the baby a couple of seats ahead of us still permeates the bus.

'Maybe we won't have to get out this time,' I hope out loud. It's all right for Victor. There's camaraderie between the men. They talk low and make little jokes. One pulled up his T-shirt to show Victor the silver ring and silver heart pierced through his nipple. The brotherhood of self-mutilation. But the women, who have changed the nappies of boys like these soldiers, and cooked their meals, and cleaned their scraped knees, close their own ranks by keeping their silence. I'm tired, I'm thirsty and I'm hungry, and I don't feel like standing by the side of the road while some kid with a rifle pokes through my things.

A soldier appears at the front of the bus and formally asks the passengers to step outside. He's young, still green and stupid, but he performs his task like a professional, like a man, like the soldiers from a thousand films. He points at us to make sure we understood. We don't move at first. You don't want to appear too eager. The bloke next to Victor taps his shoulder. 'You have to get off, too,' he says. 'Everyone.'

We're two of the last out. The men have already been shunted to one side of the soldier sitting at the table under the tree and the women stand in a weary circle on the other. The boy at the makeshift desk checking documents and the ones searching each man as he leans against the bus with spread legs and open arms are all performing their jobs like professionals, too. They've all seen the same movies. They, like most of us, don't so much become a thing – a soldier, a doctor, a bank clerk, a parent, a partner, an insurance salesman – as act the part. We learn what's expected by watching others; like learning the words of a song in a language we don't understand.

One of the soldiers waves his rifle in front of Victor as though he's John Wayne or Harrison Ford.

Victor hands me Roy's bag. 'Take a picture this time,' he orders.

Something like cardiac arrest seizes me. Although I agreed to wear the camera around my neck for easy access, I did it so as not to miss any scenic shots of what it's like to be a quarter of an inch from the rim of a precipice in an overloaded bus, not to document the death of my travelling companion at the hands of a fascist military.

'Are you nuts?' I hiss. 'I'm not taking a picture. I—'

But he's already striding towards the soldier, who is motioning him on with the barrel of his rifle.

Victor, of course, wouldn't hesitate to use the camera. He lets no one cut in front of him in ticket queues, no one shove him aside when everyone is trying to board at once, no one gazump him at checkouts. Unlike some of us. Victor's legs are spread, his hands flat against the side of the bus. I glance down at the camera. All I have to do is push the button. For God's sake, given the known nervousness of gringos when hauled from their seats at gunpoint, even the Colombian security force would believe it was an accident. What's the worst they would really do? Take the film? Smash the camera? How do you say it wasn't my fault, it went off accidentally, in Spanish?

The woman with the baby comes flying down the steps, the two of them covered in vomit, one of them crying and the other close to tears. When I look back at Victor, he's at the back of the line of men waiting to show their documents. A man in a red shirt is laying a silver revolver in front of the boy at the table. The boy gives it a quick, uncurious look and hands it back.

The wailing infant makes the soldiers nervous – or convinces them that we're not as dangerous as we look. When the one checking inside emerges, they send the women back on board after only a glance into one or two pocketbooks.

I give the woman with the baby my last towelette saved from the plane, and slip the camera from around my neck as I walk back to my seat. It's not too late to prove that I am a person of courage and character, the sort of person given posthumous awards for her photographs of war-torn El Salvador. Victor is still waiting his turn.

Not quite sitting down, I stare through the window across the aisle, watching Victor, a flamingo among the penguins, move up in the queue. The women don't say anything as they settle again, but the men returning to their seats are talking and exchanging jokes.

Sit down, I urge them silently. For God's sake, get out of my way. Victor steps up to the makeshift desk. Clutching the camera, I stand up. Coolly. Casually. Stretching my legs. Despite the racket being made by my heart, no one looks at me. I push the button as Victor leans forward to point his passport number out to the soldier. Exhausted by my bravery, I collapse back into my seat. I'm pretty pleased. Let someone try jumping the bank queue on me again. But I'm pleased only for the half a second it takes the camera to realise that it's at the end of the reel. The sound of the automatic rewind thunders through the bus. Everyone is looking at me now.

Maybe it's Victor who should have the camera.

We're getting used to personal questions. Where do you come from? What's the weather like? How much did the trip cost? How long did you save for it? What do you do? How much do you make? Are you

married? Do you have children? Why aren't you married? Why don't
you have children? What do you eat if you don't eat meat?

But Carlos José isn't asking us questions. He's giving us a lecture
on the Tao while his assistant, a girl wearing a white lab coat like
Carlos José's, sits on the stairs at the back of the tiny shop because
there is nowhere else to sit. She looks as though she's probably heard
this lecture before.

Outside there's a party going on. San Gil is covered with a haze of
smoke from a constant if random explosion of fireworks, its streets
decked with streamers and white and blue flags, its doorways lit by
tiny candles, sparklers glimmering like stars. But in here it is quiet
and dark. We came in here because the sign outside says Vegetarian
Food – Homeopath. The vegetarian food is six dry-looking biscuits
in a case at the front with the ginseng and the books on how to suc-
ceed in life and muscle-building. The homeopath is Carlos José.
Carlos José is a young man, bright and enthusiastic, dedicated to his
profession and true to his convictions. There is no certainty, no tran-
scendent truth, nothing worth knowing that can be known with the
mind. Carlos José must feel a little lonely here among the smoke,
lights, certainty and truth of the Catholic world.

'Ask if he's got any *chichonella*,' said Victor when we realised there
really was no food to be had.

But there hasn't been a chance.

I feel that I've grasped quite a bit of what Carlos José has to say
about change, which is the nature of the universe; about the Tao,
which cannot be named or understood by reason; about the nega-
tivity of eating meat and the interconnectedness of all things, but
suddenly he jumps streams.

'There is only one way for a man and woman to have a truly
loving and fulfilling relationship,' I think he says. 'And so there must
be only one partner.'

I move half a step closer to Victor. 'What are we talking about
now?' I whisper.

'Stone me,' says Victor, 'but I think it's the Taoist Way of Sex.'

Carlos José starts explaining the role of the penis in the making of
love. It is the Taoist Way of Sex. I glance at the assistant as Carlos
José describes the importance of ejaculatory control. She looks more
bored than she was when he was discussing cosmic flow. It obviously
isn't as interesting as you might think.

'One man and one woman,' says Carlos José. 'That's the only true
way to find sexual fulfilment.'

At least I think it's the only way to find sexual fulfilment. It may be sexual something else. I'm filling in the gaps as best I can.

Behind Carlos José, over the cupboard of medicines, is an over-sized wedding portrait of him and his bride. 'A man who sleeps with many women debilitates himself,' I think he goes on. 'Instead of using his orgasmic energy he throws it away.'

The assistant slips a sweet from her jacket pocket and puts it in her mouth.

We both nod whenever Carlos José pauses for air.

Victor moves half a step closer to me. 'Do you understand what he's saying?' he asks, smiling as though he's saying something else.

'Bits,' I admit. *Mujer* and *hombre* I have no trouble with. *Sexual* I understand. I feel pretty confident about my guess on what *miembro* means, but the finer points of the lesson are lost on me.

'Four, five hours of the most beautiful sex,' Carlos José is saying. 'That's what happens when you learn not to come.'

Four or five hours sounds a little excessive to some of us. I glance up at the wedding photograph, wondering how many shopping lists have been compiled while Carlos practises penis control. I glance at the assistant again. She thinks it sounds a little excessive, too.

Carlos José returns to the ill effects of promiscuously squandering your sex. Of destroying your true spirit. Of not living in harmony with the rest of the universe. Of thinking about your life as some-thing personal and particular to you and not simply as another manifestation of the cosmic whole. Of failing ever to see what your life really means.

I look over at Victor to see if he thinks there is anything odd in our being in a small Colombian town on the feast night of the Virgin taking a course in Tao for beginners, but Victor is asking Carlos José a question. 'What about the mother?' he says, and though I'm not sure if he's talking about Mother Earth or the female role in Taoist philosophy and ejaculation management, I'm pretty impressed. He's understanding more than I am.

'Never heard of it,' says Carlos José, quicker to understand that Victor means not mother the earth or mother the mother but mother the restaurant. 'You should always prepare your food yourself,' he tells Victor solemnly. 'That way you know that it's pure.'

Intrepid travellers, discouraged by nothing, we tread on, attracting considerable attention as we navigate the crowds. 'In this country,' the man selling fried plantain and potato chips shouts out to us, 'only a bull wears a ring in his nose.' The brightish lights of the town centre begin to thin out, the paved road dwindles. We hover indecisively while half a dozen kids race by us, screaming as the firecrackers they've just thrown explode in the road.

'Maybe we should go back,' I suggest. Being shot through the heart by guerrillas is one thing. My agent and my editor, already disappointed that no one gunned us down in Mississippi, would be thrilled if we were wounded by the enemies of capitalist oppression. What a story. Being blinded by a badly aimed firecracker would thrill them less. 'It must be the other way.'

'Is this your unerring sense of direction speaking?' Victor points into the darkness straight ahead. 'It might be up there,' he says. 'Let's keep going.'

We keep going until we reach the last lit-up shop.

'We might as well get some stuff for the morning,' says Victor, not looking at me as he adds, 'then we'll go back.'

We step out of the carnival night where the feast day of the young Jewish girl who gave birth to God in a stinking stable in Bethlehem 2,000 years ago is being celebrated by the descendents of adventurers and sun-worshippers and into suburban America in the sixties where every garage has a car and war is on the news. *The Wonder Years* is on the television. 'I get by with a little help from my friends,' sings Joe Cocker through the chatter and laughter of the street outside as Kevin and Paul fool around for the camera.

Victor steps up to the counter, but I stand by the display of Pringle's potato chips and Oreos made in Venezuela, my eyes fixed on the neat white house and the mown green lawn, suddenly understanding that the further you get from what you know the easier it is to tell what you know, which is precious little; suddenly yearning for home.

The teenage girl left in charge of the store has straight dark hair and thick black glasses held together with sellotape. She doesn't look as though she wants to be here any more than I do, but since she is here, she, like I, would rather be watching the show. Half hidden behind her glasses and her fringe, she eyes Victor not curiously as most of the girls unaccustomed to white men with nose rings and hair to their waists do, giggling nervously and trying not to blush, but warily, terrified that he might actually speak.

He speaks. 'Do you have apples?'

For at least half a second, she doesn't move, her expression blank as fresh snow. Then she reaches into a box by the register and holds up a banana.

Victor gives me a nudge. 'Should we get bananas?'

Kevin's mother is cooking something that looks like macaroni cheese in her bright and cheery kitchen. She is confident and content as she grates the cheese and drains the noodles and tests the sauce for pepper and salt. She is busy in her present, safe in her role, secure in her routines. If she is aware of the uncertainty around her that she has no idea what will happen in the next two seconds, never mind the next twenty years, that her life has no more or less meaning than the life of a fruit fly, it doesn't show.

I look over at Victor. 'They don't have apples?'

'Why are you asking me?' asks Victor.

'You don't have apples?' I ask the girl.

She picks up another banana. 'Banana,' she tells me.

'I know it's a banana,' I say. 'Don't you have apples?'

She looks from me back to the fruit in her hand. 'You don't want any bananas?'

Victor steps in. 'We'll take them both,' he says, sure of that much. 'Two bananas.'

I point into the cold case. 'And water.'

Now she really looks wary, holding the two bananas in her hands as though she can't imagine what she's supposed to do with them. '*Qué?*'

'Water,' says Victor. 'Four bags of water.'

She puts down the bananas. 'Water?' she asks. 'You want bananas *and* water?'

Kevin's mom is happy, you can tell by the way she stirs the casserole. This is the life she expected to have. She knows what to do. Take care of her home, take care of her husband, take care of her children. It all makes sense. It's the life every girl I knew expected to have. Two kids and a dog.

'Four waters,' says Victor. He points to the slices of cake on the counter. 'How much for one?' he wants to know.

The girl freezes in the act of taking a bag of water from the shelf of the cold case. 'It's cake,' she tells him.

'How much?'

She blinks behind her glasses. 'You don't want the water?'

'Four waters,' says Victor. 'And four slices of cake.'

Kevin's mother doesn't think that thirty or forty years from now she may be sitting by a window in a nursing home, watching other people's visitors getting back into their cars to go home for macaroni cheese and war on the news, wondering what happened to her life, thinking of all the things she never did and won't do now.

The girl puts one slice of cake in a small plastic bag.

'Four,' says Victor. 'Four slices of cake.'

She can't fit four slices in the small plastic bag.

Victor, patient until now, takes several sheets of paper from the stack beside the box of cake and starts to wrap it for her. He holds up one piece. 'What do you call this?'

She looks at her watch. 'A quarter past eight.'

On the way out, we ask her mother, talking in the street with two other women, if she knows where La Mama is.

She knows. 'Vegetarians,' she says. Her friends laugh. She points back the way we've come. 'Go past the church,' she directs. 'Two blocks past the church, make a right. There's a juice bar on the corner and then a pharmacy. La Mama is across from that.'

Clutching my daughter's AT&T calling card in one hand and the receiver in the other, I stare at the instructions on the telephone. This is my first attempt to phone home since we left California. According to the AT&T USA Direct ad in the guidebook, this is going to be easy. According to the ad, I can use any telephone in Colombia to make my call, but some may require a coin or debit card for dial tone. This one, from what I can gather, requires a coin. I turn to ask Victor for a 50-peso coin and smack into the man in the Batman T-shirt waiting so close behind me that he has probably identified my shampoo.

'Tell him to move back,' says Victor, handing me the money. 'He's practically eating your hair.'

'Could you give me a little room?' I ask politely. 'Por favor.'

The man stays where he is, which is pretty much where I am, and doesn't answer.

'You want to talk?' Victor asks him, jabbing a finger at the receiver. 'You want to talk to Tommi?'

The man doesn't want to talk to Tommi. He shakes his head.

I want to talk to Tommi. Now that I know that there is nothing to know except for the fact that there'll be no steamed vegetables tonight. I want her to tell me that she's watching *Cheers* and eating salsa and tortilla chips and drinking a Corona. I want Tommi to tell me how their building has been decorated in wreaths and styrofoam candy canes for the holidays. I want her to tell me what she and Jack are doing for Christmas and whether or not they've already bought their tree from the lot outside the toy store on Seventh Avenue. I want to know if she's worn the reindeer socks I gave her yet, the ones that play 'Jingle Bells'.

Still aware of the aroma of chicken and tobacco behind me, I put the coin in the slot. I have 50 pesos' worth of credit. I dial the number as directed by the ad. The busy signal bleats. I debit the 50 pesos and try again. The signal bleats. I debit the 50 pesos and try again. The man in the Batman T-shirt shuffles off and is replaced by a man in a grey suit. He's been eating pork. Out of the corner of my eye I see the nose of the man in the suit poking over my shoulder and Victor wandering off down the street as the telephone in Brooklyn finally starts to ring.

I can see Tommi, sitting on the floor in front of the TV, put down her beer and get to her feet. I see her walk the few feet to the phone, red and green tinsel twisted into its coil of wire to match the colours in her hair, and reach out her hand. The phone continues to ring. I see Tommi come racing from the bathroom with a purple towel around her, shouting at Jack, tangled in lengths of coloured lights, trying to get them to work, that he could have answered the fuckin' phone. The man behind me closes the half-inch gap between us. I see Tommi and Jack's apartment – the old Navajo rug and the overstuffed cushions on the floor, the blue neon light that says SMILE on the wall of the kitchen, the cat asleep on top of the laundry basket in the bathroom – but they're not there, where they're supposed to be. They could, of course, be sleeping or taking out the garbage. But maybe not. Maybe they're fandangoing in Prospect Park. Maybe they're hitching through the suburbs, checking out the house decorations. Maybe they're on their way to Tangiers. Nothing stays where you left it. That's the nature of Tao – and of everyday life. Not even you. But if you believe that things can stay the same, if you live like a snail in your personal present, cramming each day with things to be done, worrying about the boiling of eggs and saving of money, not thinking of things that can't be seen or touched or used or stashed away, then you lose all the rest. Lose the real present, unpredictable as a hadron; lose those sudden sharp moments of irrational joy brought on by an impossible sunset or a sliver of moon, by the way a child leans into its mother or someone whistles 'Good Night, Irene' as he walks down the street.

Victor comes back as I'm hanging up the receiver, his hands filled with something steaming in oily waxed paper. 'Come on,' he says. 'Our table's waiting.'

We sit on the stoop of La Mama, the door boarded, the window thick with dust, a single chair left inside under what looks like a photograph of a table full of vegetables, eating the *arepas con queso* Victor bought on the street.

'Jesus, this is good,' says Victor. 'I think we should get a couple more.'

Light fountains over the town, laughter weaves through the night. Someone's whistling 'Silent Night'. Kevin's mother will be doing the dishes now, getting ready to take her seat in the living room, take up her knitting while she watches TV, but Tommi is dancing around the war memorial thousands of miles in the past and the future and Victor and I are sitting in the Andes where there are ghosts in every tree. I lick Tabasco sauce from my fingers, no longer yearning for home.

'It's nice to be here, isn't it?' I say.

Victor nods. 'You mean instead of where we're supposed to be?'

15

PARADISE AND LUNCH

'"As capital of the colonial vice-royalty of New Granada,"' Victor is reading above the love song playing on the tape deck, '"headquarters for the investigations of naturalist José Celestino Mutis and site of the first astronomical observatory in South America . . ."'

'Can't be.' I tear my eyes away from the flow of bicycles, most of them ridden by boys in baseball caps, entering and leaving the city to look over his shoulder. 'What about the Mayans? They were sophisticated astronomers. They must have had an observatory.'

'Central America,' says Victor.

'The Inca?'

He pulls the book out of my view. 'Are you going to let me finish this or not?' He's not sure about the Inca.

'"The city was an early intellectual centre of the arts and scientific learning,"' he goes on. '"The nineteenth-century German scientist and natural philosopher Alexander von Humboldt called it the Athens of America."'

I return my attention to what lies outside the window of the bus. Even allowing for the lack of pollution, flyovers, billboards, plastic bags looped through the trees, heaps of rubbish and beer cans flattened along the road in Humboldt's day, comparing this to Athens strikes me as a bit of a stretch.

'So there you are,' says Victor.

So here we are.

Though Quesada never found El Dorado you have to give him credit. He did get close. As close as Bogotá.

You know at once that you're in the capital: besides the cows and horses at the side of the motorway there are advertisements for Japanese electronics companies and Miller Draught and battalions of policemen. You can see the air.

'Just remember to hang on to your bags and don't talk to anyone,' says Victor as we pull into the bus station past a plot of young trees marked with a sign that says '*Hechos No Palabras*'.

Deeds, not words.

Three – or six, or ten, depending on who told you the story – Israelis got off the bus in Bogotá and were robbed of everything they owned before the doors closed behind them. Two – or five, or seven, depending on who told you the story – Dutch got off the bus in Bogotá and were mugged at knifepoint before they reached the terminal. Sixteen Americans stepped off the bus in Bogotá and were arrested by the police – or a bunch of guys in uniforms with guns pretending to be the police, depending on who told you the story – and never seen again. Che was arrested in Bogotá.

Hanging on to our bags and not talking to anyone, and as inconspicuous as a couple of chickens strolling through a group of picnicking foxes, we search for a bus to take us near our hotel. There isn't one. I start at one end of the line of buses loading up outside the station and work my way to the end. 'Not this one,' says each driver in turn, waving behind him with the same vague gesture. 'That one.'

Side by side, still hanging on to our bags and wearing the nervously dazed expression that arriving somewhere new produces no matter how casual or jaded you try to appear, Victor and I stand among the throng of people pushing their ways on to buses, trying to decide on our next move.

'Let's just take any bus that's going towards the centre,' says Victor, 'and walk from there.'

I pull on his arm. 'Now,' I say with a certain amount of urgency. 'Let's take it now.'

Approaching from Victor's other side is a gentleman in uniform wearing the hat of the mounted police and accompanied by a German Shepherd who can tell the difference in smell between chalk and cocaine. This man is not a member of the Policia Juvenal, whose job seems to be to train young children in fluorescent pinnies in public parks for street warfare, or a boy soldier, or a traffic cop. This man is something else. Although I have no idea what the date is and have to think hard to remember where we were two days ago, the warning in the handbook comes into my mind, clear and complete: under state-of-siege legislation police may shoot and kill a suspect during any narcotics operation and it will be automatically classified as self-defence. A large number of would-be drug traffickers have been killed in this way.

And presumably a certain number of non-would-be drug traffickers as well. As a way of dealing with a complex problem, even I have to admire the effectiveness of its simplicity.

'Now what?' asks Victor.

But it's too late to bolt. The officer and the German Shepherd are standing between us. The dog is looking distinctly disinterested, as though patrolling the bus terminal isn't all the fun you would think it would be – *Dios mío*, not more dippy hippies – but the man is speaking. To me. He's asking me for my documents. How do I know if he's really a policeman, who might let us go for a reasonable bribe, or just someone pretending to be a policeman to rob us? Does it matter?

'*Qué?*'

He repeats himself. '*A dónde van?*'

Where are you going?

Confident with relief, I answer almost coherently. 'We're going to El Dorado.'

In San Gil we were kept awake most of the night by the television outside our room and the continuous conversation of the *dueño* and his card-playing friends. In Socorro we were awoken at dawn by the parrot who lived outside the kitchen and the sawmill located outside our window. In Tunja guests who were never seen in the morning arrived after midnight, friendly, happy people having a good time, glad to be welcomed by our jovial host and the local pop station that never went off until 4 am, when the baby started to cry.

But things are different at the Hotel El Dorado. At the Hotel El Dorado everything keeps us up. The dripping tap, the radios that blare all night long, the television in Reception, the artificial fir tree in the lobby that plays 'White Christmas' at irregular intervals from dawn to dawn, our room's grimy red and pink splendour still visible in the dark, the city itself. The loudly drunken argument between the man next door and a person I assume to be a friend of his that is taking place outside our door.

'How do you say "shut the fuck up" in Spanish?' asks Victor.

Victor may have been dreaming about conjugating irregular verbs, as I was, but now he is lying flat on his back, as I am, staring up at the shadows playing across the ceiling, as I am, probably waiting for a cockroach to walk across his face, as I am, too.

'I don't know,' I say. 'The dictionary doesn't extend to "fuck".'

Someone crashes into the wall in the corridor and the argument stops suddenly. Almost immediately, the radio goes on next door, Glen Campbell informing the Athens of America that he's a lineman for the county. As if in answer, the music outside, more typically Latin – guitars, a flute and a plaintive wail – grows louder. Nobody here cares about Glen's life or the problems it might cause him, the holidays are upon us and the mood in the *calle* is festive and free.

'Jesus,' says Victor. 'They're bloody dancing in the streets now.'

It definitely does sound as though the revellers not shouting at each other are dancing.

'What do you think that is?' I ask as another sound joins the pre-dawn chorus.

'Skateboarders,' answers Victor. 'They're skateboarding down Calle Fifteen.'

Several lorries rumble past, flattening the skateboarders as they race each other out of town. I pull the hood of my sleeping bag more tightly around me, still hoping to get back to my nightmares of the imperfect and present subjunctive. If you don't have to touch the sheets of the El Dorado with your body it's probably just as well not to.

Victor reaches for the travel clock. 'Jesus,' he says. 'Somebody must've killed the bloody rooster. It's nearly four and it hasn't started yet.'

Encouraged by this piece of good news, I try closing my eyes, but I can still see the geometric patterns of the curtain on the window, saved from the fifties with the Chevies and the Buicks and sent down here. Earth Wind and Fire take over from Glen.

'He's probably waiting for the noise to die down.'

We have heard travellers speak quite fondly of Bogotá. 'Oh, Bogotá,' they say. 'I stayed with a reporter friend of mine there. We went to some of the greatest bars where all the gringos hang out . . .' 'Oh, Bogotá,' they say. 'My mother's friend has this incredible apartment on the outskirts of town. You wouldn't even think you were in South America.' 'Wait till you see the parks,' they say. 'The museum, the churches, the Plaza Boliva,' as though, once seen, you will feel that you had never seen a park, a museum, a church, or a Plaza Bolivar before. 'Bogotá,' they say. 'It's a real city.'

The people who speak quite fondly of Bogotá describe a cosmo-politan metropolis of sophistication and elegance whose hotels, shops and restaurants – charging 18 per cent value-added tax and another 5 per cent for tourists – will still the longings of the most homesick traveller; whose historic sites will keep the most dogged occupied for days. The people who speak of Bogotá the Beautiful, where foreign businessmen in for a conference wear plastic name tags so they don't get lost and the people who serve them, men with good manners in immaculate suits and well-turned-out women trimmed in gold, are *muy Español* – more Spanish than the Spanish – don't tell you that you'd get around Bogotá faster if you walked on top of the buses rather than sat inside them, or that the bus drivers have all the charm of mercenaries as well as the bloodlust, or that the only way to get on or off a bus, or, indeed, across a street, is to hurl yourself quickly, no matter what the bus or the traffic is doing, and not expect anyone to stop for you. No fan of the city has ever said to us, 'Hey, man, there's a section of Bogotá's going to remind you so much of Canal Street you'll be looking for the guy who sells the crawling GI Joes.'

Hell is probably a few notches up on Bogotá. Not that Bogota is so dangerous or evil, just that it is so scuzzy and dull. You can imagine the devil arriving here with all his aluminium luggage and his new baseball cap and Ray-Bans, taking a look around and saying, 'You've got to be joking, call this a view?' He points to the rubbish being burned in the middle of the road and says, 'You dopes think this town is hot?' Someone offers to sell him drugs and he laughs. 'Cocaine? Marijuana? What, you think you guys are big time? I deal in souls!'

Neither Victor nor I like Bogotá, but despite this we are both speaking quite fondly of it at the moment. Further uptown, where the better hotels are, the buildings are strung with lights and para-chuting Santas dangle from the ceilings of offices and banks, but though down here a bit of tinsel or a plastic bell are as good as it gets we're in a festive mood.

'Now what?' asks Victor as the door of the cafeteria shuts behind us. He gestures up the weekend-empty street, settled over with black fumes like clouds. 'The city is ours.'

Bogotá may have none of the charm of Amsterdam or Barcelona, none of the excitement of New York or London (excluding drug wars and random violence) and fewer of the amenities, but it does have one thing that interests us greatly: good vegetarian food. The Cafeteria Vegetariana, though less attractively decorated than the Govinda up the block and lacking the atmospheric background music, offers such a variety of meals and in such quantity that not even its soup-kitchen atmosphere, the mice scuttling back and forth behind the serving counter, or the fact that many of the other customers – earnest non-meat-eaters who give the impression that vegetarianism is some kind of penance – look like they live in one room and that their underwear's dirty can dull our present happiness.

'Maybe we should go back to that Indian market. Get smaller bags.'

Victor touches the boots hanging over his shoulder. 'Maybe we can find someone who needs these on the way.'

At 5 am, having exhausted other topics of early-morning conversation such as the number of police cameras in London and what videos we'd like to see when we get back, we decided to jettison all excess baggage, our respectable bags that can be carried as hand luggage in places where backpackers and hippies are looked on askance included. What we can't give away or dump we're mailing back to Tommi. From now on we're travelling light. So we can go into the jungle. So we can ride a raft down the Amazon. So Victor doesn't have to complain about how much junk we've got any more.

We walk.

A crowd has gathered in the small square off Carrera Seven to watch a fire-eater torment his body while other guys try to sell them sweets and cigarettes or pick their pockets. Tonight the same crowd will be gathered round the Hare Krishnas on their evening chant, but they won't be watching with the same rapt attention.

'There are a lot of street people around here,' I point out, needlessly, as we step around several.

'They're too small,' says Victor, ignoring the shoeshine boys hopping beside him, wanting to know if he wants the boots he's wearing round his neck cleaned and whether the ring hurts his nose. 'And, anyway, half of them don't have all their feet.'

We walk on.

'At least we've found out what they do with all the rubbish,' says Victor. Just visible between the block of cars, fires burn and smoulder on the traffic islands of the avenue. 'Must save them a bomb on trucks.'

'Jesus.' I point to the other side of the street, to the man leaning against a wall with his dog. 'Even the vagrants have Rottweilers here.'

'Undercover.' Victor pulls me back as a motorcycle cop on a Suzuki 125 steams past on the pavement. 'In Bogotá the police lead by example,' says Victor.

In the Mercado Indigenista we squat between stacks of jumpers and ethnic bags and talk to Laura, whose baby sleeps beside her on a pile of rugs. Laura is an Otavalan Indian, an evangelist and a hard bargainer. Because she likes us, because we're *amigos*, she gives us a special price on the two woven bags and the one that comes from Guatemala. Victor takes this unexpected opportunity to practise his Quechua, language of the Inca. 'Good afternoon,' he says. 'How are you? Am I going the right way?' Laura's impressed, though more with the phrasebook than with Victor's fluency. She wants to know where he got it so she can learn some more English, the language of commerce. 'Teacher,' she says. 'How do you do?'

'We bought it in London,' says Victor.

'My husband and I are going to London one day,' says Laura. She takes a wallet from Guatemala just like the ones they sell in Camden out of the pocket of her long, dark skirt and removes a mint-new $100 bill. 'You see? We're already saving.'

Mint-new bills are a feature of the day. Not a block from the market there's a 5,000-peso note lying on the pavement, waiting to be found.

Rule of the Road number 15: Never pick up money from the street.

I look at Victor. Victor looks at me. We both look around. There's no one else in sight. I look at the note. Victor looks at the note. It looks real. We see no strings.

Victor makes a mock-motherly face. 'Remember the Israeli who stopped for a wallet on the ground and when he came to they'd even taken his belt,' he clucks.

I pick up the 5,000 pesos and put it away. 'That was in Peru,' I remind him.

Victor slaps my pocket. 'That means you're buying the beer.'

Just around the corner, there's a man lying on the pavement. Victor gives him the boots. 'Do you think that'll make up for all the bad karma I've got killing roaches?' he asks me.

'Not if somebody murders him for them, it won't.'

We turn another corner and come out on to a crowded street

market. We shuffle up the pavement. Sunglasses, pottery, ethnic hair
ties, Peruvian earrings, Guatemalan belts, Nepalese caps. Except for
the Indian kids wearing Santa Claus hats and selling bows and
arrows, we might be on Camden High Street or Lower Broadway on
a sunny summer afternoon.

We stop in front of a couple selling jewellery. He's black and
dreadlocked, she's white and wearing hair wraps and a gold star in
her nose.

'Look,' I say to Victor. 'These are almost the same as the earrings
I'm wearing.'

Victor, however, is already deep in conversation with the guy,
whose Spanish is as broken as ours, and doesn't hear me.

The girl shoots forward. 'You can try them on,' she says, holding
out a hand mirror. 'I make them myself.'

'They're like the ones I'm wearing,' I tell her, pulling back my hair.

'Where did you get them?' she demands. 'In Lima?'

'In London.'

'London! You two come from London?' She pushes bags of beads
and coins aside and pats the space beside her on the blanket. 'Come
on, sit down.'

Rule of the Road number 16: Don't hang out with dubious characters who might bring you to the attention of the constabulary.

I look to Victor for guidance. He's already sitting down.

'I can't believe we have the same name,' says Diana. Diana is
Colombian but she's been roaming the continent for the last seven
years. She doesn't like to stay in one place too long. She wants to
travel, to see the world. She says we'll love Peru. Not only is it
magical, it's cheap.

Diana reaches across me and taps Junior's knee. Junior is from
Brazil. He's been travelling for nearly three years. He breaks off from
showing his string of monkey teeth to Victor, who is regarding them
with something less than interest.

'Qué?'

'Don't you think it's incredible?' she asks him. 'We have the same
name.' Not waiting for his answer, she grabs my hand. 'What's your
star sign?'

'Cancer.'

She nearly throws her pliers in the air. 'Me, too!'

Diana has a friend who lives in London. She reaches into one of
her many bags and pulls out a stack of postcards tied in coloured
strings, and removes one of an old red phone box. ''Ackney,' she

reads from the back. 'Is that near you?' Diana would like to visit
England, but she isn't too sure about the weather. 'Does it really
rain all the time?' she wants to know.

I'm deep in my explanation of how the English weather has
shaped the national character when Junior and Victor, tired of arguing about endangered species in words of one syllable, suddenly get
to their feet.

'We're going for a walk,' says Junior.

I look up. There are some men who can say, 'We're going for a
walk', and you know instantly what they mean. They're going for a
walk. There are other men who when they say 'We're going for a
walk' mean they're on their way to Mauritiania and they're assuming
you'll keep their things till they return. 'I'm just going for a walk,'
says Gary Cooper, reaching for his hat and gun. 'I'll be right back,'
and you can bet your last beer that the next sound you hear is going
to be shooting and that the next time you see him he's going to be
lying down. And there are guys like Junior and Victor. Going for a
walk? Going for a walk to where?

Diana doesn't look up from trying to sell the trendy young girls in
the ripped Levis and generic Dr Marten's who have been watching
too much American television a bracelet made from loops of metal
and old coins. 'Don't be too long,' she tells him.

'You want to come?' Victor asks me.

Rule of the Road number 17: Never do drugs on the streets of
Bogotá.

'You don't like to smoke?' Diana asks me after she's made her sale
and everyone's gone.

Before I became a wild woman, the chances of my sitting on a
sidewalk in Bogotá with a hippy traveller whose hotel room cost
even less than ours were anorexically slim. I don't want to blow my
new image right away. 'Not in public places in broad daylight,' I say.
'It makes me nervous.'

She laughs. 'Me too. It's not worth it.' She gives me a look I have
seen at least two million times before. 'Men,' says Diana. She shrugs.
What can you do?

Victor says that I have to get over my shyness of speaking Spanish.
It was he who found out where to send packages to the States. It is
always he who stops people from cutting in front of us in queues. It
was he who asked the woman selling cigarettes and sweets where
she got her cardboard boxes from. It is he who usually inquires after

directions. It was he who asked the woman in the bookstore if we could have some boxes. The fact that I contributed the modifier 'empty' doesn't count. What if we're separated for some reason? What if, for example, he and Junior had never made it back from their walk? How would I have got him out of jail – or even found out where they were keeping him – if I'm too shy to speak? If I don't get over my shyness, says Victor, my Spanish is never going to improve.

'The reason my Spanish isn't improving,' I say defensively, 'is because nobody listens to what we're saying anyway.' Which is true enough. Even when I'm speaking sentences I can easily handle – How much does it cost? How much does it weigh? Do you have peanuts? – I have to repeat myself so many times that by the end my accent's so strong you'd think I was speaking Brooklyn.

'They can't listen if you don't say anything,' reasons Victor.

It's Victor I'm not saying anything to as we lug our boxes, packed but not sealed in case we need to shift things around, into the Avianca office.

There were a few touchy moments when we were making the final decisions as to what was going and what was staying that have left a little tension in our personal air. I was reluctant to part with the sleeping bags. They may not afford any real protection from tarantulas or scorpions but they do keep the sheets at a distance. Victor, for his part, is convinced that our towel is too big. 'Do we really need this big a towel?' he kept asking, waving it over my head. 'It's summer. Why do we need such a big towel?' Victor also reckons that the dictionary is a waste of space. 'What's the point of hauling it all over the place with us?' he kept asking, waving it over my head. 'The minute you look something up you forget what it said anyway.' Thirdly, Victor, personally, isn't bothered about playing backgammon in the evenings while we have a beer. 'Look at how heavy it is,' he kept saying, shaking the set over my head. 'It's made of bloody wood!'

The Avianca office, decorated for the holidays with tinsel and tiny coloured balls and cardboard Santas who don't look South American, is as busy as Grand Central Station on Christmas Eve.

There are two queues for international mail.

'You get in that one and I'll get in this one,' says Victor.

I get in that one and start praying that Victor's moves faster than mine does.

A man wearing a baseball cap and a very large gold crucifix materialises in the space between the two queues, and slides in front of

Victor. Thank God he didn't try to get in front of me, I'm too busy rehearsing what I'm going to say in flawless Spanish when it's my turn at the counter to switch into a different conversation now. *Excuse me, but we'd like to send these packages to the United States. Can you tell me, is there a weight limit? Do the boxes have to be a certain size?*

Victor taps him on the shoulder, putting on his best eat-shit grin. 'I'm waiting, too,' he says loudly and clearly.

The man gets behind him. My line moves up.

We're sending these packages to the United States. Is there a weight limit? Do they have to be a certain size?

The young woman with the Christmas corsage pinned to the lapel of her suit jacket isn't smiling at me but she is looking. 'Next!' she commands.

I pick up the box and march forward. 'We want to send these packages to the United States,' I say almost perfectly.

'*Sí.*' She nods. '*Los Estados Unidos.*'

Victor comes up beside me. 'What do they have to weigh?' I ask, still within range of a passable accent.

'No more than two kilos,' she says. Victor and I are looking at each other, but she is looking at the package in his arms. If it's less than two kilos the box is empty.

'If it's more than two kilos, you have to send it from over there,' she says. 'From the express counter.' She points down the room.

'What about the size?' I start to ask, only then realising then that I have no idea how to say size.

'*Qué?*' she asks, stopped in the act of ordering the next customer forward.

'*Dimensiones particulares,*' I say. It sounds right to me. '*Hay que tiene dimensiones particulares?*'

It doesn't sound right to her. '*Qué?*'

'*Dimensiones particulares?*' whispers Victor in a pretty good impersonation of a Spaniard with a Flatbush accent. 'Are you making that up?'

It doesn't sound right to anyone else, either. Both queues are giving me their undivided attention, wondering what I'm trying to say.

I can't believe *dimensiones particulares* is wrong. What else would it be: *sizeo correcto?*

'*Dimensiones particulares,*' I say again, enunciating every syllable.

Several people, seeing their lunch hours dwindling, sigh.

She turns to her co-worker at the next desk. 'What does she want?' she asks him.

'What do you want?' he asks me.

Victor holds up his box. 'Is this too big?' he asks. He points to my box. 'Is this too small?'

'The size doesn't matter,' says the co-worker in English roughly on a par with our Spanish. 'What matters is the weight.' He, too, gestures towards the end of the room. 'You can weigh them down there.'

We have to reweigh the smaller box three times to get it under two kilos, stuffing things into every extra millimetre of space allowed by the sleeping bags. We seal both boxes with the tape we've brought and approach the express counter. Señora Hoya, a large, confident woman who, were she English, might pass for one of Bertie Wooster's aunts, the one who makes strong men tremble, weighs the package again and then pushes her glasses back on her forehead in a way that suggests disapproval. 'What's in it?'

'Sleeping bags,' says Victor. 'Books, a tent, old clothes, a camp stove.'

'Open it.' Señora Hoya pushes a form at him. 'And fill that out.'

We fill out the form while Señora Hoya removes every item from the box. The sleeping bags, the dirty tent, the carbon-covered stove, the souvenir bottle-openers, the bag from Guatemala, our dirty clothes, *One Hundred Years of Solitude* with a hole burned in it from the Honda's exhaust. We both watch her warily, waiting for her to discover something we're not allowed to send through the post. It's just as well we're not drug smugglers – neither of us would survive the anxiety. When she's done, she puts everything back.

'Tape,' she says.

Victor hands her the tape.

'Paper,' she says.

Victor stares back at her. 'Paper?'

Not bothered by the fact that we are gringos with a grasp of the language that could kindly be called rudimentary, Señora Hoya launches into an explanation of what she means by the word *papel*. She means that we must wrap each box in plain brown paper. She means the plain brown paper we can buy at the shop a few doors down, or a few blocks down, or perhaps on another road.

I race outside and go right, which is one of the two possible directions indicated by Señora Hoya in her rushed but comprehensive summary of packing and mailing procedures in Colombia. It's the season of miracles. Three doors down, just as, I think, we were promised, is a large stationery store. I ask the young woman at the counter for brown paper to wrap a package that I'm sending to the United States. I ask her again.

She lifts a tube of paper from the box behind her. '*Papel manila?*' '*Papel manila,*' I agree.

She writes '*papel manila*' and the price on a piece of paper and hands it to me.

Because I have bought 50 cents' worth of bicarbonate of soda in San Gil I am not as thrown by this action as I might have been. I pick up the order and move the metre down the counter to where the cashier sits behind a glass window, examining her nails. I hand her the paper and the pesos. She rings it up and hands me back the paper and the receipt. I go back to the salesperson. She hands me the roll of papel manila. I run back to the Post Office.

Victor is filling out labels while a small but restless queue forms behind him and Señora Hoya reseals the package with our roll of tape. They both look up as I make my triumphant arrival.

'What took you so long?' asks Victor.

Señora Hoya throws a cardboard roll into the waste-basket. 'Did you get more tape?' she asks me.

Someone wants to know how long this is going to take.

I dash back to the stationery store for more sellotape.

The young woman writes down 'one roll of tape' and the price and hands me the slip of paper. I take the paper to the cashier and give it to her with the money. She rings it up and hands me back the slip of paper and the receipt. I go back to the salesperson and give her the receipt. She hands me the tape.

Señora Hoya is just yanking the box out of Victor's hands with an abrupt, 'Let me do it,' as I land with the tape.

'We're going to need more paper,' says Victor.

16

WHEN YOU'RE LOST IN THE
RAIN IN JUAREZ . . .

I'm standing in the middle of the town I grew up in, right outside the five and ten. It's Christmas. Strands of coloured lights hung with stars swing over the street in a frosty wind. Angels and snowmen smile down from the lamp-posts. There isn't a shopfront on Main Street that isn't decorated for the holidays: mangers and tiny villages nestle among the fishing tackle and displays of toys and small appliances, streamers loop around the painted names of lawyers and accountants, candles flicker in the windows of the jeweller and the antique store, a scene from 'The Night Before Christmas' is painted in glass polish on the windows of the pharmacy. Even the mailbox outside the post office is twisted with red and green tinsel. I stand outside the five and ten for a few minutes, watching snow fall on the town like glitter. The cars are moving slowly up and down the street, their windshield wipers schlurping; the pedestrians are hurrying, hoods and collars up and arms filled with shopping. There's Miss Richardson, who teaches first grade, putting up her umbrella as she emerges from the deli. There's Officer Novotony, a doughnut and container of coffee from the diner tucked under his arm, warning a man in a red plaid lumberjacket and matching hat with ear flaps about double parking in front of the bank. There are already young boys on the pavement shovelling the walkways clear, their breath like smoke in the night.

This is not a town where much ever happens. Sometimes the bay freezes over in the winter, sometimes a barbecue or bonfire will get out of control, and one spring the man who owned the hardware store had a breakdown and beat a stray dog to death with an industrial flashlight, but otherwise things are flat and quiet. It is with a certain amount of idle interest, therefore, that I notice a bus pull to a stop in front of the war memorial at the end of town. There is a bus that goes to and from the hospital that stops by the harbour, and there is a bus that goes to and from the railroad station that stops by the harbour, and there is a bus that goes to and from the shopping mall that also stops by the harbour, but none of them are painted red, blue, yellow and green – and none of them are decorated in fairy lights or have a picture of the young Christ, before he started looking so worried, stuck on the back window. Curious, I stay where I am, staring down the block.

The doors of the bus open and passengers start getting out. My friend Kathy comes up beside me. Her eyes follow mine. 'What's up?' she asks.

'Nothing,' I say. 'Just some people getting off the bus.'

'Nothing?' Kathy peers over my shoulder. 'You don't think there's something odd about those people?'

Kathy's right. There is something odd about them. To begin with, none of them are dressed quite right for a Long Island winter. No boots, no waterproof mittens, no hooded parkas, no six-foot scarves. Just thin jackets, cheap, flimsy shoes, straw hats, black felt hats and a shawl or two.

'Maybe they come from Florida,' I suggest.

'They look like they come from a charity shop,' says Kathy.

She's right again. Although, except for their lack of winter clothing, the bus passengers are more or less dressed like everyone else, there is something that suggests that they not only come from a warmer climate but that they shop in second-hand stores, or discount stores in Nebraska.

I'm about to ask Kathy if she thinks there's anything else about these people that is a little out of the ordinary when someone comes up behind us. I smell candy canes and Avon perfume. It's the cashier from the five and dime.

'They look very short to me,' says the cashier, biting off a piece of a green and white cane. 'People around here aren't that short.'

'Or that dark,' says a man carrying a brand new shovel with a paper bag taped around its blade. He stands beside the cashier and draws on his pipe. 'Don't they look a little dark to you?' he asks her.

I watch everyone from the bus desperately trying to get at their bags at the same time.

The cashier watches too, chewing and crunching. 'What do you think they're doing here?' she wonders aloud.

Once they have their bags, the passengers huddle together like cows in a field. 'Maybe they're lost,' I suggest.

'They can't be lost,' says the man. 'They're here.' He chews on the stem of his pipe. 'Where do you think they're from?' he asks.

'Someplace where they like chickens,' says Kathy.

My attention taken by the variety of luggage of the passengers – not just battered old suitcases but cardboard boxes, sacks and large, unwieldy bundles wrapped in blankets as well – I hadn't noticed the chickens until this second, but Kathy is right yet again: at least three of the women are carrying chickens. Many of the women not carrying a chicken have a small child or baby lashed to their backs with old lengths of cloth.

'Look,' says Kathy. 'A goat!'

The only time I've seen a goat in this town was when my third grade class went on an outing to a children's zoo. I look to where Kathy is pointing. It is a goat. We didn't see it before because of all the baggage and the bed on the roof, but the driver has climbed up on top of the bus and is lowering a small goat to the ground on a washing line.

'They look a little nervous,' I say. The dozen or so short, dark, inappropriately dressed people from the bus, clutching their boxes and bundles as though they might be stolen out from under them, are now grouped around a man whose head is bent over a thick book. Except for the man who is trying to read through the snow melting on his glasses, the new arrivals glance edgily about them, as though they've only just realised that they've landed on the wrong planet.

The man closes his book and looks around, first south down Main Street, then west, then east, then north at the pier. He points through the hedges and trees that enclose the park and starts striding past the war memorial, gesturing the rest to follow.

Kathy grabs my arm. 'Come on!' she hisses. 'Let's see where they're going.'

'You two be careful!' the cashier calls after us. 'Don't get too close!'

The people from the bus go to the bandstand in the park. Its white wooden banister is trimmed with pine boughs tied with large red plastic ribbons. The people from the bus stand in front of the red-roofed gazebo, talking and nodding.

'They're speaking Spanish!' I whisper to Kathy when we get close enough to make out their voices but not close enough to catch anything nasty. I recognise the language because I'm taking Spanish in school and I'm a fan of Zorro.

'What are they saying?' she whispers back.

'I don't know,' I admit, wishing I'd paid more attention in language lab. 'It sounds different from them.'

She gives me a shove. 'You must be able to understand something,' she insists.

You'd think so, wouldn't you, given all the hours I've spent memorising irregular verbs? I lean forward, straining to hear. 'They're talking about either summer or winter,' I inform her confidently.

The only words we definitely understand are 'George Washington'.

I'm so close to Kathy I can feel her breath. 'I wonder what they're saying about George Washington,' I murmur. George Washington camped here one summer? George Washington took refuge here that bad winter? George Washington's friend once lived in a house on this site?

'George Washington slept here,' guesses Kathy.

I look at her. 'In the bandstand?'

She shrugs. 'He slept everywhere else,' she says. 'Why not there?'

Still keeping close together, the passengers from the bus walk uncertainly on to the dock. They stand at the edge and gaze out across the bay. The man with the book reads something out loud as he points to the lights across the water. There's a murmur of appreciation as everyone nods.

They leave the dock.

We leave with them, strolling as though we were going their way to begin with. There are people grouped in doorways and faces at every window along Main Street, watching the passengers from the bus trudge through town under the weight of their baggage and the bad weather. It's hard to tell from their expressions whether they're waiting for the visitors to do something spectacular or to start spreading some disease.

'Hey, Buddy!' someone calls from a parked pick-up. 'You wanna rent a truck?'

'Hey, pal, you need a room?' shouts someone else.

'You want some waterproof boots?'

'You looking for something to eat?'

'Hey, Joe, how much you want for that hat?'

Mr Patsky, the jeweller, raps on the glass as we pass his window.

'Look at this!' he cries, smiling enticingly as he holds up a black velvet board covered with watches. 'I bet you've never seen anything
like this before!'

We reach the white clapboard Baptist church and the modern
brick Catholic church at the end of town. The passengers from the
bus stare at each church in turn, pointing to the war memorial in
front of the Baptist church and then to the sign that says BINGO
WEDNESDAY NIGHT! in front of the Catholic one. They look disappointed.

Father Downey comes out of the church, rubbing his hands
together against the freezing night. The bus passengers, not accustomed to near-zero temperatures, shiver in sympathy. A few of them
are already beginning to sneeze. The man in charge of the guidebook
steps forward and addresses the priest in troubled English. 'Ow
mooch to see the altar?' he wants to know. 'Whair, *como se dice en
Inglés?*, are the men that sell candies and *amuletos*?' He gestures to
the town. 'Ju 'ave no biggers ear?' he asks the priest.

Father Downey, smiling and nodding as only someone who hasn't
understood a single word would smile and nod, explains that though
the new church was erected in 1969 there has been a church on this
site since 1902.

'Not even a hundred years!' says the spokesman jubilantly.

Father Downey sells them tickets for the Christmas raffle.

There is a lot of confusion about change and currency. Father
Downey stands beneath a streetlamp, holding up each of the coins in
his hand in turn. 'This is a dime!' he screams, flashing ten fingers.
'This is a nickel!' flashing five. 'This is a quarter – twenty-five!' He
flashes two fingers, then five more. 'Twenty-five.'

There is a rumble of incomprehension from the travellers.

As we all troop back down Main Street, several small children run
alongside the visitors, asking questions. 'Are you an Indian?' they
want to know of the man with the single black braid, the white
espadrilles and the felt hat bound with a woven band. 'Why don't
you have a stroller?' they ask one of the women with a baby strapped
across her back. 'Do you ride in cars?' they ask the others. 'Do you
have electricity? Do you eat hamburgers? Have you ever heard of
McDonald's? Do you celebrate Christmas?'

Everyone already in the luncheonette looks up as the visitors
enter. Mr Mirsky, proprietor and grill chef, comes bustling from
around the counter with a dish towel in his hands. 'This is the oldest eating establishment in town,' he informs them, his hand

sweeping around the room with its ceiling fans, old glass counter of chocolates and soda ads and calendars on the walls. 'Been here since 1906.'

'Not ninety years!' says the keeper of the guidebook, beside himself with amazement. He translates for the others. They shake their heads and murmur in appreciation, not even ninety years, imagine that!

Mr Mirsky tells them to sit where they like, and they do, dragging several tables together in the middle of the room, ignoring the fact that everyone is still watching them from behind their cups and menus. Somehow, there seem to be more of them inside the luncheonette than there were outside. Also, although they still look short, they seem larger, too, taking up more space than they should. Two of the men spit on the floor and Mr Mirsky drops his dish towel.

The man who speaks some English orders several large bottles of Coke.

'We don't have bottles of Coke,' screams Mr Mirsky, still nervously eyeing the spit on his black and white floor. 'Only glasses.'

The group jammed into the centre of the luncheonette with their bags and their children and their chickens stares back at him blankly.

'Glass!' shouts Mr Mirsky, grabbing a glass from another customer. 'Only Coke in glasses!'

'Okay,' says the man with the English. 'Coke in glasses.' He gives Mr Mirsky a friendly, perhaps even hopeful smile. 'And sixteen *platos* of Cuban rice.'

'Cuban?' frowns Mr Mirsky, no friend of communism. 'Cuban rice?' He hasn't sold cigars since the Bay of Pigs. He looks around him to see if everyone else has heard this incredible request. 'We don't have no Cuban rice.'

Mr Mirsky doesn't have any rice, as it turns out. No rice, no *arepas*, no *empanadas*, no *frijoles*, no roast chicken.

The spokesperson asks him, reasonably if incoherently, what he does have.

'What?' booms Mr Mirsky.

'Wot du ju 'ave?' the man asks again, forced to scream.

Mr Mirsky shakes his head. 'What?'

The group representative mimes eating, jabs a finger towards the pictures of sandwiches stuck to the mirror behind the grill. 'Wot tu eat? Wot tu eat?'

It's the season for miracles. 'Hamburgers,' shouts Mr Mirsky in sudden understanding. 'Chicken salad, tuna, cheese melts, French fries, omelettes.'

When the food comes the bus passengers regard it with suspicion. There's a certain amount of consultation over the guidebook and peering under hamburger rolls and into bowls of relish. Mothers start scraping pickles and ketchup from the bread. Several of the diners, too hungry to be cautious, fearlessly bite into their sandwiches and fries. '*Dios mío!*' they gasp, fanning their mouths and turning various colours. '*Dios mío!*' The food's too hot. They reach for their Cokes, gulping down the liquid and then spitting it back out. Too much ice. Mr Mirsky runs towards them with a mop.

Without having left our stools at the counter, Kathy and I are in the pink and white ladies' room. One of the women from the bus comes in. She stands at the door, her expression worried as her eyes take in the pink and white wallpaper, the shining pink sink, the pink paper cup dispenser, the pink stalls, the tiny vase of flowers next to the soap and the mirrored wall. She thinks she's in the wrong room.

I explain that this is the baño. 'You go in there,' I tell her, pointing to the stall. '*Adentro.*'

The woman goes adentro. She doesn't lock the door. We can see her in the mirror, squatting on top of the toilet seat, her feet gripping the rim and her skirts up around her.

'Good grief,' I whisper. 'What if she falls in?'

Kathy jams her fist in her mouth so she doesn't laugh out loud.

When the woman comes out, she goes straight for the paper cups. She pulls one out and fills it with water from the tap. She goes back into the stall and pours it in the bowl. She comes back and fills another cup.

I make a move to show her how to flush the toilet, but she pushes me away. 'I do not whant tu buy anyting,' she tells me sharply. '*Nada.*'

Kathy backs into the hand-dryer, setting it off, and the woman screams.

And then, as they do, the dream changes. I wake up on a bus just like the one that stopped in front of the war memorial, my head against the dirty red rayon curtain at the window. This bus has also stopped, but in the middle of the road, in front of a wooden shack with tinsel looped across its porch. A group of musicians sits on the grass and rocks outside the house. The reason the bus has stopped here is because a noisy gathering of devils with pitchforks, spiked tails and penises the size of truncheons have barricaded the road.

Gibbering shrilly, they storm the bus and the musicians pick up their instruments and follow them on.

Everyone laughs as the devils take over the bus. The devils are pranksters. They sit on laps and snatch at bags of sweets and biscuits; begging for money, they cajole and coo. The *músicos* start to play and some of the passengers sing along. One of the devils comes to a halt next to our seat. He puts an arm around Victor and rests his penis on Victor's knees. It looks as though it's made of old pyjamas. '*Dame un propio!*' he squeaks, seductively stroking Victor's shoulder. '*Dame un propio.*'

For a man quintessentially negative about anybody putting a penis on his lap, Victor is taking this demonstration of affection pretty well. He isn't reaching for his change, but he is smiling. He kicks my foot. 'Quick,' he hisses. 'Take a picture!'

Feeling a lot safer with demons than the military, I fumble to take a picture. It isn't until the flash goes off in our faces that I realise that I'm no longer asleep.

'It does seem to me as though the poor Queen is having a very, very bad time,' Sister Geronimo is saying. 'All this trouble with her family . . .' She lowers her already soft voice and says musingly, 'How difficult motherhood must be . . .'

Sister Geronimo is sitting in the window seat across the aisle. Behind her is nothing, as though the bus is riding on a ledge, which, indeed, it more or less is. There is horizon in the distance – more mountains, more green, more banana trees, more patches of corn and coffee and a hut – but between us and that horizon there is only emptiness, the drop is sheer.

One of the turkeys in the bag in the aisle makes a sound that is eerily sympathetic. The poor Queen, it seems to be saying, and I thought I had problems . . .

The bus lurches as the driver, his hand steady on the furry blue and green material that covers the shift as well as the dash, the horn pull, the trim of the mirror and the visor, goes down one last gear, and descend along a trail of rubble which pitches us so sharply forward that the moustachioed man standing by the open door with the bottle to his lips almost falls out. Everyone screams.

The conductor has been conversing intently with the driver, holding on to the back of his seat for those sudden jolts and turns, but now he breaks off and jumps forward.

Between me and Sister Geronimo, Sister Alma Teresa catches her breath as the conductor hauls the drinker back by his belt. 'I do hope they're not going to buy any more after that bottle's gone,' says Sister Alma Teresa, her blue eyes worried behind their spectacles. Each time we stop the man with the moustache and his friend, Juan, stagger off for another pint of *aguardiente*. They have already bought four.

'It's Prince Charles I feel sorry for,' says Sister Maria José from behind me. 'He always struck me as such a nice young man.'

I am trying hard to concentrate on what the nuns are saying, not just because they are being friendly and patient with my Spanish, but because I know I'm not dreaming this time. We are on our way to San Agustín, a place you really have to want to go to if you ever intend to get there. I'm hoping that talking with nuns will keep disaster at bay.

'We all have our trials, don't we?' says Sister Geronimo. Her eyes shift past me and come to rest on the man wearing the Save the Whales T-shirt who is leaning over the back of his seat, talking to Victor. This is Juan. Juan is telling Victor all about himself between slugs of *aguardiente*. Juan owns a jeep, if we want to rent a jeep in San Agustín. He owns horses, if we want to rent horses in San Agustín. He is a guide, if we want a guide to show us around the astounding sites. He is an artisan, if we want to buy souvenirs while we're there. Juan, like his buddy, is very drunk.

'You come see me, *amigo*,' he is saying, his voice rising with passion. He pounds his chest. 'I'll give you a good deal.'

Sister Alma Teresa leans across the aisle, her habit touching my arm as she whispers, 'What is he trying to sell him?'

'Beads,' I tell her. Beads or stories, the words are similar.

'Oh.' She nods. 'Beads.'

The man with the moustache puts his arm around Juan, passing him the bottle. 'You're good people,' he tells him loudly. 'Good people.' He waves a hand in benediction over our heads. 'They are all good people.'

The gears grind and we take a forty-five-degree turn straight up a cliff face.

'They haven't started rattling their rosaries yet, have they?' asks Victor, glancing at the nuns.

'Not yet. We're discussing the problems of Queen Elizabeth at the moment.'

'Let me know when they start getting worried about the ride,' says Victor. He closes his eyes.

Juan and his friend begin a robust conversation about the Catholic religion. I know this partly because the sentence 'Yo soy muy Católico' is making regular appearances in their competing monologues, and partly because they have finally managed to take Sister Geronimo's attention away from Her Majesty. She watches them over the rims of her glasses like a silent prayer.

'And how are you liking Colombia?' asks Sister Alma Teresa as the man with the moustache launches into an explanation of what's wrong with priests.

'We like it very much,' I answer. 'It's very beautiful.' I add, 'Very tranquilo.'

Juan holds up himself and the almost empty bottle. 'Yo soy muy Católico,' he shouts. 'Muy Católico.'

'Sit down!' warns the conductor. 'Sit down!'

'Eres buena gente,' his companion assures him as he falls back down. 'Buena gente . . .'

The statue of the Virgin on the dash tilts backwards as we start our descent.

'Where have you been so far?' asks Sister Maria José.

I tell her where we've been. Cartagena. Bogotá. Tunja. Socorro. Silvia. Garzon.

'Not Santa Marta?' she asks. 'I come from Santa Marta. It's very, very nice.'

'Yo soy muy Católico!' the man with the moustache is reassuring us emotionally again. 'Muy Católico . . .' and then says something I don't catch about the clergy. Something not particularly flattering.

Juan's face lurches over the back of his seat. 'Not you, Sisters,' he says thickly, breathing aguardiente fumes across us. Thank God no one's smoking. 'He doesn't mean you.' He holds the bottle out towards the nuns. 'Have a drink,' he says. 'For Christmas.'

The bus, slowing suddenly, lurches as well. Juan disappears.

Victor opens his eyes. 'What is it? Another aguardiente stop?'

I lift myself up so I can see through the windscreen. There are eight or ten uniformed soldiers in front of us, and with them several women in flowered dresses. Two of the women are holding a length of yellow rope across the road, the rest are holding tin cans. 'Military checkpoint,' I tell him.

We wait for the soldier to come on board and tell us all that we have to get off the bus, but he doesn't come. Instead, one of the soldiers and one of the can carriers come to the window to talk to the driver.

'I'm not a rich man,' laughs the driver, patting his pockets. 'I'm poor.'

If it occurs to me that the reason I can hear the driver so clearly is because everyone else on the bus – including the turkey, the children and Juan and his very Catholic friend – has shut up. I don't pay much attention to the thought.

The soldier bobs his rifle; the woman doesn't smile.

Victor looks over at me, almost as though he's never seen me before. 'What makes you think this is a military checkpoint?' he asks.

The conductor leans across the driver to hand some money out of the window.

'Colombia isn't Peru,' says Sister Geronimo conversationally as the bus pulls away, watched in silence by the soldiers and the women. 'The guerrillas in Colombia don't hate tourists, it's the oil companies that they hate.'

Sister Maria José touches my shoulder. 'Look,' she points as we bounce over a narrow steel bridge. 'We're crossing the Magdalena.'

17

IT'S CHRISTMASTIME
IN THE CITY

The tallest of the shoeshine boys, the one in the faded Bart Simpson T-shirt, is arguing with me. 'But it's Christmas Eve,' he finally says in exasperation. 'You should have them cleaned for Christmas Eve.' His comrades in rags and Shinola nod in agreement. Treat yourself, it's Christmas Eve.

It doesn't feel like Christmas Eve. It feels like a summer day, despite the Stars of David dangling across the streets from strings of tinsel.

The boy points his wooden box at my dirty Docs with a certain amount of intrepidity. 'I can make them look like new, señorita,' he assures me. His own shoes don't look as though they've been new for several years. 'I can make them shine.'

'I don't want them to look like new,' I say, trying to sound as rational as he does. 'I don't want them to shine.' The three boys roll their eyes in horror. 'I like them the way they are.'

'Like that?' they shriek. 'You like them like that?'

It's eight in the morning on La Noche Buena, but already the square is filled with kids with cardboard trays of sweets and cigarettes, or shoeshine boxes under their arms, drunks anticipating the fiesta to come, and guides offering horses and jeeps and trips to see the statues, *muy* cheap. A family of three passes the plaza on a motorcycle, the child in front of the father, the Christmas branch in front of Mum. Victor and I, although we have a rule about tours and guides and visiting ruins, are waiting for the jeep arranged by the

Oficina de Turismo to come and collect us for our tour of the ancient Indian sites. Both the guidebook and the woman in the tourist office have made the tour sound pretty interesting, six or seven not to be missed relics of a vanished, mysterious culture, plus a genuine jungle waterfall. It's Christmas, we can break our own rule.

'But señorita,' pleads the youngest of the boys. 'I'll give you a very special price. Just for you.' His T-shirt says AMERICAN AND PROUD and he wears a silver Star of David around his neck. 'A special price because it's Christmas and you're my friend.'

'I don't want a special price,' I tell him once again. 'I don't want my shoes cleaned.'

The tall boy turns to Victor. 'Where are you from?' he demands, picturing, perhaps, a country full of filthy boots where he and his mates could make a fortune. 'Germany?'

'England,' Victor smiles. 'But she's American.'

The boys exchange a look. 'Ah, Americana . . .'

Her lipstick is red enough, her eyes are shaded in the right amount of blue, her foundation is even and smooth. Having finished checking her make-up in the rear-view mirror, she tosses her hair and readjusts the baseball cap on her head as the driver takes his seat beside her. She was smiling when the jeep pulled into the plaza, and she was smiling when she was looking in the mirror, but she isn't smiling now. It seems likely from her expression that, without consulting her, the driver has just locked a couple of goats in the back of the jeep. 'Are they coming with us?' she demands coolly, nodding ever so slightly behind her at us and not quite meeting his eyes. She is accustomed to dealing with the help.

Alberto starts the engine. He isn't meeting her eyes either. 'Yes,' he says flatly, with just a hint of Native American fatalism. 'They're coming, too.' He is accustomed to dealing with visiting royalty.

She turns to the large, sunburned German in the white slacks and pink sports shirt sitting behind the driver. In much slower and more painstaking Spanish, and in tones much warmer, she explains the situation to him. 'They're coming with us,' she says, and makes a face.

Since *they* are actually in the back with the German, knees almost touching, it seems likely that he was already aware of this, but he nods as though the information is new. He is accustomed to dealing with her.

The jeep starts to roll.

She sits with her back to the door so that she can speak to the driver and to her boyfriend at the same time.

'What about swimming?' she asks the driver, almost glancing at us. 'We're still going swimming, aren't we?'

Alberto's eyes appear in the rear-view mirror. 'The first thing we will see is the narrowest point of the Magdalena,' he informs the back of the jeep. He clears his throat. 'We will stop at the river for half an hour. *La señorita y su amigo quieren bañarse.*'

'Half an hour at the river?' comes the response from everyone but the German. 'Half an hour?'

The driver glances at the road for a second – which is just as well as it allows him to miss the woman crossing with her pig, and returns his eyes to the mirror. 'You can swim, too, if you want,' he offers.

But *they* have no swimsuits, no towels, no desire to dare death by jumping into the narrowest stretch of the Magdalena on Christmas Eve. *They* don't want to swim.

She turns up the volume on the tape deck, swaying in her seat while everyone in the back bounces on the hard benches as the jeep leaves the main road. 'This is typical Colombian music,' she says to the German, her gold bangles jangling in agreement. 'We Colombians love music. It is part of our soul.'

Her boyfriend nods. '*Sí, sí.*'

There is another jeepload of tourists already at the site, staring over the precipice admiring the statue of the Virgin that marks this remarkable point of the Magdalena.

The drivers synchronise their watches. 'Ten minutes,' says the driver of the first jeep. 'You have ten minutes to see the river.'

'Ten minutes?' *they* ask. 'But we thought the others were going swimming.'

'No, no swimming,' says Alberto as la Colombiana and the German disappear down the dirt trail, she shrieking and taking his hand. 'It's much too dangerous.'

The drivers sit smoking by their jeeps while the tourists scrabble on the rocks of the riverbed that looks spectacularly similar to quite a few of the planet's other riverbeds, and not as nice as some. The Swiss couple sit on a boulder, making out, while the Americans take pictures of the Virgin and la Colombiana takes off her shoes and wades at the river's edge, carefree as a child and just as noisy. 'Colombians love nature,' she tells the German. 'We love to swim. We are a very physical people.'

Her boyfriend nods, 'Sí, sí.'

There are several thousand miles of rocks and ruts between the river and the first excavation, but it's well worth the trip, says Alberto as the jeep bucks and sways.

She leans back, holding on to the window frame and the edge of the driver's seat as she explains to her boyfriend why no matter where she might travel she will always return to Colombia, home of her heart.

At last, close to nowhere, the jeep comes to a stop in a small village of several mud houses and a fenced-off square. Chickens stroll by.

'That is the first site,' says Alberto. He points to the square. There's a sign on the grass that suggests that he is right.

Everyone but Alberto gets out and troops into the square. There are three holes in the ground.

She takes off her sunglasses. 'This was made thousands of years before Christ,' she tells the German as they stare into the first hole.

'So much history,' she tells the German as they stare into the second hole. 'We are an amazing people.'

'Colombians have a lot to be proud of,' she concludes as they stare into the third hole.

Everyone but Alberto, who is still behind the wheel, gets back into the jeep.

She puts in another tape and turns up the volume just a little bit more. 'Doesn't this music make you want to dance?' she asks her boyfriend.

The German, holding a handkerchief to his face because of the dust, just nods.

No one else feels impelled to dance either.

This lack of enthusiasm doesn't dampen hers. 'I'm from Cali,' she informs the jeep at large. 'In Cali we start dancing in the streets at six on Christmas Eve.' She snaps her fingers in time to the music. 'Just wait till tonight,' she goes on. 'Tonight the whole town will be partying.'

'Sí, sí,' nods the German.

The other jeep is already parked with two others at the archeological park, their drivers all standing together inside the entrance, watching their charges sign the register and follow the signposts up a steep hill.

'I'll wait for you here,' says Alberto.

'We may have to kill her,' says Victor as we follow the rest of our group up the hill. He tosses his head and laughs in a way that has become familiar in an astoundingly short period of time. 'Are *they* coming with us?' he screeches. He kicks a stone that might just possibly be thousands of years old out of the path. 'Why is she sitting up front like she's some kind of princess?' he wants to know. 'Just because she's Colombian and has music in her fuckin' soul?'

'We may have to kill them both,' I counter. 'No matter how much I shove back he takes up most of the bench.'

At the top of the hill are several more holes in the ground and quite a few of what the official brochure describes as 'large rough-hewn stone figures of men, animals and gods, dating from roughly 3300 BC', gathered from other sites and positioned carefully, precisely and meaninglessly around the excavations.

The pairs of visitors follow the signposted path as though painting by numbers, stopping to take a picture of this rough-hewn stone figure of a priest or a wild cat and that rough-hewn stone figure of a god or a pregnant woman, stopping to look appreciatively into another hole filled with relics that used to be somewhere else.

'Jesus Christ,' says Victor. 'It's not bad enough we're stuck with la Princesa and Po-Face, this isn't even half as interesting as Tierradentro.'

I stand beside him, staring into the hole, thinking about the nameless people who thought they'd buried their dead with dignity, sanctity and safety, protecting them with rituals and prayers – protecting themselves – not imagining that 5,000 years later a bunch of foreigners in trainers and jeans would be admiring their craftsmanship and embalming techniques while they wondered where they'd be stopping for lunch.

'You've forgotten that by the fourth tomb, Tierradentro wasn't half as interesting as Tierradentro,' I remind him.

'This waterfall had better be good,' says Victor. The only falls we've seen so far have resembled sewer drains more than spectacular crystal torrents. 'It'd better be big and it better not smell.'

'I think I've reached my vestiges of ancient cultures limit,' I say as we peer into the largest of the holes. 'Let's go back down.'

Back down, the guides are all sitting under a tree eating sugar cane and talking about life. We sit with them.

In answer to their questions, we tell them that we come from England, that it's very far, that the plane ride over cost us *mucho plata*, how much *plata* the air fare cost, how long we had to save for the trip, and that we like Colombia a lot.

Alberto breaks off another piece of cane. 'You don't like the ruins?' he asks.

'It's boring,' Victor says simply. 'Seen one hole and you've seen them all.'

Alberto looks over our heads as the rest of our little tour appears at the top of the path. 'It may be boring for you,' he says, 'but for us it's a lot of work.'

The men all agree. The same difficult road, the same five sights having to be approached each time with new enthusiasm and pride.

'And the tourists,' says Victor. 'It must be difficult having to deal with the tourists.'

'That's not so bad,' one of the guides generously offers.

'No,' agrees Alberto. He spits out bits of cane. 'The tourists are usually all right.' His eyes scan the hilltop behind our heads. 'Most of them can't speak Spanish.'

As we cover the few thousand more miles over rocks and ruts to our next destination, la Colombiana shares out sugar cane between her and her boyfriend. '*They* don't want any?' she says to the driver.

Alberto looks over his shoulder. 'You don't want any sugar cane?' he asks Victor.

'We don't like sugar,' says Victor. He smiles at la Princesa. 'Bad for the teeth.'

She leans her head against the window. 'Colombians love sugar,' she sighs. 'It shows a sweet nature.'

'What it shows is a toxic dependency,' mutters Victor.

The German gives him a look.

We come to another village, larger than the first, and stop outside the restaurant El Rincón.

Tossing back her hair, la Colombiana turns to the German with an encouraging smile. 'We're going to have lunch now,' she tells him.

He brushes some dust from his trousers on to me. 'I'm not hungry.' Something related to a smile plays on his lips. 'All that sugar.'

She considers this for a split-second. 'No,' she says, 'neither am I.' She leans towards Alberto. 'We're not really hungry,' she informs him with a certain amount of finality. 'We don't want to stop for lunch.'

Alberto switches off the engine. 'We are stopping here,' he says and nods his head towards Victor and me so that she knows whom he means by 'we'.

The bracelets sound as she turns around in her seat. 'Do you want lunch?' she says in her asking-the-servants-their-opinion voice.

Since she isn't looking at me, but at Victor, I don't say anything. Victor doesn't say anything either.

'You see?' she says to the driver. 'They're not hungry either.'

The jeep carrying the Swiss and American couples from site to site pulls up beside us. Alberto tells the other guide that we're not stopping here for lunch.

The other driver argues. This is the stop they'd arranged. The food is ready. The agreement made. 'They're expecting us,' he finishes. 'We have to go here.'

It is impossible to see the expression on Alberto's face as he says, 'We're not hungry,' but not impossible to imagine it.

Ungracious in defeat, the other driver guns his jeep ahead of us through town and over a few thousand more miles of ruts and rocks that wind up the mountain to a gravel lot perched above the river. He's already sitting on a bumper, smoking a cigarette, when we pull in beside him. He's glaring.

'I don't believe this,' I say as we stagger out of the back. 'It's another restaurant.'

'No it isn't,' says Victor, pointing to a sign that points to the Magdalena. 'It's the falls.'

The owner of the restaurant, as delighted by the unexpected arrival of gringos with money on la Noche Buena as Mary and Joseph were by the unexpected arrival of the Magi with their gifts, comes rushing across the terrace with several small children in her wake, rattling off the blue-plate special as she comes.

'We're not hungry,' says la Colombiana, cutting her off before she can get past chicken. 'We'll just have juice.' She raises an eyebrow at the German. 'Juice?'

He nods. '*Sí, sí.*'

'We're eating,' says Victor. It isn't a question or even a suggestion. I look over at him, but he is looking towards the river as though he's never heard one before. It's my turn to do the '*somos vegetarianos*' spiel.

'*Somos vegetarianos,*' I say, aware that I have finally captured the attention of our fellow sightseers. '*No comemos carne, ni pollo, ni pescado, ni nada con el sabor del carne.*'

'No problem,' the proprietress assures us, Mary willing to accommodate a couple of shepherds as well as the kings – just stand at the back. 'Thirteen hundred pesos for a vegetarian meal.'

As though I'd asked her a question, la Colombiana nods at me. 'That's very cheap.'

The German rocks on his heels.

The Swiss and the Americans are already on the path leading away from the restaurant, cameras ready, laughing and talking loudly.

'You can go down with them and take pictures,' says the *dueña*, 'and by the time you get back your lunch will be ready.'

By the time we catch up, everyone else has reached the landing at the end of the path. They're leaning over the railing, taking pictures of the falls and the river still far below.

'At least it's not brown,' says Victor as he strides past them to where the trail, steeper and overgrown, continues.

No one comes after us as we carefully descend, passing the place where the empty crisp and candy wrappers stop and going on until we are on a ribbon of rock and trampled dirt almost lost in the bushes. The next time I look up there is no one on the terrace, no one on the scenic overlook.

I look up again when we get as far down as we can without a machete, but all I can see up there now are trees. In front of us are the falls.

'She's going to be mad,' I say to Victor as we sit on a rock, watching the water tumble down the mountain, pretending we are far from jeeps and tourist restaurants.

'I don't give a fuck,' says Victor. 'So am I.' He lights a cigarette and leans back. 'This time she's waiting for us.'

As with most things, it's harder going back up the mountain than it was coming down. The distance has doubled, the path has become steeper, the air a bit thin. Every time I collapse on the trail, gasping for breath, Victor says, 'This is good practice for Machu Picchu.' It's not such a comforting a thought. If it takes me this long to get back to the restaurant, how long is it going to take me to reach the Door to the Sun? About as long as it'll take me to reach the gates of heaven at the rate I'm going.

There are several children watching us from the patio as we finally stagger to the top. Breathing restored to normal at the scenic overlook, we glide up the path to the dining room. 'Did you go down?' they want to know. 'Did you go to the river?'

'Yes,' says Victor. 'We went down.'

Heads shake. '*Es muy lejos.*'

Victor grins. 'It's not that far.'

Rush hour is over. The tables are empty again, the Swiss and the Americans already gone, the rest of our party sitting in front of the remains of their lunch at the bar, looking like a couple who thought they were going on a tour of stately homes and wound up on a tour of prisons instead.

We enter smiling. No one smiles back. We stroll across the dining room and carefully choose a table as the rest of our group start banging around, impatiently demanding to pay their bill. We slowly eat our lunch, waving pleasantly at our fellow tourists as they go back outside to admire the view some more.

'If you won't do it, I will,' says Victor when we get back to the still empty jeep.

Although I'd been hoping to spare him this glimpse into my true character I admit that I won't. 'I can't,' I say as I get into the back. 'I don't want her to yell at me.' As a token protest, instead of sitting in my usual place, pushed into the corner by the spreading German, I sit in his seat, behind the driver.

Even before we see the three of them come round the bushes, we can hear la Princesa complaining to Alberto that she had wanted to go swimming today, but that she knows you can't think only of yourself and what you want to do when you're travelling with a group, you have to consider the others, too.

Alberto watches the ground as he listens to her, but when he reaches the jeep he looks up, grinning. 'Did you get down to the river?' he calls.

'Almost,' says Victor. 'As far as we could.'

'I went all the way down once,' says Alberto as he opens his door. 'But that was a long time ago.' He stops in the act of climbing in, surprised to find that la Colombiana is standing right beside him.

She doesn't give him a chance to ask her what she wants. Her eyes go from Alberto to Victor, smiling innocently if comfortably from the passenger seat, then back to Alberto. 'Is he staying there?' she demands.

Alberto looks over at Victor. 'Are you staying there?' he asks.

Victor nods.

Alberto turns back to la Princesa. 'Yes,' he says. 'He's staying there.'

Doña Silviana's is a small farmhouse up the mountain behind San Agustín, well beyond the point where the street signs end. To find it you have to climb to the very top of the town and then follow the dirt road past other small farmhouses with caged birds on the porches and Christmas decorations shining through open front doors. The houses have no names or numbers. To find Doña

Silviana's you must ask on the way, stopping to say where you're from, where you've been, where you're going and how much the plane fare to Colombia is, or to have a cup of *tinto* while you sit among the chickens, explaining why you don't have children. Doña Silviana's house is the one just before the small white cross at the side of the road where the soldier was murdered.

There are fields on either side of Doña Silviana's house, and fruit trees at the back where the wood-burning clay oven, the chicken coops and the pig pen are. There is a courtyard at the centre of the house, its walls covered with Disney characters dancing brightly across the whitewash. The toilet stall, the shower stall and the sink all share the courtyard with the dining table, a big old armchair, a big old sideboard, a very tired Chihuahua who sleeps in the armchair, quite a few chickens and, for this week at least, a nativity scene and a Christmas branch trimmed with lights and glass balls. Five rooms and a kitchen open off the courtyard. Once these rooms were filled with children and the things and noise of children, the kitchen always busy and smelling of home, but now Doña Silviana lives here alone, her husband dead and her children grown up and moved away, even as far as Bogotá. She spends her days looking after the animals and her vegetables and children from town, and at night she sits in the armchair with her supper, watching television while the dog sleeps at her feet and the chickens sneak into the garbage.

But Doña Silviana is not alone today. Today is Christmas Eve and the house is loud and crowded. Doña Silviana and her daughters make *tamales* at the sideboard, sweep the floors, look after the children, chase chickens from the garbage, shake fruit from the trees, and, from time to time, abruptly march into the dark with lengths of garden hose over their shoulders, while the men sit around eating bread soaked in honey and knocking back the *aguardiente*. In fact, the house is more crowded than it was before. Besides the sons, daughters, sons-in-law, daughters-in-law, and grandchildren, there are gringos in the room with the three pedal sewing-machines.

Though not at the moment. At the moment the gringos are sitting at the dining table, drinking freshly squeezed juice and eating cheese bread hot from the hearth.

Alberto, Doña Silviana's youngest son, comes back from his unsuccessful attempt to find the bit for the hot water heater that attaches into the head of the shower – giving the uninitiated the opportunity of washing and drying off at the same time – and sits next to Victor. 'It's Christmas,' he says. 'Who needs hot water at

Christmas?' He pours out three shots of what is needed on Christmas. '*Aguardiente*,' he explains. 'The drink of Colombia.'

Alberto used to work for one of the petroleum companies, but now he is an industrial mechanic. He likes meeting people from other countries. He has a friend in Australia who sends him post-cards and another in Germany who writes every birthday to see how he is. Alberto wants us to have a good time in Colombia. He has never met vegetarians before. 'But what do you eat?' he wants to know. Everything except meat, Victor tells him. Cheese, eggs, veg-etables, rice, noodles – he helps himself to more *pan con queso* – bread . . . Alberto, not convinced that this is enough to support human life, gives up and starts to explain Christmas to us.

'Tonight is Christmas Eve,' says Alberto. He gestures to the nativ-ity and the Christmas branch and the women stuffing *tamales* near the door to the kitchen. 'The whole family gets together at Christmas to celebrate. We eat *tamales* and *pan con queso* and drink *aguardiente*, and at midnight the children open their presents.'

'It's the same in England,' says Victor.

Alberto looks surprised. 'Really? You have Christmas in England?'

Victor embroils himself in trying to describe a Christmas tree while Alberto pours out three more drinks.

'The entire tree?' Alberto shakes his head. 'And you decorate it, too?'

Victor becomes enmeshed in describing the gross capitalist com-mercialism of the birth of Christ in the Western world while Alberto pours another round.

'Big business,' says Alberto. 'They're all the same.'

Victor opens the discussion on government while Alberto fills the glasses again. Jaime, the husband of Doña Silviana's eldest daugh-ter, joins us.

'Big business and the government work together,' says Jaime, usurping the role of bartender.

There is general agreement that no government is interested in more than money and power.

'That is why you have nothing to fear from the guerrillas,' says Jaime. 'They have nothing against tourists – it's the government and the multinationals they're fighting.'

Jaime opens a new bottle while I become involved in a defence of the guerrillas and Alberto and Victor discuss the ELP.

'The ELP are more into blood than using their heads,' says Jaime.

'It's the same in our country,' says Victor.

'Really?' asks Jaime. 'You have terrorists in England?' I can almost hear him thinking, *with the Queen?*

A starburst of pink and white explodes in the darkness behind him, over the lemon and orange trees and the snoozing pig.

'More than here,' says Victor.

'You see?' Jaime turns to Alberto. 'It's what I always say. Colombians don't have enough contact with the outside world.'

Maybe it's the tension of taking a cold shower more or less in the living room, praying all the while that you don't suddenly fart or lose your underwear on the wrong side of the door, or maybe it's the liquor, or maybe it's a combination of the two, but sitting in our room, waiting for the kitchen to be free, the idea of using one of Doña Silviana's sewing machines to make hidden pockets for our trousers suddenly seems like a good one. Quicker and easier than sewing them by hand.

'Except,' I point out, 'that there isn't a chair.'

You discover a lot about another person when you travel with them, hour after hour and day after day. You discover what they're like on their tenth day of cold rice and beans or their tenth hour in a bus without air conditioning or shocks. You discover what they're like when they're bored with the monotony of travel or anxious because they forgot to shut their mouth in the shower. You discover who has never used a pedal sewing-machine before.

'So what?' says Victor.

'So I have to sit down to make it work.'

He looks from me to the ancient Singer and back to me.

You also discover how resilient they are in the face of buses that never come because the road is washed out. How resourceful when there's nowhere to do the laundry or hang it when it's done. How imaginative in finding a chair when you don't want to ask your hostess because she's busy making cheese bread and *tamales*.

'So I'll be the chair,' says Victor.

So Victor's the chair. It takes me a few minutes to get the knack of the machine. The chair has to get up to rethread three times, because the seamstress can't see the eye of the needle even with her glasses on. The second pocket is done with only one halt for rethreading. The third is done in seconds. I'm on the last seam of the last pocket when the lights go out.

'Uh-oh,' I say.

There's a knock on the door and it opens just enough to let me see Doña Silviana standing in the hall with a candle in her hand.

'Jesus,' says the chair.
'I brought you a candle,' says Doña Silviana. 'The electricity is out.'

It still doesn't feel like Christmas. It's a gentle day in the mountains around San Agustín, soft with sunlight and sleepily quiet. Barefoot children in shabby clothes stand among the flowers, holding hands as they watch us pass. We follow the map we got from the Oficina de Turismo across the mountains to see the sites we couldn't reach by jeep the day before. We slide down rocky dirt trails. We clamber across fields. We wade through streams. We crawl up cliffs. We get lost six times, having to flag down jeeps or men on horseback or shout into open doors for directions. 'Excuse me, but is this the way to El Tablón?' 'Good day, can you tell us which direction Chaquira is?' 'Merry Christmas, how do we get to Peolita?'

El Tablón is a few more relics and a hole in someone's field. Chaquira is a large carved stone looking down at the river as though waiting for the return of the men who made it. We never make it to Peolita. Instead we stop halfway down the mountain in a patch of red flowers and yellow butterflies to eat saltines and *aji* and the vegetable omelette made the night before while most of Doña Silviana's family watched in curious amazement, *you're putting salad in the eggs? You eat vegetables on their own?*

'Christmas,' says Victor, his eyes on the green, turquoise and purple lizard scooting across the path. 'What's your worst Christmas memory?'

The Kodachrome photo-card of a snowy window bright with coloured lights and a tree gleaming with icicles and shining balls that I've been carrying around in my mind the last few days finally fades, revealing the Christmases inside.

Worst day of joy? It's a difficult choice. 'I think it's a toss-up. It could be the year my parents had a fight about the roast and my dad stormed out of the house, got in the car, and drove into the stone pillar at the end of the road.'

'One year my mother refused to come out of the kitchen,' says Victor. 'I think it was something my grandmother said.' He picks a flower redder than a holly berry and hands it to me. 'What's the other one?'

The grey streets of London hover over the emerald landscape, lonely rooms, no one talking but the radio or the television, laughter coming from the flat next door, sitting on the sofa with a frozen dinner on your lap, wondering why your life isn't like the life you were told you should have, the life everyone else is having, happy, prosperous, and loved.

'The year the woman in the flat above me killed herself.'

'Shit,' says Victor. 'What's the best?'

'Oh, that's easy,' I answer, as I march into the bushes for a pee. 'The year my mother and her sister got smashed on sherry flips and insisted on dancing to old Glenn Miller records.'

'That was the best?'

'Uh-huh.' It isn't easy to hold a flower and pee in the bushes at the same time. 'They fell into the tree.'

Victor turns to see if I'm joking.

'Really,' I say, balancing carefully. 'They brought the whole thing down. You should've seen my father's family. They acted liked we'd had the anti-Christ to dinner.' I have to look down to aim. 'What about you?'

Victor doesn't answer for a few seconds. 'I think this could be it,' he says. He almost sounds as though he's trying not to laugh.

I look up.

'A Kodak moment,' he grins. He has the camera up to his eye. 'This is one Christmas memory I intend to keep.'

At a small blue house with a Cola sign nailed to the side we sit on the porch trimmed with tinsel, staring in at the two bare rooms beyond the open doors, and drink warm *gaseosas* while the farmer asks us how much *plata* the trip from England cost and tells us about the guerrillas 'up there' and the high cost of living here in the hills, and the farmer's wife, in a sad blue satin dress, nods, and his little girls hang on to their mother's skirt, silently waiting for the *gaseosas* they've asked for that they're not going to get.

We trek on to the Parque Arqueologico, the most important and interesting place in San Agustín, according to the guidebook. The guidebook uses the words 'mysterious' and 'unforgettable', describing a trove of ancient treasures, tombs, sacred burial mounds, sarcophagi, and the Bosque de las Estatuas, where thirty-five statues of different origins have been assembled along a footpath that snakes through the forest.

'Um,' says Victor as we stalk past the stalls selling replica El Tablóns and *idolos*, San Agustín tea towels, friendship bracelets and snacks.

'Um,' say I as we stare into another hole in the ground.

We follow the signs past families eating ice-creams and taking pictures and the occasional Germans or Swiss standing together looking impressed at the Bosque de las Estatuas.

'Well,' says Victor as we stop on the well-trodden path through the fringe of the forest to read the placard on another statue.

I'm trying to imagine where this jaguar was 700 or 800 years ago today, what it looked like then, who was watching it, but my imagination fails. I'm unable to picture the jaguar anywhere but here at the side of the gravel path dotted with candy wrappers and trampled flowers. 'I can't decide whether this is worse or better than Tunja,' I say at last.

In Tunja, the mysterious ancient statues were in a small park by the side of the motorway next to El Restaurante Chibcha. There was no one else in the park but a woman, a boy and a cow.

'This is,' says Victor.

It isn't until we're leaving that we find something worth the price of admission. The toilets. The toilets aren't in the middle of the living room, they are in private cubicles where you can squat on the rim of the bowl in peace and no one can hear the state of your bowels.

'Now that was unforgettable,' says Victor as he emerges from the Men's.

'There's an old travellers' saying,' I tell him. 'It's the little things that mean the most.'

'There's a better one,' says Victor, heading towards the exit. 'Beer.'

'Go away!' I say in my firmest Spanish. 'Go away!'

God, I hate this. This doesn't come close to what I consider broadening my horizons or opening up my world. Right at this moment I should be standing in the weary queue in front of the telecom building, waiting – again – to put in a call to Brooklyn while Victor discusses politics with someone else loyally waiting for a friend to shout a few unintelligible words into the plastic receiver before the line goes dead or the people shuffling behind him force him to hang up. But I'm not.

Where I am is at the back of the telecom building, halfway up a steep hill covered with rubbish, wishing I were still in the bar. Behind me is the San Agustín basketball court and outdoor auditorium, deserted on this sacred afternoon. Somewhere to my left, on a roof behind the stage separated from my hill by a ravine that has to be jumped, is Victor, kneeling in the broken glass. Across the road a few chickens wade through the shrubs of a small house. Between me and the chickens are three dogs – one brown and scarred, one black and scarred, one dirty white with patches of grey – none of whom like me. They move forward, growling with more teeth than seems normal.

'I mean it,' I say, my tone still firm. According to the survival manual read by my travelling companion, the way to discourage possibly rabid dogs from savaging you is to crouch down and pretend to eat. The human brain is indeed a wondrous thing. Even in times of definite peril and overwhelming doom it continues to function, to think, to reason, to ask pertinent questions. The chickens disappear into the bushes, firecrackers go off in the centre of town, and my wondrous human brain asks, 'Why?' Why should miming a person eating her dinner on a hillside protect me from being ripped apart by creatures closer in spirit to their savage ancestors than to the beribboned and bandannaed man's best friends of home? And even though part of my wondrous human brain is looking around for something to climb or throw, another part is saying, *maybe it taps into some primal memory . . . you know, the half-starved wolf watching the man hunched over his fire, gnawing at a hunk of woolly mammoth, suddenly understanding that if he is patient and doesn't come on too strong with the fangs and the snarls he may get not a club between the eyes but a still-warm bone and a place within range of the flickering flames.* It could make sense. Or, my wondrous human brain goes on, it could be the certain ancient knowledge that to disturb someone tucking into her dinner is to ask for trouble. This could make sense, too. To me, scoffer of the need for rabies shots, both explanations make quite a bit of sense. It could work. And I could do it. I could crouch down and pretend I'm eating roast potatoes and gingerbread men. But I'd rather just shoot them. 'Go away!' I scream again. 'Go away!'

The dogs edge forward. I edge back.

Someone who isn't me begins to scream. It's Victor. 'The meat!' he's saying. 'I forgot the meat!'

I allow my eyes to wander from the dogs just long enough to take in Victor, crouched on the dodgy-looking roof where condoms and candy wrappers float in dark puddles, his arms in the air.

'The meat!' he shouts again. 'It's in the bag!' In the bag hanging over my shoulder.

Victor and I have been travelling together long enough now for me to know that he does these things on purpose. It was he who first saw the stray dog with the small plastic bag full of bottle tops tied to its tail. He who dragged me out of the bar, where I was perfectly happy, to follow it for nearly an hour, while men and small children threw rocks at it and kicked it, their laughter bell-like in the after-dinner stillness. When the dog, panicked and desperate, finally cornered itself on the roof with no way of escape, it was Victor who jumped the four-foot gap to reach the dog, but left the packet of meat intended to instil trust in the bag with the woman who'd rather be back at the bar.

My eyes return to the dogs who've been following me. There is less space between us than there was a few seconds ago.

'For Christ's sake!' screams Victor. 'What's keeping you?'

'What's keeping me?' I shout back. 'What the hell do you think is keeping me? Cupid, Donner and Blitzen?'

'They're not going to hurt you,' Victor assures me. 'They're just dogs. You're bigger than they are.'

I am bigger than they are, but they have all their own teeth. Don't let them know you're afraid, I tell myself. They won't attack unless they think you're afraid.

The two larger dogs don't know I'm afraid. Accustomed to being kicked and stoned, they growl but hold their ground. The smallest of the three, however, does know I'm afraid. I can tell this by the way he's attached himself to the bottom of my jeans.

'Just kick him away!' orders Victor. 'Show him who's boss.'

But we both know who's boss.

'Kick!' yells Victor. 'Give him a kick!'

I would like to kick him, I really would, but I can't see how I can do this without falling over. I pull instead.

'Today, Dyan! That soldier will be coming back soon.'

I don't want to be arrested by the young man stuck with guarding the telecom building while his comrades are all in the bars or back home eating *pan con queso* and drinking *aguardiente* any more than I want to be left shredded across the hillside. Half hopping, half hobbling, I carefully cross to the point where Victor jumped to the roof, dragging the one dog with me while the others follow, quivering with excitement.

Victor is squatting a few feet from the bony brown mutt, talking softly. Victor isn't looking at me, but the dog, lying quietly now, is. He's wondering what the hell is going to happen next, what new form of human torture this might be.

I take the oily paper packet from the bag. The growling simmers beside me as six dark eyes watch me with new interest, the grip on my jeans slipping just a little.

'For Christ's sake,' Victor hisses. 'Throw the damn thing!'

I was never good at sports. When teams were picked, I was always the player chosen last. Once chosen, I was the player no one else would allow near the ball. I throw. The packet bounces off the black head and lands in the road. The three dogs spring after it, snapping at each other.

'You see what I mean?' Victor says to the dog beside him. 'She does it on purpose.'

It really is a day for miracles. After only four attempts, the satellite connects the phone booth outside the telecom building in San Agustín – where whole families queue up to take turns screaming *Feliz Navidad* into the echoes and static – with the black beetle phone in Tommi's kitchen in Brooklyn. Jack answers.

'Perfect timing,' says Jack. In the background I can hear not Bing nor Elvis but some band named after something either toxic, depressing or illegal shouting out 'Silent Night' in broken English and decimated German. 'We were just going to eat.'

'Stop winding her up,' screams Tommi. 'Wish her Merry Christmas then come and put the stuff back in the oven.'

'Merry Christmas,' says Jack. 'You get arrested yet?'

'Not yet,' I admit. 'But there's still time.'

Tommi grabs the phone from him, imitation sleigh bells ringing as she puts the receiver to her ear. She's full of news. The snows have started, the boiler broke down, the landlord was taken away by the police for smashing up the car of his ex-wife's new boyfriend with a sledgehammer, the new tenants have a pet iguana, Jack has another scar over his eye from falling off the front of a Ford while intoxicated, they went to a great party on Christmas Eve where Jack played Santa, there are lights across the building and a wreath on the door, the man across the street has outdone himself this year with a moving diorama of Rudolph the Red-Nosed Reindeer, and my agent would like me to call her when the holidays are over.

'What about you guys?' asks Tommi. 'You're the ones on the big adventure. What's happening?'

Our daily lives are made up of hundreds of incidents and crises. Back in London – back in my daily life – I would know what to say to the question, what's going on? I would report on the progress of the wall in the bathroom, or what happened at dinner the night before. I would complain about deadlines or troublesome plots. I would detail the disasters of the last few days – blown lights, lost keys, missed appointments, unexpected bills, disagreements with friends, flooding washing machines and air in the shower head, the dog next door in the garbage again. I could fill up several minutes with an anecdote about the stray cat that comes in and eats Elvis's food while he watches in alarm or an argument had with the chap at the gas board, what do you mean he can't come until Tuesday? Half an hour could be taken up with a description of the really appalling show just seen on the telly or my conversation with the young man trying to sell me dishcloths and clothes pegs as an alternative to begging on the street. But this isn't daily life, traumatic but dull. This is an adventure.

I stare across the telecom plaza. The outside tables of the bar across the way are full, the streets crowded with families and gaggles of teenage boys and girls. Men stand on the corner, hugging each other and laughing, the shoeshine and cigarette boys hovering behind them. Victor is sitting on the kerb with a guy in a green tracksuit, smoking a cigarette and discussing the cost of a ticket to Colombia.

'Well?' she prompts.

I can't think of anything to say. The details I remember – the things that catch my attention – are not the things adventures are made of. That people step over the bags of turkeys and sleeping children on the floors of the buses without seeming to notice them? That we saw a pig strapped to the back of a van? That Victor finally untied the bag of bottle tops from the sad-eyed dog and leaped from the roof with the dog in his arms? That we passed a couple dancing on their porch on our way back to Doña Silviana's last night while the midnight fireworks exploded and the night echoed with shouts of *Feliz Navidad*?

'Not much, really.' Victor and the young man beside him, joking with the boy in the faded Raiders T-shirt trying to sell them cigarettes, lean their heads back, laughing, squinting up at the sun. 'It's Christmas.'

18

DEATH IS NOT THE END

He sits with his face to the window, as intent as a doctor studying an X-ray. The way he holds his shoulders says that this isn't what he'd expected, that there's something wrong. 'Things are different, but still exactly the same.' His whisper is both astounded and resigned. 'When I was young, I never imagined things would turn out like this.'

The *colectivo* passes a vacant lot dotted with buzzards and a mural on an old stone wall, its colours faded but its figure clear, those big buggy eyes, that high square head, that flippant mouth.

'Who's that?' asks the man crammed beside me, pointing with a finger that hasn't been properly washed in days, maybe months.

'Bart Simpson,' I answer.

'Who's Bart Simpson?' He turns for a last glance. 'A football player?'

'No,' I say. 'He isn't a footballer.'

He sits back. His fatigues are black with dirt and sweat and blood and smell like the death you're hoping to avoid. 'He's not a politician, is he?' he asks suspiciously.

'No, he's not a politician. He's a cartoon character.'

His voice changes from suspicion to fatalism. 'American.' Several books and speeches on the nature of American are contained in his nod. He knows what American means. 'What did the caption say?' He is not a man who takes too much for granted any more.

The caption, copied from a T-shirt or maybe a mug, says: Underachiever and Proud of It.

'Typical American cultural subversion,' he doesn't so much say as spit. Give the oppressed a hero who relishes failure, who embraces losing. 'It's not enough that you control our governments and economies. You want to control our hearts and minds as well. American television, American clothes, American food and drinks and films.' He gives me a glance. 'American tourists, corrupting our children and destroying our traditions.'

He himself is an over-achiever, inspired by challenge. Afflicted with chronic asthma from childhood, he forced himself to excel at athletics, to become a traveller undaunted by hardship, deprivation or the lack of hot food, to finish his studies in three years instead of six. Turned down for military service on medical grounds, he went on to lead an army of his own.

'This may surprise you,' I say, 'but you're expressing the establishment opinion when it comes to Bart.'

It does surprise him, but he doesn't let it show. He has been surprised before. He slowly prepares a cigar. 'How's that?' he asks.

I tell of the public outcry over Bart's eschewing of under-achievementdom in a land where success is measured in how much more you have than everyone else.

'Really?' he asks, weighing this with his mistake about the revolutionary zeal of the Indians and peasants, his miscalculation in the Congo, his total fuck-up in Bolivia.

'Really,' I say. 'The middle-class parents of America went apeshit.' Decrying this communist subversion, railing against this contempt for their values. 'My friend's husband won't let her watch *The Simpsons* because he says it attacks the American family.'

'*Qué es* "apeshit"?' he wants to know.

'Remember the Bay of Pigs?' I wave smoke from my face. 'That's going apeshit.'

He exhales a perfect ring that disappears over the heads of our fellow passengers like a dream. He remembers the Bay of Pigs.

Far from any town, the houses are huts of mud, laundry spread out on the bushes to dry. A man in swimming trunks bathes in a barrel at the side of the road while his children wait for traffic to pass. Music fills the *colectivo* as we ride through the rainy mountains of Ecuador – swirls of grey, bursts of green, distant glimpses of blue – on a road that might have been carved, songs about love with an up-tempo beat or a tear in the throat, if it doesn't save you it will kill you for sure.

I glance at my companion, a man who's known love. All I can see is the back of his head, the silvered hair long and matted.

'Look at them,' he's saying, pointing to the children running shouting beside the van, palms outstretched. These are not the children from a Coca-Cola billboard, one multiethnic world filled with love and good dress sense, but from a poster for Unicef, You Can Help. 'This is what I fought for,' he says. 'So our children could beg and wear the cast-off clothing of their enemies. For the Third World, where people must live without dignity.' He doesn't add – as he, a man whose body was hacked apart by his killers and displayed like a trophy, buried, disintered and finally burned, well might – and die without dignity, too.

I'm not sure I totally agree. You can't deny the poverty and lack of choice, but the concept of the Third World as another planet, populated by downtrodden aliens, both violent and backward, who believe in ghosts and witches and useless gods, is beginning to elude me. Once you get used to livestock on public transport and toilets in the ground, cold showers and rampant child labour, a limited choice in food and television programmes, the difference between the first and the third is less than two. We all have our superstitions, our ghosts and witches and useless gods; we are all trapped and defeated in our different ways.

'What dignity is there in living a life of monotony and mediocrity, a slave to your credit rating, your personal details on a computer, your dreams bartered away for a pension you may never live to see?' I ask.

There was a time when this statement might have gained me a lecture on the inevitable birth of a moral world, with the revolution as midwife, but that time is past. He is an old man now, his beard grizzled, his body corpulent, his eyes as cloudy as the patchwork mountains.

'Perhaps you have a point,' he says. 'The only true dignity is in fighting against what tries to crush your spirit in whatever way you can.' His smile has lost some of its charm. 'From behind a plough or a deep-freeze, it's all the same.'

We jolt into a small village, pass several people walking their goats and the office of the Ecuadorian Socialist Party, and stop at the Plaza Bolivar, surrounded by hedges sculpted into birds and men and elaborate columns. The woman in the bright yellow suit with the parrot gets off.

'Bolivar,' says my companion, but it is difficult to determine what he means. Bolivar, dangerous in life? Bolivar, safe as the Queen in death?

My companion and Bolivar have a lot in common. Determination. Ideals. Vision. I mention this to the man beside me as four more people and a sack of empty brandy bottles take up the space left by the woman and the bird.

'*Claro*,' he says, gazing out at the weathered statue of the Liberator in the centre of the square. 'We're both dead.'

'That too,' I agree. I look on the bright side. 'But death made you both legends.'

It isn't that bright.

'Now that is losing,' he says, laughing as he hasn't laughed in years. 'Bolivar must be raising hell. Instead of a united continent he has parks and plazas named after him.'

'Then perhaps you did win,' I say. I point to the black face stencilled on the whitewashed wall beyond his window. The legend lives.

'"8 Octubre – 25 años,"' he reads, only then recognising the man he used to be. His eyes take on the look of an administrator used to calculation. 'Are there T-shirts?' he asks.

I nod. 'All over the West. Posters and stickers, too.'

'It's like being shot with your own gun,' he says. He turns his eyes, still narrow and dark, on me. 'What about Fidel?' he goes on. 'Are his T-shirts on sale in the First World?'

'No,' I say. 'He's not a legend, he's a thorn in their side.'

'You see,' he says. 'I lost, too.' He spits out of the window into the dust of the road.

Groaning and grinding, we descend dark green mountains, riding through clouds.

He stands up, readjusting his beret after banging his head on the ceiling, cigar ash drifting from his clothes. 'Let's get off,' he says. 'There are no gringos here, just simple peasants living as they have always lived.'

Sunlight glints off television antennae and battered tin signs for Coca-Cola and Black Cat shoe polish. The unbeaten path at last. Tripping over a basket of potatoes, I follow him out of the van.

The town of Mira, population 5,000 plus livestock, is in no danger of being overrun, corrupted or ruined by Yanqui imperialism or busloads of sunburned tourists looking for cheap souvenirs. The good citizens of Mira can rest easy on that score.

The woman who owns the *residencia* eyes us silently, two small children hanging on to her skirt, an infant sleeping in her arms, standing back from the smells of stale blood and sweat emanating from my comrade in travel, her back to the wall of the *sala* that is crowded with the furniture from more elegant days.

No stranger to stubbornness, my comrade's voice is gentle but persuasive, admiring the *dueña's* baby, discussing crop rotation and the price of coffee beans, telling her a story about a Christmas in the Sierra Maestra.

She isn't fooled. 'What is it you want?' she asks when he's through.

'A room,' he says.

She isn't fooled, or perhaps she just didn't understand him, defeated by his accent. '*Qué?*'

'A room,' he repeats. 'A room for the night.'

Fear is one of the few things stronger than greed. 'You have papers?' she asks.

He shakes his head. 'No,' he says. 'I'm a citizen of the world.'

This cuts less ice than a paper straw. 'You have to have documents,' she insists. 'It's the law.'

And one time he might have argued this, tried to teach her that unjust laws have got to be broken, but that time, too, has passed. He knows why he lost; knows now that most of the people he was trying to free wanted nothing more than to be left in peace. He reaches into the pocket of his jacket and pulls out an ancient passport, more dead than he is.

For once, the ignorance of the people is in his favour. She takes the passport, staring blindly at the words and numbers, trying to match the faded, yellowed photo with the faded, ragged face in front of her. 'What do you do?' she demands.

I wait to see what he will say. Teacher? Theorist? Major? Minister of Industry? Liberal icon? '*Médico,*' he says.

'*Médico?*' She knows he's lying, you can see it in her eyes. Doctors do not wear broken boots or wretched clothes, their beards are not knotted with dirt. Doctors dress in suits and ties, their nails are clean and manicured, their faces immaculate and smooth. She hands him back the battered book. 'You'll have to go somewhere else,' she says.

We walk up and down the quiet, empty streets of Mira, past courtyards filled with flowers and caged birds, twice around the plaza with the statue of the Cardinal in its centre, searching for a room that doesn't exist. There is nowhere else.

We stop in front of the stone Cardinal, smiling perpetually and benevolently on the blue and beige concrete of the plaza and the dustbins painted to look like clowns.

Naturally enough, my travelling companion is sensitive to the vanity of the clergy. 'Why do you think they portrayed him with his glasses on?' he asks. 'To make him seem more human, more kindly, a friend and not a foe?'

'Because no one would have recognised him without them,' I answer.

He strides on. 'We can sleep in the hills,' he says, stalking past the three little girls watching us warily as they chase each other around the pastel benches. 'Let's get something to eat.'

We walk down and up the staring streets of sleepy Mira, past empty restaurants and tiny shops stocked with only sweets and biscuits, packets of crisps and plastic barrettes on thin sheets of cardboard, a few bananas and a bag of dried corn, dusty tins and bottles of sauce, the afternoon as quiet as a tomb.

El Restaurante Rio has no food. The bar near the plaza, decorated with pictures of blondes in bell bottoms and bathing tops, doesn't sell beer, never mind meals. The *picaderia*, five tables, a calendar with a topless blonde on the wall and one sign for Sprite, is deserted. La Boascia has only meat, but not today. In El Comedor Rayenza, a small unlit room consisting of four tables and a counter and the last restaurant in town, we try again.

'Let me ask this time,' he says, stepping forward as the proprietress emerges from the courtyard, drying her hands on her skirt. 'You speak Spanish like a gringo.'

He pulls himself up to his full height, smiles politely and speaks clearly, sounding nothing like a gringo. 'We would like to eat,' he tells her, 'but we don't eat meat, chicken, or fish. Do you have anything we can eat?'

The dark head nods. '*Sí* we have chicken.'

'No,' he says patiently, 'we don't eat chicken. We're vegetarians. We don't eat chicken, meat or fish.'

She shakes her head sadly. 'We don't have fish.'

'That's good,' he says, as though she's finally absorbed his explanation of dialectical materialism. 'We don't eat fish.'

I back him up. 'We don't eat fish, chicken, or meat,' I inform her, still the one sentence I can say without having to think. 'Do you have anything we can eat?'

Again she nods. '*Sí*, we have sausage.'

'No rice?' he asks. 'No beans? No lentils? No eggs?'

'Chicken,' she answers. 'But it won't be cooked until tonight.'

'That was always the problem,' he mutters as we trudge back into the street. 'People won't listen.'

There's a wheeled stand selling potatoes, roasted corn and charred flesh in front of the empty bus office. The Otavalan behind the glass wears black trousers and his hair in a plait that reaches his waist, his dark eyes are blank. My companion calls him *amigo*. '*Amigo*,' he says, 'six potatoes and a bag of corn.'

Dumbly, the Indian fills a brown bag with corn.

'*Amigo*,' he says, 'do you grow these things yourself?'

But the Otavalan doesn't want to discuss crop rotation or the market price of corn any more than the woman in the *residencia* did. 'Twenty sucres,' he says, and holds out his hand.

The corn is salty, the potatoes dry. 'I'll ask this time,' I decide as we step into the darkness of the tiny shop.

He gestures me ahead of him, as gallant as a Don. 'Be my guest.'

I have bought water before. '*Se vende agua aquí?*' I ask the old man dozing in the chair with the cat on his lap.

'*Qué?*'

'Water. Do you sell bags of water?'

'*Qué?*'

My companion steps forward. 'Water,' he says. 'Do you sell water?'

The old man studies his lips for a few seconds. 'Water wheat,' he says at last.

We look at each other, then back at him. 'What is water wheat?' we ask as one.

The old man shrugs. 'I don't know.'

'Now I know why I spent so much time in the mountains,' he says. He isn't speaking to me.

It might be the setting of a fairy tale – or it might be that of a myth. Dark snow-capped mountains nudge the clouded sky, and tucked into the valley at their feet lies an aged city, its narrow cobbled streets and steep stone stairs twisting and dipping up the hillside. It is a city of spectres; doomed soldiers and desperate priests, the descendents of the sun, sure in their universe, and the homesick maidens of Madrid, bored in the Andes; natives and invaders, drunk and sober, blood-mad and placid, hacking apart their enemies and quietly pursuing a life of survival. It was here that Rumiñavi, a general as great as Crazy Horse, a resistance leader as determined as Che, murdered Quilliscacha and turned his body into a kettle drum, burning the city of his people's dreams behind him as the Spanish, undaunted by their heavy crossing of the Andes, finally drew near. Here that the conquerors built their own city and put their names on its walls. Here they tortured Rumiñavi and his warlords and executed the passionate resistor in its centre square. Here, as in Bogotá, they built the first astronomical observatory in the new world.

Here is where I stop.

'You go on,' I gasp, collapsing on a broken stone wall scribbled with the legends of lovers long gone. The street smells of urine and things biodegrading. 'Leave me to die.'

When the guidebook said that Quito would leave you breathless it wasn't the view that it meant. Across the valley, the Virgen de las Americas looks down on a city as filthy as the useless Machangara, on the black air and the endless traffic beneath it, on garbage strewn across broken, pitted steps, on the dead rats in the heaps of refuse that ring the market.

Victor stops and looks back. 'We can't quit now.' He points the opened guidebook behind me to the hundreds of steps we've just climbed. We should have known that an area called Tola Alta would be straight up a bloody mountain. 'We must be nearly there.'

'There' is not, of course, where we're really supposed to be.

It is the nature of man to make plans, and the nature of God to fuck them up. Bolivar had planned a united land, liberal and free, but instead his legacy is a gaggle of unstable countries where CIA agents pretending to be salesmen and oil representatives drink imported whisky in the bars of their hotels and where the borders are heavily patrolled by armed youths. We had planned to ride through the Andes on a Honda 750 with the wind in our hair and the sound of pan pipes in our ears, but instead we travel cramped on buses, entertained by young men with guitars and shabby children reciting poems when not being deafened by the pop music on the cassette player. Che had planned to recreate the world, but instead it was the world that recreated him. We planned our route through Ecuador with excitement and purpose, sure that here we would discover the reason we'd come. At last we were out of Colombia, so white, so Western, so much like a poor sister of Spain, and in the South America with an older soul. We would go first to Otavalo, with its Indians still steeped in their traditions and crafts, then spend New Year in Quito, leave what we didn't need at the *residencia* there, then go on to the rainforest to boat up the river. Instead, we came straight to the city, sent here by the heavy hand of fate, searching not for magic and unconquered ghosts, but for a dentist who speaks English.

I'm still gasping. 'You go on. I'll find you if I ever start breathing again.'

'Casa Patty,' chants Victor. 'Use of kitchen. Hot shower. Friendly, clean, safe. Will store luggage. Highly recommended.'

The sanitation of Quito might leave a certain amount to be desired, its main streets might be a jungle of beggars, sellers, pick-pockets, bag-slashers and boys shouting out 'gringo' and '*amigo*'; its air might be thin and threatening, and its Inca ruins don't exist, but it still has its treasures.

Like a half-dead conquistador, drawn past reason and endurance by the promise of glory and gold, I feel hope shoving me on. I'll be all right once I've had a hot shower. I'll be all right after I've had a hot meal. I'll be fine if I never have to leave Tola Alta.

'And anyway,' says Victor as I stagger to my feet, 'this is nothing next to Machu Picchu.'

'You have to pay a little more if you want to use the kitchen,' Doña Patty is saying. Doña Patty is a short, nervously energetic woman who speaks loudly and with emotion, managing to convey both competence and impending chaos at the same time. We are gathered around her at the dining table in one corner of her immaculately frightful living room. The curtains of Doña Patty's living room are floral, the sofa and armchair are floral, the carpet has great swirls of colours that may be flowers and that, like the colours of the curtains and furniture, matches nothing else. The formica shelves are lined with cheerful ceramic animals and plastic plants. In the centre of the table stands a large, glossy photograph of a middle-aged man with a dark moustache and tired eyes. 'You wouldn't believe what they charge for the gas.'

Having already heard what they charge for the electricity, garbage disposal and beef, we probably would.

'We'll——' says Victor.

'I don't really cook for myself any more,' Doña Patty tells me. 'When my daughters are here or my grandchildren, but not when I'm alone.' She nods towards the artificial tree by the television, whose lights are turned on only once, on la Noche Buena, because of the price of electricity. 'I could eat for a week on what it cost to cook Christmas dinner.'

Victor, busy filling in the register, gives me a glance over his shoulder. Despite the expense of eating, Doña Patty is in no imminent danger of starving to death.

'We'd like to use the kitchen,' I say.

'English,' she continues, reading over Victor's arm as he writes.

'I've always wanted to travel myself, but who has the money for things like that? I've never even had a cup of your famous tea.' She sighs. 'There's another English couple downstairs, and two Australian students at the top.' The table is covered in a cloth of plastic lace. Doña Patty looks at it and heaves a sigh even more heartfelt than the first. '*Dios mío*, those girls,' she moans. 'Food poisoning! One of them got food poisoning at Christmas. Do you know how much it costs to get your stomach pumped in Quito?'

We both nod sympathetically.

'Doctors!' cries Doña Patty. 'I can't afford to get ill.'

This time only I nod understandingly. Victor is hesitating over the next entry to be made in the book. He can never remember what '*estado marital*' means.

'*Soltero o casado?*' she prompts. 'I am a widow,' she goes on. 'Five years – can you imagine? – Five years. And here I am, my hair grey with worry, working my fingers to the bone.' She looks at the photograph. 'Poor Armando,' she says. 'You never intended this to happen, did you?' Armando smiles back in death as he probably smiled back in life – silently. 'You can't imagine how hard it is to make ends meet in Quito,' says Doña Patty.

As a general rule, it is always easier to understand another language than it is to speak it. Which means that we have an unexpected advantage in conversing with Doña Patty since she doesn't require that we actually say anything.

'Mmm.'

'Mmm.' Victor hands me the pen.

'A writer?' says Doña Patty from close to my elbow. 'I should write about my life. The stories I could tell you . . . People stay here from all over the world, you know.' She makes a sound that is less wistful than it is reminiscent of the air being let out of a tyre. 'But who has the time? I have too much to do just to keep the roof over my head.'

She stands up and takes a set of keys from the back of the living-room door. 'I haven't had a chance to get the room ready yet,' she apologises as she bustles us downstairs. 'The Germans only left this morning.' She sighs again, and marches us towards the back of the house. 'It's one thing after another from morning to night. The life of a widow is not an easy one,' she says.

We follow her into a small, dark courtyard. There are three rooms facing out on one side, one on the other, an old stone sink in the centre and a thin wooden door with a key in the lock at the end.

Victor breaks the Doña Patty sound barrier first. 'Is that the bathroom?' he asks. 'There's hot water?'

In answer, Doña Patty hooks a sharp right and opens the door. 'This is the bathroom,' she says. 'But you have to be careful with the shower. You can't put it on all the way.' She steps back to let us look inside. 'And you can't use the hot water for washing clothes. *Dios mío!*' She sighs again. 'You have no idea how expensive the electricity is.'

We poke our heads through the door. The toilet is blue and seatless, the electric showerhead is also blue, its wires twisting around the water pipe, the Frankenstein switch beside the tap.

'Let it trickle,' says Doña Patty. 'And don't stay in too long.'

'And is that where we can do our laundry?' I ask as we move away from the loo.

'No, no,' says Doña Patty. 'The laundry is up on the roof.' She marches to the door of the centre room. 'But it's really for the students who live here. You can't use it unless you stay for more than eight days.' Her sighs are becoming longer and more heartfelt by the second. 'The water in Quito costs an arm and a leg.'

'This is the key,' she says, handing it to Victor as she pushes open the door. 'You have to leave it upstairs whenever you go out. I can't afford to have them lost.' She motions us inside. 'Do you know how much they want just to copy a key?'

The room we are lucky to get because the Casa Patty is so popular that it is causing Doña Patty's hair to go grey, flesh to whittle and her daughters to worry about her is large and clean, and opulently furnished with three single beds, a wardrobe and a table and chair.

Doña Patty collapses on the bed by the window. 'Sometimes I don't know myself why I do it,' she says. 'My daughters say, "Mama, you've worked hard all your life, you deserve a rest now."' She appeals to Victor. 'But what can I do? I'm a widow. Armando wouldn't want me to be a burden on them.'

Victor, who has stoically if silently stood through our first episode of the life and trials of Doña Patty for nearly half an hour despite the considerable pain he's in, doesn't nod sympathetically now.

'Do you know of any dentists nearby?' he cuts in. 'Any dentists who speak English?'

'Dentists?' Doña Patty clutches her heart. 'You don't need a dentist, do you?' *Dios mío*, they charge more than the doctors.'

Doña Patty, possibly to save money, is unfamiliar with the bus system of Quito, but the maid, who can't be more than fourteen, says that the bus marked 10 de Agosto will take us near the English-speaking dentist recommended in the guidebook. We stand on the kerb of the road that leads back to the bus station, deliberately trying not to breathe this time, waiting and waving at the buses that say 10 de Agosto as they belch by, moving far more rapidly than you'd think possible in the swarm of traffic.

'Maybe they think we're just being friendly,' says Victor as two more 10 de Agostos pass without pulling over. 'Are you sure we're at the right stop?'

I go into the electrical shop for a lesson in how to catch a Quitan bus. Yes, the young man assures me, the 10 de Agosto or the 6 de Deciembre, either will take you to Colón. Yes, they stop right outside.

Victor doesn't believe me. That is, he knows I think I'm telling the truth, but he doesn't feel I can be totally trusted. He hasn't forgotten who it was who thought the woman at the Govinda in Bogotá said that the sticker we admired came from a conference in Venezuela when what she'd actually said was that it came from a bookshop on Calle Venezuela. Or who was so certain that the girl at the bus station in La Plata said the bus would stop at Tierradentro for ten minutes and not drop us off in the rain, three kilometres up a mountain in the opposite direction. Or who it was bought a kilo of raisins when she wanted half a kilo of nuts.

'I'll just ask those women over there how much it costs,' he says, and strolls over to the two middle-aged matrons dressed for a day out in shiny skirts and blouses and rhinestone sweaters.

The darker one shakes her head as he speaks. 'No, no, no,' she says. 'The 6 de Deciembre doesn't go to Colón.'

'Colón . . .' mutters her friend with a look of concentration. 'Which bus goes to Colón?'

A sleeve the colour of buttercups juts into the air, shaking frantically. 'That one!' shouts the first woman. 'That bus goes to Colón.'

The woman with the Madonna shopping bag grabs her arm, even as the bus that has been flagged down emerges from the fumes, aiming towards the kerb, slow enough to be considered stopping. 'No, not that one,' she says, shooing the driver back into traffic. Her own arm, blue as the sky over Quito must once have been, starts thrashing at the air. 'That's the bus to Colón!'

Her friend disagrees. 'No it's not.' She points at yet another bus. 'That's the bus to Colón.'

But the second woman is shaking her head. 'I don't think so. I think the bus to Colón is—'

Heading more or less straight for us is a 10 de Agosto. I still feel pretty confident about the 10th of August. I wave my hand. In the quantum world, anything can happen, though that doesn't mean that it will. In the material world, things are supposed to happen in a certain way, though that, too, doesn't mean that they will. But sometimes, against all the laws of Mr Murphy, they do. The bus stops inches from the kerb.

Both of our advisers start shrieking at once. 'You don't go to Colón, do you?'

The several people squeezed into the seat beside the driver all nod. Sí, sí, Colón. 'Siga! Siga!' screams the driver. The bus starts to move again. 'Siga! Siga!' Jumping for the stairs, we hurl ourselves through the open door.

It's not as though I've never been on a crowded city bus before. We have crowded city buses in New York and London. Most of them are not what my mother would call 'so clean you can eat off it', and most of them give even the most casual passenger a chance to determine the body type, perfume or aftershave and last thing consumed by everyone around you. But the buses of Quito add a new dimension to the concept of full. We squeeze our way up what must be the aisle, stepping over the shoeshine boys sitting on their boxes and trying not to knock the cardboard trays out of the hands of the boys selling sweets, Victor stooped over to avoid hitting his head on the ceiling. Ecuadorians do not share the English timidity about physical contact. No one moves, or pretends to move, or tries to move out of our way.

'Christ,' says Victor as we push into two seats at the back. 'All this and toothache, too.'

I'm beginning to remember how much I hate uncharted territory, how many miles I have walked through the wilds of Brooklyn or Streatham, forced to retrace my route because I had no idea where I was going and was too shy to ask.

'How will we know when we get there?' I nervously ask my travelling companion.

My travelling companion doesn't answer me. He's studying the map.

A middle-aged couple, dressed for a meeting with their solicitor and looking as though they'd be more at home in a BMW than the multicoloured 10 de Agosto, sit down beside me. The man leans towards me. He can't really be wearing Old Spice. He says something unintelligible.

Flattered that he should assume I'd understand him, I say, '*Cómo?*' in my very best accent.

'Do you have the time?'

The fact that he still has confidence in my ability to speak his language gives me confidence. Victor's not the only one who remembers my mistakes in Spanish. I'm the one who wound up in the men's loo at the depot in Popayan, the one who never found the loo in bleedin' Ipiales. 'No, I don't. I don't have a watch.'

He nods. 'Nor do I,' he says. On my other side, Victor, pushed to the limits of endurance not by greed or the thought of a hot shower but by pain, mutters at the map.

Sometimes courage makes you do the impossible: for example, it made Crazy Horse, Che and Rumiñavi keep on fighting when anyone with any sense had already left town. And sometimes courage makes you do the dreaded but mundane: for instance, ask for directions.

'Don't worry,' says my new friend. 'I'll tell you when we're there.'

As we grind our way through the new city, where the charms of Quito are less apparent, he points out things of interest. The park. The shopping district. The Banco Central. I'm more interested in the writing on the walls – YANQUIS HIJOS DE PUTA . . . LIBERTAD O MUERTE.

TERRORISMO

ECOLOGICO

X

A

C

O

ECUADOR NO ES SUYO, the face of Che; OLVIDENSE DE LO QUE SONARAN SUS SUENOS YA FUIERON VENDIDOS – Forget your dreams, they've already been sold.

'Look at that,' I say to Victor, pointing to a scrawl of red paint. SHIT HAPPENS.

Victor looks. 'Another Taoist,' he says.

The section of town where the dentist who speaks English polishes his mirrors and sharpens his drills belongs, at a guess, to the people who bought those dreams. Well-off businessmen and professionals who drive new cars and live behind walled gardens, affluent tourists and foreigners with expense accounts who frequent the English pubs and the tapas bars, the chic cafés and expensive restaurants.

The dentist's office is in a large, elegant house of Spanish influence, set behind a stone wall and a locked wrought-iron gate. I immediately feel relieved. Visions of medieval torture chambers where men in dirty white smocks chisel at the teeth of their victims without benefit of jet drills or sterilised needles haven't made it any easier to persuade Victor that sawing off the cast on your hand with your Swiss Army knife in a hotel room in Colombia is one thing, but wrenching out an infected wisdom tooth in Doña Patty's back bedroom with a piece of string and a doorknob something else. This is where the wives of Texaco honchos come to have their teeth capped and polished. He won't get AIDS or bleed to death here. Victor rings the bell.

We wait on the quiet, tree-lined residential street, far from the belches and bleats of the traffic, listening to a violin concerto drifting gently from the house across the road. Nothing happens for several seconds. Victor rings again. We peer through the bars, expecting a frazzled maid to come running down the path with the keys jangling in her hand. Nothing happens for several more seconds. And then a man appears at an upstairs window. He isn't wearing a starched coat, white as the snow on top of a volcano, or even an impeccable suit with a London label. He's dressed in combat fatigues.

The sight of him dampens my sense of relief. 'Jesus,' I murmur.

Victor, however, takes this in his stride, as though he has suddenly realised that the one thing missing from his life was a dentist who carries a gun. 'We're looking for the dentist,' he shouts. 'Are you the dentist?'

The man shakes his short-cropped head. *Gracias a Dios*. He may be a mercenary guarding the dentist's drug cupboard, or he may be a psychopath holding the dentist and his family hostage in the master bedroom, but he is not the dentist. 'Next door!' he shouts back, jabbing his finger leftwards. He seems accustomed to being mistaken for Dr Roberto Mena. 'Next door.'

Next door is locked and boarded.

Victor gets out the book.

The second English-speaking dentist recommended by the guide is located in a modern office building among the sleek and gleaming stores on the very busy, very cosmopolitan Avenida Amazonas.

We push past the outstretched hands of an Indian woman and her little girl to get through the glass door and into the wood-panelled foyer.

'He isn't here,' says the *portero*. 'He went away.'

We aren't grass-green gringos any more. We know that this could mean anything. We have learned that phrases like 'a half hour's walk' or 'just over the hill' are open to interpretation. Half an hour if you're used to climbing mountains at high altitudes with forty pounds of baggage on your back; just over the hill and twenty kilometres on. 'He isn't here' and 'He went away' might mean the dentist is out getting drunk or has been arrested by the police.

'Forever?' asks Victor.

'*Sí, sí,*' nods the *portero*. 'He doesn't practise any more. His heart.'

But there's a dentist across the street. No, the *portero* doesn't know the dentist personally, but he knows that he's there.

'Pot luck again,' mutters Victor.

'With dentists as with life,' say I.

The office building across the street is the grandest on the block. Its doors are trimmed in brass, its foyer marble. A young man sits behind an enormous reception desk, reading a newspaper.

'*Hay algunos dentistas,*' he says when he finally understands the question. He points to the directory near the door.

We study its listings. Accountants, solicitors, travel agents, dentists. 'Pick a dentist, any dentist,' says Victor. There are at least eight doctors of dental surgery somewhere above us.

'Do any of them speak English?' I ask.

The young man stares back at me. '*Qué?*'

'Is there one who speaks English?'

He blinks.

There are quite a few things I imagined South America would be: dangerous, exotic, spiritually renewing. What I hadn't imagined was that it would be like engaging in one continuous *Cheers* conversation. 'Is there one who speaks English?' asks Norm. 'One who speaks English?' asks Woody. 'One what?'

'Yes,' I say. 'Is there a dentist in the building who speaks English?'

His responses have been restrained so far, but now he shouts. 'Manolo!'

I'm half expecting Manolo, the dentist who knows how to say 'impacted wisdom tooth' and 'it's not going to hurt' in the language of the Queen, to jump out from behind the desk.

But it is the young man who jumps. 'Manolo!' he screams, racing to the back door. 'Manolo! Which is the dentist who speaks English?'

Manolo appears in the doorway. Like the concierge, he can't be more than twenty. He is wearing a Bon Jovi T-shirt and holding a bottle of Coke. 'Perez,' he says. 'Jaime Perez.'

The first young man turns to us. 'Perez,' he repeats. 'Jaime Perez.'

'But he may not be there,' says Manolo.

All three of us look at him. 'Why not?'

Manolo grins. He could use a dentist himself. 'Because he often isn't.'

Victor gives me a smile. 'With dentists as with God,' he says.

Dr Perez is a dignified, silver-haired man in his sixties, dressed not in jungle fatigues but in grey trousers and a blue-white shirt. His cross, his cufflinks and his Rolex are gold. We will never know what miraculous configuration of planets has caused Dr Perez to be in his office and not at lunch in the restaurant of one of the better hotels around the avenue, or at the barber's having his hair trimmed, or playing chess with a friend in a private club whose walls are lined with portraits of dead Spaniards, but today he is. He listens to Victor's tale of pain and inflammation, glancing at his watch as though he wishes that he weren't.

Dr Perez's English might not get him much past page one of *Finnegan's Wake*, but it is good enough to cover, if superficially, the really vital things such as abscess, wisdom tooth, antibiotics, painkillers, and it will have to come out. Chatting about the weather of England, Dr Perez leads Victor through the frosted-glass door to the treatment room and shuts it behind them.

For a while, I can still hear the murmur of their voices, the nervous laughs of a man trying to convince someone that he isn't going to cause him pain and of someone trying to believe him, but then everything goes silent. And stays silent.

How long does it take to extract an impacted tooth? I'm learning that there are quite a few questions whose answers I don't – and may never – know, but I thought I knew the answer to this. Five minutes or so to administer the anaesthetic and let it take effect. A minute or two to judge the angle needed for the elevator. A few more minutes to lift out the tooth – according to my dentist in London a simple procedure that requires no special strength: the secret is all in the wrist.

There are several neat stacks of magazines on the formica coffee table. I have plenty of time to leaf through them while I wait, discovering quite a few things I didn't know about summer fashions, Michael Jackson and the bird life of the Orkneys.

Dr Perez's receptionist, Eugenia, sits in the next room behind her closed window, filing her nails while she reads a magazine of her own, her red lips moving. She isn't accustomed to being interrupted. I finally catch her attention by rapping on the glass.

Eugenia raises her blandly pretty face from the article open before her. She forgot I was here.

'Is everything all right?' I ask.

She has no idea of what I'm talking about. '*Qué?*'

I elaborate. 'With my friend. Is everything all right with my friend?'

Eugenia, who hasn't stirred from her seat since she let us in, and who can't see the treatment room from where she sits, nods, her finger tapping on the photograph of a beautiful young couple who seem to be exchanging saliva. 'Of course,' she assures me. 'He won't be long.' She goes back to her reading. I sit down.

Off the waiting room is a private toilet for the use of staff and patients. I have plenty of time to ascertain that the hot-water tap doesn't work and to search the cupboard for toilet paper, too. The waiting room is still empty when I return.

Dr Perez got his degrees in Buenos Aires. I also have plenty of time to study the diplomas reassuringly hung around the walls between the framed prints of paintings by van Gogh and Matisse. Indeed, since time seems to have ground to a total halt, I will probably be reading these diplomas for the next hundred years.

I start to worry. If I were someone else – someone like Eugenia, for instance, earnestly absorbed in learning all she can about the secrets of a good relationship – I probably wouldn't worry. Eugenia knows that the secret of a good relationship isn't lust but mutual trust and respect. She also knows that no one dies because he has a tooth taken out. But I am not Eugenia. I know that mutual trust and respect don't have the chance of survival of a snowball in hell when lust starts strutting her stuff. I know that life is an ironic bitch.

Death might have met Victor on any sharp and rain-swept curve in London. It might have reached him on the bullet of a cop who was shooting at someone else, or a soldier who wasn't. Death might have stabbed him in an alley or punched him through the window of a wild party. It might have run him over as he was crossing a street on his way to phone his mother. All of these deaths have tragic, not to mention romantic possibilities. But not this one; death by dentist. Imagine if Che had been killed not fighting in Bolivia but while having his teeth filled in Havana. Forget the T-shirts. No one would remember his name.

The door opens suddenly and Dr Perez steps through it. He's wearing his suit jacket and carrying a panama hat. He isn't a dark man, but he looks decidedly whiter and closer to seventy than I'd thought before. He dabs at his forehead with a blue handkerchief and puts his hat on his head. He gives me a smile. 'I'm exhausted,' he laughs. 'That was some job.'

Victor doesn't emerge from the other room until Dentist Jaime has left. Victor, too, looks paler and closer to seventy than he did before. He's holding a piece of gauze to his mouth with one hand and a prescription in the other.

'Let's go,' he mumbles, already at the door.

'Well?' I ask as I hurry down the stairs after him. He doesn't want to wait for the lift. 'What happened?'

'What do you think happened?' Pain may kill the appetite, crush desire and obliterate happiness and hope, but it doesn't make a dent in sarcasm. 'We had a party. I'm surprised you couldn't hear us. Cold beer, hot food – you should've been there, Dyan, you would've loved it. Springsteen provided the music.'

'It was worse than you imagined?' I guess.

Victor strides across the marble foyer and into the street lined with stalls selling colourful crafts and fried plantains. 'It was worse than the devil could have imagined.'

An Otavalan, strands of gold glass beads and coral looped around her neck, stops beside him. She is carrying a metal tray heaped with ice-cream in an improbable shade of pink, cones stuck on top like miniature mountains. Strapped on her back in a woven blanket is a baby. She holds out the tray. '*Helado,*' she says. 'Gringo, *helado.*'

The gringo shakes his head.

I was raised as a woman. I played nurse when I was a kid. I know how to be cheerful and positive when a patient is tetchy and depressed. 'But he got the tooth out, didn't he?' I ask as we suddenly stop at the kerb. 'That's what's important. You'll feel better soon.'

Victor doesn't care about soon. 'Yeah, he took it out.' He spits a mouthful of blood and tooth shavings into the gutter.

The tray touches my arm. '*Helado,*' she repeats. 'It's very good.'

I pull my arm away. '*No, gracias, no.*' I don't know what's in this ice-cream, soft and streaky and far from a freezer, but I don't want it on my clothes.

'He took it out with a chisel.'

Cheerful, positive and sympathetic. I hand Victor a wad of my ill-gotten toilet roll to wipe his chin. 'A chisel?' I repeat the word because I'm sure it can't be what I heard. 'He couldn't have used a chisel, Vic. He was using an elevator. It's a precise dental instrument that—'

The mound of ice-cream veers towards him again. 'With a hammer.' Victor spits another mouthful of blood and tooth chips into the street. 'A chisel and hammer. It's about as precise as a chisel and hammer.'

'*Helado*,' she insists. '*Es muy bueno.*'

'A hammer?' The Otavalan is between us now. The baby gazes back at me passively. 'Are you sure it was a hammer?' There are parts of the past that you want to get in touch with but the tortures of the inquisition are not among them.

'Bloody close enough.' He runs his finger along his gums, dislodging more of the remains of his tooth. Bloody close indeed. 'He practically had his knee in my chest,'

'Señorita,' wheedles the ice-cream vendor. 'Señorita, it's strawberry. Very refreshing.'

Victor, trying to avoid being hit by the baby, steps back on a small girl with her hand out to him. She speaks in the same sing-song whine as the woman. 'Give me a present, Señor.'

'His knee?' This is not the time to laugh. A woman dispensing cheer, positivity and sympathy should not laugh at a man whose life's blood and second teeth are part of the debris on the major shopping avenue of Quito. 'He had his knee on your chest? Where was he sitting, on your lap?'

'Try it, Señorita. Señorita, just one.'

'Señorita, give me a present.'

'It's not funny,' says Victor.

'I didn't laugh,' I say indignantly.

'You want to,' he accuses.

'*Señor, un regalo. Señor, tengo hambre.*'

'No, I don't.' Which is true enough. I don't want to. Only an insensitive cow would laugh at another's ordeal. 'It must have been horrible.'

'*Señorita, por favor . . .*'

'Señorita, it's very good in the heat . . .

It was horrible.

'I had to hold my jaw steady.'

That tears it. The image of Jaime Perez on Victor Sanchez's lap, Victor trying to hold his head still while the good dentist hacks at his mouth with a chisel and hammer, blood on the Rolex and sweat appearing under the arms of the blue-white shirt, is stronger even than the subtle gender teachings of childhood. It's the magic potion of a horror story. Nurse Nancy and Cruella De Ville.

The woman, the baby and the girl all stare at me, that crazy gringo look in their eyes.

'If you don't stop, I'm going to make you eat one of those cones,' mutters Victor. 'Then we'll see who laughs last.'

19

LET'S BUNGLE IN THE JUNGLE

Otavalo was a market town in pre-Inca times. Here nameless Indians, uninterested in conquest or power and famous for nothing, brought jungle products from the eastern lowlands and traded them for highland goods. It would have been a long walk up those richly coloured mountains, so serenely beautiful that they don't look real. They would have camped here for days, the women selling and weaving, cooking and minding the children, catching up on deaths and births and other news as they worked, the men getting smashed on maize liquor and swapping stories as the sun moved across the deep, high sky.

And it is still a market town. 'Justly famous for its friendly people and their Saturday fair,' as the guidebook puts it. Here busloads of tourists from the better Quitan hotels come on Saturday mornings, bringing fistfuls of sucres to trade for blankets, baskets, bags and weavings, and state-of-the-art cameras to take pictures of the friendly natives in their traditional dress. In pre-Inca times, there would have been no Plaza Bolivar or 24 de Mayo, no museums or churches, no artisan shops, nowhere to rent a horse or a jeep or a canoe or cash a travellers' cheque.

'Jesus,' says Victor as we come into the square where the market will be held in two days' time. Nor would there have been a vegetarian restaurant and a Hard Rock Café on the Plaza de Ponchos. 'We're back in the States.'

We look in the window of the restaurant. It's whitewashed walls are decorated with pictures and woven hangings, its tables and chairs are polished pine and topped with a candle, a profusion of plants hangs from the ceiling. It reminds me of three restaurants I know in London, four in New York, and every restaurant in Santa Cruz. It's packed with gringos, easy to spot not just because of their height and their colouring and the state of their teeth, but because gringos are the people in South America who wear ethnic sweaters and Guatemalan trousers.

'What do you think?' asks Victor.

Usually we shy away from the company of gringos on the grounds that if we wanted to talk to Westerners and eat spaghetti we would have stayed home, but the familiar decor and a room full of people who already know how much silver it cost you to get here is unexpectedly inviting.

'Well, at least we're seeing some Indians,' says Victor as we walk through the door.

And he's right. There aren't only gringos here. There are two young women with bronze-ruby skin and near-black eyes, just about as beautiful as humans can get, dressed in the traditional Otavalan long dark skirt and white peasant blouse, strands of gold and coral around their necks, and four young men, equally high on the list of good-looking humans, in short white trousers and woven waist-coats, their hair in a single plait to the waist. The girls are the waitresses, the young men the musicians.

There are four German students at the large table by the window, a young American couple at the small table near the door, an English mountaineer behind them, a middle-class American family – mother, father, noisy son and sulky daughter – next to us, and two Australian travellers to our right.

Another American, decorated in silver and turquoise like a display for Navajo jewellery, bursts into the restaurant and hurls herself into the empty seat at the table beside us. Her hand-knitted sweater is decorated with llamas, her hat has a glittering woven band. 'God, am I bushed.' She drops a new carpet bag with Inca motifs on the floor. It isn't empty. 'You have to bargain for everything, it's harder than working.' She waves the waitress over. 'Coffee!' she says in English, but loudly so that the girl will understand her. 'Coffee and apple pie!'

The girl says, '*Qué?*'

She picks up a menu and points. 'Coffee!' she shouts. 'Apple pie!'

Her friends want to see what she has bought, though it would probably be quicker to see what she hasn't bought. She shows them the bag – 20,000 sucres – and starts pulling out her other souvenirs: smaller bags (10,000 sucres, 15,000 sucres, 8,500); patchwork shirts (18,000 each); a wall hanging of Indians napping in the sun (30,000, reduced from 60,000). 'Not as cheap as Indonesia or India,' she decides, 'but better than what you'd pay at home.'

'They're beautiful,' says the mother. The boy wants another brownie, the father wants to know if she saw any pottery, the girl mumbles something about MTV.

The mountaineer asks the American couple how their meal was. They say it was good. He starts describing the food poisoning he got in Peru.

'I just hope all this isn't changing their way of life,' says the mother.

The woman who shops doesn't think so. 'How would they make a living if it weren't for us?' she wants to know. Ecuadorians don't want traditional crafts, they want American jeans and electric blenders.

The Australian woman says to her husband, 'Tourists. If she knew what she was doing she could have got the whole lot for twenty thousand.'

The musicians start tuning up.

'*Cwando tocaumos?*' shouts the mother, with a friendly smile.

'Now,' answers the drummer.

A fat white man out of a Graham Greene novel in a seersucker suit and panama hat comes in, seating himself at the table abandoned by the Germans. He snaps his fingers at the waitress behind the till. He orders cake and coffee in very good Spanish. She writes down the order, not looking at him. He snaps his fingers again. '*Café con poco, poco leche,*' he says impatiently. '*Poco, poco leche.*' She nods, but still doesn't look.

'He's got to be a CIA agent,' I say to Victor.

Victor picks up his juice. 'Too obvious.' He smiles. Smugly. 'I know who the agents have to be,' he informs me.

'The Australians?' I hiss.

He shakes his head.

'The English geezer?'

'Uh-uh.'

'Well, who?'

Victor nods behind him. 'The Indians.' He smiles again. 'They're the only ones who look out of place.'

*

George says that the same thing that happened to me in Doña Patty's shower happened to him in Bolivia. 'Nearly fell into the sink, the shock was so bad,' he laughs, a seasoned traveller himself. 'The joys of the simple life.' George is the Australian from the restaurant, staying, it turns out, in the room next to ours.

'I got bitten by a dead scorpion,' says his wife. 'In Misahuallí. It was in my sock.'

I step around them with my wet wash. The hotel not only has a real hot shower, it has a double stone sink for laundry and clothes lines strung across the roof terrace outside the first-floor rooms.

'Lynn was bloody lucky,' says George cheerfully. 'We met a bloke in Cuenca who was bitten in the arse.' He grins. 'Couldn't sit down for days.'

Victor, sitting across from them, his wash already hung, drying his hair in the sun, asks them if they've been to Peru.

They've been to Peru, three days in Cuzco, two days in Lima.

George shakes his head. 'You aren't seriously going overland through Peru, are you?'

'Everyone we've met just flies into Cuzco and then to Lima and then out again,' says Lynn. 'Like we did.'

'Not that we didn't have a great time in Peru.' George leans back in his garden chair. 'But you have to be careful. Lynn had forty thousand sucres stolen from her in the hotel in Lima.'

'It was my own fault,' says Lynn. 'I shouldn't have left it in the room.' She picks up her Coke from the white metal table. 'But that's nothing to some of the stories we've heard.'

Three Israelis were travelling through Peru on a bus. At the town where they were to change buses they refused to listen to the driver, who advised them to stay on the bus till the next one arrived, got out, and were immediately robbed of everything they owned.

Six Israelis were travelling through Peru on a bus. The bus drew near to a military checkpoint. The driver told the Israelis to get on the roof and hide among the baggage. The Israelis refused. When the bus stopped at the checkpoint the police stood the Israelis by the side of the road and shot them dead.

'What about the Dutch blokes we met in Cuzco?' George asks Lynn.

'Oh, Jesus,' sighs Lynn. 'You wouldn't believe it. After we heard that, we only took a little cash with us when we left the hotel.'

Six Dutch guys, checking out the market in Cuzco, were jumped by twelve Ecuadorians, beaten up and picked clean.

George shrugs. 'We just made sure we never went out in groups of less than ten, and we were fine.'

'You might have been jumped by twenty guys,' says Victor.

George doesn't reply. He's greeting another Australian who is in a room at the other end of the balcony, the one who thinks he's Mel Gibson. 'We're talking about Peru,' George tells him.

'Jesus, Peru,' says Mel. He sits down next to Victor. 'I know a bloke in jail in Peru. Bought some cocaine from a couple of chaps he met in a bar. Turned out they were cops.' He opens his beer. 'He was a nice guy,' says Mel. 'So I guess he must've tried some.'

Mel has a friend who got drunk at the carnival in Rio, went into a portable loo and sat down to take a shit. A fat black woman came in, also the worst for the celebrations, didn't see him in the dark, sat down on his lap and shat all over him.

'You aren't related to a guy named Ron Castlewhite, are you?' asks Victor.

Mel asks the Australian where they're going for supper. 'It's too bad there isn't a kitchen here,' he says. 'I find I eat better when I cook my own food.'

'Oh, us too,' says Lynn. 'We try to cook for ourselves every so often, even if it's only a cheese and tomato sandwich.'

'What about you guys?' George asks Victor. 'You having a few drinks tonight?'

Victor starts to explain about his tooth and his course of anti-biotics, but there is something in George's tone that makes me suspicious.

I turn from trying to fit my jeans on to the crowded line. 'What day is this?' I ask.

Everyone looks at me.

'Friday,' George answers.

'It's not Thursday?'

Mel, Lynn and George all shake their heads. 'Friday,' George says again. 'New Year's Eve.'

Victor and I look at each other. We counted each day carefully, several times. Sunday in Mira, Monday in Quito – Tuesday in Quito, Wednesday in Quito – today should be Thursday.

'It's Friday,' says Mel. 'New Year's Eve.'

'We forgot Popayan,' Victor tells me. 'Sunday was Popayan.'

George is philosophical. 'It's easy to lose track of the days,' he says.

Guy Lombardo. In the years of my childhood, New Year's Eve

belonged to Guy. My mother would make devilled ham sandwiches on miniature slices of rye bread and Californian onion dip to go with the potato chips. The four of us would gather round the television, watching the couples dancing to the tunes of their youth and Guy in his shiny cardboard hat and tux leading the band, smiling encouragingly at the camera every few minutes to let everyone know that this was his party, that the New Year was going to be a good one, full of music and confetti and everyone being happy. At 11.55 my mother would hand out the hats and noise-makers and my father would get the bottle of sparkling wine from the fridge. Poised for action, we'd watch the countdown at Times Square – ten, nine, eight, seven, six, five, four, three, two, one. On the small screen in the corner, hundreds of people hugged each other and screamed joyously, as though the death of the old year solved all their problems, erased any disasters lurking in the shadows of the future; in the centre of the carpet, my mother, my father, my sister and I shook our rattles and blew our whistles, embracing and shouting out, 'Happy New Year!' The dog usually hid under the couch.

There is a band on the Plaza de Ponchos, spirited and enthusiastic and playing old tunes danced to by couples in the road between the plaza and the Hard Rock Café, George and Lynn among them, but it isn't Guy's music and it isn't Guy's band. The plaza itself, and all the main streets of Otavalo, are jammed with people.

'It's more like Hallowe'en,' I say to Victor as we struggle through the crowds.

Half of the people filling the streets are wearing masks – clowns and cats, goats and gorillas, dinosaurs and Oliver Hardy, princesses and devils and, of course, Bart Simpson. Gangs of children block the traffic of trucks, cars and pedestrians aimlessly cruising through town, begging *limonosas*.

Victor gives 10 sucres to a short witch in plastic sandals. 'Guy Fawkes,' says Victor.

It's more like Guy Fawkes' Night too. There are booths all along the kerbsides, some containing scenes of everyday Ecuadorian life or political satire, tape-decks behind them blaring out the story, others hold effigies made out of old clothes and stuffing and faced with a plastic mask. Fireworks punctuate the uproar of the night.

One of the effigies looks like Fidel. I give Victor a nudge. 'I wonder what Che would think about that.'

'About what I think of that,' he answers. A few of the vehicles slowly circling the town are new black Land Rovers, their windows tinted, neon purple lights shining beneath their chassis. All the young men in the cars, laughing amongst themselves and calling out to friends, wear black felt hats with woven bands and a single plait of black hair down their backs. It's The Last Picture Show, Otavalan-style. There are 35,000 pure-blooded Indians living in and around Otavalo, and quite a few of them are here tonight. Ten of them, teenagers, are hanging out on one corner of the Plaza de Ponchos. Their hair is impossibly long and impossibly black, their eyes are dark, their skin burnished, their beauty as casual as the beauty of a condor. The girls are wearing the long skirts, white blouses and gold beads of their mothers, but the boys are in baggy jeans, trainers and American sweatshirts, baseball caps clamped down on their heads.

We sit on the kerb with our beers and a packet of tortilla chips. 'You can think of it either as progress or cultural imperialism,' I decide.

'Cultural imperialism,' says Victor, much as Che himself might have said.

Time speeds up the older you get, and the older the planet and species get, too. Things once changed so slowly that you could live out your life and never notice the steps that were taking us from the bubbling swamps of our past to our shrieking, hi-tech future. But now you can see what's happening, what's getting lost, what will soon not even be a memory – the rainforests, the ozone layer, the older worlds still grimly surviving within ours. Nonetheless, you can't really blame Americans for the twentieth century. They may be in its vanguard, but they are not its sole creator. Blaming them is like killing the messenger.

'Everything passes, everything changes,' I say to Victor.

He laughs a sigh. 'Tao again.'

'Bob Dylan.' Bells begin to ring and the sky to ignite. We sip our beers and watch the revellers welcome another year.

'Happy New Year,' says Victor.

We touch cans.

And Happy New Year to you.

I have seen enough films to know what to expect.

A whitewashed hut stands on a small clearing not far from the river. It has one large room with two paneless windows, bamboo doors and a floor of mud. Hanging from the centre of the ceiling is an old fan, its blades painted green. It turns slowly, buzzing like a mosquito, futilely batting at the humid, heavy air. The only furniture in the room is a large wooden desk, three wooden chairs and a dented metal filing cabinet, rusting at the edges. There are two men sitting at the desk, drinking whisky and playing poker. The one facing the door wears the uniform of a border patrolman; the other, dark and unshaven, a thin once-white shirt, dirty khaki trousers and a canvas cap that has fallen in the river one too many times. A blue and yellow parrot sits behind the policeman on a shit-covered perch. There's a small grey monkey on the other man's shoulder. The sound of their voices is rougher and lower than the sound of the fan.

'I wouldn't go if I were you,' the policeman is saying. 'There's been a lot of trouble upstream lately.'

The other man's eyes are on his cards. 'If you were me I'd be the one stuck at this desk just because the job comes with three meals a day and a bed.' He laughs. 'Me, I don't mind a little trouble. Trouble always comes to pass.'

You stand in the doorway for a few minutes, waiting for one of them to notice you, then quietly make your way across the room, tentatively approaching the man whose back is to you. You've heard about his reputation. 'Excuse me,' you say, stopping beside him. 'I understand that you have a boat.'

'Full house!' he roars, slapping his cards down on the table.

The policeman laughs wryly. 'I thought you were bluffing.'

'You always think I'm bluffing, José,' says the second man, scooping up the coins from the table.

You consider tapping the winner on the shoulder, the one without the monkey on it, but you think better of the idea. 'Excuse me,' you try again, 'but I was told that you have a boat.'

'Of course I have a boat.' He doesn't give you a glance. 'How else do you think I got here? By flying?'

The policeman smiles, his eyes darting to you.

You press on. 'I want to go upriver,' you say. 'I was told you were the man to take me.'

'Yeah?' He shuffles the deck as though that, in fact, is the only thing he does. 'Who told you that?'

'The captain of the cargo boat I came here on,' you answer quickly. 'He said you were the only man who knew the river well enough to make the trip.'

He begins to deal. 'The only white man,' he corrects you. 'There are dozens of Indians in the village who could take you as well. Why don't you ask one of them?'

'I have,' you admit. 'But they won't go as far as I want to go. They all said it's too dangerous.' The river's up, the rapids are treacherous, there are too many crocodiles, hostile tribes . . .

But once again my expectations are wrong. Nowadays, if you want to see the jungle you start in Quito on the Avenida Amazonas.

The office is furnished only with a wooden desk, three chairs, a low table against the window. On one side of the desk sits Luís Alberto Garcia, a small, chunky man with long black hair held down with a headband, a sincere smile and a good command of English. 'Of course we cater for vegetarians,' he is saying now. 'And we carry mineral water. If you can leave the day after tomorrow, I have a party ready to go.'

Luís Garcia runs Emerald Forest Tours. He comes from Misahuallí. He was recommended by the American guy at the Explorers' Club. But even more of a recommendation – and despite the fact that the guidebook suggests that Luís could use a few lessons in environmental conservation – he studied with David Neil at the biological reserve Jatun Sacha, just as Barbarann in Campmore in New Jersey had. The dirty white walls around us are decorated with posters of the Real Ecuador – a chap in red feathers with a bone through his nose, an unfettered parrot, flowers falling down a mountain like confetti, and a map of the jungle large enough to serve dinner on. New Jersey seems a long way away. Just about as far as the rainforest's heart.

'I am different to the other guides,' Luís assures us. 'I won't take you where everyone else takes you.'

'Where will you take us?' asks the ever-wary Sanchez. There are as many tour guides on Avenida Amazonas as sunglasses salesmen, which means that nearly every other window or doorway bears an advertisement for a Real Jungle Tour. You're invited to get to know the wonderful world of the Ecuadorian jungle, prodded to go for nature, assured that Ecuador is the best place for adventurers, urged to explore and have original experiences, reminded that the forest is to be treasured, not trampled.

Luís smiles the smile of a man you can trust. 'It depends.' He stands up and strides across the room to the map. 'You can go for three days, or five, or seven, or even longer if you want.' We stand up and follow. 'If you choose the three-day tour we take this route,' he says, his finger moving eastwards along the river. 'The first day we go from Misahuallí to Coca – lots of rapids on the river. The second day we stop and walk in the jungle for two or three hours – lots of flowers and birds. That night we stay with an indigenous family. On the third day—'

'That isn't very deep into the jungle,' says Victor. 'What about the five-day trip?'

'Ah,' breathes Luís. 'If you choose the five-day tour we go to Coca on the first day. On the second we walk through the jungle, on the third we spend the night with an indigenous family, on the fourth we camp under the stars.' Luís moves from the map to the table. He opens a photo album and starts to show us pictures of happy jungle explorers swimming in a river, eating fish around a campfire, smiling beside an indigenous family.

'What about animals?' asks Victor. 'Will we see any animals?'

'Lots of birds, butterflies and snakes,' says Luís. 'If you want to see anything more you need at least seven days.'

'How much?' I ask. Sanchez isn't the only one who is wary.

Though still trustworthy, Luís's smile is now modest as well. 'Sixty dollars a day each – food, mineral water and equipment included. But if you want something stronger than fruit juice you have to bring it yourself.'

'The guidebook says twenty-eight dollars a day,' says Victor.

'The guidebook must be old,' says Luís.

If you fail to find a guide in Quito you can, of course, moving steadily towards the jungle, try in Tena.

We try in Tena. Amaronachi Tours is located in a small bamboo hut near the river. Under a sheet of glass on the desk, there are photographs of smiling, sunburned Europeans having adventures, and a baby boa constrictor lies in a basket on the floor by its side. There are, says Patricia Uribe, a lot of other tours in Tena, but Amaroncachi doesn't go where the other tours go. And Amaronachi is reasonable, only $35 a day. The first night on the trip we will stay with an indigenous family, all of whom play traditional musical instruments, even the children. The second day we pan for gold. The third we walk through the jungle, seeing butterflies and learning about medicinal plants. Animals are more difficult. Yes, says Patricia, it is possible to go deeper into the jungle, but it is dangerous and uncomfortable. She points to a picture of a large blond man gazing at a large black and yellow reptile. If we want to see animals we can stop there. Victor asks where 'there' is. Patricia doesn't smile. 'It's a hotel.'

If you fail to find a guide in Tena, you can push further on into the jungle till you reach Jatun Sacha, where Barbarann from New Jersey worked.

David Neil is not at Jatun Sacha, but his second in command, Alejandro Suarez, is. He can't help us find a guide, but for only 14,000 sucres we can wander through the marked trails of the reserve and its comprehensive garden of medicinal plants, information sheet included. Not only are there a lot of butterflies and birds to be seen at Jatun Sacha, but for another 16,000 sucres we can have lunch as well.

And if, having got lost in Jatun Sacha's garden of medicinal plants, you still want to get into the jungle, you can try at Misahuallí itself. There are scores of guides at Misahuallí. Elias will take you walking through the forest to see butterflies and birds. The first night you'll stay with an indigenous family who will cook you a meal with mineral water and explain the uses of medicinal plants. The second day you'll watch natives panning for gold. On the third you'll swim and fish for piranha. Socrates will on the first day, take you to Jatun Sacha, where you can walk through the primary rainforest. On the second he'll take you to the Hotel Anaconda to look at animals. Jonas, too, can take you to see butterflies, indigenes using blowpipes and panning for gold and monkeys like the ones that hang out by the river.

'Fuck this for a lark,' says Victor. 'We'll get the next launch to Coca and try there. Let's spend the rest of the day exploring the jungle around here.'

We step back into Main Street, muttering about building a raft, but stop abruptly at the unexpected sound of someone calling our names.

A familiar short, squat figure in a T-shirt and red headband is charging towards us.

'Jesus,' I say. 'It's Luís.'

'Small world,' mumbles Victor.

Luís has just sent off a group of gringos to see butterflies and birds. He had too many Cubra Libres last night in the bar, and is going back to Quito.

'Still looking for a tour?' he asks us.

'No,' says Victor. 'We're going for a walk.'

We look and look, but we never seem to find. Not just small, inconsequential things like food and places and people, but the larger, things too. No parallel realities; no worlds that might have been.

Things are not going well. The boat to Coca never showed up so in the end we abandoned the jungle for the time being, our hopes now on Peru, and have come back to Quito to be greeted by Doña Patty as though we were her dead husband's ghost.

'You!' she cries from the first-floor window, her expression a mixture of several emotions, none of them full-throttle joy. 'You're back.' She throws down the keys, just missing Victor.

She is sitting at the table, fiddling nervously with the register as we reach the landing. She asks us where we were as we fill in our names, occupations, marital status, the place we're coming from and the place we'll be going. She hands us the key to room number 2. And then, just as we're leaving, she starts to talk, quickly even for her.

I look at Victor. Victor looks at me. We both look at Doña Patty. '*Qué?*' I say. '*No entiendo.*'

She tries again, faster this time.

'*Qué?*' I ask again when she finally comes to another breathless halt. My Spanish, it seems, is not getting better, it's disimproving. Apparently at a rate of knots. Doña Patty can't possibly be saying what I think she is saying. But, though God knows I'm trying, if she's saying something else I can't understand what it is.

'*En la basura,*' she says again. '*La eché en la basura.*'

Maybe it's the fact that she's smiling at me that is making it so difficult for me to understand what she's saying. Surely she wouldn't be smiling if she were saying what I think she's saying. If she were saying what I think she's saying she should be close to tears.

'*Qué?*' I ask for the third time. '*Qué hizo?*'

'Ooooh,' moans Doña Patty, 'I'm such a silly woman. This wouldn't have happened if Armando were here. But how could I know? You didn't tell me you were coming back. I thought you didn't want it any more.'

Victor has been silent through this exchange, as confused as I by her sweet, shy smile, but now he speaks. 'You threw away our bag?' he says. 'Threw it where?'

'*En la basura,*' she says once more, pointing towards the street. She wrings her hands. She has missed her calling. She could have been big on daytime TV. '*Dios mío,*' she groans, turning to me, an unfortunate woman like herself, for sympathy and understanding, 'how could I have known?'

But my gender identification system has broken down; I'm all out of sympathy and understanding for the time being. She's thrown

our things away. My notes, our thermals, Victor's socks, our dictionary, my spare glasses, our yeast tablets, our receipts, the keys to my
flat in London, my Docs, and the bag itself, intrepid traveller that
made it through South America with poor old Roy only to end up in
the trash in Ecuador. The only thing I want to give her right now is
a good sock in the jaw.

'How could you not know?' asks Victor, a lot more calm than he
would be if Doña Patty were a London motorist who'd cut him up at
a light. 'We told you we were going. We talked to your daughter and
the maid. The storage room was locked. They said it was all right to
leave it under the bureau.' He turns to me. 'She did it on purpose,' he
says in English. 'The stupid cow.'

Doña Patty holds her head with both hands. She may not understand his words but his tone has got through the language barrier
without any trouble. '*Dios mío*,' she groans. 'No one told me. I found
the bag in the hall. I thought you didn't want it any more.'

'My notes,' I say, as my brain finally fully accepts what she's been
trying to tell it for the last few minutes. Three months of notes gone
with the rats and rubbish of Quito. 'My glasses. My boots.'

Doña Patty sits up a little straighter. 'Oh, not the boots,' she says,
as though it is I who is the stupid one. 'I kept the boots.'

'You kept the boots?'

'I told you she did it on purpose,' says Victor. 'Because she knows
we washed clothes in the shower.'

She nods. 'They're good boots,' she says. 'You can't get boots like
that here.'

Normally my Spanish has all the passion and emotion of a bank
manager. 'Then why did you think I didn't want them any more?' I
demand. 'Why did you think I was throwing them out?' Maybe I'm
improving after all.

But Doña Patty doesn't answer this question; she is on her feet and
rushing out of the door.

The boots are still in the locked storage room with the washing-
machine and the ironing board. 'See?' she says, holding them up.

'I bet she was going to sell them,' says Victor.

She hands me the boots as though she's giving me a present.
'They're good boots,' she tells me. 'I didn't throw them out.'

'But everything else is gone,' persists Victor, refusing to return her
smile.

'I gave the socks to one of the German girls,' says Doña Patty. 'You
could get them back.'

'And the notebooks?' He is nothing if not persistent. 'You threw them out too?'

If Doña Patty were a sky she would be a sky gone suddenly hazy. She's thinking. 'Maybe . . .' she murmurs, and is through the door again without even remembering to turn off the light.

The notebooks are in the bureau in the hall where Doña Patty keeps the books and magazines the gringos leave behind. So are the glasses.

'But it doesn't make sense,' I argue later. 'If she knew we were coming back she knew she wouldn't get away with it.'

'Then it must be that she's stupid,' says Victor.

'But that's ridiculous too,' I counter. 'Nobody could be that stupid and manage to live.'

Victor makes a face. 'And this from a woman who comes from a country where Ronald Reagan was President.'

'I just wish we'd go,' I grumble, absentmindedly watching the several people, including the driver and the conductor, who are trying to haul the usual load of TVs and beds on to the roof. The tape machine is already playing – Freddie Mercury singing, 'It's a Kind of Magic'. 'I feel like we've been here for hours.'

'We have been here for hours,' says Victor. He turns a page.

So eager were we to get out of the city, to reach Quilotoa, perched between volcanos, its lake like an emerald in its long-quiet crater, that we were either six hours early for the bus to Latacunda (where we catch the bus to Quilotoa) or two, depending on which company we chose – the one said to be reliable or the one that isn't – so we sat in the empty burger bar at the back of the bus station that didn't have tea, or fruit juice, or *envuelitas*, playing backgammon before an interested, if critical, audience of shoeshine boys. One of them, another nine-year-old going on forty, stayed behind when the others moved on, wanting to see some coins from our country. Victor pulled out a handful of change.

'Where's that from?'

'America,' said Victor.

'And that?'

'Inglaterra.'

'And that?'

'Ecuador.'

He reached out his hand. 'Let me see.' He took the coin and examined it closely. 'It's from Costa Rica,' he decided.

'No it's not, it's from Ecuador.' I took it back. It was from Costa Rica. We waited for him to ask for a gift, but instead he just stood there, his fingertip touching the gold of a British pound, the silver eagle on the US quarter. 'Here,' said Victor, pushing a dime into his hand. 'Take it as a souvenir.'

'Listen to this,' says Victor. 'It says we might not be able to get a bus to Quilotoa. The drivers don't like to take you if you're not going all the way to Quevedo.'

'That can't be right. They'll take you, your turkeys, your extended family and your bike as long as they can squeeze you all on.'

'Then we'd better hope it's a lot less crowded than this bus,' says Victor.

The rather tired-looking man whose wife died and left him with seven children to raise, and a failing farm, wishes us a safe journey, puts the few coins he's been given into his pocket and shuffles down the steps. His place beside the driver's seat is immediately taken by an almost dapper, almost young man in a white shirt, clean beige trousers and a black moustache. He reaches up and turns down the volume on the player just as the Mamas and the Papas begin to belt out 'California Dreamin' '.

'Good morning, ladies and gentlemen,' he shouts. 'I beg for a few minutes of your time, minutes that you won't regret giving me.'

Everyone, even the kid squeezing up the aisle selling chocolate, gives him their attention.

'I have here a bargain you can't afford to miss.' He holds up a thin silver-plated chain. 'This exquisite, delicate necklace, plated with real silver, is yours for the incredible price of only two thousand sucres.'

A woman undecided about which seat is hers steps into the aisle, blocking his view of the back of the bus.

'Señora!' he shouts at her. 'Señora, sit down! How can people see me if you're standing in the way?'

The woman sits down.

The salesman holds three small cellophane envelopes above his head. He is enthusiastic; he is sincere; he is happy to be able to give us such a great deal. 'Not only am I offering this beautiful necklace for only two thousand sucres –' he shakes the necklace – 'but I will give you these three charms for no extra charge if you take the chain.' He spreads the envelopes in a fan. 'An anchor, a cross, and the sacred heart of Jesus – free! *Absolutamente libre!* And there's more!' Like a magician, he makes another object appear in his palm. 'I'll even throw this in as well,' he says. 'A silver ring!'

Several late arrivals, clutching children and bags, appear in the doorway behind him, trying to push their way through.

He holds up the hand with the fan of charms. '*Un horarito!*' he orders. 'Can't you see I'm working here?'

'Jesus,' Victor mutters. 'I don't believe she's going to do this.'

I take my eyes from the chain salesman and turn to the window. Between our bus and the next a woman is lifting her long black skirt and dropping her pink knickers. She moons at us and pisses casually on to the pavement.

'See?' says Victor. 'That's how you do it. I told you you should bring a skirt.'

20

THE MAGICAL MYSTERY TOUR'S WAITING TO TAKE YOU AWAY

You could almost forget that there are such things as polluted cities where the dimensions of your dreams are measured in concrete and glass and rules printed in black on plain sheets of paper as you climb the deep green mountains ducking beneath a ceiling of clouds. 'This is better,' says Victor. 'It may not be Peru, but it's better. I feel like I can breathe again.' We share an orange as we each silently read *Catch-22*, bought for a price in Quito, and gaze out at the passing scenery, the green occasionally broken by a herd of cows or a lonely farm and a small straw hut. At one point, near the two large military installations between us and Latacunga – both of which feature a huge bronze statue of a noble soldier before its gates – dozens of young men in suits and sunglasses, basin haircuts and freshly laundered clothes appear, walking along the road with bags over their shoulders, going home on their first leave. At another, a woman milking a goat into a plastic cup while the man beside her reaches into his pockets for change catches our eyes. 'At least he knows where it came from,' comments Victor. We pass another white cross along the roadside. On it is a picture of Christ, his hand to his head, weeping dear tears. 'Oh, no, not Julio,' cries Victor in his best impersonation of Jesus distraught. 'He was one of my finest works.'

The conductor, a small, swarthy man in a Terminator T-shirt, stands by the door, urging more people to get on board. '*Siga! Siga!*' he shouts, and rattles off names that to the untrained ear sound more like the clatter of a typewriter with a monkey at the keys than a list of destinations.

'Quilotoa?' asks Victor.

The conductor nods vigorously. '*Siga! Siga!*' The typewriter keys begin to rattle once more.

Victor doesn't move. We have walked several kilometres uphill in the rain with our packs before because an enthusiastic conductor *siga*-ed us on to the wrong bus. 'Quilotoa?' he repeats. '*Se va a Quilotoa?*'

The conductor breaks off in mid-commentary to nod some more. '*Sí, sí. Siga! Siga!*'

The bus can safely be considered full. Groups of men sit at the back, talking loudly and drinking rum out of plastic shot glasses, whole families squeezed into two seats, the children eating ice-creams and outrageously coloured candies, old men and women eating *empanadas* and bags of corn and beans. Sacks, baskets, bags, food vendors and extra children clog the aisle. It's Saturday. They're all going back to the hills from the market.

'This makes a change,' says Victor as we carefully force our way to the last two seats at the rear.

Apart from the chickens, who are travelling up on the roof, we are the only white people on board – or trying to get on board. Wandering through markets and shops, we've seen several hundred colourful paintings – soft, round shapes and warm, bright shades, perfect for that spot over the mantelpiece or the far wall of the kitchen – of natives in felt hats and ponchos placidly going about their daily lives. This is not one of those pictures. The faces are sharper, the eyes darker, the colours dirty and dulled. Their lives may be everyday, but they're lived on the edge of a very high cliff.

Still talking, drinking and eating, every last person watches us as we struggle up the aisle, trying not to hit anyone with our packs. It isn't just curiosity.

Our behaviour still being monitored, we fight our way out of our packs and cram ourselves into the seats. 'At least it's not too late,' says Victor. 'It'll still be light when we get there. We'll be able to find this guy who rents the hut without too much trouble.'

I gaze back at the dark, don't-give-it-away eyes that are still watching us. What makes him so sure?

When at last there are so many people and things in the aisle that were something to happen none of us would be able to get out of the door, the bus pulls off.

The conductor slowly makes his way up the length of the bus, checking tickets, collecting money, magically finding clear spaces large enough for his feet without having to look down the whole time. '*A dónde van?*' he asks when he reaches us.

'Quilotoa,' says Victor.

The conductor shakes his head. 'This bus doesn't go to Quilotoa. It goes to Zumbahua.'

'Zumbahua?'

'But you said it was going to Quilotoa,' says Victor.

What it would take a politician two hours to say the conductor says with a shrug: so sue me. 'It goes to Zumbahua,' he says firmly. 'You can get to Quilotoa from there.'

The immutable carved mountains stand like guardians of time as we climb higher and higher and the electric century, frantic with activity, vanishes from the memory of the world. I stare out of the window, watching an Indian woman dig in the soil, a baby with a yellow cotton bonnet on its head tied to her back. So lost in the landscape am I that it takes a few seconds before I realise that Victor is muttering, this time not to himself.

'I wish I wasn't a gringo,' he's saying. 'If I wasn't a gringo I'd straighten those creeps out myself.'

I look over at him. 'What?'

'Those creeps,' says Victor, jerking his head backwards. The creeps being discussed are the men, loud and swaggering on rum, sitting behind us, their laughter a menace. Everyone else is making a point of ignoring them. 'Haven't you heard what they're saying?'

I'm lucky to hear what people are saying in Spanish when they're talking slowly and to me. 'What?'

Between spitting on the floor and swigging their drink, they're making dirty jokes and comments, some directed at us, some at the girl unfortunate enough to be sitting in front of them, in the aisle seat behind and to the left of Victor. The girl clutches her bundle on her lap, eyes straight ahead, body rigid, pretending she isn't aware of them any more than the elderly couple in front of us are, that she isn't afraid. Christ, it's like taking the 36 to Harlsden late on a Saturday night – why don't you come home with me, darlin'? and barfing on the steps.

'Hear that?' hisses Victor. 'If I wasn't a gringo . . .'

But he is a gringo. Unmistakable and friendless, different and foreign, unprotected by the rules of this particular road. It's at times like this that you know exactly where you are: free-falling through a hostile environment. You could disappear as quickly and remorselessly as a mosquito or a moth.

The bloke with the bottle, the loudest and most aggressively drunk of the lot, starts rubbing against the girl. She stops pretending that she isn't upset. Beside me, the gringo who has only to step off the bus and into that landscape abandoned by time to have never existed tenses. 'Vic—'

As though shot, the girl suddenly jumps to her feet. The man makes a grab for her, catching her trailing shawl.

'Vic—'

The scene is more like a market painting now, still and unbreathing, all heads down or facing away, peaceful daily life.

Victor lifts himself out of his seat, leans towards the girl, his eyes calm and on the man. He pulls her shawl free. There is an ice-cold second in which anything could happen. The drunk mumbles something in which the only words I understand are 'gringo' and '*maricón*' and starts to laugh. His friends join in. The girl hurries past us to the front of the bus. Everyone else goes back to their placid lives. The man in front of us looks over his shoulder. '*Borachos*,' he says. No good for *nada*. The bus rattles to an unexpected halt.

'Zumbahua!' the driver shouts over the voice of Sting.

We look out of the window. We're back in nowhere, in the middle of the dirt road between two short rows of mud huts. A few chickens and a handful of men hanging out in front of one of the huts watch the bus stop with incidental interest.

'Zumbahua!' scream the driver and the conductor. 'Zumbahua?'

We exchange a glance. 'This is Zumbahua?'

'Sí,' nods the old man, touching Victor's hand. 'You get off here.'

On Saturdays, says the guidebook, the cluster of forty houses by an old *hacienda* that make up Zumbahua have a fine morning market for produce and animals, not tourists' goods, but rated, it says, as one of the most interesting and colourful in Ecuador and not to be missed. Llamas on view.

'Be fair,' says Victor as the bus disappears in a cloud of dust and killer fumes. 'It doesn't actually say who rated it so highly.'

I don't see any llamas. But there is a woman, standing at what out of necessity could be described as the corner, watching us warily. 'Is this Zumbahua?' I ask her. Shy as a jungle cat, she admits that it is.

'How do we get to Quilotoa?' asks Victor.

At the sound of his voice her shyness becomes pathological. She looks at the ground, her face colouring, her own voice dropping below a whisper. 'You go down there. To the *carretera.*'

'Down there's a steep, rocky path through patches of crops. 'That'll do,' says my travelling companion. 'The book says there's a bridge and a fork in the road. Maybe that's the *carretera.*'

The hillside is dotted with women with goats, children and sacks of vegetables. 'Is this the way to the main road?' calls Victor, but the minute he speaks their eyes drop to the ground. The only ones who will speak to him are the drunks staggering up the trail in the other direction, who warmly shake his hand and ask for money. At least we must be heading towards the centre of the town.

Eventually we locate Zumbahua's small and dusty heart, several dark shops, herds of scruffy chickens, a couple of guys staggering along under large pieces of furniture, and a crowd of men standing around a bus and a taxi in a dirt clearing. They look suspicious in both senses of the word.

Victor smiles as though oblivious to the fact that they are watching him with expressions hovering between amusement and contempt. 'Is this the bus to Quilotoa?'

The man wearing the Lakers cap and leaning against the bonnet of the bus spits on the ground. 'There is no bus to Quilotoa,' he says flatly. 'You have to take a taxi or a truck.' A smile shimmers for an instant. 'Five thousand sucres.'

'We'll walk,' says Victor in English. 'At least we know we'll get there.'

We go into the nearest shop for water. 'Sure there's a bus to Quilotoa,' says the proprietor. 'The last one's at four.'

'How far if we walk?' asks Victor.

He shakes his head. 'Not far. Eight or nine kilometres, straight up the road.'

The road is neither straight nor easy to find. It crosses the river, starts climbing and twisting up the mountains, and abruptly cuts across the surface of the moon. We stop to study the deep grey canyons, strange and wondrous as lunar craters, carved into the variegated green of the mountain in every direction.

'Water?' I guess.

'Probably lava,' says Victor.

This part of the moon is inhabited. Here and there a field of sheep or sudden clutch of vegetation in the stretching grass, thatched, windowless mud huts built into the earth and hillsides, not an aerial in sight.

Children appear out of bushes and in doorways. 'Gringos! Gringos!' 'Give us a sweet!' 'Give us a present!'

Traffic picks up. Three little girls, looking like midgets in their long skirts, hats and shawls, are herding sheep down the road. The oldest stops Victor. '*Saca una foto!*' she orders.

'*Mi saco?*' says Victor, holding up the bag. 'You want to know about my bag?'

'No, no,' she insists. '*Saca una foto de nosotras.*' She holds out her palm. 'Fifty sucres.'

'You take a picture of us,' teases Victor. 'You pay us.'

Just in sight of a minor village, a small boy on a large bike joins us. 'Where are you from?'

'England,' we tell him.

'*Es muy lejos.*' He nods. 'A lot of gringos come up here.'

There may be no billboards for Coca-Cola, no fast-food restaurants or episodes of *Renegade*, but this much we already know. The path to Quilotoa may not be as beaten as the one to Quito, but there are heavy footprints in the dirt.

'Why do they come?' asks Victor.

The boy starts to accelerate. 'Who knows?'

The clouds get closer and closer. We stop along the road for water and raisins, gasping for oxygen in the thinning air. The book described this as a two-and-a-half to three-hour walk, but it didn't mention that it was all uphill or how many hours to add if you were carrying two loaded packs.

'Christ,' sighs Victor. 'I hope this is the right way.'

It starts to rain.

I hold out my hand to count the single drops. Seeking a less ignoble past, we are learning to read the messages of God. 'You think this is a sign?'

And to interpret them correctly. 'If it is, it's not a good one.' Victor looks right to the dark clouds steaming towards us, almost close enough to touch. 'Maybe we should put on our wets.'

The drops are getting heavier and faster, and not so lonely now. By the time we've struggled into the baggy green plastic trousers and cumbersome tops our bags are soaked. One pack under Victor's jacket, one in my arms in a black bin-liner, we continue up the road.

Smoke curls into the rain, sheep shuffle together, a farmer passes with a llama, a woman steps out of the bushes, a boy watches from under a tree, a jeep heading back to Zumbahua with two gringos in the back pulls up short.

'How far to Quilotoa?' we ask each in turn. 'Do you know Jorge
Lataconga?' The guidebook says that though there is no accommodation in Quilotoa, Jorge Lataconga has a hut near the emerald lake
that he will rent out to travellers.

'Another three hours.'

'An hour.'

'Jorge Lataconga? No, I never heard of him.'

'I'll come back and take you. Twenty thousand sucres each.'

Finally, to still my fears that we've missed the turning incidentally
mentioned in the guide, Victor asks the little girl standing in front of
her house holding a small pig if we're on the right road. '*Pagame*,' she
says flatly.

To me, Victor says, 'Jesus.' To her, 'No.'

She tosses her head. 'This isn't the road to Quilotoa,' she snaps
back. 'You're going the wrong way.'

With as much dignity as travellers clumsily dressed as frogs can be
expected to muster, we trudge coolly on.

Jaime Rodriguez Quebar de Mendoza and his brother, Alberto
Gustav, wearing identical imitation leather and sheepskin hats,
though otherwise ill equipped for the rain, are stopped in the middle of the road, discussing whose turn it is to ride their rusty bike.
Jaime reckons it's his, but Alberto Gustav isn't so sure. Jaime is about
to end the debate by knocking Alberto off of the bike when he spots
two green hulks slogging through the drizzle. 'Gringos!' he cries, letting go of the handlebar to hold up his hand. '*Buenas tardes! De
dónde vienen?*'

'*De Inglaterra*,' I answer.

Jaime Rodriguez nods knowingly. '*Es muy lejos.*' Alberto nods,
too.

Both of them are staring at Victor. 'Do all the men in your country
wear rings in their nose?' asks Jaime.

'Only the witches,' says Victor.

He might have said, 'Only the tall ones,' for all the impact this
information has on them. Witches, suggests their response, are as
common as sheep around here.

They fall in step beside us, Jaime next to Victor, his brother pushing the bike. Jaime, who has never heard of Jorge Lataconga,
effortlessly takes on the role of guide. This is where he plays football.
He likes volleyball and basketball too. That canyon over there is where
his brother lost his shoe. His cousin lives over that hill. His school is
up the road. His other uncle lives back towards Zumbahua in the hut

with the tyre by the door. The rain's been bad or the road would be better. There are fewer jeeps and buses when it rains. When we get to the basketball court in the next village we should take the left.

Victor points to the etched ravines, ghostly in the dull and fading light. '*Por qué es así?*' he asks.

Jaime shrugs philosophically. 'Because it is.'

'Bloody Taoists,' laughs Victor, as Jaime takes the bike from his brother and pedals back down the road, Alberto running behind him. 'They're everywhere you go.'

The village that boasts the basketball court is small enough that within minutes of our hoving into view a large percentage of its population is on the street, staring at us with open amusement. Even the men and boys having an informal game on the court break off to clock us in.

'They mustn't get as many tourists as we thought,' I say above the squeaking of our trousers. 'Not in plastic, anyway.'

We stop around the bend to get out of our wets. Victor is helping me out of my trousers with a marked amount of gracelessness when Jaime and Alberto reappear beside us. They find the sight of me hanging on to Victor while he tries to yank the trousers over my Docs one of the funniest they have ever seen.

'Maybe we should've brought pictures to hand out,' says Victor. He glances up at them, holding on to each other to keep from falling over with laughter. 'You want to take a picture?' he asks in English.

'Take a picture,' mimics Jaime Rodriguez. '*Qué significa* "take a picture"?'

Victor gives one last tug that lands me in the mud. '*Saca una foto,*' I say, but the boys don't hear me. They're laughing too much.

We trudge straight on, walking through clouds, the packs getting heavier, the temperature getting colder, the sky getting darker, the huts becoming fewer and fewer and farther and farther between.

'*Más arriba,*' says the family returning from their field when we ask them where Jorge Lataconga lives. '*Más arriba.*'

We slog on *más arriba*, dogs barking, our breath now visible, some of us finding it increasingly difficult to walk and breathe at the same time.

Materialising out of the chiselled grey stone, two little girls and a boy suddenly appear beside us, the red of their shawls and poncho glowing in the mist. They slow their pace to match ours, staring at us silently until we turn their way. Then the girls look at the ground and the boy kicks a stone into the bushes.

'Jorge Lataconga?' asks Victor. 'Do you know Jorge Lataconga?'

The girls giggle, blushing and bumping into each other.

'Give us a gift,' says the boy.

They disappear around a craggy bend, dematerialising in a swirl of cloud.

'Maybe we should ask her if she knows Jorge Lataconga.' Victor points up the high embankment to where a woman is bent over the ground, either taking something out or putting it in.

'Sure,' I start to say, but my answer is lost in hysterical barking.

'Christ,' says Victor. He grabs my arm. 'Keep moving, but don't run.'

Keeping moving, out of the corner of my eye I watch four mangy dogs, teeth bared and their eyes on us, charging across the field where the woman continues to work as though the afternoon is still quiet and calm, frantic to reach us and tear us to shreds. If I could run, I would, no matter what Victor says, but by now I can barely walk.

'Don't stop,' cautions Victor as the dogs, too incensed to show any caution themselves, hurl their thin bodies over the embankment. He picks up a couple of stones. 'Aim at their feet,' he tells me. 'You don't want to hurt them.'

Oh yes I do.

Sticking together, the dogs circle around us, their barks now turned into low, thick growls.

'Go away!' shouts Victor, raising his arm. He throws a stone near the largest. 'Go away!'

'Why don't you hunker down and pretend to eat?'

'More walk and less talk,' says Victor, and suits his actions to his words.

The smallest of the four takes the initiative and launches himself at my ankle. I scream. 'Get him off! Get him off!' I feel teeth against my bone.

'Kick him away!' orders Victor, still walking. 'Kick him away!'

Terror is making me forget that I am a guest in Ecuador, and should behave as such. 'I can't,' I shriek. The middle dog has attached himself to the cuff of my trousers while the small one snaps at my foot. 'Jesus wept!' I whack him with my bag.

Victor stops and turns around. 'What are you doing?' He sounds like an anthropologist who's just discovered a primitive nomad doing something curious with a stick and a bloody bone.

The dog is still holding my bag, back feet dancing on the mud, as

I try to take it away again. The growling from the vicinity of my cuff has reached a fever pitch. 'I'm trying to get him off me, aren't I?' I shout back.

It starts to rain. But this time it's a shower of pebbles. 'Get away!' shouts an authoritative female voice. More stones fall around us. 'Leave her alone!' At last we've caught the attention of the woman on top of the bank.

Still growling, the dogs back off.

'*Gracias!*' I gasp. '*Gracias!*'

'Do you know a man named Jorge Lataconga?' asks Victor.

Giving no evidence that she's heard either of us, the eyes of the woman stay on our faces for a full and empty second; then she turns and goes back to her work.

Stuffing stones into my pockets and silently praying that the dogs will be dead by the time we come back in the morning, I follow Victor up the mountain and into the rolling clouds.

Outside a concrete house set back off the road stand a girl with a baby strapped to her back and a man with a bicycle.

'You go,' says Victor. 'They react better to you.'

I stay where I am. 'You don't see any dogs, do you?'

'Go on!' He gives me a push. 'Ask if they know where he lives.'

'Half an hour up the road in a two-storey house on the right,' I report back.

'You see?' says Victor. 'And you were worried we'd gone the wrong way.'

Half an hour further up the mountain, nothing to be seen now but the caverns beneath us, the road bends into clouds.

I'm still worried that we've gone the wrong way. 'We must have missed a turning,' I say as we take the bend. 'We're getting farther from everything. There's nothing up here.'

The two of us come to a sudden stop. I was wrong, there is something up here.

Curiouser and curiouser, said Alice.

A man in a black and white poncho and a black hat sits on a ledge above us like a caterpillar on a magic mushroom, whittling a piece of wood. He looks up and smiles. '*Buenas tardes,*' he says. '*De dónde vienen?*'

Victor finds his voice first. He tells him that we come from London, England, that we've travelled across the United States, Colombia and a good deal of Ecuador, that we're looking for Jorge Lataconga and the liquid jewel in the volcano's crater.

'Jorge Lataconga lives just fifteen minutes away,' he says. 'In a one-storey stone house.' He points over our shoulders. 'They'll accompany you.'

Now what? wondered Alice.

We turn around. Three small boys in dirty purple ponchos and brown felt hats are standing behind us, silent as spectres.

We start to walk. They follow. When I stop, Victor stops; when Victor stops, they stop, the four of them waiting patiently while I try to breathe again. A young girl in a red shawl and long dark skirt emerges from a path on the right, the gold studs in her ears glinting like stars. As though invited, she joins our little group. She doesn't speak either. When I stop, and Victor stops, and the boys stop, she stops, too.

Volcanos surround us, some crowned with snow, all caught in rain clouds, bits of gold and dark blue sky tearing through the grey. We stop to wait for the children, whispering together as they come up the road; flute music drifts up from the valley, as smooth and flawless as the passage of a condor.

Victor's voice is no heavier than air. 'How are you going to write about this?'

Clouds tumble towards us, woven with song. The little girl shrieks as one of the boys throws something at her. They all begin to laugh.

It is not often, and often almost never, that a single moment – a moment heartbreakingly perfect, a moment clear as crystal – will step out of the millions of other moments and overwhelm you with the pure and simple joy of just being alive.

'I don't think I can.'

Victor and I stand in the middle of the road, looking to the right at the three mud huts grouped together on a rocky dirt clearing, smoke from the largest mingling with the clouds, and to the left at the cinderblock house twenty metres beyond them. 'Are you sure he said stone?' I'm saying.

'Are you sure he said right?' says Victor.

There are no streets signs or house numbers or mailboxes to read for clues. 'Maybe it's a little further up,' Victor is saying.

I point across the semi-barren land that stretches into mountains behind the three huts. 'There are some more houses over there,' I say.

Three small boys, barefoot, filthy and underdressed for the chill of the evening in T-shirts and trousers from a bag of rags, come charging across the muddy yard, shouting and waving their arms. Victor and I step back on a couple of chickens. 'Gringos!' scream the boys. 'Gringos!'

Victor has to shout to be heard above the noise of the boys. 'Is this the house of Jorge Lataconga?'

'Sleep here!' the boys are yelling now. 'Why don't you sleep here?'

Victor tries again. 'Is this the house of Jorge Lataconga?'

Another boy, older, comes walking towards us from the house. He can't be more than fifteen himself, but he carries himself more like a man than a child.

'We're looking for Jorge Lataconga,' says Victor.

'He's not home,' says the boy. 'He just went by drunk.'

'We understand he has a place where we can stay,' Victor explains. He gestures to the darkening sky. 'For the night.'

The boy points to the windowless hut only feet from the road, a weathered sign – Artesanía – hanging on its door. 'You can stay here.' I glance at Victor. Victor glances at me. We're right at the top of nowhere, and as far as we know the only other person who has any accommodation to offer is either lying in the shrubs or barfing in a ditch. Our options are not limitless.

The boy turns to his brothers. 'Get the key,' he orders.

'Well . . .' demurs Victor.

The boy extends his hand. 'Mario,' he says.

'Victor.'

'Diana.'

'It's very comfortable,' says Mario as the other three come racing back with the key. 'Very safe.' He points to an upright wooden box on the opposite side of the road. 'That's the *servicio*, very convenient.' He gives us an encouraging smile. 'You see the room first,' he says. 'And then you decide.'

The very comfortable, very safe hut contains two old kitchen chairs, a hanging shelf in one corner with a wooden chest underneath it, a cluttered table and a box of corn. While we get accustomed to the darkness, two young girls come in, dragging a bamboo mat across the dirt floor, hoping that if they don't meet our eyes we won't actually see them. The girls keep their distance, but the boys crowd around us, watching every movement, waiting like kids at a circus to see what will happen next. A woman who is neither old nor young joins us next, carrying a well-used rectangle of cardboard that she puts under the mat for extra insulation.

'My mother,' says Mario.

Mario's – and presumably everyone else's – mother smiles and makes her exit.

'What about a candle?' I ask. 'Do you have any candles?'

'Get a candle,' orders Mario.

One of the boys runs out for a candle.

Mario turns to the other two. 'Clear that table,' he orders.

The boys remove the scales and the old tins from on top of the table so we can put down our bags.

Mario's mother reappears. This time she's carrying a worn feed bag. She sits on the edge of the bamboo mat, slowly removing objects from the bag and carefully unwrapping them.

'My father, José Segundo, is a painter,' explains Mario as his mother spreads the paintings out on the floor. 'He sells them in Quito and Baños. He is president of the *artesanos*.'

The girls lean against one another, giggling softly, the boys jostle around us, their mother nods and smiles.

Victor and I hunker down on the floor, examining the rectangles of sheepskin on their wooden frames. There are small ones and larger ones, some scraped clean, some whose backs are thick with wool. Tiny figures in red and pink ponchos and deep white hats lead long-necked llamas up steep mountain passes, work with bent backs in terraces of pink and yellow, blue and green; white huts with red roofs sit placidly under high clouds and the snowy peak of Cotopaxi; an emerald lake tilts into a wall of volcanos. Despite the gloom of the hut, the colours of the paintings are vibrant and intense, the colours of the world the way you hoped it might be. We've seen dozens, if not scores, of paintings very much like these in the tourist shops and markets, but none as lovely as those painted by Mario's father.

Having made our selections, Victor tries to hand the canvases back to Mario. 'We'll pay you in the morning.' Neither of us is about to dig into our body belts for money with José Segundo's entire family watching us.

Mario pushes them away. 'No, no. You keep them, they're yours.'

Mario's mother repacks the unsold paintings and, silent as a cloud, disappears once more.

'You're cold,' announces Mario, looking at me, hunched in my sweater, my hands buried in my armpits. 'We'll build a fire.'

I squint into the corners of the hut, searching for a chimney or a stove that I hadn't seen before. I still don't see it.

'Go get wood,' Mario orders his brothers. 'Wood and kerosene.'

While we wait for the return of the boys, the girls sit in silence at the edge of the mat and Mario keeps the conversation going. He only comes home at weekends, to help his father with the farm. Five days a week he goes to school in Quilapungo from six-thirty in the morning till six at night. He's studying to be a carpenter. 'But I also study maths and *castellano*,' says Mario. 'And next year I'm learning English.' The school is an evangelical one, run by Italians and Peruvians. 'My father is a very religious man,' says Mario. 'He hasn't touched a drop of liquor in twenty-five years.' Mario speaks both Castilian and Quechua. His oldest sister does, too, and his youngest brother is learning Quechua and is doing very well.

The boys tumble back into the hut. Mario introduces them. Juan Umberto, Juan Nelson, Juan Calvino. We shake each grubby hand in turn. 'And I am Juan Mario,' says Mario. He gestures to the girls. 'The oldest is Maria Ilsa,' he tells us, 'and the other is Maria Suela.'

'What odds are you taking on the mother's name?' I whisper to Victor.

Juan Umberto lights the candle. Juan Nelson lights a tin of kerosene. The girls laugh, pretending to shield their eyes from the flames.

Mario teaches us some words in Quechua while Victor and I, trying not to step on any children or torch ourselves, take out our hammocks and string them across the room.

Tired, cold, and very definitely hungry, we wait for the children of José Segundo to leave. They stay.

The fire lit, the hut filled with smoke, the stars now out in a blue-black sky, we wait for the Juans and Marias to wish us goodnight. The boys play with the fire, the girls lean against each other, Juan Mario tells us the schedule of his school day: breakfast at five-thirty, lunch at noon, supper when the chores are done at six.

There's a knock at the door. We hope it's Mario's mother, wondering why her children are late for their supper. Mario goes to the door. It isn't his mother. Two couples follow him in, barely glancing at us as they step over the girls and walk over the mat to the far side of the room. Mario takes bread from the chest, scoops out a bag of corn, haggling over the price the whole while. Victor and I start to take more things from our bags, hoping they take this as a sign that we're ready for bed.

When the couples have trooped back across the mat and into the night, Mario sits back down at the fire. 'I'm so tired,' I say to the room at large.

Mario starts telling us stories about thieves in the cities. Maria Ilsa and Maria Suela squeeze in between their brothers.

We give up and sit down, too.

'My older brother was mugged in Quito,' says Mario. He describes the dark street, the white men stepping out of a doorway, the flash of the blade. The little boys lean forward in the firelight, their faces blurred by the smoke, eager to hear every word.

'And my friend who is a bus driver had a robber hold a gun to his head,' he goes on. Mario's older brother carries a gun now himself. 'All the Indians who go into the cities carry knives,' says Mario. 'Even my father.'

Victor says that he doesn't believe in weapons.

'Me neither,' says Mario. 'If the Indians catch a foreign thief they just burn him.'

There's another knock at the door. This time I'm sure it must be their mother, wanting them all in bed. Maria Suela opens the door. It isn't her mother. It's José Segundo.

José Segundo is a tall, solid man in a brown poncho. His voice is quiet, his bearing calm, his manner gentle and polite.

'I am pleased to meet you, Señor,' he says to Victor. 'Welcome to my home.'

'Victor,' says Victor, shaking the large, hard hand.

'Señorita,' says José Segundo. 'Just tell me if there is anything you need.' He eyes the hammocks. 'A blanket?' he suggests. 'Do you need a blanket?'

'Thank you,' I say quickly. 'I would love to have a blanket.'

And el Señor?

Wilderness Man declines. 'I'm fine,' he says. 'I have my jumper.'

The smoke must be cutting off the oxygen to his brain.

José Segundo nods. Of course, a hammock and a sweater; what else do you need? He sends the girls off for a blanket.

'I am a very religious man,' says José Segundo. 'My family and I live by the Bible.' He gives me a reassuring smile. 'You are safe here,' he tells me. 'No one will bother you here. If you want to go off for a day or two you can leave your luggage with us.' He waves smoke from his face. 'All men are brothers,' says José Segundo.

Victor tells him how much we like his paintings.

'I just paint the place where I live,' he says. 'I paint what I see.'

When he leaves, he takes his children with him.

'Alone at last!' says Victor. He heads for food bag. 'If I don't get something to eat soon I'll die.'

I'm putting the tortilla we made last night with the bread we bought from Mario when there's a knock at the door. 'Now what?'

It's Mario, a rough length of brown wool in his arms. 'My father says you should have a blanket, too.' He hands it to Victor. 'My father says it gets cold at night.'

Victor's just cutting the bread when there's another knock. 'Your turn,' he says.

Juan Nelson is standing in the doorway, behind him a wall of stars. 'Here,' he says, thrusting something into my hand. 'This is for you and el Señor.'

He is gone before I can thank him.

'What is it?' asks Victor, coming up behind me.

I open my hand. On my palm, in a creased and dirty red and green wrapper, is a chocolate caramel. He must have been saving it since Christmas.

Victor picks up the sweet and looks at it for a few seconds. 'I think we picked the right hotel this time,' he says, and puts it back in my hand.

It's a dark, cold night.

The candle has died, the room is just a shadow. Wearing everything we have and clutching our blankets around us, we lie flat on our backs, afraid to move in the poorly hung hammocks in case we tumble out, our mosquito nets suspended over us for the illusion of warmth and protection. In the post-big-bang stillness, creatures scurry across the room.

My guess is scorpions. 'Don't forget to shake out your boots in the morning,' I remind Victor.

Victor thinks it's rats. 'You should have put your hammock higher.'

It's a night that crawls.

Every fifteen minutes or so Victor farts and checks the time. Nine o'clock. Nine fifteen. Nine forty-five.

'Do you think there's a place for the helicopter to land if I need to go to hospital when I fall out and break my back?'

Victor farts. 'Ten,' he announces. 'Christ, it's cold.'

Something rustles in the thatch. Maybe it's not scorpions or rats, maybe it's bats. Victor lies with his arms folded across his chest, his hood up, staring at the ceiling. I pull my blanket over my head. My feet stick out.

'Ten fifteen,' says Victor. 'Ten thirty . . .'

'You think we'll ever sleep?'

'I'd build a fire, but I'm not sure it's worth it for the little heat we'd get.'

Gingerly, I pull my knees up. The hammock tips. 'It's not worth it.' The most we could hope for is asphyxiation from smoke inhalation.

'Ten forty-five,' says Victor, and farts.

I can hear something moving across the ground so clearly that I almost think I can see it.

'The net's a waste of time, isn't it?' I say. 'It's like a puppy with his head under the bed thinking no one can see him because he can't see them.'

'Or a kangaroo,' says Victor.

I cautiously turn my head to face him in the dark. 'Do kangaroos stick their heads under the bed?'

'In the ground.'

'I'd just stick it in my pouch.'

'Not kangaroos,' says Victor. 'Ostriches.'

'What time is it now?'

The tiny light of the travel clock flicks on. 'Eleven.'

'At least time isn't standing still.'

I'm following Victor up a narrow, rutted trail. One side is walled in jungle, the other is empty to the river below. The night is noisy, the air sharp as ice, the sky moonless but snail-trailed with stars. Victor is well ahead of me, striding on. He disappears behind a bend. Small, busy creatures with big, bright eyes are scrabbling through the underbrush; birds are calling in the trees. The river rumbles and something howls. I stumble to the bend. Always he'll wait if I've fallen behind, but there is no Victor around the corner. 'Vic!' I hiss. 'Vic!' A single star falls from the sky. 'Vic!' The birds cease their yammering; the underbrush stills. The sweet lament of a faraway flute threads through the howling. I force myself to climb faster, but my pack is growing with every step I take. 'Victor!' I look up ahead to where the path rises steeply and suddenly ends, flat against it that shining sky. 'Vic!' He is standing with his back to me, a shadow in the shadows, but he turns his head.

'Listen!' The howling has changed while I wasn't listening. Now it's a song – but it's not Sting, or Phil Collins or Freddie Mercury or Vilma and the Vampires this time – it's a song without sex or timbre, a strangulated cry that suddenly tapers into laughter. 'Look!' he says, taking a step towards the stars. 'There's no reason we can't fly!'

'Victor!'

'Do you hear it?' He is rolling out of his hammock, hurriedly making his way to the door.

I'm awake now, but I still hear, slipping through the voice of a flute that rides along the mountainsides, the voice of my dream. It's the voice of something that can't have a voice, something neither animal nor human, something with no knowable purpose, as though the world itself, so ununderstandable, so unfathomable, so huge and uncontainable by logic or reason, is speaking in the night. It's a voice from the non-reality, possessing both the qualities of ordinary reality and the qualities of an ordinary dream, but equal to neither. It's a voice straight out of the teachings of Don Juan.

Victor has the door open before I hit the ground. 'Shit,' he whispers. 'Look at that.'

The voice simmers in the silence, the peaks of sleeping volcanos lie flat and black against the sky, dipping between them a sliver of moon, haloed by its own ghost. Stars crowd the sky. This is a night you could walk into – and if you dared, you would never fall, would never get lost, could never die.

'If a *brujo* gives you a gift, don't waste it,' says Victor softly, quoting from Don Juan.

We stand close together, two cold and tired gringos, far from the world they know, strangers in the strangest of lands. I've never felt so safe in my life.

21

KEEP ON ROCKIN' IN THE FREE WORLD

Don Juan says that a man has to be tricked into becoming a man of knowledge, that men of knowledge are born and not made. He is chosen by forces outside himself. Anyone who wilfully undertakes the task of becoming a man of knowledge is a fool, he doesn't count.

'Maybe this is part of the trick,' says Victor, holding on to his hat as the jeep bounces into, out of, and over ruts.

The two men talking about football as they stand on the tailgate hold on to their hats, too. I manage to recapture enough breath to be able to speak. 'Everything's part of the trick.'

Victor laughs, causing quite a few heads to turn. 'Maybe we'll find out if we ever get to Huancabamba.' Huancabamba, says our invaluable guidebook, is the headquarters for the *brujos* of Peru. Huancabamba, we believe, is a doorway to the non-real world. We're coming to the end of our time in Ecuador, drifting towards that invisible door.

One of the fifteen people jammed into the back of the jeep, the woman on Victor's right, leans her head out of the window and starts to vomit. I hang on to him as the rear wheel loses the road. 'Or not.'

Don Juan says that becoming a man of knowledge is a matter of learning; of discipline and intent. He says that most of us confuse the world – the real world – with the world of man, with what people do.

We nose up another hill and the milk canisters slide forward, stretching the rope meant to hold them in and banging into Victor.

'Christ, I wish we had the bike. Doesn't Don Juan say something about motorcycles?'

'Don Juan says something about everything.' My hip is grinding into the spare tyre, but there's no way of moving out of its way. Don Juan makes a joke about motorcycles when Castenadas asks him if he's ever seen an ally driving a car or a bus. He tells him he should have asked if Don Juan had ever seen an ally driving a motor vehicle, not just a car or a bus. 'You don't want to forget the motorcycles, do you?' he teases. Or the jeeps.

The canisters jerk forward again. 'Umph,' mutters Victor. He grabs on to me, just managing to stop himself slamming against the infant strapped to the woman who sits between him and the men on the tailgate, terrified that if the baby isn't already dead of suffocation, he's going to crush it.

One of the three people up front with the driver begins to sing an American love song in Spanish. The mother of the infant nods her head in time to the tune. The mountains are blurred by clouds.

But the things people do, says Don Juan, are, in truth, no more than the shields they hold up against the forces that surround them that they can neither apprehend nor understand; they comfort us and make us feel safe, but they are only a shield.

'It's the kangaroo under the bed again, isn't it?' says Victor. The jeep descends and we both slide back.

'Or the ostrich.' It's easier to stay with your chin on a shoe and your eyes closed than to go and see what's out there in the waiting dark.

Don Juan says that the world is incomprehensible, and that a man of knowledge understands this and accepts the world as the endless mystery it is; he gives into it instead of shielding himself from it. It is the things that people do, says Don Juan, that the man of knowledge treats as endless folly.

The jeep comes to a sudden stop. Everyone else starts to get off, climbing over us as though we aren't there.

The driver looks back, sees us still wedged against the side, and shouts loudly and rapidly. He points through the windscreen at the long and hopeful wooden bridge two or three hundred metres away that trembles over the dirty river below. This, it would seem, is as far as he goes.

Victor jumps over the now-raised tailgate and I fall over it after him. He helps me up.

We start cautiously down the mud-covered rocks towards the

bridge. There is no motor vehicle – car, bus, jeep, or bike – waiting for us on the other side.

'It's lucky it's the journey that counts and not the actual arrival,' says Victor, quoting from Don Juan again.

The guy with the earring, the ponytail and the poncho decorated with laconic llamas has worked this joint before. We saw him here last night, attaching himself to every manless table, smooth, smiling and charming as a double-glazing salesman who's been in the job too long. He joins the two gringas at the table next to ours. Where you girls from? Where have you been? Bolivia? I've been there. Chile? I've been there. Where you going next? The jungle? He's just come from the jungle. And after that Peru? He orders another coffee and makes himself comfortable, stretching his legs so the toes of his boots touch the trainers of the girl across from him. Let me tell you about Peru. Peru, says Poncho, isn't like Ecuador. Look at a place like this. Ecuador is civilised.

Victor's eyes are on his menu. 'Welcome to the civilised world,' he mumbles.

Peru, says Poncho, is dangerous, though he, it was true, had no trouble at all. But you have to know the ropes. Forget riding overland, he tells them. It isn't worth the hassle. Nobody with any sense goes overland. You fly into Lima or Cuzco, and fly out of Cuzco or Lima. You don't want to be caught by the Shining Path. Or the military. Or the hostile natives. You want to stay where the tourists are, though Lima itself is treacherous and the police are warning tourists not to walk the Inca trail.

'Really?' asks one of the girls. 'Because of terrorists?'

'Bandits,' says Poncho. 'Whatever you do, don't do it alone.' He tells them the best hotel in Lima, the best guide to get in Misahuallí, and the coolest bar in Cuzco, his arm brushing the arm of the prettier girl.

'Jesus,' Victor mutters. 'This guy should come with a government warning.'

Still torn between the cheese omelette and the banana pancake, I glance over my shoulder. DON'T BE FOOLED BY THE WAY I LOOK, I'M WORSE THAN THAT.

We've been forced into town for our breakfast, to the vegetarian restaurant run by the American and his Swiss wife – bamboo walls and lampshades, ethnic crafts on the walls, ZZ Top and David Bowie on the tape deck, chocolate cake and spaghetti with tomato sauce on the dinner menu, and a gringo at every pine table – because the Germans are in the kitchen again; as far as we can tell they've been there all night.

'Now I know how Alice felt when she woke up back in the garden with her sister,' I whisper.

Victor gives me a glance. 'You mean depressed?'

Nuestra Señora de Santa Agua, the local hero, draws the pilgrims to ask her for favours, to see her clothes and the paintings of the miracles she's performed in the museum, to buy medals and holy pictures, charms and candles from the stalls hunched around the Basilica, to eat the taffy that hangs in doorways and drink the *aguardiente* with cinnamon, lime and water sold on the streets. The hot springs, miracle workers themselves, bring the holidaymakers and tourists. In Baños you can eat pizza, pasta, pancakes and sandwiches, you can buy friendship bracelets and Peruvian earrings, you can hang out in bars and restaurants with rock music on the tape deck and plants in the windows where the only non-gringos are the musicians and the dishwasher, you can stay at hotels where English and German are spoken, and parrots squawk in the garden, prevented by chains from flying away.

We've come to Baños because it's on our way.

We've come to Baños because it's on our way and has, unexpectedly enough, as the guidebook promised, a hotel with a kitchen for guests, large clean rooms and a hot shower – though it doesn't mention, of course, that there are no curtains in the bathroom, that you're best advised to flush with your foot because the toilet's always blocked with paper, that the shower was bought cheap when they shut down Alcatraz, that despite all the signs taped in the hallway asking you to be considerate of fellow guests the hotel is noisy till dawn, or that there are always Germans in the kitchen.

Poncho leans slightly forward but doesn't lower his voice as he tells the gringas where to go to get drugs in Baños.

Victor pushes his menu aside. 'Let's go somewhere else,' he says. 'I feel like I'm in a Camden pub.'

We go to the Italian restaurant across from the market, where the sign in the window promises *pan y mermelada*, mussly and *ensalada de frutas*.

'Never mind the homeopathic medicine,' Victor's saying as we study the menu. 'When we get to Peru, we're having coffee.'

I can see us sitting in an outside café overlooking a Plaza Bolivar, sipping dark, aromatic coffee never tasted in New York or London from white china cups. The blood should show up nicely when the soldiers open fire on the square.

'Excuse me,' says a voice that belongs to neither Victor nor the waiter. We both look up. Two of the Germans have left the kitchen. One of them is sitting by the window with a bowl of mussly and the other is standing beside us with a shyly pleasant smile. 'Excuse me, but possibly you know where we can buy cocaine?'

Wherever men are gathered in his name, there is Christ; and wherever men with backpacks and ethnic hats and sweaters are experiencing life, there are drugs.

Victor looks at me. 'Where to next?' says Victor.

We buy some fruit, cakes and water in the market and head out of town. Gingerly descending the hillside behind the sugar-cane stalls that line the main road, a small child in what used to be a party dress glides towards us over the rocks.

I squint down the path. 'That little girl isn't carrying a machete, is she?'

Victor jumps a minor tributary of the Pastaza, sliding a few feet in a spray of gravel. 'I doubt it.'

'Then what is she carrying?'

He looks up. 'A machete.'

We cross the tentative-looking bridge, and start up the mountain on the opposite side, talking about mescal. The cactus down here is free for the picking. What does it look like? What if we find some? Should we make some tea ourselves? Victor knows that he said no drugs, but mescal is different. It's natural; it's there; it would be an experience foolish to pass up. That is, it would be foolish for Victor to pass it up. I, however, should probably stick to rum. I've never taken a trip in my life that didn't depend on motorised transport. Victor says that the Germans were making mescal tea in the kitchen last night when he went to see if there was a burner free. 'If they didn't piss me off so much I would've asked them where they got it,' says Victor.

Civilisation drops behind. The steep, muddy trail is banked by small farms – a hut suddenly appearing among the banana trees and blocks of maize, a yard brown against the neat squares of green, corn laid out to dry in front of the house, a few chickens scrabbling through the bushes, pigs sleeping in the shade. There are no gringos up here. The only other traffic on the track is a farmer, his son and a loaded donkey, making the long trek into town. We stare at them and they stare at us. But there have been gringos up here: 'Hello!' says the boy. 'Goodbye!'

We sit on a sunny slope beneath a sky of an improbable blue, surrounded by dozing cows as black and white as chessboards, talking
about Peru. Witches. Condors. Inca ghosts. Machu Picchu at dawn.

I am not immune to the lure of wild magic and ancient phantoms – if I were I wouldn't be sitting on cow pats and lethal-looking
insects up an Ecuadorian mountain – but I am still my mother's
daughter, no matter how hard I try not to be. 'Do you think it's as
bad as everyone says?' I wonder aloud.

From the shack halfway between us and the valley music begins
to play, a song familiar from more than one bus ride – Freddie
Mercury singing, 'I don't want to be on my own'.

'Jesus, let's hope so,' says Victor.

The tiny shop can accurately be described as a hole in the wall. A
hole in the wall that is packed from floor to ceiling with junk and
antiques. Chipped clay relics and old knives, dulled ceramic figurines and brass door-knockers, crumbling stacks of magazines and
cracked glasses that once sat on lace tablecloths and were filled with
the deepest red wine. We leave the food we've just bought on a
carved wooden chair and inch along the shelves and cabinets, pointing out beads and spoons and blackened silver jewellery. The old
man sitting behind the counter fixing a shoe shows none of the
interest in us that the market sellers show, shouting '*Siga no más!
Siga no más!*' and foisting bananas and tomatoes, avocadoes and
onions on us – 'How much do you want? A kilo? Two kilos? Why
not take them all?' – unlike the woman in the store across the street
who threw us out because we asked to see something before we
would buy it. He hammers away, humming along to a love song on
the radio that is nearly as old as he.

At last he looks up, and catches me admiring the one thing in the
shop that I really want. We saw it from the street, hanging in the centre of the far wall, the last place you would expect to find it, and had
to come in. His hat and hair have faded to blue, his skin to a watery
pink, but it is the same face, young and determined, more sure and
more certain than Christ ever felt.

'*Es Che,*' says the old man. 'Che Guevara. You know who he is?'

'Yes,' says Victor. 'We know who he is.' It's not a print and not a
clipping from a magazine, but an actual photograph. Victor glances
at me. 'Is it for sale?'

He shakes his head. 'It's not for sale. I've had that photo a long,
long time.'

'Why?' I ask.

It is difficult to stand on Broadway in the squawking traffic and imagine Iroquois braves walking softly up a wooded trail. Difficult to watch the news and understand another way the world could be. Difficult to look at your life and picture one of the other lives it might have been. And it is difficult to look into a face, worn soft and slow and set by time, and see in it the face it was, sharp and quick and capable of everything. But it happens now and then. Now he is an old man in shabby clothes, sitting out his days in a dusty shop of memories, most of which are none of his, but once he had youth and dreams on his side; once he might have tried to cross the Nancahuasu with a laden pack and swollen feet and defeat hanging thickly in the air, following a man who never grew old.

He looks from the photograph to me. 'Because I admire him,' he says.

The bus taking us out of Sucia, our dreams of paddling through the jungle finally defeated, is more cosmopolitan than the bus that took us in. For one thing, it is larger and was made after the Second World War. For another, it has real seats, though not, of course, enough to go around. No one carrying a machete is selling freshly cut guava pods; no one is paying for their fare with a chicken. We don't even have to get off the bus when we come to a bridge. It's not all good news, though. The bus is so tightly packed that every time it sways, bucks or pitches, which it does more often than it doesn't, we shift left, right, back and forth like a block of ice. Cosmopolitan but within the parameters of tradition.

Eventually, we leave the bamboo huts, empty basketball courts and faded political posters of the jungle villages behind and start climbing through the clouds towards Cuenca.

The man in the beige leisure suit and the blue baseball cap, tired of watching the impossibly beautiful landscape through the dirty window, leans towards Victor, who is sitting on the arm of my hard-won seat, forcing his way between the two men beside him, one of whom is an American. 'Where are you from?' asks the man, his voice loud enough to be heard over the noise of the crowded bus and the volume at which Bob Marley is singing.

'England, says Victor.

The man nods. 'Ah, Inglés.' He points to me. 'And she?'

'She's American,' says Victor.

He glances at the short-haired young man in the plaid shirt and chinos, whose expression is both friendly and noncommittal, and gives me another, disbelieving look. He knows an American when he sees one. '*Si?*'

My fellow countryman smiles.

'But she comes from England, too,' explains Victor.

This seems to satisfy him. 'Ah . . .' His wife, pressed against the window with a small girl in a pink organdy dress and gold jewellery on her lap, stretches forward to get a look. 'Where in England?'

'London.'

He considers this. 'London. That's very far away. How much did it cost you to get to Ecuador?'

The men beside the American, effortlessly able to straddle their luggage and remain standing despite the terrain, stop the conversation they've been having about football and turn their eyes on Victor. The gringo takes a small bag of roasted corn from his pocket and starts to eat it, slowly and thoughtfully, giving his mouth something to do.

Victor explains that we started in New York, flew from LA to Barranquilla, and are leaving from Lima, and, editing slightly, tells him how much it all cost.

His whistle catches the attention of several other passengers. 'That much? That's very expensive.' In case she, or anyone else didn't hear Victor's answer, he repeats the figure to his wife. She thinks it's very expensive, too. He throws up his hands. '*Dios mío*, do you know how long I'd have to work to earn that much?'

Victor explains how hard and how long he has had to work to save enough for this trip. He explains that the most expensive part of the trip is the airflights, that the only reason we can afford it is because hotels and food in South America are cheap compared to what they are in England.

Victor's new travelling companion ignores this irrelevant information, and moves straight on to the next questions. 'What do you do in London? How much do you make?'

It may be that he has a curious and ever-questing mind, that he is a man eager to learn about the worlds he'll never see himself; either that or he is an undercover cop, flawlessly camouflaged by his nervous wife and whining child, who will slip something into our bags should we be stupid enough to leave them behind when we make the next rest stop.

Freddie Mercury takes over from Bob, but everyone else falls silent. The American slips another piece of corn between his lips.

'I'm a motorcycle courier,' says Victor, riding an air CX500. 'I deliver packages and letters.'

'You're a postman,' nods the man in the stained brown hat.

'No, no,' says the man whose hip is pressed against Victor's shoulder. He rides an air CX500 of his own. 'Vroomvroom. *Mensajero en moto.*'

The gringo will soon be out of corn.

'Ah . . . And how much do you make?'

Victor, still editing slightly, tells him how much he makes for driving a motorcycle in and out of London twelve hours a day, five days a week, in weather with an attitude and traffic with a vendetta. 'It's very hard work,' says Victor. 'It's very cold. It rains all the time.'

'What do you pay for rent?' continues el Señor Inquisitor.

Victor starts to explain that he doesn't pay rent, he squats, that there are thousands of homeless people in London both ignored and victimised by the government while buildings lie empty and politicians pick lint off the sleeves of their Saville Row suits and talk about law and order and rising crime, and that for this reason, if for no other, it is important to fight for squatters' rights.

El Señor cuts him off. 'How much is a flat?'

'At least one hundred pounds a week,' says Victor.

A bee-like hum rumbles around us. A hundred English pounds . . . a hundred English pounds a week . . . *Dios mío*, a hundred English pounds . . .

The American, a buyer from Long Island, who has yet to find little of real interest to ship back home, gives us a look. It's a they'll-be-asking-you-how-much-you-weigh-next kind of look.

'How much is that in sucres?' asks the man.

Victor tells him how much that is in sucres, how much a week's groceries in London costs in sucres, how much for gas, electricity and water in the currency of Ecuador.

Heads shake up and down the bus.

'And what does she do?' el Inquisitor would like to know.

'She's a writer.'

He shoves his head between the elbows of the men in the aisle, tilting one into the woman with the parrot on her shoulder. The parrot bites him. 'A writer?'

The American stares down at his feet as though a platoon of ants is marching back and forth across his Reeboks.

'What do you write?' he demands. '*Libros scientíficos?*'

You what?

'No,' I say quickly, aware that even the parrot has stopped watching Victor and is now watching me. 'Not science books. I write novels. Novels and books for children.'

'*Qué?*' shouts someone at the front. '*Qué tipo de libro?*'

'*Libros para niños,*' the woman in front of me answers. 'She draws the pictures.'

'And are you married?' El Señor asks Victor.

Victor says that he isn't married.

'And you?'

'*Yo tampoco,*' I mutter. I do not like the way this conversation is going.

He waves a finger between us. 'And you are a couple?'

'No,' we both say at once, so fast that it seems likely that we not only aren't a couple but are travelling together under duress – either he's bringing me in, or I'm bringing him. 'No, we're just friends.'

The bees buzz.

He focuses on Victor. 'How old are you?

Victor tells him his age.

'*Y la señorita?*'

The tape ends. You can hear the parrot poop in the silence.

I never thought I'd become the sort of woman who refuses to tell her age, but I have. At least to an audience of sixty. I step on Victor's foot. Men have died for less than this.

Victor shrugs. 'I don't know,' he says in clear and faultless Castilian. And adds, even more clearly and perfectly, 'It's none of my business.'

El Señor hesitates for a second, considering this information, then changes his mind. 'And do you have children?' he now wants to know.

Victor says that he has no children, which seems to be no more than our fellow passengers expected from an Englishman with a ring in his nose.

Fed up with the inquisition, I say that I have no children either. They expected more of me, *Dios mío,* I'm a woman after all.

'Why not?' asks the Inquisitor, speaking for the rest of the bus. He yanks his daughter forward, something that looks like curds and whey dribbling down her chin to the pink ruffles of her dress. 'This is my fifth child,' he says. He holds up five fingers. 'My fifth and last. They are the greatest blessing God can give.'

As far as I'm concerned, the greatest blessing God could give right now would be that trick he does with the annoying human and the pillar of salt.

I smile back, thinly and dumbly.

'Why not?' he repeats. 'Why don't you have children?'

Victor looks at me out of the corner of his eye. The American bloke, head still bent forward, raises his eyes. The moment is pregnant.

If I were in London and for some reason the British vow of silence on anything considered personal information was not in force so that I found myself in this situation – without, perhaps, the parrot and the smell of vomit in the air – I would tell him to mind his own bloody business, and not worry about all my mother's injunctions about good manners and being rude. But I am not in London. I am in a bus rollercoasting through the mountains surrounding Cuenca, a visitor in a foreign country who must always remember to be calm and polite and never offensive. God forbid I should hurt his feelings or embarrass him. So instead I lie. I tell him that my husband and infant son were killed in a car accident one stormy Christmas night. I mime the hairpin turn, I imitate squealing breaks, I touch my broken heart. 'That's why I'm not married,' I tell them. 'That's why I have no children.'

It's a moving tale, even in broken Spanish with a Brooklyn accent. Victor buries his face in my shoulder. A few whispered *Dios míos* weave through the crunch of passengers like mosquitos, but otherwise the silence is stunned. Though not for long.

'And why didn't you marry again?' the man asks.

Victor presses his mouth in my arm. The other gringo laughs.

Señor Bolivar puts down the copy of *Reader's Digest* he's been reading as the three of us stagger through his office door. Max, the laughing gringo from Long Island who agrees with Victor that I should give up illustration and become a real writer, drops the baskets he bought in Sucia for his mother's crafts store in front of the desk. Victor and I throw our bags on a cracked leather chair. 'Welcome to the Hotel Colombia,' says Señor Bolivar, and rises to his feet. 'How can I be of service to you?'

Señor Bolivar is a tall, thin man in his late fifties dressed in a lightweight suit and neat striped tie who, like the Hotel Colombia itself, seems left over from a different time; one more genteel if not more gentle. A time when the hotel's tiles were brightly coloured, its doors solid, its central courtyard filled with plants and birds that shone in the sunshine; a time when Señor Bolivar's bearing wouldn't have seemed old-fashioned and formal but elegant and correct.

Max says that he wants a single room. Victor that we want a double. We don't even ask to see them first. It's nine at night, we've been travelling for nearly ten hours, and the hotel next door is twice the price.

'*No hay ningun problema*,' says Señor Bolivar. He takes a ragged register from the shelf beside the desk, opens it carefully, and hands Max the pen. 'If you will just fill in the information the government requires . . .' he says, and then, when he sees him write 'American', begins to tell us of the winter he spent in Queens, visiting the World's Fair. 'It was very cold,' he says, wrapping his arms around him and shivering. 'Very, very cold. But I enjoyed myself very much.' He smiles at Max. 'I liked the coffee and those breads with the cream cheese.'

'Bagels,' says Max.

Señor Bolivar snaps his fingers. 'Bagels, *eso es!*' He closes the register and recaps the pen. 'My *empleado* will show you the rooms.' He looks over our heads. 'Oscar!' he bellows. 'Oscar! Show these weary travellers the rooms above.'

Oscar, Señor Bolivar's employee, whom we passed on the way in, ironing in the courtyard while he sang along to the South American rap song on his Walkman, comes running up the stairs. Oscar is also leftover from a different time, but his is a time when Cuenca was known as Tomebamba, white men were no more than spirits in a dream, and it never occurred to even the most gifted shaman that one day a descendant of his might be wearing Levi jeans and a Public Enemy T-shirt.

Oscar shows us to our room. It is large and green, as safe as pitching a tent in Central Park, and at the other end of the balcony that overlooks the plaza from the cell he shows to Max.

'And the shower,' says Victor as Señor Bolivar's *empleado* gives us the key. 'It's hot?'

Oscar grins. 'Sometimes.'

'I smell dope,' says Victor, stopping in the doorway, sniffing the air.

I barge past him. Victor's mind has been on drugs ever since Baños, but mine is on the two red plastic shot glasses already laid out on the table at the foot of the bed and the bottle under my arm.

'You're hallucinating,' I say. 'It's lack of protein.' Unlike other South Americans the Chinese do at least stretch to vegetables – indeed, if it hadn't been for the need for cheap labour to build the railways in the nineteenth century, at least two more vegetarians might have starved to death in the twentieth – but tofu has yet to become what you could call popular, or even existent. 'It's probably that chicken place across the street.'

Victor locks the door behind him but doesn't move. 'No,' he says. 'I definitely smell grass.'

I crack the top. 'Well, I smell rum.'

He stands where he is for a few seconds more, looking like a hound that's just hit the river. 'You must be right,' he finally decides. 'It's gone now.'

We fluff up the pillows and get on the bed with our rum and our book. Victor reads, because my reading puts him to sleep.

We are far away from Cuenca and not far away at all, in a Colombian town of colonial houses and cobbled streets much like the ones here, deep in the story of a persistent love, when someone starts banging on our door.

'Sí?' shouts Victor. '*Quiénes?*'

'*Buenas noches!*' a female voice shouts back. '*Buenas noches!*'

Victor puts down the book. We look at each other. 'Who is it?' he demands.

There's a flurry of giggling and then another female voice says, 'It's us!'

'*Buenas noches!*' calls the first voice again. '*Buenas noches!*'

'You have the wrong room,' says Victor.

The giggling escalates. 'No we don't. *Son extranjeros, no?*'

'Jesus,' mutters Victor, hurling himself over me and grabbing his trousers from the chair by the bed. 'What do you have to do on this continent to get any peace and quiet?'

He opens the door no more than a crack. The giggling becomes slightly hysterical, but all I can see is the side of his head as he says, 'What do you want?'

'*Buscamos una pareja de extranjeros,*' gasps one of the women.

'Wrong room,' the other squeals.

Victor gets out of his trousers, climbs back on the bed, picks up the book, takes his fresh drink from my hand and begins to read again.

There's a knock at the door.

'Wrong room!' shouts Victor.

The knocking persists.

Victor throws down the book. 'Wrong room!'

'*Policia!*' comes the reply.

Victor gets out of bed, puts on his trousers, and goes to the door. He opens it only a crack, so that all I can see is the side of his head as he says, '*Sí?*'

Now I can hear the heavy footsteps and male voices marching through the hotel. The soldiers want to see our passports; they want to check our bags.

'Just a minute,' says Victor, and slams the door in their faces. 'Get dressed.'

Reluctantly, I put down my rum and get dressed.

We pick up our bags and go to the door. There are two soldiers standing in the dimly lit hallway with Oscar beside them, his head-set around his neck, his eyes on us. 'You can go now,' the larger soldier tells him.

Oscar hesitates. '*El señor me dijo—*'

'You can go now.' The soldier gives him a shove

Still looking at us, Oscar backs into the dark.

The soldiers go through our bags. Out come the backgammon set, the cheap camera, the ketchup container filled with brewers' yeast tablets, the toilet bag and our dirty clothes.

'What's this?' asks the one calling the shots. He's scrutinising the small plastic bottle he's holding with a certain air of suspicion. He squeezes a blob of white on his finger.

I wait till he's put it to his lips before I answer. 'Shampoo.'

He recaps the bottle and throws it back as though I hadn't spoken. He hands me back the bag. '*Pasaportes.*'

We hand over our pasaportes. He looks at Victor. 'Wolverhahmtone?'

Victor blinks. '*Qué?*'

'Wolverhahmtone. *Usted es Wolverhahmtone?*'

Victor moves forward to see what the soldier is reading. 'No,' he says. 'Wolverhampton, that's where I was born.' He turns the page. 'That's my name,' he points. 'Victor Ernesto David Sanchez.'

The soldier stares at Victor's name. 'And what is your surname? Dahveed?'

'Sanchez. Victor Sanchez.'

The soldier, still staring at Victor's name, bites his lip thoughtfully. 'And where are you from? *Los Estados Unidos?*'

'Inglaterra.'

The soldier nods, as though just testing, and begins to flip through the pages. 'So you came from el Oriente . . .' It isn't a question. He snatches my passport out of the hands of his comrade and starts scrutinising that. He looks from the photo page to me. '*Inglesa*,' he says.

'*Americana*.'

He turns several pages. Doors are shutting on the other floors, boot-steps are descending the stairs. At last he raises his eyes to ours. He smiles, as apologetic as a snake who's about to crush your chest. 'I'm afraid there is a little problem,' he says. 'Your papers are not in order.'

'What are you talking about?' asks Victor, forgetting about the politeness and respect recommended when dealing with representatives of the military police.

'This.' He holds out our *pasaportes*. 'You have a stamp from the Oriente.'

'Uh-huh . . .' We nod. Not that we had much choice about it, but you would have assumed that it was the thing to do.

He smiles again. I wish he wouldn't. When they smile like that it means you're going to have a chance to meet the commandante and see what headquarters are like. I don't want to go to jail tonight. I want to stay where we are and finish the rum.

'But it isn't signed.' He indicates the line at the bottom, unfilled by the border guard's signature. 'It has to be signed.'

'But we have the stamp,' says Victor. 'What difference does it make if it's signed or not?'

It makes, apparently, a great deal of difference.

'I am sorry,' he says, with as much sincerity as you might expect in the circumstances, 'but you will have to go back and get it signed.'

'Go back?' says Victor.

The second soldier is glancing over the balcony, trying to see what the others are doing.

He closes the passports, shaking them in his hand. 'Yes. When are you going back?'

In an Eddie Murphy movie, the answer would be, 'Try never.' But we're not in an Eddie Murphy movie. That's not the answer in Cuenca.

'Not for at least five days,' says Victor. 'We only just arrived.'

The soldier taps the passports against the air. 'Five days . . .' He turns to his comrade. His comrade shrugs without opinion. 'Five days . . .' He turns back to us. 'I'm afraid we'll have to keep the passports until you have the signature.'

He doesn't seem afraid.

'But that doesn't make any sense.' I can recognise a shakedown when I see one. 'How can we get the signature if you have the passports with the stamps in them?'

Victor can recognise a shakedown, too. 'You're not taking our passports,' he says flatly. 'Not without us.'

The soldier turns to his comrade again. His comrade shifts nervously. He turns back to us. Another smile disturbs his face. 'You foreigners think that we want to cause you trouble, but we don't.' He holds the passports out to Victor. He shakes Victor's hand and then he shakes mine. 'We are your friends.'

'Well, thank God for that,' says Victor in English.

Once more we lock the door to our room. Once more we take up our rum and our book and get into bed. Victor starts reading again.

This time the knock is at the French window that overlooks the plaza.

'Now what?' Victor jumps over me to the floor and pulls his trousers back on. 'This is worse than the place with the oil workers. This is worse than the place with the movies in the lobby.' He thumps across the room. He peers around the edge of the curtain.

'Is it the cops again?'

'No.' Victor pulls aside the curtain and opens the window.

Max is standing on the balcony, holding a hand-rolled cigarette in front of him. 'You guys smoke?' he wants to know.

'See?' Victor says to me. 'Why don't you ever believe me?'

'They just wanted money,' Señor Bolivar is saying. 'They're the scum of the earth.' His hand pushes the air in a gesture of contempt. Badly educated, greedy, stupid, largely indigenous . . .

Night has dropped over the plaza like an old cloth. Rubbish lies about in drifts. The crowds of people who spill across the plaza from the market during the day – the Indian women with their cauldrons of food, their children sitting on the ground beside them, playing with broken toys or doing their schoolwork, the musicians who break Victor's heart by destroying his favourite song, the vendors selling socks and plasticware and vegetables and fruit, have all gone till the morning, but, interestingly enough, the queues of people we'd earlier assumed were waiting for buses are still there, patiently inching their way to the kerbside.

'I always tell my employee to shut the door at ten and not let the soldiers in,' he continues.

Beside him, his employee, Walkman in place, stares out at the road, singing along to 'Hotel California'.

'When they come in, they look at the register.' Señor Bolivar points to his eye, he focuses it on a phantom register in front of his stomach, his expression calculating and intent. 'They see who is foreign, where they've come from . . .' He smiles in happy surprise, pointing at the air. 'They knock on your door.' Señor Bolivar raps against the night. He sighs. 'They're just after money,' he says. 'That's all they really want. When I'm here and the soldiers ring the doorbell at night, I look out of the window.' He acts out looking out of the window with a certain panache, pulling aside the curtain, opening the double panes, leaning his head over the narrow balcony. '"What?"' He puts a hand to his ear. '"You want to come up?"' He is puzzled, bemused. '"No, no, no," I tell them.' He shakes his hands. '"There's nothing for you here! Come back tomorrow!" But my empleado . . .' He shrugs.

'What a lovely plate . . .' sings his empleado.

At the head of each queue, camped right on the kerb, is an Indian woman with a hillock of leafy branches and a small fire beside her. The queue steps up to her, person by person, family by family, mother and child. I'm listening to Señor Bolivar, but I'm watching them. The women dust each petitioner with a fresh branch of leaves and flowers as he or she steps before them. Then they break the branch and scatter leaves over shoulders and head. Then they take a mouthful of water and spit it over head and face. Then they make a cross on the forehead and a dot on either temple with ashes, a circle around the navel, and spit on each symbol twice. All the while they chant almost under their breaths, a sound like flowing water.

'The same thing happened to my son,' Señor Bolivar goes on. Señor Bolivar's son has long hair and plays the guitar, but he's a good boy. He's not into drugs. He works hard and does well at school. He calls Señor Bolivar 'Papi'. 'He was taking a friend home from a party one night. It was dark and he wasn't sure of where he was.' Now Señor Bolivar is driving down an unfamiliar, unlit street, looking for the house of his friends. He stops the car. 'He went past the house and decided to back up rather than turn around.' Señor Bolivar, a careful, cautious driver, backs up his car. 'And then what happens?' He doesn't wait for us to guess. 'The police stopped him!' he cries. 'I'm woken up by the telephone ringing.' He starts, rubbing his eyes. He picks up the receiver. '"Hello? Who is this, please?" It's the police! My son has committed a grave crime.'

'And what happened?' asks Victor.

Señor Bolivar slides his hands into his pockets. 'I paid the bribe.'

'Butter never leeve,' sings Oscar.

Smoke drifts over the heads of the people at the kerb.

'What's happening up there?' I ask Señor Bolivar.

He gives up there a cursory glance. '*Curanderas*,' he replies. 'The Indians, they still believe in those things, in healers and shamans and spirits who are out to get you.'

'Chucachucachuca,' rumbles Oscar, imitating the chant. 'Chucachucachuca.' He pretends to spit.

A kid wearing his baseball cap backwards cycles past the *curanderas*.

'*Curanderas*,' repeats Victor. '*Brujas*.' We were expecting to find witches in the mountains of Huancabamba, but not halfway into traffic off a plaza in Cuenca.

'*Brujas* are evil,' says Oscar. 'These are just *curanderas*.'

Señor Bolivar glances at his *empleado*. 'Superstition,' he snaps. He smiles at Victor. 'Do you know anything about hypnotism?' he asks. There was a famous hypnotist on the television recently who hypnotised half of the home-viewing audience. For days afterwards, ordinary, respectable citizens would cluck like a chicken every time they heard a bell. 'It was very impressive,' says Señor Bolivar.

'Chucachucachuca,' whispers Oscar.

'And where are you off to now?' asks Señor Bolivar.

Victor slings his bag over his shoulder. 'We're going to the movies.'

'What film do you want to see?' asks Señor Bolivar.

'We don't want to see any film,' answers Victor. 'We just don't want to be here when the police come back.'

Señor Bolivar thinks this is hysterical.

'Chucachucachuca,' says Oscar.

When you travel the mundane takes on new importance; the ordinary becomes special; the simplest task becomes more difficult than cleaning out the Aegean stables with a wet toothpick. We decide to clean out the stables before we go to the film.

It is only because we tried this before that I know what to do. There's no way I'm sitting passively on a plastic chair for an hour tonight, patiently waiting for a booth to become free. No way I'm letting one of the bored, bossy women passing sweets and cakes to one another behind their glass-enclosed counter to push me around. Not two nights running.

The waiting room is already half-filled with people waiting. I choose a different retired Gestapo officer from the one I went to the night before, a round munchkin of a woman with bright red curls and an orange dress, her black glasses decorated with rhinestones. She's painting numbers on large glass marbles with polish the identical colour to her nails.

'Excuse me,' I say. 'But I'd like to make a call to the United States on my AT&T card.'

Not looking at me, she carefully sets down the marble and returns the nail polish brush to its bottle. She picks up a pen and holds it over her records sheet. 'Name?'

Sometimes I give Victor's last name, to make life a little easier for everyone, but tonight I decide to spare her nothing. 'Sheldon.'

Now she is ready to look at me. Just long enough to see that I've taken the notepad and pen she's shoved under the grille for me.

I write Sheldon, and push the pen and pad back to her.

She copies it on to page 2 of her list. 'Go wait in the *sala*.'

'For how long? Last night I—'

She picks up the brush and the marble. 'Go wait in the *sala*.'

I go back to the *sala*. It's more than half-full now.

'You should just grab a booth,' says Victor as I sit down beside him.

'It wouldn't work. They have to put the line through.'

We sit back and wait.

'Did you tell her you're using your AT&T card?' asks Victor.

'Yes, I told her.'

We wait some more.

I become absorbed in the sign taped to the wall that explains how easy it is to call the United States simply by dialling 119. At the bottom, in smaller print, it says something about *salas de prensa*.

'What do you think *salas de prensa* are?' I ask Victor.

He glances from the sign to me. 'Did you really tell her you're using your AT&T card?'

We continue to wait.

All countries have things in common. The same sun. The same sky. Problems making the trains run on time. Tannoys that can transform any human voice into an amorphous crackle. The tannoy of the Cuenca Eitel office begins to crackle. Señor Trrerdeqssssssdo . . . Señorita Mmmmdzzz . . . Señora Prrrzzz . . .

'You did tell her you're using your AT&T card, didn't you?' asks Victor.

I choose a different woman this time. 'Excuse me,' I say. 'But I'm waiting to make a call to the States on my AT&T card. What are *salas de prensa?*'

She turns to the woman beside her and asks her something about either Saturday or sheets.

I go back to the woman in orange.

She looks up from the marble she's working on now. 'What do you want?'

'I want to call on 119.'

'Then go wait in the *sala.*'

I move back against the wall, but otherwise I stay where I am.

When, at last, she waves me forward it is to hand me a large multicoloured marble with the number 12 painted on it. And to think that I thought she didn't take her job seriously.

I gesture to Victor and he follows me into phone booth number 12. I dial 119. An American operator asks me what I'm trying to do. I tell her that I'm trying to call Brooklyn on my AT&T card. Victor presses his ear to the receiver as the phone begins to ring. Ringring . . . ringring . . . ringring . . . ringring . . .

'We're not answering the phone right now,' says Jack's voice. 'Leave your name and your shoe size and maybe we'll call you back.'

'I'd like to see him try,' says Victor.

Oscar, finished with the morning sweeping, the sheets already hung out to dry in the courtyard, is sitting in his room – the cupboard under the stairs – listening to the radio. He nods to the bags in our hands. 'Are you leaving?' he asks.

'Yes,' says Victor, shaking his hand. 'We've come to say goodbye.'

Oscar shakes Victor's hand, and then mine. 'Will you come back?'

'Not this time,' says Victor. 'We're going to Vilcabamba, then straight to Peru.'

The bare lightbulb hanging over the bed that fills the cupboard flickers as Oscar considers going to Vilcabamba and then straight to Peru. He gestures towards the radio with his head. '*Se dice* please dohn't go . . .' he says.

22

THE COPS DON'T NEED
YOU, AND, MAN, THEY
EXPECT THE SAME

It is a dark and stormy night. Rain shakes the wall of trees on either side and floods the treacherous, unpaved road. If you could see out of the windows there would be nothing to see, not even the gas lamp of a distant hut, but you can't so it doesn't really matter.

I give Victor a nudge. 'It says here not to travel in Peru by train or bus at night,' I tell him. Not by train or bus at night, and never alone. Outside the main centres, it's always advisable to go as a group. When travelling on buses in the mountains, says the guide-book, there is the likelihood of the transport being stopped, either by guerrillas or by *comités* of villagers who will ask for 'donations'. The guidebook suggests that it would be foolish not to give. Ever helpful, it offers recommended reading: *How Not to Get Robbed in Peru*, a pamphlet issued by the South American Explorers' Club. I know Victor well enough now not to add, 'Or at any time by motorcycle,' or he won't rest until we've managed to rent one.

Victor, worried that the driver is paying more attention to the young woman squatting beside him, tossing her hair and rattling her jewellery while she discusses music and films, than he is to the road, doesn't take his eyes from the windscreen. 'We're not in Peru.'

But we're as good as. When we stop at a dimly lit village, the other passengers don't scrabble out for drinks, or food, or a piss in the bushes as they usually do, but stay huddled in their seats, glancing at their watches or trying to go back to sleep. When we stop at a dimly lit checkpoint, the other passengers shift restlessly in their places, sighing impatiently as Victor and I, lugging our sodden baggage, get out and trudge through the dark and stormy night to have our gringo passports checked again by bored young men with nothing else to do. It may be the weather, or it may be something else, like the proximity of the border. With a little luck – or no really bad luck – we'll be in Macara tonight, will walk into Peru in the morning.

'The books says to take special precautions.'

The guidebook, while striving to be reasoned, balanced and unhysterical, isn't all that positive on Peru. Though it makes a point of reassuring us that most Peruvians, especially those outside areas affected by crime or terrorism (thieves, the book qualifies, just to put our minds at rest, are active only in markets, streets, hotels, buses and trains, but, it admits, the activities of Sendero Luminoso and Tupac are spreading), are friendly.

'We're always careful,' says Victor, who by his lights always is. But not by the lights of the handbook. The lights of the handbook illuminate the words SECURITY, ANOTHER WARNING and NB. Avoid visiting places where guerrilla activity is reported as particularly active, it warns. Since Sendero Luminoso has been linked with the drugs trade, police and army searches have increased under state-of-siege legislation, it further warns, adding that you should be careful what you photograph and if possible carry an official letter stating your business. It speaks of curfews and martial law.

The bus stops suddenly in the hostile night. The dark, muddy street looks as deserted as the ruin of a vanished jungle tribe. The book advises the sensible traveller who would like to be alive when he or she uses the return half of his or her airline ticket to make inquiries about the state of siege whenever he or she arrives in a new place, but there is no one here to ask. We only know we're in a town because the travelling salesman with the black vinyl sample case and the fake Rolex gets off hurriedly.

'Shit,' says Victor, squinting through the waves breaking over the windscreen at dirt roads, shabby two-storey buildings and covered wooden sidewalks sprawling in front of the bus. 'It's Dodge City.'

But without Chester and Matt Dillon, without the charms of Miss Kitty and stampeding cattle.

Victor leans forward and taps the driver. 'Where are we?'

The driver, absorbed in rewinding his favourite casssette with a pencil, answers, 'You don't have to get out here. There's no checkpoint.'

Victor taps him again. 'Where are we?'

The driver looks over his shoulder. Isn't it enough that we've had to stop every forty-five minutes and wait while you two prove that you're not spies or drug smugglers? asks his expression. Do I have to be a tourist agency for you, too? '*Qué?*'

'Where are we?'

Finished rewinding, the driver sticks the pencil behind his ear. Where the fuck do you think we are? 'Macara.'

Gateway to Peru.

There are a few small buildings stuck in the mud on either side of the short concrete bridge that spans the river dividing Ecuador and Peru. Chickens tiptoe along the roadside, dogs, boys and men gather in doorways and around dirty jeeps. The chickens are clucking, the dogs are barking, the boys are shouting 'Gringos! Gringos!' and the men are calling out, 'Dollars! Dollars! You want to change dollars?' We pay them no mind.

'Now, remember,' Victor is saying as we slog through the mud towards the one-room, single-storey concrete building just before the bridge, 'we don't let them separate us, we don't let them take our passports or our bags out of our sight, and we make sure we get a receipt and a name and number if they demand any money.'

'Gotcha.' This is not something I really need to be told twice. According to the guidebook, because fewer travellers choose Macara as their route out of Ecuador, there is less likelihood of bureaucratic hassle or of drug pushing than at the more popular Huaquiles, but there the good news ends. Because the officials have less to do, they are likely to create work for themselves. The traveller should be prepared for extensive searches by bored officials. Every bag searched, every tube of toothpaste and dirty sock laid out and examined, every book and photograph passed around. What's this? What's that? What do you want with this string? these eye hooks? the balloons covered with stars? We may not pay any attention to the guidebook's views on churches, cathedrals and museums worth a visit, but we're paying attention to this. We've heard of gringos held up for hours, held up for days, unceremoniously sent back to whence they'd come by soldiers familiar with the state of their underwear and the contents of their sewing kits.

Shoulder to shoulder, we approach Passport Control, doing our best, despite lack of sleep and food, to appear sharp and sussed and sure of ourselves. Attitude, says the guidebook, is very important. You don't want to look like a turkey if you can possibly help it –

policemen, like muggers and dogs, will go for the frightened and weak, but a friendly attitude can help you out of trouble. No matter what, says the guidebook, never be discourteous to officials. Your fate is in their hands.

There is one soldier, well out of his teens, behind the glass window, sipping a cup of coffee while he reads yesterday's paper. Despite the early hour, he already looks pretty bored.

He gets up heavily and comes to the open door. '*Buenos días.*' He looks us up and down without interest. He holds out his hand. '*Pasaportes.*'

'*Buenos días.*' We hand him our passports.

He opens mine and studies the information as though he is actually able to read it. '*Americana,*' he says, glancing at me.

'*Sí, Americana.*'

Slowly, he flicks through the pages, glancing at the stamps. When he gets to the back of the book he looks at me again. 'What's this?' he wants to know. He holds out the passport with the £20 note held to the inside cover with an elastic band.

Victor looks at me, too.

'*Dinero inglés,*' I answer promptly. 'For when I return to my country.'

As though defusing a bomb, he removes the bill and hands it to me. 'You should keep that safe,' he says. He opens Victor's passport and repeats the process. '*Inglés,*' he says. He reads, he flicks. He holds out the page with the £20 note held in place by an elastic band. 'What's this?'

Victor tells him what it is.

The soldier carefully slips the bill free with two fingers and passes it over to Victor. '*Momentito,*' he says, and disappears into the office. Momentito is one of those words like 'freedom' and 'love' that might mean something and might mean nothing; that might mean anything. He may be back in a moment, or in ten moments, or in a day and a half.

'It can't be this easy,' I say softly. 'He's gone for reinforcements.' Or chains.

He's back in a moment, our exit stamps in place. Have a good time in Peru.

'Is there somewhere we can change money?' asks Victor as the soldier hands back the passports.

For the first time genuine interest bends the guard's mouth into a smile. '*Dólares?*' he asks. '*Quieren cambiar dólares?*'

We shake our heads. 'Sucres,' says Victor.

The smile vanishes, but he nods. 'I'll change them.'

'You?' The way I speak Spanish usually eliminates any nuance of emotion, but even I can hear the surprise in my voice. This is what happens when you maintain an army without a war to keep it busy. It finds other things to do.

'What's the exchange?' asks Victor.

He doesn't have to think even once about this.

Victor turns to me. 'What did he say?'

I'm not sure either. 'I think he said that a sol is worth a mil sucres.'

Victor gazes back at me, wondering how he could know me so well and not know I'd lost my mind. 'You're crazy,' says Victor. 'One sol for a thousand sucres?'

The guard removes a sol from the pocket of his uniform and holds it against the 1,000-sucre note in Victor's hand. '*Uno por uno*,' he elucidates.

Victor's Spanish is better than mine – he can combine surprise and contempt. 'One for one?' He waves the note in front of the guard. 'That's impossible.' He points to the sol. 'Are you saying that one of these is worth one of these?'

Yes, that's what the soldier is saying: 1 sol is worth 1,000 sucres.

But Victor's memory of the guidebook's advice is worse than mine. He doesn't care if the soldier knows we think that he's lying. Victor stuffs the bill back in his pocket. 'We'll change them somewhere else,' he says.

The guard shrugs. Suit yourself.

Peru, when we get to the other side of the bridge, looks remarkably like Ecuador: a dirt road, a huddle of mud huts, boys and men hanging out on a slab of concrete that seems to be the village square. The only real difference is that the official buildings are newer and more impressive in Peru: the police headquarters, painted white, the customs office, painted pink, each have an official sign and a neat flower garden out front.

'Gringos! Gringos!' chant the boys.

'Dollars! You want to change dollars?' scream the men.

We stop by the garden of the border police. 'Is this where we go?' asks Victor.

The man propped against the door shakes his head. 'Not here.' He points across the street. '*En el edificio azul.*'

We follow the direction of his hand. Across the street, its flaking walls covered with faded, peeling posters, is a derelict building with a chicken on the porch.

'That can't be it,' says Victor as we start across the road.

'It's the only blue building there is.'

'Dollars!' the onlookers chorus. 'You want to change dollars?'

'It's not blue,' says Victor. 'It used to be blue.'

'But he did say blue.'

He stops a few yards from the crumbling blue building. 'He can't mean *that*,' says Victor again. 'That's where they dump the bodies to get them out of the road.'

The chorus changes. 'In there!' the men are shouting now. 'You go in there!'

We glance over our shoulders. Several hands are pointing at the *edificio azul*. 'In there! In there!'

'They'd better not be winding us up,' mutters Victor, all the good advice of the guidebook totally forgotten. 'This had better not be a joke.'

'*Sí, sí*, in there! In there!' the men urge us on. Childish laughter, not all of it coming from children, rolls down the rutted road.

God knows what's in there. The jail? More chickens? Victor carefully steps over the dark pellets scattered over the broken stone stairs that lead to the porch. A goat?

We stop at the door and, cautiously, peer in. The room is bare and less than immaculate, the only furniture a worn wooden desk and a small metal table. In the room are two men, drinking coffee and smoking cigarettes in a let's-kill-some-time sort of way. One wears the uniform of the Peruvian army, the other the uniform of the rest of the world.

Victor turns to the soldier. 'Is this where we get our passports stamped?'

'Passports,' says the man at the desk, the one in the Raiders T-shirt and jeans. 'Give them to me.'

Although it seems unlikely that we really have a choice in the matter, even I don't think this seems like such a good idea. We both look back to the man whose government trusts him enough to give him clothes, a leather holster and a gun.

He doesn't smile reassuringly. 'Give them to him.'

God knows who the man in the T-shirt is, but we give them to him.

He examines the jackets, running a calloused finger over the gold lion and the eagle with the symbol of peace grasped in one foot and

heavy arms grasped in the other. He examines the names and birth-
dates and addresses and numbers. He looks at Victor's photograph
and then closely at Victor. He looks at my photograph and then
closely at me. He reads each page slowly, checking every arrival and
departure, thinking about where we've been and when we were
there. He is thorough, meticulous. He doesn't think Victor's name is
Wolverhampton or confuse the passport number with his date of
birth. He may not be dressed for it, but he takes the job seriously.
'Barranquilla . . . Ipiales . . . Tulcan . . .' There is no clock on the wall,
loudly counting each minute, but we are still aware of the loris-like
passage of time as he notices every unsigned stamp, every unexpected dip and turn in our journey; as he judges whether or not we
pose any threat to the state, whether we're likely to have friends who
would miss us if we never reached Lima. 'Pastaza . . . Loja . . .
Macara . . .'

At last he raises his eyes to ours. 'You have dollars?' he asks.

There is no bus. We've walked the length of the *pueblo*, children sliding past us with baskets, bags and open mouths, but the bus, we are
told, *no hay*. The heavy rains have washed out the road. 'When will
there be a bus?' we ask the one woman not quick enough to duck
back into her doorway away from our questions. '*No sé.*' We can get
a bus from the next village, but the next village is far away. 'How far?'
asks Victor. Very far. Some of us don't want to walk very far on a road
like pea soup in a country where even riding on a crowded bus can
be considered an act of faith. We go back to the river to wait for a
colectivo. There are more people sitting on the slab of concrete, a
couple of guys winding between them selling juices. Everyone is
laughing at the goat stranded on the roof of the restaurant, cornered
by a skinny dog with a maniacal bark. No one seems to have much to
do. We sit on the painted white rocks surrounding the flagpole in
front of the *edificio azul* and eat bananas, aware that some of the
onlookers' attention has shifted from the terrified goat to us. 'They're
up to something,' says Victor, staring back. A bomb explodes near my
feet. I scream. Another flies past Victor's shoulder, bursting behind
him. The men across the road think this is even funnier than the
panicky goat. Victor shakes the water from his hat, forgetting to
smile. The door to the police station suddenly opens and two soldiers
emerge, backs straight and heads high, marching right for us.

'Now what?' I wonder aloud.

'Get out of the way,' says the soldier not carrying the flag.

We get out of the way.

'Take off your hats.'

We take off our hats.

Everyone stands, eyes solemnly fixed on the flagpole, while the banner of Peru is launched into the air.

Everyone stands, bareheaded, while the Ecuadorian flag is raised across the bridge.

'Do you think we can sit down again now?' I ask Victor.

He shakes his head. Striding towards us from the customs office is a large, middle-aged man to whom the Peruvian government has supplied not only a very smart uniform but quite a few bits of metal to decorate it.

'I knew we should've walked to the next village,' mutters Victor.

The officer doesn't so much as glance at me. He walks straight to Victor, raising his hand. For a very long second I think that he means to hit him. A hand like a hunk of meat claps Victor's shoulder. The second gets longer. Every cell in my body freezes. He isn't going to hit him, he's going to take him in. The soldier grins. 'You want to change dollars?' he asks.

Horacio thinks that we'd be foolish to wait for the bus to Chiclayo. It isn't leaving for another two hours. The bus station is dirty and full of thieves. The bus will be crowded and take hours to cross the desert. The bus will be uncomfortable and noisy. Sure, maybe it's 9 sols more to take a cab, but it's worth it, says Horacio. We'll be safe; we won't have to worry about a thing. We can sit up front. We can put our luggage in the boot. His car has air conditioning. It has a radio. It can get there in half the time the bus would take, well before dark.

'What do you think?' asks Victor.

Other cabs, cabs I really want to ride in – Volkswagen Beetles and motorcycle rickshaws, not vintage Buicks with a picture of Jesus stuck on the dash – pass us on both sides, staggering along with the traffic, jamming into the pick-up area in front of the bus station. 'Why can't we take a moto-taxi?'

'Across the desert? Haven't you had enough dust for one day?'

Probably I have. Six hours in the back of a truck with a chicken crawling up your trousers – no matter how exciting crossing rivers without the aid of bridges, no matter how spectacular the rice pad-dies and the lunaresque landscape of the desert – doesn't make the prospect of a ride through sand on a motorcycle a truly pleasant one.

'What about a Beetle?'

'Too small,' says Victor. 'If we're going to get packed into a Volkswagen we'd be better off on the bus.'

The streets are lined with stalls – Slush Puppies, ice-creams, drinks, plasticware and fruit – jammed with people, blocked with traffic and solid with noise. We'd be better off in Chiclayo with a room and time to get supper and beer. It would be nice to travel in comfort for a change – comfort and style.

'Let's take the cab.'

Victor turns back to Horacio. 'All right, we'll go with you.'

Horacio beams. 'We just have to wait for a few more people.'

He shakes Victor's hand. 'Are you German?'

'No,' says Victor. 'I'm English.'

Horacio nods. 'Ah, *Inglés*.' His eyes wander to two men in cotton suits and nylon shirts carrying suitcases. 'Chiclayo!' he shouts. 'Chiclayo!'

The businessmen pause beside us. They ask the price. They ask how long it will take. They ask when he's leaving. '*Prontito*.' Horacio gestures to us. 'They're coming,' he says. 'We only need two more.'

The men look at me and Victor. They pick up their suitcases. They'll try the other depot.

'What other depot?' I ask. 'You mean there's another bus company?'

Horacio's gesture is dismissive. 'They're both the same,' he says to Victor. 'It won't get you there any sooner.'

Horacio and Victor discuss the high cost of living and the problems with drugs and guerrillas, blaming it all on the President. 'He's Japanese,' explains Horacio.

'He's not Peruvian?' I interrupt.

'He's Peruvian,' Horacio assures Victor. 'He was born in Peru, but he's Japanese.' It's not the same.

I've noticed that Horacio doesn't speak to me. He speaks of me. Is she English, too? Are you travelling together? Did you meet in Ecuador? He gives me a glance. 'Are you a couple?'

'*Somos amigos*,' says Victor.

The woman selling bottles of warm soda from a wooden cart laughs.

Horacio shakes his head. 'We're religious people,' he tells Victor, 'In Peru a man and a woman cannot be friends. A man has a wife, and that's it.'

The soda seller agrees. Peru is not like the wicked West. It's very bad to have friends of the opposite sex.

'We're friends,' repeats Victor. 'I have friends who are men and friends who are women. It's the same thing.'

Horacio and the woman exchange a look. They don't think it's the same thing at all. They know about England and America. They've seen movies. They read the tabloids. In England even the future King fools around.

A woman with two small children and a good deal of baggage appears around the Buick's gleaming bumper.

'Chiclayo!' booms Horacio. 'Chiclayo. *Vamanos horatito.*'

They haggle over the children's fare while Victor and I gaze down the road, wondering about the other bus station.

The woman and the children go off. Horacio turns back to Victor, and begins the now familiar dialogue about how much it cost us to get here. Victor tries to explain.

'It's all right for you,' Horacio says. 'I couldn't travel like you do. I could never save that much money.'

'We had to work hard for our money,' says Victor. 'We saved a long time.'

Horacio, however, is still talking. 'Even if I could save the money, it wouldn't matter. I only get two weeks' vacation a year.'

'I don't get any vacation,' says Victor. 'I work for myself. If I don't work, I don't get paid.'

I can tell from Victor's look that they have reached that point in the conversation where he is tired of being told how hard it is for the working Hispano, how easy for the rich gringo. It's the same look he had when the man on the bus to Piaru, the man who entertained the passengers by sticking needles through his neck, demanded money from him. 'You're rich!' screamed the human pin cushion, needles flashing. 'Give me some of your money.' Victor said, 'No.' A single word, as effective at stopping an argument as a bullet if your eyes are as hard as a gun.

'Then you must make a lot of money at your job,' says Horacio.

Victor reloads. 'Everyone thinks we're rich, but we're not,' he says loudly. Several of the other street vendors turn our way. 'In my country, I'm poor.'

Horacio smiles. 'But you're here.' The soda seller nods.

'Look at my shirt,' shouts Victor, tugging one of his two shirts, the red one riddled with holes. 'Look at my shoes.' He holds up his Converse, bought just before the trip but already shredding and losing its sole.

'Would I be dressed like this if I were rich?' demands Victor. Horacio makes a face. The woman bursts out laughing.

An elderly Chevy pulls up behind the Buick. The driver gets out and comes over to Horacio, greeting him warmly. 'How's it going?' They discuss the journey to Chiclayo. The gringos are going. The woman and the two children are going.

The second driver spots a couple dashing through the honk of traffic towards our concrete island of litter and carts, arms around each other. 'Chiclayo!' he shouts. 'Chiclayo!'

The young man is quiet and nodding, the young woman considers the price. 'What do you think, *querido*?' she asks the young man. He nods. She questions the time. She hugs the young man. 'What do you think? Does that sound all right?' He nods. She wants to be dropped off at her hotel. 'No problem,' says the driver. She examines the car. She has to sit in the front. The driver nods. 'Of course.' She looks over at us. 'Are they coming with us?' she wants to know.

I'm about to say that we're not going with her, we're going in the Buick, when Horacio suddenly grabs our bags and heads for the boot of the Chevy. '*Siga! Siga!*' he calls. 'You're going with them.'

It isn't the moon. It's further from the planet earth than that. The white and grey desert spreads to distant dunes. A clump of vegetation. A hut made of mud, a shack made of cardboard, gas lanterns shining like torches through the gloaming. Every so often, we pass a solitary figure wrapped in black rags walking along the vacant road like an Old Testament prophet.

'*Star Wars*,' says Victor.

The little boy makes another lunge for Victor's nose. 'Take it out!' he shrieks. 'Take it out.'

Victor ducks back, pressing me into the window. Up front, the couple kiss and coo and the radio crackles.

'Manolito,' says his mother with all the passion and emotion of a twitch. 'Manolito, stop it.'

Manolito whacks his sister in the head with his GI Joe.

The kissers break for air. 'Can't you get a better station?' asks the girl.

'Manolito.'

The little girl resumes crying, kicking Victor in the knee.

'Take it out,' shrieks Manolito and lunges again.

The Chevy comes to a sudden stop.

'Police,' says the driver, opening his door.

The driver and the soldiers talk at the back of the car. The driver opens the boot. The police look inside.

Manolito pulls his sister's hair. She continues to cry.

'If they arrest anybody I hope it's him,' says Victor.

The girl sticks her tongue in her boyfriend's ear. If anybody's arrested, I'm praying it's them. Arrested, tortured and never set free.

The driver gets back in and starts up the car. We bump back on to the ribbon of road tentatively holding its own against the ocean of sand.

We pass a bus, a couple of cars, an open-backed truck loaded with men. The land is both flat and rising, a few stars nicked into the purple sky. For half a heartbeat, the headlights illuminate three figures hunkered down together in the sand, as motionless as though they were always there.

'I'm hungry,' whines Manolito. 'I want a drink.'

His sister decides to vomit.

Another police car pulls us over to the side.

The couple up front pull out of their kiss.

'Didn't I tell you we should take the bus?' says Victor.

By the time we finally reach the outskirts of Chiclayo the sky is black, hazed by smoke and gouged with stars. Traffic swarms over the pitted road: overloaded trucks with broken headlamps and dented bodies, oversized American cars held together by force of will, careening moto-taxis, Beetles and bicycles, plodding horse- and mule-drawn carts; motley clouds of people drift along the shoulders, buying from the street hawkers, loitering in front of the shacks selling food and drinks, gas lanterns nailed over the doors. The driver, tired of having to wait in traffic, leaves the right-hand lane and steams across the traffic island and down the left, squealing to a sudden halt more or less in the middle of a street that looks the way Broadway might after the holocaust.

My head bangs against the window. 'Surely it can't be legal to drive like this.'

'No,' says Victor. 'But it's effective.'

Like Barranquilla and the Hotel Zhivago, neither Chiclayo nor our hotel look any better in the morning than they do at ten at night. Chiclayo is still shabby and crowded, the roads clogged and filthy and the pavements thick with *ambulantes* waving wads of bills in your face and vendors selling lighters and watches, old electrical parts and dyes, rasta jewellery and T-shirts, beads and plastic toys.

Our hotel is still shabby and noisy, a row of men permanently occupying the old plastic sofa in the foyer, dozing or watching the television behind the desk, two small stuffed deer on top of the set gazing back at them. The street is the better option of the two.

El Mercado Central is a full-block square, stalls and carts spreading like a puddle all around it. Crowds gather round the geezer with the monkey and the chap nimbly shifting a nut between three plastic cups. They can't believe that the monkey looks so human in its yellow trousers and red jacket or that the nut is never where they think it's going to be. We fight our way through the aisle of shoes and stationery, up through bags and material, over through meat, olives, dried fruit and eggs, back through cookies and alcohol, up some more past clothes and toys, stepping over all the squashed things and dead things and wet things that litter the ground.

By the time the vegetable market hoves into view we have six small boys with us, bumping into each other as they step on our heels. None of the boys is more than eight, all are dirty and dressed in clothes that are either too big or too small and broken shoes. All of them look like people seeing ice for the first time as they shuffle beside us, their ears straining for every strange sound we might utter, their eyes wide to see what we'll do next.

We stop for avocados.

The boys stop with us.

The avocado seller scoops up half a dozen fruits and thrusts them into Victor's hands. '*Muy rico, muy barato. Riquísimo . . .*'

The boys nudge and jostle each other.

Victor and I juggle the avocados between us, testing for ripeness. 'What do you think?' he asks me.

The boys start to giggle.

'This one's all right.' I hand him the one that's all right.

The boys poke each other.

Victor squeezes the one that's all right. 'So is this one,' passing it over.

The boys edge closer, rocking back and forth together, grinning like kids watching chimps use forks.

Victor holds the two avocados out towards them. 'Well?' he asks.

They jump back, laughing.

Armed with avocados, chillis, garlic, coriander, tomatoes and lemons, we sidle through fruits and vegetables, refusing offers of the richest melons, sweetest oranges and blackest corn at the cheapest prices in Chiclayo.

We turn a corner and Victor stops so abruptly that our escort piles into us with shrieks of surprise.

'Jesus Christ,' says Victor. 'There it is.'

I follow his stare. Before us stretch dark cramped stalls laden with herbs and bottles of coloured liquids, dried bear and monkey claws, toucan heads and necklaces of bone, amulets, charms, medals, candles, wads of fresh tobacco, magic spells and tarot cards.

It's the *mercado de los brujos*, the biggest market of its kind in the Americas.

'Witches,' says Victor with new enthusiasm. 'Let's go.'

The eight of us go, the boys jostling around us whispering, '*Brujos, brujos*,' and the gringos ogling everything like a couple of street urchins let loose in F. A. O. Schwartz. What's that? Look at that! Do you think that's real?

We get distracted by a display of wooden sticks carved with skulls and snakes and hands and twisted symbols. '*Son chuntas*,' explains the old man behind the stall. '*Son muy raros*.'

The boys crowd closer.

'What are they used for?' asks Victor.

The old man waves his hand in a way that is vague and specific at once. '*Brujos*,' he says.

'*Brujos*,' echo the boys, their eyes on Victor; their breath on Victor too.

Victor wants the large redwood *chunta* carved with skulls, I want the small black snake for Tommi.

The seller wants $10 for the skulls, $6 for the snake.

'Six for both,' says Victor.

The boys come even closer.

'Six?' cries the man. 'Six? You are mad. You won't find another like this. Look at the wood.'

'Seven,' says Victor.

'I can't sell this *chunta* for less than ten,' says the man, shaking the redwood stick. 'Look at the carving! Look at the detail!'

'Eight,' says Victor.

'Look at this wood,' says the man. 'This wood is hard. It's specially treated. It's—' He breaks off as he realises that there are several small heads between him and his customer. He starts shaking his fist. 'What are you doing?' he screams at the boys. 'Are you crazy? Get back!'

The boys scatter.

We pay for the *chuntas* and turn to go.

Victor grabs my arm. 'Do you see what I see?' he asks.

I see a glass dome packed full with beans, kernels of corn, bits of bone, pictures of Jesus and Mary, a brightly painted crucifix, stones, leaves, twigs, something's tooth, feathers, glitter, a tiny plastic angel and a ceramic skull. The only thing missing is a likeness of Elvis. But this isn't what Victor sees.

He points. Stacked up on the tables are heaps of cacti, like logs on a woodpile. Some fire.

'Cactus.'

'Mescal.'

According to Don Juan, mescalito is not just another ally. An ally, says Don Juan, is not a guardian nor a spirit but an aid. Mescalito, however, is unique and powerful. Mescalito, says Don Juan, is a teacher. An ally can be trained and used, but not so Mescalito. Mescalito shows himself in many forms to whomsoever, whether that whomsoever is a *brujo* or a clerk in Woolworth's. If mescalito likes you he can teach you how to live; if he doesn't you're in deep shit.

'It can't be. Just out in plain sight for sale like that?' Don Juan says that few Indians have the desire to learn about mescalito, but this is ridiculous. If they sold it like that in Camden there'd be a three-day queue.

'This is Peru, not England,' says Victor. He gives me a look. 'And anyway, what else can it be?'

It's a good question, as questions go. What else could it be?

'Well, it could be some kind of medicinal cactus . . .'

He gives me another look. 'You mean like a cure for haemorrhoids or arthritis?'

Well, it could be.

Or it could be medicinal like mescal.

Victor strides forward. He stops at the first stall. 'What's this?' he asks, pointing to a bag of herbs.

'That is for the heart.'

'What's this?'

'That is for the liver.'

'What's this?'

'Tobacco. You soak it in *pisco* for a week and then inhale the liquid. It gives you dreams.'

'And that?' asks Victor. 'What's that?'

'San Pedro,' says the man. 'The shamans use it.'

'What for?' asks Victor.

'*Para levantarse.*'

Out of the corner of my eye, I see Victor glance at me out of the corner of his eye.

'How do you use it?'

'You boil a piece in water for an hour. Then you drink it.'

We try another stall. It's San Pedro. The shamans use it to see. You cook it slowly for half an hour. And another. You cook it rapidly for twenty-four hours. And another. You slice it lengthwise. And another. You slice it like a cucumber. And another. You simmer it for ten hours. You simmer it for five. You cook it in a little water. You cook it in a lot of water. You leave it overnight. You drink it right away.

'What do you think?' I ask Victor. 'Do you think we should get one?'

He picks up one of the ribbed ears and hefts it in his hand. 'Do you think we should try that tobacco, too?'

23

ONE SIDE MAKES YOU BIGGER, THE OTHER MAKES YOU SMALL

A man goes to knowledge as a warrior, says Don Juan. The nature of knowledge leaves no alternative. If you stay in ordinary reality you protect yourself with surface illusions, with the illusion that things have meaning, with the illusion that what we do matters, with the illusion that the world we've created is the only one there is. But a man going to knowledge enters non-ordinary reality. Illusion stops. And so he must lead a warrior's life. So he must possess fear, respect, alertness and self-confidence. Maybe we aren't going to knowledge, exactly, but we are going to Huancabamba. Of Huancabamba the guidebook says little – it was once an important colonial town, it is said to 'walk' because it is constantly slipping down strata, it is flanked by a series of lakes 40,000 metres high, and around it live the most famous witchdoctors of Peru – but our image of it is clear: a small, half-forgotten village unspoiled by the modern world and untrodden by time, where tradition is part of the fabric of life, not the packaging. We reckon that going to Huancabamba, tucked high into the Andes, has to be considered a pretty similar thing to going to knowledge.

The journey to the centre of mythos and magic is never a simple one. You should pack carefully, plan your route as much as possible, be prepared for surprises and delays. Journeying to the centre of mythos and magic is not like going to Catford or Boston. You don't jump in the car and toodle over to Camelot or Brigadoon. You don't take a cab to El Dorado, catch a bus to Xanadu. The way is never straight and direct, clearly signposted, lit, repaired or well paved. You

can forget about rest stops and gas stations, scenic overlooks and
picnic areas. You can throw away your *AA Guide*. The road is always
steep and arduous and mined with obstacles: is always devious and
hidden. There is rarely a map. When there is a map, it's sure to be
wrong.

So far, so good, you might say.

The air is filled with clouds and love songs as the bus slowly
rides the edges of mountains, crawling in and out of ruts, speeding
up for a few feet when the road is suddenly – momentarily – smooth.
Through the tattered strips like gauze, small mud houses and tiny
farms circled in patches of garden emerge and fade, the hillside suddenly catches spectral colours; spikes of purple, flames of red, bursts
of yellow, streaks of white and swirls of blue. Through the drifting
haze a small girl in the pinkest poncho waves, unsmiling, from the
back of a donkey. Two men and two oxen plough a field, their faces
to the gradient green of the mountains, shifting and glinting in the
knife-like sun.

The bus stops on what in most places would be a hairpin turn
perched within a cloud, but which here in the Peruvian Andes is just
a turn, and the little boy in the Fido Dido T-shirt who rides on the
stairs picks up the large rock under the dash and jumps into the
road.

I watch him run around the side of the bus. 'What's he doing?'

Victor looks out the window. 'He's putting on the emergency
brake.'

The driver and the conductor climb down after the boy and the
three of them stand at the roadside, gazing at the rear tyre in the way
that men do. The passengers continue what they've been doing for
the past six hours – eating and laughing and talking – the chickens
continue to cluck, the parrot travelling with the old man and the girl
calls out, '*Con permiso! Con permiso!*'

The express bus to Huancabamba – eight hours, one rest stop for
soup, chicken and rice and to stand in the courtyard where the wild
cat is caged waiting for one of the holes in the ground to become
free – is better than full. Seats have been unfolded into the aisle to
make the most of extra space, but still the roof is overloaded and
there are people standing at the front.

'It looks like they fixed whatever it was,' says Victor.

'What'd they do?'

'Kicked it,' says Victor.

By the time we arrive, pitching down the mountain to the neat village square of orange-flowered trees and hedges shaped like a cowboy, a band of musicians and a giant chicken, military head-quarters at one end and the church at the other, we are three hours late and there's a crowd of people waiting in the road.

'Try to look inconspicuous,' says Victor, banging his head against the ceiling as he ducks down the aisle. 'I don't want to be hassled.'

'You mean like use my magic powers to make myself invisible?' I gasp as I struggle after him.

'Just try not to draw attention to yourself,' says Victor.

It's like arriving at Kennedy Airport in the traditional costume of a Lapland reindeer herder. The Huancabamba equivalent of New York gypsy cab drivers, a gaggle of young boys in T-shirts and jeans, is waiting just feet from the bus. It might be my pathological in-ability to keep from bringing attention to myself – or it might even be Victor's height or long hair or purple hat or the silver hoop in his nose – but at the sights of us the boys all begin to scream, 'Gringos! Gringos!' They draw around us as though they're bees and we're the hive. 'Gringos! Gringos!' They pull on Victor's bags and sleeves.

'You need a hotel?' asks the tallest. He has a game eye and an intense, not to say desperate, manner. He reaches out and shakes Victor's hand. 'My name is Juan. Let me help you find the best hotel. If you want to visit a *curandera* I will take you to the *maestro*. People come from all over the world to see him. Friday is the best day. Do you want to go Friday? Four am.'

'No,' says Victor, to shut him up. 'We don't want to go Friday.'

'Saturday, then,' says Juan cheerfully. 'We can leave at seven. Or, if you want to see the lakes, I have a friend with a jeep. We can go Friday. We'll pick you up at five-thirty.'

'What we want is a hotel,' says Victor. 'A hotel with a kitchen. We're vegetarians. We need to cook our own food.'

'No problem,' says Juan, shoving a couple of his compadres aside so that he can lead the way. 'But first you must register with the police.'

Juan and his friends are waiting outside when we emerge from the yellow colonial building that houses the military police. He steps into stride beside Victor, leading us down the raised sidewalk. 'The El Dorado is the best hotel in town,' he assures us. 'Very nice rooms, very reasonable. El Señor will let you use the kitchen.' At the end of the sidewalk he turns into a doorway. El Dorado. He leads us into the lobby, several refrigerators and pieces of old furniture in a dusty room once painted white, a couple of old formica kitchen tables and chairs, an Inca Kola es Nuestra sign, an ad for pilsner beer and one for Pepsi, a long wooden counter across one end of the room, a rusted ceiling fan that doesn't move. You can imagine what the hotel must once have been. El Señor, a small, slender man in his fifties, nearly dapper in his old white suit and floral tie, doesn't move either.

'Don Jaime,' says Juan, 'Don Jaime, I've brought you Americanos.'

'*Ingléses*,' corrects Victor.

Don Jaime looks up from the book he's reading with tired eyes and a smile as faded as the El Dorado's days of glory. Juan explains that we're Americans, that we want a double room, that we want to use the kitchen. Don Jaime won't let us use the kitchen.

'Don't worry,' says Juan. 'They have a restaurant upstairs. The *cocinera* will cook whatever you want.' He gestures elaborately. He's been watching old films. '*A su gusto*.'

We pick up our bags. 'We want a kitchen,' says Victor.

'I don't know about a kitchen,' says Juan, running after us. The other boys run after him. 'I don't think this may be possible. The visitors who come here don't usually want to cook.'

Although no one has done that much talking to me so far, I decide to join the conversation. 'We need a kitchen,' I insist. 'We're vegetarians. We want to make our own meals.'

Juan looks over his shoulder. 'Luís,' he says to one of the other boys. 'What about your mother? Wouldn't she let them use her kitchen?'

The El San Pedro is a few blocks up from the El Dorado, newer, slightly cleaner, purpose-built. There is no pink dining room overlooking the main square, its walls lined with pictures of the *dueño*'s family in Las Vegas and California in 1964. It was never sophisticated and elegant, never had a curved wooden reception desk polished till you could see your shoes reflected in it as you waited to pay your bill. It doesn't have a restaurant, never mind a kitchen. It didn't have a toilet seat in the loo until the manager noticed our footprints on the rim of the bowl. But we have not, of course, come to Huancabamba for ambience, we have come for old-world charms, for nights that speak and secrets out of time. Victor reckons that the name of the hotel, despite its lack of a kitchen, must be a sign. A good one. And it does, it is true, have its voices in the dark.

We lie on our beds in the shadows cast by the street bulb outside our window, listening to them: faceless, disembodied, shapeless, fluid sounds that can't be caught, laughter that has no imaginable source, words whose meanings are as lost as a flake of skin in wind.

At 1 am, Victor asks me if I'm still awake. I'm still awake. 'Well, it sure ain't Quilotoa,' mumbles Victor.

Most of the other guests at the San Pedro seem either to be pilgrims come to have their illnesses cured or Peruvian anthropology teachers and students in neat cotton clothes, come to research the *curanderas*. By day they walk briskly through the streets carrying folders and attaché cases, heads bent together as they earnestly confer, but at night they sit on the balcony talking and laughing, comparing notes. Labourers thump in from late-night card games, loud with beer. Every rooster in the village is crowing.

At 2.30 another group returns, singing Happy Birthday with uninhibited zest.

'What are we going to do about finding a kitchen?' I ask Victor as the second celebratory chorus starts up.

'Maybe we can rent a camp stove,' says Victor. 'There's a market. There's a hardware store. We're bound to find something.'

Somos vegetarianos. No comemos carne, ni pollo, ni pescado. Though this is not why we want a kitchen. After a lettuce omelette in the terminally empty dining room of the El Dorado – our second in a country where 'vegetable' can, apparently, be interpreted in only three ways: lettuce, tomato or onion – we arranged that in the future the *cocinera* would cook for us whatever we brought. No, we want a kitchen so we can make our mescal tea. *Somos hippy viajeros. Tomamos lo que hay.*

'At least it gives us a focus for our day.'

'That and finding a shaman,' says Victor.

At four several men wearing heavy boots start running through the hallway, banging on doors. One of them bangs on our door.

'Go away!' shouts Victor. 'Go away!'

'Maybe it's the police.'

'I don't care,' says Victor. 'I'm knackered. If they want us they're going to have to come in and get us.'

Men start whistling outside the window.

'It must be the jeeps to go to the lakes,' I say.

'The lakes and the *maestros*,' snorts Victor.

In the course of one brief afternoon we met at least a dozen people who could get us a jeep to the lakes or take us to the *maestro curandera*. Forty soles for either trip. What you pay the *curandera* depends on how long you stay, what treatment you have, whether he's a *maestro extraordinario* or just run-of-the-mill *ordinario*. But if you're economically minded, you don't even have to leave town. We've passed several shops with painted signs swinging over the entrances, Maestro Curandera, step inside. 'It's like God taking a shopfront in Camden,' said Victor. Come here for your miracles and doses of divine wrath.

At 7.30, strong male voices suddenly sound outside our window, half singing, half shouting.

I sit up. 'What is that, Vic? Do you recognise that song?'

'No,' snaps Victor. 'No, I do not recognise that song.'

An image of Grace Kelly, blonde and graceful as an art-deco nymph, drunkenly running an ivory arm through a chlorine pool while Bing Crosby croons and a toy sailboat lists across the water floats across my mind. It's 'True Love'. The army recruits are running through Huancabamba in their green shorts and T-shirts singing 'True Love'. The voices fade and then come back; come back and fade.

'It's a love song, isn't it?' asks Victor.

I pull the sheet over my head as the soldiers return, singing a different song now, 'You know how I love you, I always will . . .' 'We haven't reached non-ordinary reality yet.'

Everyone in Huancabamba seems to have a *curandera* – a *maestro*, there are no semi-skilled or apprentices here – they would be willing to take us to visit for forty soles, but no one has water.

'*Agua mineral?*' we ask in the first shop on the square.

The clerk looks behind her at the shelves as though seeing them for the first time. '*Agua mineral? No hay.*'

'*Agua mineral?*' we ask the woman behind the counter in the second shop on the square.

'*Qué?*'

'*Agua mineral?*'

Her eyes run over the bottles of Inca Kola and orange soda. '*No hay.*'

The man in the third shop on the square purses his lips, frowns, squints at the six bottles on the shelf behind him, lips moving as he identifies the Pepsi, the three Inca Kolas, the strawberry pop and the one dusty beer. He shakes his head. '*Agua no hay.*'

We spread our nets wider.

On the street going down to the market, where an old man sits on the pavement selling sandals made out of old tyres and the Indian women stroll by with baskets of wax-perfect lilies on their heads or sit at their stalls, keeping the flies off the food with brushes made of shredded plastic bags, we try first one miniscule shop and then another.

We go the other way, down a side street near the church, rutted from the last rains. Halfway down, a rusted Inca Kola sign and an open doorway suggest a store.

'We might as well try in here,' says Victor.

Tripping over the raised sill, we step on to the dirt floor of the one large, dark room.

Shelves run around three walls, and, unusually enough for the back roads of the Andes, most of them are full. The counter is loaded with bags and boxes; sacks and barrels take up most of the floor space. A dark shadow shimmers past us, tail flicking.

'*Hola!*' shouts Victor, as our eyes adjust to the sluggish light. 'Is anyone here?'

There is no one here but the cat.

We walk up to the counter, stopping in the space between the glass case of biscuits and the piles of fruit. The signs stuck on the shelves are all from the 1960s and faded, refreshing drinks and sparkling teeth. Through the open doorway we can see a chicken standing on top of a goat in the yard behind the house.

'Hello?' I shout, stretching towards the chicken and the goat. 'Hello? Is anyone here?'

There's a rumble behind us. 'What do you want?'

We both jump round.

'Jesus,' says Victor. 'Where did he come from?'

Tucked into the corner to the left of the door beside a burlap bag of corn sits an old man. His white hair touches the collar of his green poncho, his face is frosted with stubble. He glares grumpily back at us from under a beaten straw hat with eyes that are clearly blue even in the dusty gloom. He doesn't look as though he's come from anywhere; he looks as though he has been sitting there forever.

Victor recovers first. '*Agua mineral?*' he asks. '*Se vende agua mineral?*'

The old man doesn't glance in puzzlement at the shelves. He spits on the floor. '*Sí,*' he nods. '*Sí, hay agua mineral.* 'Maria!' he bellows. 'Maria!'

A middle-aged woman suddenly shoots out of the back like something launched by a spell. She's dusting off her hands and smiling.

'You ask,' says Victor. 'Woman to woman.'

I ask.

'*Qué?*' says Maria.

The old man spits on the floor again.

'*Agua mineral,*' I repeat. 'You have mineral water?'

'*Qué?*'

'*Agua mineral!*' barks the old man.

Maria ducks behind the counter, surfacing again a few minutes later with two small bottles and two dingy glasses. The cat jumps up beside the bananas to watch her snap off the lids.

She wants to know if we're German. She's never met anyone from England before. Are we here to see a *curandera*? She looks from one of us to the other. She hopes there isn't something wrong.

'Of course there's something wrong!' growls the grumpy old man. 'There's always something wrong.'

Personally, I couldn't agree with him more, but his daughter doesn't. 'Don't be silly, Papi,' she says. 'You're dreaming again.'

The rocking chair creaks. 'And you're not?'

'We're interested in talking to a *curandera,*' explains Victor. 'We don't want to consult one for an illness. We just want to listen and talk.'

Maria nods. 'Professors and students come from all over for just that reason,' she says. 'They write books and papers about all that they learn here about medicinal plants.'

'Books! Talk!' The old man spits on the floor. 'What good is any of that?'

With an uneasy glance towards her parent, she smiles at us. 'So you're students?'

Victor corrects the impression that we are somehow part of the brigade of note-takers earnestly tramping through the hills with tape-recorders over their shoulders, preparing their papers on pre-Colombian uses of plants and herbs in a religio-medico context. He shrugs, his arms a question. 'But it's difficult, isn't it?' he says. 'There are so many *curanderas* around here – so many *maestros*. How can you tell which is the best one to go to?' he puts down his glass. 'There isn't a *curandera* you could recommend, is there?'

She considers this for a few seconds, as though, in fact, she and Victor had been talking of the difference between the climates of England and Peru and this sudden conversational detour has confused her. 'A *curandera?*'

The rocker moans and another dark shadow detaches itself from the green poncho and hurls itself across the room with an almost human cry. Another cat.

'Papi,' says Maria. 'Papi, what's the name of that *curandera*? 'Frederico . . .? Genaro . . .?'

'Manolo, Luís, Garcia . . .' Papi mutters, beginning to rock in earnest. 'They have all the names, just pick one you like.'

Maria stops in the act of taking up the empty bottles and puts them back down with a triumphant snap. 'Francisco!' she smiles. 'Francisco Gomez!'

'Panchito!'

She looks over at the figure in the corner. 'Panchito?'

He's waving his hand at her. 'Not Francisco. Panchito. Panchito Gomez y Navarra.'

His daughter shakes her head. 'No, Panchito is the other brother. It's Francisco who's the *curandera*. Panchito just runs the farm.' She shrugs, the shrug of a woman whose father, like a long dirt trail, is getting less and less clear the further he gets from his beginning.

'How old is this Francisco Gomez?' asks Victor cautiously. The last *maestro* we were offered was twenty-two. Sixty soles to get there and you can use the nearby lake as well.

She looks to the corner again. 'Old. He's an old man.' She lowers her voice. 'They've been friends since boyhood. Though of course they never see each other now.'

This sounds a little more hopeful. The Dalai Lama gets the job pretty young, it's true, but we'd feel more comfortable with a *brujo* with enough years on him to allow for experience as well as divine choice. We exchange a look of cautious hope. Travelling also teaches that the arrival of a bus at 3.45 when you were expecting a bus at 3.45 does not necessarily mean that it is your bus. 'Where can we find him?' we ask her. 'Does he live far?' Forty soles into the mountains? Sixty-five with lunch?

'It's not far,' she says, gesturing vaguely. 'Just up the road. It's not far, is it, Papi? Isn't it Culanca?'

'If you come from here it's not far,' says Papi above the edgy creaking of the rocker. 'If you come from England it's far.'

Maria's still running her hand through her hair. 'If it isn't Culanca, is it Culeba or Plata? Or maybe it's San Geronimo . . .' The glasses click as she takes them from the counter. 'No, I think it's Culanca – but maybe it's not . . . why can't I remember the name?'

The cat stretches across the pitted wooden counter, picking up crumbs and dust with its tail.

'Which direction is it?' asks Victor. 'Maybe if you just point us in the right direction . . .'

'Oh, of course.' Maria laughs at her own foolishness. Why didn't she think of this before? She stares over our heads at the door behind us, her eyes narrowed, thinking. Left or right, she's thinking. She's thinking it depends on which road it turns out to be. 'If it is Culanca, then it's left,' she says. 'But if it isn't . . .'

'If it isn't it's right,' says the old man. His eyes are almost closed. 'Or maybe not.'

'Just go back to the plaza and ask anyone where Francisco Gomez lives,' his daughter decides. 'They'll tell you how to get there. He's well known around here.'

'But that doesn't mean they'll find Panchito,' says her father. 'He'll be home now, but even if they go to Culeba they might not find him.'

'It's not Panchito they're looking for,' Maria shouts at him as we step over the threshold and turn towards the square. 'It's Francisco!'

'Bah!' the old man shouts back. 'What do they want with him?'

We want a glimpse of something else, a glimpse of other, that's what we want. Not a twelve-year apprenticeship, not an intensive course in sorcery, just a glimpse. Just to sit in the ordinary sunshine on an ordinary chair in the shadow of an ordinary mountain with a person as common as sheep or bananas and for just a sliver of a second to feel that time and space are not what hold you up but what you might possibly learn how to slip into in order to get free.

I've met witches in New York and London, socially, usually, at a party or in someone else's kitchen over cups of herbal tea, and Victor and I met one in California whose article for the monthly wiccan magazine was overdue because the computer was acting up, but as personable and enthusiastic as they tended to be, these were people with keys to their cars, keys to their houses and apartments, keys to their bikes and steering-wheel locks – and one in the West Village had a key to her wine cellar – but they were not in possession of the keys that unlock that passage to the unreal world. They might run around in the moonlight at the solstice, or light the night with candles and coal-like dots of incense, hang crystals in their windows and decorate their rooms with stars, but when it comes to unreality they will never find the door. If they bump into it by chance it won't open. If it opens they won't step through. They are anchored in the romance and nostalgia of the real world, where knowledge, pre-sweetened and easy to digest, is an expedient, and what we know of what we can't apprehend has come down to us in cartoons and children's stories, paperbacks and black and white movies, and a few cautions about picking things on Midsummer's Eve. Like us – like most of us – the witches I've met with their decks of cards and little blue bottles of essential oils long for something more than man has created, but – also like most of us – they decided what that was before they had a chance to discover if they would ever have a chance of finding out what it might actually be. Like all of us, they whisper their practised incantations, brew their special teas and potions, joke about the accident or piece of bad luck that happened to someone who got in their way, take out ads in the right magazines, discreetly let their names be dropped. But they, too, are as powerless as the President, as worried about their mortgages as the Methodist butcher next door. Like the rest of us, if they really knew what they were doing, they wouldn't let anyone else know.

There's a man selling cigarettes on the corner of the plaza near the statue of the strapping Eastern maid in her blue blouse and red skirt, a jug of water on her head. Victor buys a cigarette and asks him if he knows of Francisco Gomez or his brother Panchito.

'Francisco Gomez?' He hands Victor his change. 'Sure, I know Franciso.'

The three young boys who came running over as soon as we stopped start shaking their heads, *sí, sí, sí,* crowding closer to the cart.

'I can take you to him,' says Jorge, twelve and a half and the eldest of the three. We know his name is Jorge because he sat with us in the bar last night when we were having our pre-dinner beer and game of backgammon. Like most Peruvians, he much prefers chess. 'If you want, I can take you now.'

'Really?' says Victor. 'You know where he lives?'

Jorge nods. 'I've taken other people.' His black and white sweater is too big and old, his striped T-shirt has more holes than Victor's red one, his trousers are thin and stop at his ankles, his sandals once graced the wheels of some American car, but his smile fits him perfectly and is as new as a dawn. He points to the hills that rise hazily behind the market. 'It's right up there.'

Our eyes follow the direction of his hand. The mountain is sealed by a spectrum of green unbroken by road.

There's a reason you can't see it from the town. The road that winds up from the valley hasn't been cut or dynamited or gouged out of the earth but worn into it by thousands of feet, most of them bare, all of them with the same destinations, for centuries so similar to one another that they might all be just one. Its hold on the mountain is tenuous at best.

Jorge, in his rubber sandals, strides easily up the stream of mud and rocks and fallen trees that divides the fields, banana groves and thickly glowing vegetation shrouding the hillsides, while I follow clumsily but intrepidly in my Docs, and Victor, in his new Giant Eagle sneakers, made in China and bought in Chiclayo, slides about like a beginner skater on wet ice. The road's negligible hold has been made worse by heavy rains.

Occasionally there is a mud and bamboo or bamboo and packing-case hut surrounded by a garden of flowers on one side of the road, but most of the houses at all visible are well in the distance, guarded by trees, no sign of watchful eyes or rabid dogs or even a curious pig or chicken peering out from the brush. Jorge talks as we climb. It takes many years to become a *curandera*. You have to be born to it. This plant is for the rheumatism, he says. This is for breaks and bruises. This is used for problems with the lungs. No, he will never be a *curandera* himself. He seems shocked at the idea.

Victor follows Jorge across a log, his arms out like wings. 'What about the San Pedro cactus?' he asks. 'Is that used as well?'

'San Pedro is for the shamans,' says Jorge. 'In order to see.' His expression – incurious, disinterested, slightly puzzled that Victor should even have thought of such a question – suggests that no one but a *curandera* would have any need or desire for sight.

Victor grabs an overhanging branch to stop himself from pitching into the mud. 'Oh,' he says.

'What about Panchito?' I ask. 'Doesn't Don Francisco have a brother named Panchito? Is he a *curandera*, too?'

Without warning, Jorge leaps to the other side of the road, nimble as a goat. Slithering between a break in a wooden and wire fence is a thin dirt trail. For cattle. For sheep. For farmers and their families. For *brujos* slipping with their allies through the night. 'This way,' orders Jorge. 'Don Francisco lives up here.'

The irregular trail staggers through a field, vanishing at the top in a jungle of banana trees. Smoke drifts up from behind the trees, but there is no sign of a house of any description. There are, however, several women, children and cows sitting under a tree at the bottom of the hill, warned by our voices to be watching for us to come around the bend. Cautious '*Buenas tardes*' are exchanged on both sides, amid a flurry of shy giggling on one.

Jorge strides on. He pulls a leaf from a small bush. 'This is for the heart,' he says, passing it behind him to Victor. He rips off another leaf from another small bush. 'This is for the liver.'

I don't see the leaves. My eyes are on the dense growth of banana encircling the hillside farm; on the deep but narrow path that leads through it. We are about to meet a Peruvian *brujo*. I'm not sure now if I believed that it would really happen or if I thought that this, like the bats of Carlsbad, the vegetarian restaurant in Socorro and the underground cathedral in the salt mines of Zipaquira, would be something else we never found. I know what I don't expect; I don't expect Robert, by day a computer programmer, or Caroline, by day a proof-reader, or Alara with her passion for the pagan Earth Mother and her necklaces of strings of stars. But I don't know what I do expect.

Twigs snap, a chicken flees through the trees.

'Do you know what you're going to ask?' whispers Victor.

'Do you?'

Victor ducks branches. 'I reckon it'll come to me when we're there.'

I'm not so sure that it will come to me. I would know what to ask a witch on MacDougal Street with a reputation for returning lost people and objects and a fax machine, or a Santa Cruz wiccan who gathers rosemary only when the ram is in the ascendant, or a sister from Devonshire with a moon-shaped paperweight and a lethal line in elderflower wine, but not one who lives centuries behind within a circle of clouds. What can I say in my flim-flam Spanish? What can I ask?

Jorge stops as a clearing appears before us. In the clearing are several mud and branch buildings, a wooden barn, a courtyard around a rain barrel, a few well-used benches against a wall awned with straw. There are two men in the barn, sitting on stools to one side of the doorway, talking lowly, heads bent together. The one in the T-shirt and jeans is young and lean and worried-looking, the other is old and heavy-set, his stubbled face unanimated beneath a worn green felt hat. The doctor is in. The young man talks quickly, hands moving; the old man watches the fire at their feet and nods. On one of the benches beneath the porch of the courtyard sits a middle-aged woman all in black, smoothing her skirt with the side of her hand, her back against the mud and straw wall.

'This is it,' says Jorge with a certain air of solemnity. 'This is where Francisco lives.' He points towards the woman. 'Sit down,' he orders. 'I'll tell him you're here.'

'It's better than waiting in a surgery in London,' says Victor as we take our places on one of the empty benches. 'At least there aren't any two-year-old copies of *Architect's News* on the coffee table.'

'It's just as well,' I say as a chicken suddenly dislodges itself from a ledge behind us, losing feathers as it panics to the ground. 'They'd only be covered in shit.'

The young man in the barn can't sleep. The *curandera* recommends hot baths, manzanilla and abstaining from coffee. They stand by the rain barrel for a few minutes, discussing the treatment. Don Francisco, slow but sure, comes across the yard to shake the hand of the woman on the bench. He sits down beside her. He folds his hands on his knee. He leans close so he can hear her. The woman's young son has colic. The *curandera* nods while she details the symptoms. He recommends manzanilla and coffee and shakes her hand again.

All the while, Jorge has been standing beside us like a farmer waiting for his pigs to be judged for the county prize. Now he gives us a come-on wave and we jump to our feet. He introduces us formally.

Don Francisco doesn't look at us directly. He seems less than delighted to meet us. If we were pigs and he the judge we'd be in the stewpot by sunset.

'Are they students?' he asks Jorge. He says 'students' in the way an invalid might say 'injection', the way a man who's been selling shoes for the last thirty years might say 'foot'. 'What do they want?'

Jorge looks to Victor.

Victor explains that we aren't students and we aren't ill. We just want to talk to him. To listen.

Don Francisco, still watching us warily from one corner of his eye, mumbles something neither of us catches and starts to walk away.

'Go with him!' hisses Jorge. 'Go with him!'

We go with the stooped figure in its old grey workpants and sweater, three paces behind as we turn the corner of the building, three paces behind as we turn the next corner into another courtyard, stopping at a respectful distance when he finally sits down on another wooden bench.

He gestures to the bench beside him. 'Sit down.' Don Francisco takes a crumpled cigarette from his shirt pocket. 'Go on,' he says, as he rolls it between his fingers. 'What do you want to know?'

My answer would still have been 'I'm not quite sure', but Victor replies immediately and easily. 'We want to know how you became a *curandera*. *Sabe usted?* We want to know how long it took, what process you had to—'

Don Francisco throws the used match on the ground. 'Don't you want recipes?' he snaps. 'What recipes do you want? For nerves? For asthma? For inflamed kidneys?' Before Victor can answer he starts giving him the recipe for inflamed kidneys. *Dos cucharaditas de inaza y tres cucharadas de cebada.*

He taps his stick on the ground between us. 'Why aren't you writing this down?' he demands. 'Write it down.'

'Jesus,' mutters Victor, but he pulls his spiral pad and a pen from his pocket.

'*Bueno*,' says Don Francisco. '*Entonces*, what recipes do you want to know?'

We don't want recipes. If I wanted a cure for headache, or a remedy for aching joints, or something to aid the digestion or the circulation I could look it up in *Culpeper*. Better yet, I could ask my friend Hayley. Hayley would look it up in *Culpeper*, too, but Hayley's advice and instructions, as well as being linked to her baroque interpretation of your astrological chart, are always more interesting and colourful than Nicholas's. Or I could ask Hayley's homeopath, Mrs Soskel, who doesn't believe in astrology but in getting down to earth.

'We don't—' I begin but Don Francisco shoves my words away with his cigarette.

'Loss of hair?' guesses the *curandera*. 'Night cough? Diarrhoea?'

Diarrhoea catches our attention. You can't depend on the buses, or the police, or the guidebook, but you can depend on that.

Fuelled by this unexpected bleep of interest, Don Francisco steams on. '*Pique en trozos, tuestelas y muela una pepa de palta*—' The stick jabs into the earth once more. 'Write it down!' he demands of Victor. 'You have to write it down.'

Victor starts writing a list of things we need to get in the market. Avocados. Tomatoes. Vegetables and eggs to bring to the restaurant of the El Dorado later for our supper. A cooking stove and pot for the making of tea.

Don Francisco starts at the beginning. Every time Victor stops writing he stops speaking, his eyes getting narrower. 'Notes!' he barks over and over. 'Why aren't you taking notes?'

We get through the cold rice splatters, headache, stomach cramp, and rheumatism in this way, Victor pretending to write down ingredients, the old man rattling off the remedies like evening prayers.

In the second of silence Don Francisco takes to yawn, Victor tries again.

'What we're really interested in is you,' he says. 'Why and how did you become a *curandera*?'

Don Francisco grinds his cigarette butt under his foot. 'My father was a *curandera*.'

Encouraged by this relatively positive response, I try as well. 'What about your mother?'

'And my grandfather. And his father and grandfather.'

I've not yet given up. 'And your brother?'

'*Quien?*'

There is something about the way he asks the question that makes me doubt for a second my ability to say the word brother, but only for a second. *Hermano*. It's one of the first words you learn in beginner's Spanish. *Hermano*. Luisa lives with her mother, her father, and su *hermano* Juan.

'Your brother,' I repeat a little louder. 'Panchito. Is he a *curandera*, too?'

Don Francisco knocks the conversation sideways. 'He's not here,' he says shortly.

Victor knocks it back. 'We heard he was. There was a friend of his in town—'

The interview is over. Don Francisco, agile for a man who will never see eighty-five again, is already on his feet. 'He's never here,' says Don Francisco. He turns his back on us and walks away.

'Jesus.' Victor's voice sounds choked, or possibly gagged. 'I don't know if I can do this.'

He is leaning against a rock at the side of the road, an Inca Kola bottle in his hand. I'm sitting beside him, opening the packet of cream crackers. A few feet away, a dog lies stretched out in the shade, not quite dozing. Both the dog and I turn to Victor.

He doesn't look as though he can do it. It's not often that you see anyone actually turn green, but I am seeing it now.

'Take this, it's good for the nausea.' I hand him a biscuit.

He eats the biscuit, eyes the bottle, holds his nose and takes another drink.

'Is it really that bad?' I know that Carlos had a little indigestion trouble when he first took peyote, but it never occurred to me to worry about something with 'tea' in its name.

Victor shoves the Inca Kola bottle at me and claps his hand over his mouth. 'It's worse.' He makes an effort not to gag. 'Christ, there's no way anyone could have discovered this shit without supernatural help.'

Soufflés. Ice-cream. Coffee. These are just three of the thousands of things we wouldn't have, had their invention been left up to me. I would never look at an egg and think about what might happen if I beat the white first. Never look at a cup of cream and wonder if freezing it wouldn't be a good idea. Never pick a few beans and come up with the perfect drink to go with eggs or brandy. But someone did. Someone not only thought of whipping the eggs but of adding the yolks and wine and dill and cheese. Someone steamed right on from thick, cold cream to adding strawberries and topping it with fudge sauce. Someone made the leap from grinding the beans to making espresso.

I put the bottle to my mouth, take a deep breath, swallow. It's all I can do not to spit the cloudy, acrid liquid right back out on to the ground. Victor is right. Who on earth ever thought of drinking this? Even at a time of high human creativity, when everyone was inventing wheels and indoor fires, figuring out how to roast chestnuts and grow corn, it is difficult to imagine how anyone came up with brewing mescal tea.

'Maybe we didn't make it right,' I manage to gasp, forcing the tea to stay where I put it. Not only does it taste vile, its texture is thick and slimy. 'I don't remember those Argentinians saying anything about it making you want to puke.'

Reluctantly – world-stoppingly reluctantly considering his attitude to recreational drugs – Victor takes the bottle from my hand.

'After all we went through, what could we have done wrong?' he wants to know. 'We cut it the way they told us in the witches' market. We cooked it the way they said.'

After all we went through, indeed. Demonstrating the determination that got Columbus to Cuba, Hannibal over the Alps and Margaret Thatcher a title, we spent an entire afternoon trudging in and out of every hardware store and junk stall in Huancabamba, trying to find a stove we could rent, bargaining over a pot, tracking down the one place in town that sold kerosene. As my mother always assured me it would, it just goes to show what you can do if you really set your mind on something. Even when, back in our room at the San Pedro, the stove spluttered out after only five minutes, we didn't give up. We went back to the side-street stall where we rented the stove. No problem, he assured us. You probably didn't pump it enough. He pumped it. The stove went up like a Roman candle, scattering small boys, gringos and one middle-aged junk-metal salesman into the street. Stove fixed, we went back to the San Pedro and another three hours hunched on the floor of our room, carefully stirring and timing the mixture and adjusting the flame, impatiently looking for some sign that the tea was ready while we waited for the cooker to explode again or the police to suddenly come banging on the door for a passport check.

'Maybe you're supposed to mix it with something.' Two pounds of sugar, a litre of Coke, a bottle of rum.

Victor takes one more serious swallow and puts his head between his knees. 'That's it,' he says. 'You finish it.'

I hold the bottle in the air, there's not that much left. In for a penny, in for a pound, as they say back in London. Shit or get off the can, as they say in Brooklyn. 'Let's just hope it works.'

'Jesus,' groans Victor. 'It had better be bloody marvellous.'

He gets to his feet, slings our bag over his shoulder, and starts walking upwards again. I follow.

'Is Pancho coming?' he asks, not looking around.

I don't look around either, but I can hear him, padding behind us, the occasional click of a claw against stone. 'Yeah, he's coming.'

'If we met him after we took the tea and not before I might be worried,' says Victor.

Pancho has been following us for at least a mile. We turned a corner and there he was, sitting by a cross at the side of the road, a small brown dog with floppy ears, scars on his legs and Bambi eyes in which fear and trust wrestled for control. He didn't bark. He didn't bare his teeth or growl. He didn't hurl himself at our ankles in a frenzy of bloodlust. He just sat there as though he'd been waiting our arrival. When we cautiously passed him he got up and started walking behind. He hasn't left us since.

Halfway to nowhere it starts to rain. 'Jesus,' mumbles Victor, looking around. There's road ahead of us and road behind us, mountain above us and mountain below us, and not much else. 'This is all we need.'

Not waiting for us, Pancho makes a leap for the steep bank beside us, heading for the solitary tree left on its own in a field of rocks and grass.

'Maybe we should be worried anyway,' I say as we scrabble up the bank after the dog. 'I'm not comfortable with the way he's adopted us.'

'He's just a dog,' says Victor, throwing himself under the tree. 'We're probably the first people he's ever met who haven't started throwing stones at him straight away.'

The three of us sit against the trunk in easy silence, watching the rain fall and the clouds drift by. I can hear each drop, I can see the shades of purple in the thick, low clouds. I don't know what's over the next rise, what lies down the mountain on the other side, what lies above us. I can imagine the windowless huts hidden among the banana trees, the people who live in them, the rhythms of their lives, the fears in their hearts, the shards of joy. Time falls away.

It isn't until Victor speaks that I realise the rain has stopped. 'Feel anything yet?' he asks.

Pancho barks softly.

'No.'

Two small girls are standing on the hillside beside us. There is blue in their hair, brown in the black of their eyes. They're both dressed in long dark skirts and ragged blouses, shawls so red they almost shine, sharp rings of gold in their ears, nothing but dirt on their feet. The smaller one holds on to the other. They might be statues, they're so still and silent, their eyes unblinking. Statues untouched by the recent rain.

'*Buenas tardes*,' says Victor.

The girls don't answer.

'Do you live around here?' I ask.

Pancho, on the other side of Victor, barks again.

Still saying nothing, the girls sit down on the grass.

Pancho puts his head on Victor's knee.

The afternoon blazes around us. There is nothing unreal about this world. No demons more terrible than the demons of the real world, no visions better. Count each bird, unseen but calling. Listen to the movement of each leaf. Feel the air. Watch the diamond pattern on the succulents vibrate, the landscape shift and dance. Blue sky, yellow sun, the mountains every hue of green, the colours clear and sharp and strong as though they are new; as though being seen for the very first time. Here, says God. This is your paradise; this is being alive.

'How are you now?' asks Victor in a voice that sounds like the rub of velvet.

'Okay. Everything just looks a little bright.'

And seems both far away and intensely close.

Pancho rolls over.

'Let me see your pupils,' says Victor.

It's like having your sight and hearing restored. What you remembered was only blurs, only shadows, only a dull, indistinguishable hum. Now you see every single thing as though there is nothing else to look at; hear every single thing as though all else is quiet. You can almost taste the colours, feel each sound. I've seen the documentaries on hallucinogenics. I've heard the drunken midnight tales. I was expecting a kaleidoscope, phantasmagoric images, visions and fantasies like Disney cartoons. But if this is the unreal world it is the same as the real, only uncluttered, cut clean. It is a world where every grain of sand is counted, every blade of grass accounted for, every second unmissed.

Three small boys are shouting as they run out of the bushes on the opposite of the rutted mud. 'Gringos! Gringos!'

Pancho sits up, growling.

The girls turn to the road.

The boys stop abruptly, staring back at us. And then, without another word, they rush back the way they came.

'So how are you feeling?' asks Victor.

'Good.' As accurate as describing autumn in West Virginia as a bunch of dead leaves.

'Yeah,' says Victor. 'I feel good, too.'

We are still feeling good hours later as we start our descent. While Victor scrabbles through the brush looking for a secluded place to have a shit, Pancho right behind him, I study the pulsating leaf patterns, watch a hummingbird hover over a yellow flower. An Indian family and their burro pass by like helium balloons. They smile when they see Victor suddenly rise from the bushes, a furry brown head at his knee.

There's a large mud hut at the point where the track up the mountain splits in two. When we passed it earlier it's door was closed, the holes that are its windows dark. There was no one around but a cat and some chickens. Now, however, the door is open and though the hut is still dark inside there are a weary-looking woman, a teenage boy in a Lakers T-shirt and a man with half a nose on the bamboo porch, five or six men in the road. The simple peasants whose traditional skills, reflecting centuries of culture, fill the pages of the charity catalogues each Christmas are, except for the woman and the boy, all drunk.

One of the men, losing his balance in the telling of some story, catches sight of us skidding down the slope. '*Amigos!*' he shouts. '*Amigos!*'

The other men laugh.

'*Amigos!*' the first man screams again. '*Amigos*, where are you from?'

Victor stops at the bottom of the hill, his hand out for me. Pancho has disappeared.

'*Amigos!*' He's a middle-aged man, heavy-set but hard with being poor. Raising the bottle of cane liquor he's holding like a torch, he staggers towards us.

The other men laugh again, one of them, small and bony and wearing a shirt that might once have gone to a wedding in a different universe, stumbling after him, echoing '*Amigos! Amigos!*' like a mechanical parrot.

The first man stakes himself in front of us. His thin mouth is smiling, but there is nothing to be seen in the flat brown eyes but our own reflections. '*Amigos!*' He thrusts his hand at Victor.

Victor puts on his Happy Hiker smile. '*Buenas tardes,*' he says, taking the shake.

'*Buenas tardes! Buenas tardes!*' cries the second man, weaving beside his friend.

The first man looks from Victor to me, and spits near the toe of my boot. 'Are you German?' he demands. He's still smiling.

Victor, polite and friendly enough to be commended by the guidebook, tells him that we're not German. We're from England.

'*Ingléses! Ingléses!*' parrots the wedding-shirt man.

The first man shuffles a step closer, so close his shoulder is almost touching mine, looking from Victor to me, his smile even stronger than cane liquor. 'Are you a couple?' he doesn't ask me. He spits on the ground, just missing my boot.

The world has lost none of its intensity. It still vibrates, it still shines, it is still vivid enough to break your heart. But now I realise that the dark parts are darker, too. What would normally be a vague feeling of dislike or unease, an instinctive but logically inexplicable pulling away, is as obvious, clear and unmistakable as a notice printed on a wall. For the first time since we left New York, I'm truly afraid. I look into the drunk's eyes. And I know exactly why. I take a step backwards, smiling unwarmly myself. Victor squeezes my hand. 'Tell him yes,' I hiss. 'Get him away from me.'

Victor tells him that we're a couple.

'And is that why you have a ring in your nose?' shrieks the skinny man. 'So she can lead you around like a bull?'

We're the only ones who don't find this remorselessly funny.

'*Amigo*,' says the man with the bottle, pressing it towards Victor. '*Amigo*, have a drink.'

Victor, glancing at the top of the bottle, demurs.

'*Amigo, te invito!*' He sways towards me. I take another step back. He pushes the bottle against Victor's chest. '*Amigo*, you have to have a drink!'

The woman on the porch calls out something, her voice low and flat.

He shakes his free hand in the air, nearly toppling. He grabs Victor's arm. 'You have to have a drink. You're my friend. I invited you.'

If Victor is afraid, he gives no sign. He casually pulls his arm free, his smile unwavering, his left hand still holding mine. 'I don't drink,' he says.

'Just one!' The man grabs him again, pressing the bottle against his shirt like a knife. 'You have to have one. Why don't you want to drink with me?'

The only one laughing now is the man with half a nose.

'I don't drink,' Victor repeats. It is a little harder this time to casually slip out of his new friend's grasp.

'Everyone drinks,' he shouts. 'Even priests! Even the Pope!'

'I don't,' says Victor. 'It's against my religion.'

He spits again, not missing my boot this time.

'Religion?' He staggers forward as Victor and I inch back. 'What religion are you? We –' gesturing with both hands – 'are Catholic.'

'*Somos muy Católicos!*' the second man squeals. '*Muy, muy Católicos!*'

The other men all nod and mutter. The woman crosses herself.

The first man takes a slug from the bottle, then raises it into the air. 'Are you Catholic?' He pushes his face so close to mine I can smell more than the liquor. 'What religion are you?'

The second man is unsteadily dancing around us, muttering, '*Muy Católico, muy Católico*,' over and over under his breath.

I would like to run. I know this would be a mistake, but I'd like to run anyway. Or magically disappear. Victor's hold on my hand tightens. 'Don't panic,' he whispers. 'Just hold your ground.'

'We have to go now.' Victor holds out his right hand. 'We have to meet someone in town.'

The keeper of the bottle slaps it away. 'But I'm very Catholic!' he argues. 'You're not Catholic, are you? Is that why you won't drink with me? Because I'm Catholic?'

Instead of an answer, there is a sudden bark, sharp and final as a gunshot. Everyone's attention is caught.

A small brown dog is standing in the middle of the road a few metres away. His body is facing towards the town, but his head is turned back, looking at us. One of his ears is up like a question. He gives the impression of having been waiting for us to leave for quite some time.

The smaller man stops dancing. He steadies himself on his friend. 'Where'd that come from?'

'He's with us,' says Victor. He holds out his hand again and this time the first man takes it.

At the curve in the road we glance back. The first man has passed out in the grass, but the others are all where they were, watching us go. To the right, at the top of the hill we came down, the two little girls are standing still as statues, the little one clutching the older girl's skirt. The older girl waves.

Victor gives me a look. 'Jesus,' he laughs. 'What kind of tea did you say that was?'

24

ROXANNE

Pizarro came this way. Pizarro and 150 men, their horses and arms. Atahualpa, camped outside of Cajamarca, invited a meeting. Pizarro accepted, and sent the Inca king two perfect goblets of Venetian glass. Like smallpox, a present from the old world to the new. And thus, their dreams driven by the success of Cortés in Mexico, the Spaniards left the maize and cotton plantations of the Northern Oases and took the Inca Trail into the Andes. Over the watershed into the treeless savannah, through narrowing canyons, posted with watchtowers, higher and higher in thinning air and slimming chances of escape. It was a rough march, the road too bad for horses, off the road impassable by any type of foot. Skilled and seasoned soldiers to a man, the invaders knew that they were vulnerable. They didn't know what to expect. They didn't know when to expect it. They were about as frightened as they could get.

We, at least, are not on foot. We're speeding from the grey dunes and dusty cliffs of the coast to the dark, looming Andes behind them. It's a landscape that makes your mind wander, makes it lose its ordinary way. A landscape that fills your thoughts with phantoms and shadows that seem like memories, that makes you try to remember things you've forgotten you know. It's a land whose ghosts can no longer be seen, whose stories have not all been told. A land in ruins. Abandoned buildings, towns left half-finished, towns left half begun. *Cristo Ya Vine. Servicentro Jhony.* Pepsi. TV aerials strapped to bamboo poles over windowless mud-brick huts. Corn and sugar-cane fields, green between stretches of wasteland, barren mountains and rice paddies shimmering at their feet. One-room shacks of sticks or bamboo. A field of smouldering rubbish studded with scavenging birds. Heady mangrove swamps. The eroded remains of civilisations no longer named. Like Pizarro and his troops, we don't know what to expect or when to expect it. Like the conquistadors, we're doing what we can with the companionship of fear.

The *colectivo* takes a curve on the left and nearly clips a guy with a bunch of bamboo tied to the back of his bike and a kid on the handlebars. I grab Victor and he, his feet on his bags and his knee nearly touching his chin, grabs the bar between him and the driver's seat. The gold-framed picture of the Virgin and the gilded angel hanging from the purely decorative rearview mirror swing recklessly. The old woman jammed in between the driver and the conductor mumbles, '*Dios mío,*' and makes the sign of the cross, something she does with a certain regularity – whenever we have to back down a mountain, or we form our own third lane of traffic, or we drag-race a pick-up, or the driver loses even the minimal interest he has in the road. '*Idiota!*' shouts the driver, all the emotion in his flailing hands, and seamlessly returns to his conversation with the conductor.

The driver's name is Geronimo, the conductor's is Luís.

Geronimo, wearing a T-shirt that depicts two cows fucking, steers with one hand. 'That's ridiculous, Luís,' he shouts above the rattle of the van and the rumbling of its engine as we come into a sudden village and he steams up the lane he's created between the two carved out by the department of roads. 'How can you say a thing like that? It's not about the Devil. It's a love song.'

But Luís is adamant. 'No, it isn't. If you listened to the words you'd know that it's about Satan. It's about depravity and sin.'

The angel and the picture of the Virgin jerk about wildly as we shoot between a bus and a jeep. 'Unrequited love,' insists Geronimo, raising his hand in a gesture of camaraderie to the driver of the bus. 'He would do anything to have her, but he knows she can never be his.' The bus toots back.

Luís is a good conductor. Spotting some likely peasants sitting with their bag, a flute, a drum and a guitar by the side of the road, he abandons the argument, pushes his net baseball cap back on his head and leans all the way out of the passenger door as the van bucks down a gear, getting ready to plough through the little gathering in the grass. '*Cajamaraca!*' he screams aggressively reaching out as if about to yank a couple of peasants on board by their shirtfronts or ponchos. '*Cajamarca!*'

The old woman sitting between Geronimo and Luís crosses herself again as the van skids to a stop.

'Shit,' says Victor. 'Where are they going to put another passenger?'

Not on the roof, which has already rejected a sack of potatoes and a wooden chair; not in a seat, since there are none left; most probably in the three or four feet left of aisle. There's always room for five more.

'You know,' I say conversationally to Victor as the newcomers battle their way on board, 'in a weird way this reminds me of Brooklyn.'

He starts to peel an orange. 'What does?' he asks. 'The rice paddies? The dead cow in the road? The pre-Inca relics?'

I can't sweepingly gesture around me because I'm still holding on, but I nod my head. 'This. We have *colectivos* just like this in Brooklyn, you know.'

Victor passes me half an orange. 'No, you don't.'

'Yes, we do.' I press closer against him as the flute and drum struggle past.

The guitarist dumps his bag on the floor and sits down on it, the guitar on his lap. He begins to strum.

He raises one eyebrow. 'Just like this?'

Okay, so maybe not just like this. 'Same basic idea.' Old vans with sliding doors fastened closed with washing line or simply left open for efficient boarding and unloading. Old vans that suddenly pull up to the kerb, the conductor leaning out, shouting something unintelligible, and people you thought were waiting for a bus to arrive or a light to change quickly jamming themselves in. Cheaper than a real bus; faster than a speeding bullet.

'Then why didn't we ever go in one?' asks Victor.

'Because you're not black.' The only people I've ever seen get into *colectivos* in Brooklyn were black. But race is no barrier to an interesting ride here. Geronimo and Luís would take anyone, dead or alive, whether they were going their way or in the opposite direction, whether they'd at least intended to get on some bus for somewhere or whether they were walking home from church.

Making up for the time lost in having to stop for two minutes to pick up new passengers, we start racing through the desert again.

'Who told you it was about the Devil?' asks Geronimo, as though there has been no interruption.

'Everyone knows that,' says Luís. 'I heard it on the radio. It was banned by the Church.'

'Pfft!' Geronimo's steering hand leaves the wheel, flicking this nonsense away. 'It's a love song, Luís. Why would the Church ban a love song?' The bus jumps as a wheel slips the road. 'Love makes the world go round.'

'Money makes the world go round,' says Luís. He leans in front of the woman to look at Geronimo. 'And they banned it because it isn't a love song. They banned it because it's a hymn to the Devil.' Out of the corner of his eye I see him notice us. He snaps his fingers. 'Gringos!' he laughs. 'They'll know!'

Breaking the rule of a lifetime, Geronimo glances in the rearview mirror, catching our eyes. 'You know The Eagles?' he wants to know. 'You know " 'Otel California"?'

'"Hotel California"?' repeats Victor as we streak through a grove of mimosas.

'Sí, sí.' Geronimo nods, his eyes darting back to the windscreen for long enough to be sure that no idiot is trying to get in his way. 'Is it a love song or is it about the Devil?'

'It's about California,' I say. This is so far-fetched that both men lose interest immediately.

'Mira!' shouts Luís, reaching across the old lady to thump his compadre's arm. 'Mira! He's wearing a ring in his nose.'

Geronimo turns around in his seat. 'A ring!' he laughs. He lets go of the wheel to allow him to point. 'Where are you from? Why do you have a ring in your nose?'

'Por dios!' I shriek. 'Keep your eyes on the road!'

The old woman has given up crossing herself. Instead she lifts the crucifix from the considerable expanse of black cotton that covers her chest and touches it to her lips. Pretty fervently.

The two men laugh. 'Calmate,' says Geronimo to me. 'I could drive this blind.'

'He practically does,' mutters Victor.

We are still well in the centre of the highway, so we don't have to pull over because of the Sud America bus stuck on the shoulder, two of its tyres deep in the sand, its enormous body tilting teasingly towards the vast grey desert. The driver is sitting by the engine, smoking a cigarette; the conductor is shovelling madly at the back wheel, trying to dig it out. The bus's passengers are shuffling down the road with their belongings. All they need is a clean-cut, concerned BBC reporter in khaki and sunblock standing beside them with a cordless microphone and a world-weary cameraman to look like fleeing refugees.

'I'm amazed that isn't us,' I say, turning back for one last look.
'Don't worry,' says Victor. 'There's still plenty of time.'

Pizarro and his men came out of the hills to find the valley of
Cajamarca green and miraculously flat below them, the tents of the
Inca's army spread across a hillside, as beautiful as any city they'd
ever seen. The valley is not so unbrokenly green any more. Instead
of the billowing tents of the Inca's army, Cajamarca is surrounded by
a bleak and dusty sprawl of storefronts and service stations. At its
centre is the city of the Spaniards, one of the picturesque colonial
towns of narrow cobbled streets, crumbling whitewashed buildings
and enough churches to make you wonder why so many priests felt
they had to leave Europe. But despite Cajamarca's considerable old-
world charm, it is difficult to hear the haunting sounds of guitars
and instruments of torture over the incessant bleating of traffic and
shouting of vendors; difficult to picture the streets more poorly lit
and jammed not with buses, cars and moto-taxis but carriages and
horses; the pavements empty but for a few elegant women in black
lace shawls out for a stroll with men from good families and faith in
their luck, and scores of men in black cassocks scurrying down the
alleyways, desperately looking for something to do. Cajamarca is,
above all, a tourist town. For a couple of bucks you can still see the
room where Pizarro imprisoned Atahualpa, or walk up the hill of the
ambush itself. For a couple more bucks, take a bus to Baños de Inca
and bathe in the waters once reserved for the descendant of the sun
and his wives.

'Gringos! Gringos!'
'Christ,' mutters Victor. 'Do they think we don't know?'
Ignoring the cries and amused stares, we continue to push our
way down the narrow pavement through the Cajamarcans going
about their business and the holidaymakers searching through the
craft shops for the cheapest souvenirs, carefully stepping over the
Indian women sitting on the pavement with their wares spread
around them, spinning wool while they wait for a sale and their
children play with bugs and bits of rubbish. Músicos wander from
plaza to plaza, serenading hotel windows and foot-tapping onlookers, loud and slightly listing young men erect dead trees on the side
streets, decorating them with toilet-paper streamers and knitted hats
and socks, people dance in the streets. It's carnival time in
Cajamarca.
'Gringos! Gringos!'

Victor flicks a hand at the young men on the corner. 'Hispanos!' he answers. 'Hispanos!'

Two small girls run beside us, hands outstretched. '*Señor . . . Señorita . . . Por favor . . .*'

There are five transvestites – ingeniously coiffed, eye-catchingly dressed, their luggage, in fake gold and leather, heaped up around them – waiting on a bench at the corner. 'Gringo!' they shout as we make our turn. 'Gringo! How are you?' 'Gringo, come say hello!' 'Gringo, we like your ring!'

A man sticks out his head from a first-floor window. 'Gringos! Gringos!'

Victor, intending to shout back, stops abruptly. Which is just as well. Splat. Splat. Splat. Several water bombs explode at our feet. We jump back, too late to stay dry. Laughter comes at us from every direction.

Pizarro and his soldiers received a warmer welcome, skinned ducks stuffed with wool and a drink with Atahualpa in his private baths.

Victor shakes water from his hat. 'If they'd treated the Spaniards like this the whole course of American history might have been different,' he grumbles.

A classic case of too little too late.

An automatic flash goes off amid happy shouts and laughter, capturing forever five smiling faces pressed together over a table of cakes and Inca Kola. Behind them the wall is looped with streamers left from Christmas and shrunken balloons. The waiter, looking like a waiter in his black trousers, white shirt and black bow tie, returns the camera with a formal bow, bumping into the clown moving among the diners selling sweets. The clown honks his horn.

'Busy place,' says Victor, placing the backgammon set on the plastic cloth that covers the red-checked cloth that covers our table. 'Maybe that means the food will be hot.'

A non-clown sidles past us, holding out his tray of cigarettes and sweets as he glances at us hopefully.

'Maybe.'

Brightly lit and throbbing, El Zarcón has the busy but frivolous air of a popular restaurant in a popular resort town. The main dining room is large but unspacious, its tables filled with families of holidaymakers devouring platters of quickly served food and locals sharing two-litre bottles of Inca Kola, a small boy with a fly-swatter

weaving between them. At the far end of the room is the desk where
the waiters rest their large trays while they tot up their bills with pre-
occupied frowns. At the opposite end is the entrance to the back
room. On the right are the toilets and a photograph of what might
very well be Lake Geneva. To the left is the glass cage of the cashier,
kerosene lanterns at the ready on the shelf beside a picture of
Jerusalem, and old-fashioned glass and wooden cases filled with
yoghurt and jellies.

A small child materialises beside us, dirty dark skin and blue eyes
staring silently from Victor to me. '*Señor . . . Señorita . . . tengo
hambre . . .*'

'Get out of here!' A waiter has appeared on our other side, slapping down menus, impersonally shooing the child away with his
printed pad. The child moves on. We order two beers.

The waiter is watching the game. 'What size?'

I roll double six, and react childishly as usual, waving my hands
in the air. 'Large.'

Another flash goes off.

The menu offers options. Four kinds of salad washed in the user-
friendly Cajamarcan water. Cheese omelette and rice. Vegetable
omelette and rice. Rice and beans. Rice and lentils. Cuban rice.
Papas fritas con salsa aji. Fried plantain. *Humitas.* Pickles. Olives.
Spoiled for choice.

The *músicos* enter, five smiling young men with plaits down their
backs wearing black and white ponchos, black hats and trousers
and the woven waistcoats you can buy in Camden. The guy with the
pan pipes stops next to Victor. '*Amigo*,' he says, slipping a leaflet into
his hand. 'We're playing later at the Bar Atahualpa. Why don't you
and the señorita come?'

Our waiter, a small, dark, cheerful man who in past lives may
have waited on wealthy Europeans at a resort in the Alps, or on day-
trippers in Blackpool, or even brought cups of *chibcha* to the Inca
himself, returns with the beers. He has never heard of backgammon,
but he plays chess with his son. His son is eleven. He is very bright,
very good at school. Soon his father will never beat him at chess. A
large, made-up woman trimmed in gold starts clapping loudly at a
nearby table. Our waiter holds up one placating hand. We order
quickly – pickles, olives, *aji*, two Russian salads, two portions of vegetable omelette, lentils and rice, one portion of chips – and he rushes
off in a flurry of '*Qué quiere señora*, is there a problem?

But nature, of course, abhors a vacuum.

'*Qué hacen?*' asks a sweet, young voice that is unusually uncajoling.

'Beating the shit out of her at backgammon,' says Victor in English, not looking up.

I risk a glance. The girl leaning on the back of one of the empty chairs beside us is small, thin, and no more than ten. Her hair is in braids and there are freckles across her nose.

'Señorita,' she says, her voice may be sweet but her manner is far from shy. Her eyes are on Victor. 'Señorita, doesn't it hurt *el joven* to have that ring in his nose?'

'No,' I say, taking in the dirty red shirt and grey sweater and the thin flip-flops. I pull back my hair so she can see my ears. 'It's just like this.'

'*Uno, dos, tres, cuatro, cinco, seis*,' she counts. 'Six earrings!' She points to the poster on the wall behind Victor. 'Even the queen wears only two!'

The poster shows last year's carnival king and queen, waving to the crowds.

'I love *los reyes*,' she informs me warmly. She is now staring at the queen in her glittering gold gown. 'Isn't she beautiful?' she breathes. 'Last year my sister and my brother-in-law took me to see the procession.' Undiscouraged by the fact that we are paying more attention to our game than to her, she goes on to describe the ride of the king and queen through the town, fireworks making the sky bright and hazy, water bombs making the onlookers shriek, the king so kind-looking and handsome, the queen like a picture in a story book. Everyone was dancing and singing. Everyone was happy. Her brother-in-law bought her a soda and she found a paper star in the plaza but her cousin ripped it up. 'You should've seen it,' she says, her eyes shining. 'It was marvellous.'

Victor, anticipating dinner, starts clearing the pieces away. 'And what about this year? Are you going this year?'

She shakes her head, her face suddenly expressionless. Her eyes stop shining. 'I don't know,' she says. She gives a little, hopeless smile. '*Depende.*'

Victor holds out his hand. 'I'm Victor,' he says. 'And that's Diana.'

She shakes our hands as solemnly and formally as a queen, be it one in a gaudy gold dress or one with a kerchief over her head and a Corgi under her arm. '*Yo soy Roxanna.*'

The guidebook recommends that if you make the walk to Cumbre

Mayo through the splendid surrounding countryside you should keep your eyes peeled for the local building method, Tapial, huts made of compressed adobe alternating with layers of stones or wood. The guidebook's enthusiasm gives the impression that a hovel constructed in Tapial is worth its weight in hummingbirds or wild flowers, but it isn't quite as fascinating as the book suggests. More fascinating, we discover as we carefully pick our way up the hill, trying to avoid the waste matter and the garbage and the demented dogs, are we. Me in my mirrored sunglasses and Victor in his hooded *chulupa* have captured the attention of the poor and oppressed of Cajamarca as no cloud forest or storm of butterflies ever could.

'They can't get many gringos in this part of town the way they all stare at us,' says Victor.

I pretend I don't see them all staring at us. 'I think this is one of those bad neighbourhoods the book says never to walk through alone.' Advice everyone else seems to have taken.

'You're not alone,' says Victor. 'You've got me.'

Faces in doorways and paneless windows, expressionless but wary, wonder what the hell we're doing so far from the dim lights and attractions of the better part of town. 'Gringos!' small children scream, racing to the road to watch us pass. 'Gringos! Gringos!' When we try to ask directions the adults say nothing or spit on the ground.

The rubble turns to rocky dirt, the examples of traditional house construction thin out, the fields and woods begin to restake their claim to the hillside.

'God, it's good to be in the country,' says Victor, breathing deeply. 'Smell that urine! Smell that shit!'

The mescal, which we had mixed with guabana soda in an attempt to make it palatable, and which tasted no better than it did without, is already taking effect. Splintered sunlight shimmers over the dusty road and dark huts; over the laundry spread across bushes and washing lines; over the empty fields and clusters of sheep. Even when we see no one, we know that they see us. We force a path through the dancing colours of the mountain, the air a bitter-sweet song played on a flute of glass.

'Gringos! Gringos!' come the cries as another gaggle of small boys runs after us. 'Gringos! Gringos!' Several dogs, snarling, join the chase.

The thought of fear falls in step. We could be ripped apart by crazed canines and no one would help us. We could be followed to nowhere and left for dead. I could be raped. But though the thought of fear trips along beside us, I'm still more interested in the flowers that shine on the black and green hills like oil in a puddle, and I can't hear it clearly above the whirring of the hummingbirds' whirrings. Fear itself is lingering behind.

Two old men wearing dark, worn-in hats are sitting on a rock at a bend in the road. They're drinking *anisado* and talking intently, but they look up at the sound of childish shrieking and the din made by the hounds of hell.

'Gringos taking a walk,' one man says to the other as we stagger by.

Lying lazy but alert among the wild flowers, observing a scene of which we're an unexpected part, we watch the two little girls as we watch the clouds and the mountains, the hummingbirds and spiders, the insects gleaming like mother of pearl. They are no more really than spots of colour – the eldest a blue skirt and purple shirt and white hat, the youngest red and green, their braids thick lines of black – but we can hear their voices, childish and disembodied, clear and comforting as wind chimes, as they tend their sheep. They remind me of Roxanna. Not because the eldest must be the same age as she; not because the three of them all wear their hair in plaits; not because they all have little-girl voices sweet enough to cut through hearts of stone. The youngest one rolls laughing down the hill, her sister runs after her, slipping and sliding, singing. That's why they remind me of Roxanna, because I can't picture her here, with a present that leads to a future.

While we lay among the wild flowers on the hill across the road, our conversation as random as an electron, the girls spent the morning in the valley, the ten-year-old sitting backwards on the mule, her little sister climbing in the trees, the sheep wandering over the riverbank, and, seamlessly perfect, the world turned slowly away from the sun.

Now the girls have crossed back to the hillside next to ours. The youngest sings while she chases the sheep. The eldest flops across the back of the mule. The day winds down while Victor listens and I write a letter to Patricia in California, longing to visit Mexico. I tell her about the mescal and the texture of the day, about the quiet intensity of each second and the way the splendid landscape makes the efforts of man seem so inconsequential, about the little girls like travellers through time. You'd love it here, I write to Patricia. Maybe next time you'll come along.

'Gringo! Gringo!' Giggles drift towards us like clouds. 'Gringo! Gringo!'

Victor props himself up on his elbows. 'What?' he shouts back. 'What do you want?'

More giggles and shrieks. 'Gringo! Gringo!'

'Hello!' calls Victor. 'What are your names?'

The younger girl, incoherent with laughter, starts to answer but the elder one is more wary and whacks her over the head to make her stop. A family of Indians with bags and boxes get out of a pick-up and head up the hill dotted with sheep. The girls start getting ready to go home for the night.

We start getting ready, too, planning our route.

'Not the way we came,' says Victor. 'Let's avoid the dogs. Let's try not to run into any drunks.' He points to the valley across the dirt road. 'Let's go through there.' He studies the steepness that leads to through there. 'You think you can make it?'

I stand up, ready to float, and gracelessly slide several feet down the slope. 'Of course I can make it,' I say, disengaging myself from a dark green shrub.

Victor glances up at the figures slipping over the hilltop. 'Just do me a favour,' he says, slinging the bag over his shoulder. 'If you fall don't make a spectacle of yourself.' He gives me a look. 'Don't scream.'

It is true that I screamed when the flying waterbug got into our room in Vilcabamba and I, on the wrong side of the mosquito net, had to get it back out. And it's true that I screamed the first time I saw a dead rat on the streets of Quito. And I screamed in Baños when my horse suddenly sat down in the mud and rolled over on top of me. And I did scream a bit when I lost my footing on the toilet rim in Chiclayo and nearly fell in. But despite Victor's contention that so many men die of heart attacks because there is always some woman shrieking her head off I don't really find this excessive behaviour.

I am about to reply, coolly, that I have no intention of making a spectacle of myself when instead I let out a scream that freezes every figure on the nearby hillside, four-footed and two-footed alike.

Victor says the same thing now that he said on those other occasions. 'What are you doing?'

I point just behind him to where the woolly Arnold Schwarzenegger of the spider world is *poco a poco* marching purposefully up the rocks.

'A tarantula!' shouts Victor. 'Quick, get the camera!'

'Christ,' Victor shouts from the bathroom. 'It's got gop in it. What does the book say if it's got gop in it?'

'Are you sure?' An aroma close to that of the Peruvian countryside drifts in from the doorless bathroom. I sit on the bed, flipping through the pocket-sized medical book, though considering the number of times I've read and reread it you'd think I'd have it memorised by now. 'It's not good,' I shout back. 'It's a bad sign.' What a surprise.

'It's not yellow, though,' says Victor. 'What does it say if it isn't yellow?'

I put down the book and look towards the bathroom. All I can see is the tiny lavender sink. 'It's not yellow? Mine's yellow. And kind of green.'

Victor isn't impressed by green. Not after Ecuador. 'But there's no mucus in it, is there?' he asks. 'It's just soft.' Squeaks and squirts and splatters. 'This is well beyond soft.' More of the sounds of nature cleaning out the system. 'I'm not so sure about the mucus, though. This last lot looks clear.'

I can see that the average person, who, even if they are part of a couple, are rarely alone with one other person for more than twelve hours and are asleep for most of that time, might find it hard to imagine what any two people, sharing each other's company for twenty-four hours a day every day for over six months, might possibly find to talk about after the first week, never mind two relative strangers travelling together in alien lands. With no jobs or workmates to complain about, no television programmes or films to encourage discussion and debate, no friends and their problems to analyse, no neighbours to distract them, nowhere to go for a third opinion – what? God, the universe and everything? Arsenal's chances in the Cup? The childhood dreams or traumas that made them the sort of people who will pitch themselves into darkest Peru together even though they know each other far less than most people choosing a companion for two weeks in Greece, meals included? When they lie awake in strange rooms, counting the hours on the illuminated hands of their travel clock, what stories do they tell each other, what pieces of information about themselves that have never been told to anyone else before?

'It may be nothing,' I say, holding my shirt over my nose as the new smell migrates across the tiny room. 'You were all right this morning.'

'Yeah,' mutters Victor. 'And I was all right in Puyo till I got into the loo.'

An hour later, the concierge, apparently thinking that Victor had hanged himself, was pounding on the door, 'Señor! Señor!', frantically rummaging through her keys for the one to the first-floor bathroom, a soldier, a salesman, an Otavalan couple and me pressed close behind her, all of us trying to talk at once while Victor shouted through the door, 'I'm not hurt. Leave me alone! For Christ's sake, Dyan, call them off!'

I've studied our conversations pretty closely over the last few months. In the best of times and the worst of times. In bug-ridden hotels with soldiers masturbating in the toilets and whores singing on the stairs. On deserted mountain roads with clouds bumping against us. On buses, in stations, crushed into a *colectivo* with some man who smells like last week's stew snoring beside us. And although we do talk about food quite a bit, and hot showers, and videos we'd like to see, and also give quite a bit of space to the peculiarities of divine and human behaviour, what we talk about most consistently is our bowel movements. Hard or soft? Existent or non-existent? Threatening dehydration or more or less under control? A day of constipation is worth several hours of dietary itemisation, two days at least six hours of debating whether or not to risk a beer. Shits that leave the loo smelling like the cattle drive passed through it can hold our attention for twenty-four hours.

Victor finally leaves his perch on top of the toilet and throws himself down on the bed. 'It's the *chibcha*,' he moans. 'They've bloody poisoned me.'

When we finally got back to town and found the shop where we'd bought the guabana soda, the mother and daughter who ran it were so disappointed that we hadn't even managed to reach the Inca ruins, thus leaving our lives without that extra depth and meaning, that they offered us a glass of home-made *chibcha* as compensation. To celebrate carnival. Judging by the colour and the dampness of my travelling companion's skin, poisoning isn't out of the question.

'It can't be the *chibcha*,' I reason. 'I drank it too.'

'Not the one made with peanuts,' he says. 'You drank the one made with corn and sugar cane. I drank the one made with peanuts.' He props himself up, scrutinising me closely. 'Exactly what shade of green is yours?'

The walls of the back room of El Zarcón are grey and green, and futilely decorated with a few dusty carnival masks, framed calendars, magazine pictures (a funky gas station in the wilds of America, a horse farm probably in Kentucky, what looks like a London street corner), and an enormous mirror facing the thickly painted grey double doors. The fluorescent lights are dingy and cheerless; the tablecloths in the back room are green and white.

'No, really,' Victor is saying as we take a table next to the door. 'How long do you think it took him to come up with that? Seriously. How many nights did he lay awake discarding ideas, tossing and turning with frustration, becoming so obsessed that he alienated his family, his friends and even his colleagues before he finally found the perfect solution?' He mimes a man of reason and intellect, ecstatic as he solves the problem that no one else has been able to solve.

There are only two tables occupied in the back room tonight, one by a group of white-collar workers drinking beer, laughing too loudly and spitting on the floor, the other by a courting couple sharing a bottle of Inca Kola, napkins over their glasses to keep out the flies. I glance back into the main room. 'She's not here,' I say.

'You want to know how long it took? Years!' Victor informs me, the clerks impatiently calling for more *cerveza*, and the couple holding hands around a bottle of soda the yellow of toilet cleaner. 'Fuckin' bleedin' centuries.' He throws his arms in the air. 'It probably took longer to figure this out than it did to come up with bubble-gum ice-cream.'

Victor is talking about honey. Well, not honey precisely; he is talking about the container the honey comes in. It's a plastic bag. Manageable, economical and practical when unopened, but a little more problematic after that.

'Maybe she thinks we left town.' I'm talking about Roxanna. Due to the curse of the carnival *chibcha*, we haven't left our room for two days, except for lightning raids on the *supermercado* for dry biscuits and plastic bags of honey.

'Maybe,' says Victor, but he smiles past me. 'Well, hello,' he continues, still in English. 'We were wondering where you were.' He pulls out the chair between us. 'We were afraid you might not show up.'

Unbothered by Victor's use of the wrong language, Roxanna glides past me and sits down. She's dressed exactly as she was the first time we met her. 'How are you, Señorita?' she asks as though she's been worrying about this. She gives Victor her best smile. 'Y el joven?'

I give her the packet of toast we also bought in the *supermercado*,

too sweet for either of us. She accepts it graciously, putting it on the
table in front of her. 'I'll have to hide it from my cousin,' she says
without complaining. 'Or he'll take it like he takes everything else.'

The waiter, a fly-swatter in one hand and his order pad in the
other, appears behind her, irresolutely staring down at the top of her
head. He looks at Victor.

'Roxanna,' says Victor. 'Would you like a fruit juice?'

Victor and I play draughts while we wait for our meals and
Roxanna explains why she didn't get to see the procession of *los reyes*
this year. It is a long and complex story, flatly, quickly and softly told,
involving her mother, her mother's husband, her sister, her brother-
in-law and her grandmother.

'Your grandmother lives with you?' I ask, trying to make sense of
her words.

Roxanna smiles patiently. '*Qué, señorita?*' she asks, sweeter than
the honey gluing the plastic bag together. '*No entiendo.*'

'Does your grandmother live with you?'

'Oh, no señorita. My grandmother's dead.'

Roxanna used to live with her grandmother until last summer,
when she died – possibly of consumption, possibly of pneumonia,
possibly of falling off a mule. That is why Roxanna is in Cajamarca;
she came here to live with her mother. She doesn't have a father.
Her older sisters and brothers have a different father. Her younger
sisters and brothers have a different father, too. Roxanna's mother
and her new husband don't really want her around. I think she says
that her mother beats her, or her stepfather beats her, or her stepfather beats her mother, or her brother-in-law beats her sister, or
even that they all beat her. Roxanna runs her finger over the packet
of toast. 'I miss my grandmother,' she says. And then, because an
explanation is obviously in order, adds, 'She liked *pan tostado* very
much.'

Victor, glimpsing the waiter, pushes the game box towards
Roxanna. 'You want to play with this while we eat?'

Roxanna smiles like a child. '*El joven* is sure it's all right for me to
touch it?' She's fascinated by the magnets, quickly sussing out that
some attract and some repel.

'Look at these,' says Victor, handing her the bag of chess pieces.
'See what you make of these.'

'Chess,' says Roxanna, setting the pieces on the board. 'My grandfather used to play.'

Some of our food arrives. Victor, whose bowels are still under scrutiny and discussion, is having a nominal meal of rice and an egg. It's the egg that reaches us first.

Roxanna is astounded, not to say concerned. 'Is that all *el joven* is having?' she asks. 'An egg?'

'It had better not be,' mumbles *el joven*.

'Maybe this means the rice will be hot,' I venture.

'No,' says Victor, his eyes on the waiter as he bustles back to the kitchen. 'All it means is that he's waiting for it to cool down.'

When the waiter returns with Victor's cold rice, my salad and my platter of *arroz Cubana*, Roxanna's astonishment is complete. 'Señorita,' she gasps. 'Is all that for you?'

While we eat, Roxanna chats and sips her juice. She likes to come into the restaurants because most of them have televisions. She likes television. She likes the clothes of the women on the American shows. She likes the cars.

'I can't eat all of these fried plantains,' I tell her. 'You want some?'

Roxanna likes chicken better than plantains, but she likes them, too. Her favourite TV shows are comedies.

'What about some of this rice?'

Roxanna used to go to school, but she doesn't any more, not since her grandmother died. Her papers aren't here. 'There was a girl in my class who got a fifteen from the teacher,' she says, going for the bit of rice with the ketchup on it.

'Is that good?' I guess.

Roxanna is either enjoying the rice and ketchup too much, or doesn't feel that a question of this calibre deserves an answer.

'What about you? What did you get?'

'I got a five and a zero and a lot of red.'

Clearing up, the waiter makes a joke about Roxanna going back to England with us. 'Their parents send them in to play up to gringos,' he explains, his kind face a gesture of hopelessness. 'They want gringos to take them back home with them.'

'What do you do all day if you don't go to school?' I ask Roxanna.

She drags the last tablespoon of juice through her straw and smiles. 'I sing.'

Inside room 14 of the El Dorado, streetlights shine weakly through the pink curtains, casting shadows on the wall.

'That pasta with the artichokes and the sun-dried tomatoes . . .' Victor is whispering. 'And marinated peppers . . . and seven-layer burritos . . . stuffed aubergine . . . sushi . . . miso soup . . .'

'How could you take a child of that age from here and bring her back to London?' I'm whispering. 'It would be a disaster. It wouldn't be culture shock, it'd be cultural cardiac arrest.'

Outside room 14, the couple fucking on the floor of the hallway breathe a little more loudly and more heavily. One of them moans, a sound less erotic than many people would have you believe.

'Mushrooms and tomatoes on toast with chips and brown sauce . . .' says Victor, still talking about what he'll eat when he gets back to England, but no longer whispering. 'Pumpkin soup . . . roasted vegetables . . .'

'I mean, I've heard of people getting children from Peru.' I'm still talking about Roxanna. 'There seem to be a lot of babies for sale. Judy's friend was going to buy one that was found in a basket by the sewer so they named it Moses. It wasn't even a week old. But a ten-year-old . . .' Ten years is too many. Too much to lose and learn again. Christ, I've known people depressed and traumatised because they moved next door, never mind across the universe.

The couple lying, one assumes, on the threadbare carpet of the hallway have clearly never heard what the Taoists have to say about sex or the female orgasm.

'Nothing's going to happen to her here,' says Victor. 'Roxanna's not stupid. Besides, she hits on gringos. Travellers aren't going to—' He breaks off as the sounds being made on the other side of the door begin to peak. They know bugger all about ejaculatory control, either.

'Al Stanton's a traveller,' I remind him. Al Stanton, twelve years on the road with his Nazi dreams and special forces training, his air-rifle in his backpack and his flick knife down his boot. 'How many missing ads on the sides of milk containers do you think he's responsible for?'

'Al Stanton wouldn't get down here,' says Victor. 'Too far from home.'

It's the silence after a storm, or after a fight, or after a man has squandered his sexual energy by throwing it into the nearest container. In this silence someone on the other side of our door strikes a match.

I pull the blanket over my head. 'Please,' I beg the creator of Al, Roxanna, Dr Jaime and the rest of the lot. 'Please don't let him start talking about his childhood.'

The next day – our last day – the rains are heavy and the lights are out. Kerosene lanterns light up the cheese shop and the drinks and sweet shop and the crafts stores and the *supermercado*. Candles wave from the counter of the hardware store and the sewing shop and the stalls in the indoor market. Only in El Zarcón, where the back room is shut and the main one nearly empty, is the electricity still on.

Roxanna arrives as we're finishing our meal. Today she's not alone. Held tightly in her hand is a small teenage doll. The doll's long plastic legs and arms are white. Her face, eyes painted blue, mouth a dark red, is an unhealthy ruddy colour. Her body in its short navy dress made by hand from a scrap of material is the bluey-grey of a terminal illness. She may once have had a long blonde ponytail but now her haircut is almost punk.

'And who's this?' I ask as Roxanna takes her seat between me and Victor with her angelically pleasant '*Buenas tardes*'.

Roxanna, I have noted, is often baffled by the things I don't know. 'Barbie,' she answers. Who else?

I want to be sure about this. 'Her name's Barbie?'

Roxanna fusses with the half-scalped hair. 'Of course,' she says. She stands her on the table. 'She's pretty, isn't she?'

This is one of those things that I can't let go. Not easily. 'But why did you name her Barbie?' I persist.

Roxanna glances at *el joven* to see if he finds me as difficult to understand and communicate with as she does. *El joven* isn't looking at either of us. He's searching for something in his bag.

'Barbie's her name,' says Roxanna in her clearest, slowest Spanish. 'What else would I call her?'

Victor takes a small plastic zip-loc and lays it on the table. We've been carrying balloons and stars with us since we left Brooklyn, but we never remember to give them as gifts. 'Here.' He shoves it towards her. 'This is for you.'

Roxanna likes the coloured stars. 'I saw a dress for Barbie in the market this morning,' she says as she sticks blue stars on Barbie's face and arms. 'But I don't have enough *plata*.' She sticks red and gold stars on herself.

'Look at these,' says Victor, whose interest in dolls and dolls' clothes, were it shared by everyone else on the planet, would have wiped the Mattel company out of human memory. He holds the glow-in-the-dark stars under the table so that she can see the effect.

'It was red and had a long skirt,' Roxanna continues as she and Victor peer under the table, hoping to see a bit of the night sky. 'She would look like the queen in it. It even has shoes.'

From under the table, Victor sighs the sigh of someone who is learning that while a man might dream of walking across the Milky Way, a woman would first consider what she would wear. 'What about the balloons?' he asks as the two of them return to the surface. One balloon is silver, one purple. The Hallowe'en balloon is orange with tiny black spiders.

Roxanna blows up the silver balloon less than halfway and hands it to Victor to tie. She doesn't want to blow it up too much in case it breaks. The others she has to hide from her cousin. She turns the Hallowe'en balloon over in her hand. 'There are a lot of spiders in my house,' she informs me the way another child might say, 'We have three TVs.' She smiles. 'Tarantulas.'

A waiter passes by with a tray of desserts. 'I like yoghurt very much,' says Roxanna, sticking a blue star on her forehead and putting on my sunglasses, mugging. 'But I don't have enough *plata* for it.'

'Okay,' says Victor, answering a question that neither Roxanna, Barbie nor I have actually asked. He signals to our waiter. 'I won't buy her a bloody dress for her Barbie doll but she can have a yoghurt.'

The waiter brings us two more beers, but forgets the yoghurt. He brings a spoon with which to eat the yoghurt, but forgets the yoghurt. He retrieves two jellies from the refrigerated case, which, unlike the house lights, is not on despite the power cut, and sails past us with them sparkling like jewels on his silver tray. 'Yoghurt!' I shout. 'We ordered a yoghurt!'

Roxanna pats my arm. 'It's all right, señorita. He is busy.'

Victor is staring at Barbie, leaning against his beer bottle, plastered with coloured foil stars. 'The revolution's all uphill,' he tells her. 'Uphill on ice.'

'Mango,' says Roxanna philosophically when at last the plastic cup is set in front of her. She scoops a chunk of fruit from the warm yoghurt, which now, I'm worrying, might be teeming with salmonella since the refrigeration's been off. 'If you get strawberry, strawberries come out,' she informs me.

The three of us are standing by the cashier while Victor pays. Roxanna and I are discussing dolls' clothes again when her eyes suddenly lock on to something behind me. She's the spider who sees the fly jump straight into its web. The hustler who spots the hick getting off the train with his life savings falling out of his pocket. The princess in the tower catching her first sight of a dude in armour on a white horse looking around for someone to save. 'Gringo,' breathes Roxanna.

I turn around. A young, soft-looking gringo on his own nods to me and Victor as he strolls into the main dining room of El Zarcón. Roxanna is two feet behind him.

On our way back to the El Dorado, we pass an Indian woman sitting on the pavement spinning wool while she waits for someone to buy a bag of peanuts from her.

'That's how Roxanna will end up,' says Victor. He stops and buys half a kilo of nuts.

Let's hope so.

25

SEND MONEY, GUNS
AND LAWYERS

There is something exhilarating about travelling at night. Something
not so much dangerous as on the edge. After all, we're not night-
stalkers or shadow-walkers like owls or wolves. It's bats, not men,
who glide through the shades and the moonshine, freewheeling as
the wind. The night world is not one we were ever meant to linger
in or see. We're light-seekers, worshippers of the sun. We're meant
to be indoors when it's dark, the blinds drawn and the door bolted,
lamps on, the TV comforting, the fire warm, the world still ordinary
and familiar, tame as a dog. In the darkness, the road is wide-open as
the sky; could take you anywhere or nowhere, could go on forever
and carry you with it. You hear your wheels as a heartbeat and stare
out the window at distant lights like fallen stars, at the pale dunes
and cliffs like statues, at the spectral huts that rise out of nothing and
dip back again, at things that can't be seen. It's a little like being a
ghost. It's being awake but set loose in a dream. Even in a bus. Even
in a bus over-full with whimpering children, with men coughing and
snoring, with songs like laments being played in the aisles.
Especially in a bus careening through the desert of Peru.

Until, that is, you aren't moving any more.

Victor pushes against my shoulder, leaning towards the window.
'Are we slowing down?'

We're slowing down.

He presses his forehead against the glass. 'Now what?'

The bus stops.

'Christ,' says Victor. 'What are we, cursed?'

We went two days out of our way because the guidebook said there was a hotel with a kitchen in beautiful Huanchaco where you could watch the narrow fishing rafts bobbing on the sea like gulls. We saw no rafts, only tables along the boardwalk selling Rasta jewellery and friendship bracelets. We ate a custom-made meal in someone's living room. We never found the hotel.

Victor cups his hands around his eyes. 'There's nothing out there,' he announces, leaning back. 'Not even a bunch of Indians with a lantern and a couple of sacks of rice. Let's hope it's a pit stop and not another flat tyre.'

We lingered for over an hour this afternoon in a village of houses with fenced-off gardens and covered patios, having a tyre changed, the men standing shoulder to shoulder behind the mechanic, staring at his back and the side of the bus, and the women sitting together in the shade, eating and combing their hair.

'It can't be another flat tyre,' I say pretty confidently. 'The odds are in our favour.'

A couple of men get up and force their way to the door, stepping over sleeping children, managing to get past the musicians without breaking a guitar. Either it is a pit stop, or they're going to help by standing around watching and nodding and giving advice while the conductor fixes the flat.

I put my face against the glass.

'What do you see?' asks Victor.

'Not a lot. There's one guy taking a piss, the rest are all in a huddle with the driver. They're not kicking the wheels or anything, though.'

Victor pushes closer again. 'What about the conductor?'

I look towards the front of the bus. 'I think that's him opening the bonnet.'

The driver gets back behind the wheel. He touches the crucifix hanging from the mirror and he starts the engine. The crucifix sways gently. The engine doesn't start. He shouts something to the conductor. The conductor, head under the bonnet, shouts back. The engine doesn't start again. The men who got off the bus get back on. An urgent whisper moves, wave-like, down the bus. But it's a wave that requires a better board than my high-school Spanish to ride. I nudge Victor. 'What are they saying?'

Victor watches the rest of the bus get to their feet, hauling their baggage from under their seats and the overhead racks. 'The bus has broken down,' he says. 'They're abandoning ship.'

One by one, taking it in turn to argue with the driver for a refund, the other passengers step out of the bus and into the night.

'Where do you think they're going?' My eyes are on the windscreen and the blackness beyond it, now broken by a cord of pedestrians, slouching towards an invisible horizon.

Victor shrugs. 'Lima?'

We sit in the front seats, debating what to do. Stay where we are? Ignore every warning we have ever heard about travelling anywhere and hurl ourselves into the dark? The driver and the conductor, both under the bonnet by now, might get the engine started. Even if they don't, in time they'll be missed. 'Whatever happened to the 7.30 express?' the clerk at the depot in Lima will wonder. Help will be sent.

There is a sudden wash of light and a bus whose name is Little Flower pulls up in front of us. Everyone on the road starts running for it.

'There's no point,' says Victor, as though I'd asked him a question. 'It's full already. We'd never get on.'

We decide that we'd never get on the second bus, either, though everyone else does.

'Maybe we should have gone with them,' says Victor as we watch its tail-lights disappear in darkness through the windscreen. The driver and the conductor are now leaning against the bumper, smoking cigarettes and talking as though they are hanging out on a street corner, as though they are men with time to kill.

When the third bus pulls over we are out of the door before it comes to a stop.

Our driver won't give us a refund. Don't tell me, tell them in Lima. The driver of the third bus makes us pay full fare. Don't tell me, tell them in Lima.

There are no seats. We balance on our packs at the front of the aisle, the only space not taken up with sleeping children or luggage, too grateful to be on our way again to mind the smell of the floor, or the effort it takes not to wind up with your head in someone's lap, or even the shower of peanut shells that falls on us from the women who talk over our heads while they eat.

At last we reach what is either the outskirts of Lima or the wastelands of the planet Zargo. The bus bucks and pitches off the road at the military checkpoint. An armed guard rushes over to greet us. He and the driver exchange a few words and then the driver looks over his shoulder and points to us. 'You two,' he says, shouting so that we'll understand him. 'Go with him.'

The entire bus sighs. How long is this going to take? Watches are consulted. Heads are shaken. Can't they go without us? Can't we take another bus? Comments about gringos are exchanged. We struggle off with all our things, and follow the young man with the rifle through the crowd of men aimlessly gathered in the parking lot and up the path to the small concrete building with the Peruvian seal painted over its door.

We stop in the entrance. The single, dingy room is minimally furnished with desk and filing cabinet. A bare lightbulb hangs from the ceiling. There are stains on the concrete floor and splashed against the whitewashed walls. There are quite a few men with guns aimlessly standing about.

'Christ,' says Victor. 'This is where they shoot you out back at dawn.'

It's clearly a slow night in Passport Control. Not many terrorists coming through; not many drug dealers; bloody few gringos. There's a pack of cards on one corner of the desk. The radio on the window ledge goes off as we step inside. The younger soldiers shift their rifles, pleased to have someone to shoot at dawn at last.

The officer at the bare desk sits up straight and smiles not quite pleasantly. He holds out his hand. Passports. Plane tickets. Health records. Someone coughs. We hike out our body pouches with as much modesty and dignity as we can muster. Judging by their grins, all the young men, and even the officer at the desk, like our body pouches.

The officer leans on his elbows while he painstakingly checks each page of our documents, savouring each stamp and scrawl, studying the instructions on the tickets – Don't Pack Aerosols in Your Luggage. Don't Carry Arms – failing to discover that we haven't been vaccinated against cholera. He holds up the passports. Are we German? Are we American? What were we doing in Colombia? In Ecuador? Why have we come to Peru? How much money do we have? What do we do? Am I going to write a book about Peru? I say no, trusting that even if he discovers the letter from my publisher tucked inside my body belt he won't understand it. He wonders what we've heard about Peru. We smile, giving the impression that all we've heard is good. He warns us to be careful. At last, he shakes our hands.

By the time we get back on the bus, there is a band in the space we'd called ours. By the time we get to Lima it is too late to eat. We take a Beetle to the youth hostel in the better part of town, the only place in Lima with a kitchen. We want a kitchen because we want to cook, and because we have one piece of San Pedro left. Waste not, want not, as my mother would say. The driver and I discuss Volkswagens – how much they cost, how they hold their value, how economical they are – while Victor goes up to the large suburban house and rings the bell. The door never opens. Victor talks into the phone on the wall. He is back in minutes. 'Twenty dollars a night!' he hisses. 'Can you believe it? A youth hostel! Twenty dollars a night!'

The driver takes us back into the centre, to the worst part of town. 'Watch out for thieves,' he warns as we hurtle through deserted, ruined streets, people walking quickly, figures sifting through the trash. 'Watch out for thieves.' The great hotel recommended by the American we met in Huanchaco has one room left, but it's not really ready for guests, though of course they'll move us when they can. We think our luck is turning. It's half the normal price. 'Because it smells like mildew,' I suggest as we shut the long double door behind us and stare at the dull blueness of the room no one else wants. 'Because it smells like mice,' says Victor. Tacked on to the door is a notice in Spanish and English.

Guests:
During your stay in Lima it is recommended you take the following precautions:
1. Don't speak with people you don't know.
2. Don't accept cigarettes or sweets for they may contain drugs.
3. Take care with false police who may want to see your passport. Take a fotocopy with you instead.
4. Don't walk or take photos in the Plaza de Armas late at night.
5. When you go out, take with you only the money or other values you really need. You can leave the rest in our safe.

In other circumstances – seeing this sign on someone's kitchen wall in Camden, for instance – it would probably be fun as well as interesting to consider to whom the foreign traveller might speak if not to someone she or he doesn't know. The foreign traveller could spend quite a bit of time in total silence, bereft of food, drink and lodging as well as of any idea as to where the Mercado Azul or the statue of Bolivar might be, searching for someone who wasn't a stranger. Fun and interesting to imagine gringos with peeling noses and hand-knitted sweaters decorated with llamas pelting across the Plaza de Armas late at night, steadfastly refusing to snap a picture. Mindboggling to consider what values you might really need on the streets of the capital. Honesty? Integrity? A firm belief in God? But in the dankness of room 2 at the back of the Hotel España it seems more like a threat.

'Welcome to Lima, City of the Kings,' I mutter.

Victor throws down his bags. 'Don't worry,' he says. 'We'll do what we've got to do and then we're gone. We won't be here long.'

It wasn't I who called Lima the City of the Kings, it was Prescott. Prescott was pretty taken with Lima. 'Amidst the woe and destruction which Pizarro and his followers brought on the devoted land of the Incas,' he wrote, 'Lima, the beautiful City of the Kings, survives as the most glorious work of his creation, the fairest gem on the shores of the Pacific.' Prescott saw Lima as a pure enchantment of colonial buildings and dwellings, 'one of the most gracious cities on earth'. But that was some time ago.

'It can't be true,' says Victor, his tone a little grim. 'Five days? This is 1994, not 1651. It can't be five days. There's got to be a way through.'

We are slogging our way up Avenida Grau. When Prescott was ecstatically wandering around Lima, bowled over by its grace and charms, Avenida Grau would, one assumes, have been broad and elegant, the windows of its grand houses looking out on a street lined with trees. But not any more. Now it is walled on either side by stalls and vendors, its pavements are filthy and littered, the avenue itself solid with traffic. Where once it might have had the atmosphere and sensibility of a viceroy's tea party, it now has all the energy and pace usually associated with a looting.

I step out of the way of a man with a monkey dressed like a better-class waiter. 'What if it is true?'

We are slogging our way up Avenida Grau because we're looking for the bus station to prove that what the boy at the desk of the Hotel España said isn't true. He said that we can't get a bus south for at least five days because the bridge is out.

'It isn't,' repeats my travelling companion, scanning the increasingly crumbling buildings for numbers that aren't there. 'It can't be.'

Day one and he's already into denial.

I'd be the first to admit that there's a lot to be said against teeming urban areas. Violence. Crime. Dirt. Pollution. High prices. Stress.

Overcrowding. Homelessness. Bad water. Lack of air. Traffic. Noise. Beggars. Hustlers. Young men with knives. Young women in short, tight black skirts and heels. But, of course, many cities – the cities you dream of on those futilely rainy nights that make you realise that the closest you've ever come to adventure was the time your flat was robbed; the closest to romance the Valentine's card you never knew who sent you – compensate for these drawbacks in other ways.

They may, for example, be uniquely beautiful. Paris. Venice. Pink Jaipur. Sure, people have been murdered making a phone call on the corner in New York, they've been shot sitting watching cricket in their living rooms on a Saturday afternoon in London, but the risk of random death is worth the sight of Manhattan, shining and magical, a city of jewels, as you come across the bridge at night; worth a pint of bitter in a pub on the Thames on a summer afternoon.

They may, for example, offer things you could find nowhere else. The shops, the food, the museums, the churches, the architecture, the bars, the book stores, the theatre, the dance, the music scene. What's a little overcrowding or pollution next to the lumpia of Singapore or the artichoke pizza of Brooklyn? What's a stolen wallet compared to Barcelona's park?

Lima, however, has none of these things. We'd rather be cow-tipping in Mississippi for five days than stuck in Lima.

In silence, we slog on. The joke in New York is that if you're riding uptown on the subway, Ninety-sixth Street is the point where all the white people disappear. We have, in a manner of speaking, hit Ninety-sixth Street. The crowds have thinned to a few men shuffling along much in the manner of tumbleweed, a few kids playing in the rubble, the occasional woman laden with bags and children hurrying home. The traffic is moving. At this end of Miguel Grau, revolutionary hero, the avenue was never elegant nor grand, and now it vanishes suddenly in a cul-de-sac of hovels and sand and unpaved streets that smell like a council lift in London. NB: Never venture into the poorer sections of Lima, especially on your own.

'I think we've come too far,' says Victor.

I think so, too. The slightly genteel squalor of the centre of Lima has given way to the desperate desolation of a bombed city, or a settlement just sacked by the invading hordes; a place the world forgot – or would like to.

I, for one, would like to forget it. Everyone, his cousin and his cousin's chicken knows we are here. They watch us from doorways and windows, they stop and turn to see us again. Even the children don't ask us for presents or money, but step back, staring. I feel like Gary Cooper turning up in Hadleyville.

We stop in front of an open doorway. It is gloomy inside and the quiet of empty. Two women sit behind the rough wooden counter. The flimsy shelves are bare except for a few bottles of soda and a faded display for plastic barrettes. The women are small and plump, and dressed in identical vintage cocktail dresses, one yellow, one blue, their short curly hair a shade of red not dreamed of by nature, their make-up cracking around their eyes. The only sound in the shop comes from their knitting needles, click, click, click, click, click. They look up as we enter, too surprised to smile.

'You ask,' whispers Victor. 'Woman to woman.'

Woman to woman, I walk up to the packing-case counter. Click, click, click. Their eyes are set but their hands keep moving. Working on the theory that hostile natives should be approached in the same manner as hostile dogs, I exhibit no fear or panic as I politely ask if they know what's happened to Avenida Grau.

'Avenida Grau?'

'Avenida Grau?'

Click, click, click, click, click.

'Sí. Avenida Grau.'

Click, click, click, click, click.

If we hadn't met a woman in Puyo who didn't know what her house number was and had to step out into the street to check it, it might have seemed peculiar to us that you could live at the end of a road you'd never heard of.

'Avenida Grau.' I insist. 'Avenida Miguel Grau.'

'Are you sure it's around here?' they ask as one.

Click, click.

Victor takes over in the next semi-empty store. This time the woman with nothing to sell and no one to sell it to nods enthusiastically. 'Behind the green wall,' she tells us.

The short, bare, nameless streets are all so similar it's like winding round a maze. Left? Right? Haven't we already passed these build-ings? Haven't we already been on this block? Is there something familiar about that dog? that goat? that garbage smouldering in the gutter? A handful of pebbles shower behind us. 'Don't speed up,' warns Victor. 'You'll only encourage them.'

Another handful of gravel falls at our heels. I speed up anyway. '*Mira!*' I shout, as though this is the reason for my sudden haste. '*Mira! La pared verde!*'

But all that's behind the green wall is another nameless dirt road bordered by trash. I hope I don't cry.

It's been a very long day. We both slept badly, disturbed by the comradely noise of the other gringos playing cards and drinking beer in the café in the lobby till late; disturbed by the mouldy aroma of the room and the mice that scampered over our beds and in and out of the bag where the peanuts and cream crackers were hidden; disturbed by the old lady in the room across from ours who started scrubbing the hall at three in the morning. We haven't eaten since breakfast – the bananas and crackers not wanted by the mice. We're hopelessly, irrevocably in the wrong place.

Victor gives me one of his looks. 'Are you going to cry?'

I am about to say that I am not going to cry when he grabs my arm. 'What was that?'

Down on the road on the other side of the green wall where children play with planks and rusted cans and skinny dogs claw through the rubbish, something large and wheeled just shambled by in a cloud of fumes and dust. A bus.

A small, compact man, as Peruvian as the President, is coming out of the shop near what could be a bus stop with an ice-pop in one hand and his other hand on the shoulder of his wife. 'Where are you going?' he calls out to us as we step into the road to flag down the bus charging towards us,

Don't speak to anyone you don't know.

We climb into the bus. As far as I'm concerned, I'll go wherever the bus is going, but Victor still has standards. 'We want to go to Avenida Grau,' he tells the driver. 'We want the bus station.'

His eyes on the mirror, the driver assimilates this information with the speed and efficiency of the real professional and removes his hand from the gearstick just long enough to wave us away. The bus starts to move and he shifts into second.

'I guess it must be the wrong bus,' I comment as we back down into the street, helped that last crucial step by the jolting of the bus as it pulls away.

The man who seems to want to help us is waiting on the kerb. His wife is gone. He smiles over his ice-pop, the Cheshire cat grinning from a tree plastered with conflicting road signs. 'Where are you going?'

I give Victor a look. Be wary of overfriendly people. They always want something.

Victor ignores me. 'We're looking for the bus station of Cruz del

Sur,' he tells the over-friendly stranger. 'On Avenida Grau.'

'Avenida Grau?' He shakes his head and points back the way we came. 'You're on the other side of town,' he says, sounding as concerned about this as I feel. 'You're miles away.' He bites into his ice. 'Come with me.'

We go with him. Left, right, left, right. We turn a corner and there it is, the back end of Avenida Grau, right where we left it. Our new friend stands with us while we wait for the bus. I'll tell the conductor where you want to get off, he assures us. You have to be careful in Lima, he warns us. How long have we been here? How long are we staying? Where are we from? He's been here ten years. He comes from Japan.

'Why are you here?' asks Victor as the three of us stand in the dust, peering up the road for some sign of our bus.

He finishes the pop and tosses the stick into the gutter. 'We all have to be somewhere,' he says.

Victor laughs. The first one we've managed between us all day. 'Another bleedin' Taoist.'

It would seem that not only do we all have to be somewhere, but Victor and I have to be in Lima. For five days at least. It's fate, it's destiny; its a pain in the ass. But the roads are impassable and the bridge is definitely down.

Every day we fight our way through the market streets to the bus stations off Avenida Grau, and every day we return without tickets. 'Come back tomorrow,' says the agent at Cruz del Sur on day one. 'Come back tomorrow,' he says on tomorrow. 'Come back tomorrow . . .' The other companies all say the same. 'Mañana. Posible.' Victor, his natural impatience tempered by the Taoist lessons we've been learning, is philosophical. We have plenty to do, says Victor. We can check in with the airline. We can buy another book in English. We can eat up for the walk to Machu Picchu. We can shop for souvenirs. We can mail back to Judy the things we don't want to lug all the way to Cuzco.

Imagine this: You have been travelling now for nearly six months, living rough, doing without the luxuries you used to consider necessities, like hot showers and comfortable beds and regular meals, and through it all you have been promising yourself one special treat. Sometimes, when the church bells are ringing at five in the morning, or you've had three days of nothing but cold rice and chips, you and your companion discuss this promised splurge the way courting couples discuss the house they'll live in once they're married or a businessman the car he'll get when he makes VP. 'In Lima,' one of you would say. 'In Lima,' the other would agree. 'Real coffee,' the first would continue. Instead of the usual smells of damp and excrement and toxic wastes, the distinct aroma of fresh coffee would drift through the room like a cloud of blossoms shaken loose by a balmy breeze. 'Christ, I can taste it,' the second would say. And the first would agree. Strong, freshly ground coffee, the best in the world, prepared by people who aren't English or American but Latinos, connoisseurs, experts who understand coffee and how it's meant to be made. Both you and your companion can not only smell and taste this coffee – the first you'll have had since you left California – but can see the cups it's served in, the pitcher of milk, glistening with sweat, the linen tablecloth, the laughing children playing in the green and pleasant square in front of the café.

'No.' Victor holds his foot up near the railing so the little boy on the other side can see that his sneakers don't need to be polished. '*Está bien.*'

'No.' I shake my head sadly as though, if I could, there would be nothing that would make me happier than to buy a box of Chiclets from the woman with the baby strapped across her back, but it's impossible right now. She pulls back her tray with a you've-got-to-try nod.

Soldiers slowly march along the other side of the road, the road running along the Plaza de Armas, on whose site in 1541 Pizarro was murdered, sombrely protecting the Palacio de Gobierno, a little too late. Shoppers shoulder each other along the arcade, beggars sit near the 300-year-old fountain, waiting for tourists coming out of the cathedral in a beneficent mood, but the plaza we're on is quiet except for vendors and people getting money from the cash machine at the bank, a mother and daughter walking along in the Peruvian way, one with a hand on the shoulder of the other.

'He's coming,' I say to Victor. Through the windows of the restaurant I can see our waiter at the counter putting white china cups on a tray.

We sit up a little straighter, our hands folded on the red linen tablecloth, absorbing each nanosecond of this, the moment we've been waiting for for so many weeks.

Our waiter is wearing a jacket to match the tablecloth and a black bow tie. He is officious and polite. Sliding and gliding rather than walking, he moves between tables like the waiter in a commercial, the tray held high with one sure hand.

Victor smiles at me and I smile at Victor. The waiter smiles at both of us. Ceremoniously, he takes the cups from his tray and places them on the table. He puts down the spoons and the red napkins and the pitcher of milk and bowl of sugar. In the centre of the table he places a large tin of Nescafé Classico, a spoon already in it.

Victor looks at me and I look at Victor. The waiter smiles at both of us.

'Come on,' says Victor. 'You've got to take a picture of this.'

Victor stops in a space in the shuffling throng between a guy selling sunglasses and a boy with several small lizards hanging on to his T-shirt like brooches. '*Muy barato!*' shouts the sunglasses man. '*Muy barato!*' shouts the merchant of lizards. Victor opens the guidebook. 'I'm sure there's one down here . . .' His finger lands on the restaurant listings. 'Here it is. La Naturaleza.'

Surprising though it may be in this, the cosmopolitan heart of Peru, we are looking for somewhere to eat. Only the Krishnas have done more to keep vegetarians alive in South America than the Chinese, but the Govinda, where everyone is friendly and you can get a three-course meal for a few soles and listen to the Krishna chant performed by dozens of different artists while you dine, is closed on Sundays.

'It sounds a little earnest,' I venture. Almost more than cold rice I loathe earnest vegetarian food.

'It doesn't matter so long as it's open,' says Victor.

Intrepid as ever, we make our way up the jammed and littered street. La Naturaleza is open. We climb the stairs to the entrance and stand together reading the menu. There's a lot of *carne vegetal* in the menu, most of it prepared in ways too elaborate for my Spanish.

A couple squeeze past us to the doorway. The girl says something to someone – or to no one – that might be 'I like your hair,' or might be something else, and laughs. We're still debating the menu of the day and what *carne vegetal con salsa criolla* might turn out to be when they come back out.

Lingering in the doorway, we're aware of them standing there, looking at us. Then the girl, as though it's us they've been waiting for, says. 'Aren't you going in?'

I turn around. She is short and dark and stocky, bright and loud, her black hair long and curly, her red mouth smiling as though we're friends. He is thin and vague and quiet, his lizard eyes closed but watchful, his smile as personal as the smile of a car salesman. 'We're thinking about it.'

Her gold earrings swing. 'Are you vegetarians?' If we are there's another vegetarian restaurant not far away . . .

'The Govinda's closed,' says Victor shortly.

'Is it?' She looks disappointed. 'You're sure?'

I nod. 'Closed on Sundays.'

She almost looks at her friend, her smile dimming for an instant. And then she laughs and shakes her hair. 'There's another one,' she says. She points through the buildings across the road towards the Plaza de Armas. 'Up there by the news building. It's better than this place. Better than Govinda.' This time she does look at her friend. 'Isn't it?'

He shakes his head. 'Great food,' he says to Victor. 'Much better than here.'

She touches my arm. 'We're going.'

He lights a cigarette. 'Why don't you come with us?'

Victor looks from her to him and then at me. 'Shall we try it?'

It's a dull and moody Sunday. The sort of Sunday you stay in bed; or break several of the rules printed on the notice tacked to the back of your bedroom door: don't talk to people you don't know, especially if they talk to you first, don't accept cigarettes or candy, or go to restaurants you don't know; make sure you left your values in the hotel safe.

Anna Maria and I walk up front, shoulders touching. Victor and Antonio walk behind. Anna Maria talks non-stop, chirpy and bubbly as a social director. Every once in a while I can make out a few words in a male voice. 'Did you party a lot in Colombia?' 'No, we're not staying long in Lima.'

Anna Maria originally comes from Lima but now she lives in Chiclayo. She works, I think, in a supermarket as a cashier, or she doesn't work in a supermarket and is a secretary. Antonio comes from Argentina. They're here on holiday, staying with her aunt. Where are we from? Where have we been? How long have we been in Lima? What have we seen? Have we been to the beach?

The really good restaurant is dark and dingy and smells like flies. Antonio shoves us towards the counter and reads from the wall. 'This is the menu of the day. Vegetable soup.' He turns to Victor and explains vegetable soup. 'Rice and lentils with vegetables.' He explains rice and lentils and vegetables to me. 'It comes with bread and a fruit juice and salad,' says Antonio.

Anna Maria is shaking her head. 'It's very good,' she says. 'Very economical.'

'I'll try it,' nods Victor. I guess I'll try it too.

'*Dos platos del día*,' Antonio tells the waiter. He looks over at Anna Maria, who only wants a drink. 'And one mixed fruit juice.'

'You two aren't eating?' asks Victor.

'We're not hungry,' says Antonio.

Antonio takes the seat facing the door. Anna Maria, sitting between him and Victor, pulls a newspaper from her bag. She gives half to Antonio. The waiter brings our soups.

While Victor and I eat, Anna Maria reveals the horoscopes for the week. Antonio's Gemini.

'Your high energy and intensity leave those who try to follow you way behind,' she reads. Antonio nods, but his reptilian stare and generic smile are on the front-page photograph of a knifing victim. 'The past month has been a difficult one for you,' Anna Maria continues, 'but things will begin to change on the sixth. Watch out for someone from your past.' Antonio gets up suddenly and goes to the loo.

Anna Maria is Scorpio. She shouldn't push herself too hard or be too trusting, and she has to curb her tendency towards impatience. Anna Maria says this is true. She can be very impatient. Venus is doing something towards the end of the week that might mean romance. Anna Maria smiles at me. What is Victor? she wants to know. What is Diana? Antonio comes back from the loo.

Besides being Taurus and Cancer, Victor and Diana are suspicious.

'Business prospects look good for the Taurean,' reads Anna Maria. 'Put your faith in your instincts and judgement. You stand to make a lot of money.'

Victor smiles and listens to his promising horoscope as though when we set out on our journey it was with the express purpose of spending our afternoons like this, tracking down our destinies in the tabloids of South America, but his eyes keep going back to Antonio.

'Cancerians are in for a hard time this month,' Anna Maria continues. 'You have to cut out unnecessary things from your life and learn whom to put your trust in.'

For my part, it has just occurred to me that though the common practice is to lure some trusting gringo into a dingy bar, drug his

Cuba Libre, drag him out in the alley, steal all his money and leave him for dead, there is no reason why you couldn't lure some trusting gringo into a dingy vegetarian restaurant and drug his vegetable soup instead.

Antonio starts talking to Victor about the party he went to at the beach last night. It was crazy. It was wild. Lots of music. Lots of drinking. His smile becomes suddenly meaningful. It is the smile one sussed and hip man of the world gives another. Lots of dope.

The waiter brings our main course.

Victor digs into his lentils and rice, smiling noncommittally. Anna Maria reads her paper. I cut up my salad. Antonio excuses himself and goes to the loo.

Anna Maria says that if we're going to Cuzco we can stay with her grandmother. Her grandmother would love to have us. She writes her grandmother's name and address on the inside of our guide-book. 'Just tell her you're friends of mine.'

Antonio comes back. He sits down, but not as though he means to stay. 'You want to come to the beach with us?' he asks Victor, as far as I can remember, apros pro nothing. 'We'll take you to a party. We'll have a good time.'

Anna Maria has returned to her reading and shows no sign of having heard.

Victor's eyes are on the back of the room, staring past Antonio's head to the passage that leads to the loo and the rear exit. I'm glancing out at the street, waiting to see if a jeep full of narcs is going to squeal to a stop outside the door. We could be on the brink of a real adventure. The sort of adventure my friends and family are terrified we might have, and that my agent and my editor would be delighted for us to have, so long as I live to write it all down. Antonio might be a cop. Or a false cop. He will take us to some party at the beach and plant drugs on us, or, considering the dullness and moodiness of the day, he might not have to plant them. Or he might not be a cop. He might just be a small-time dealer who makes extra money wandering the streets of Lima in search of gringos who look as though they know how to roll a spliff – or look stupid enough to follow him to a deserted beach..

Antonio smiles the sort of smile that makes me wish that he wouldn't. 'You haven't lived till you've been to a party in Lima.' Or died, or gone to jail, either.

One of the advantages of living closely with another person for an extended period of time is that it isn't always necessary to speak in order to communicate. Victor breaks a roll in two and gives me half. 'We can't,' he says. 'Diana has to make a phone call.'

'Jesus,' says Victor, taking in the fifty telephone booths on our right and the jam of bored but expectant callers waiting to hear their names all around us. 'This is going to take a while.'

I stare at the wall of glass over the counter of tellers that stretches along the width of the room. Behind the glass a bunch of men wearing headsets sit in front of piles of paper, microphones gripped in one hand. 'What do you think that is? Traffic control?'

There's a loud cackle of static from the several speakers positioned around the room. One of the men high over the crowd picks up a piece of paper and leans into his microphone. He says something. He says it again. A young woman jumps up from one of the benches and rushes off to a call box.

'I think I'm going out to have a cigarette,' says Victor.

I start on the right. 'I want to phone America on my AT&T calling card,' I say. She says, '*Qué?*' and I tell her again.

'I know nothing about that,' she assures me. She points to the next man along. 'He'll tell you what to do.' The next man along is sorting out some forms, an activity he continues to pursue while I explain that I want to phone America on my AT&T calling card. 'America?' He glances up. 'That's not my department,' he assures me. He jerks a thumb towards the next man along. 'Go to him, he knows what to do.' The next man along says there isn't any problem. He takes a 10-soles deposit, has me write down my name on the list for him, and tells me to go and wait.

I wait. I stand by the wall, watching the other callers as they talk and eat and drink and check their watches, straining to make some sense of the abandoned-spacecraft crackles coming out of the tannoy. At last, distinct among the Mendozas and Quesadas and Riveras, I hear my name. Seldone. Several heads turn my way. I straighten up as though I know what I'm doing, only I don't know what I'm doing because I can't make out the number of the booth. The thin, balding man reading out my name and cabin with the efficiency of an assembly-line worker putting the cherry on top of the cupcake doesn't notice me waving and miming incomprehension, though everyone else does. He reads them out again. I still don't catch the number. He moves on, his voice suddenly clear and distinct as the voice of Jehovah wanting you to eviscerate a son. 'Wilson Cristobal, number 48.' I race back to the first clerk. 'I can't understand him,' I bleat. 'What number did he say?' She doesn't know.

'Don't worry,' she says. 'Go back where you were. He'll say it again.'

I don't go back to where I was. I move to a spot that is under a speaker and easily seen from the control room. Minutes pass, and then, like a marble thrown among the pearls, 'Seldone.' I look up at the speaker, as though this may help. It doesn't. 'Seldone,' he says again. And then a number that might be any number between twenty and sixty. There's nothing like a little desperation for breaking down the inhibitions of decades. I don't care what the seventy or so people in this room think of me. I don't care if they all go home and tell stories about the mad gringa in the Entel office. I don't care if their opinion of America and its fine, freedom-loving people suffers as a result of my behaviour. 'I can't understand you!' I shout back. 'I can't understand what number you're saying!'

The man with the headsets and the microphone and the magic number laughs at something said by the chap next to him. My tearducts feel shaky. And then I hear it. 'Forty-three!' 'Forty-three!' 'Forty-three!' coming from all directions. I look around. 'Forty-three!' everyone around me is shouting. 'Forty-three!' If only I knew where forty-three was. The man with the parrot gets up and opens a cabin door. 'Señorita,' he shouts. 'Forty-three!'

The second Entel office is long and narrow, purpose-built for economy and practicality, formica counter, linoleum floor, fluorescent lights, the not recently painted walls adorned by a few calendars – a blonde in a bathing suit, a small child, also blonde, with a puppy, a basket of kittens – and a clock that tells the wrong time. It reminds me of a bus station; a bus station with two dozen open telephone booths lined up along one wall. At least half the phones are being used by people talking a little loudly, banging receivers to clear the static, dropping coins on to the problematical metal shelves.

'This could take a while,' says Victor. 'I'm going outside for a smoke.'

Though there are three people being busy at desks behind it, there is no one actually manning the counter. I decide to try the window at the far end of the room that says International Calls. The woman behind the window that says International Calls is reading a photo-novel, but she looks up at my greeting, putting one nail the colour of stage blood under the picture of a weeping woman with a handkerchief up to her eyes. 'Sí?'

I explain to her that I want to make a call to the United States using my AT&T calling card.

She shakes her head. 'I know nothing about that,' she says. 'Go to the desk,' she advises. 'Ask for the manager.'

I go to the desk and ask for the manager. The manager is a smiling, genial man who exudes a calm sense of authority and control. Here, I feel – and it is not a feeling I have often any more – is someone who knows what he's doing. I tell him that I want to make a call to the United States using my AT&T calling card. He smiles and nods, and when I'm through he says I can't do it. I tell him that I can. I tell him that, as it turned out, I couldn't at the Entel office off the Plaza San Martín, that having finally gotten into a kiosk I spent fifteen minutes arguing with the long-distance operator because she claimed I didn't have a correct AT&T number and I insisted that I did, and another five minutes discussing the situation with her supervisor, who told me that I couldn't phone from there on my card but I could at the other Entel office.

'This,' I say, summing up like a prosecuting attorney, 'is the other Entel office.'

He can't, of course, deny this. It is the other Entel office. But I still can't dial America direct on my AT&T calling card. Not here. Not in Lima, once the grandest, most sophisticated city in South America, still the capital of Peru.

'You can make a collect call,' he says with authority, with the confidence of a man who has been doing his job for ten or twenty years, who is here five or even six days a week, who has never once in all those years seen a gringa call Brooklyn on her AT&T card, 'or you can pay the cashier, but that's all.'

He goes back to his desk. I go over to the phones, wondering what sort of welcome a collect call from Lima will get from Tommi. I read the instructions taped on the phone. It tells me when and where to put the coins. It tells me when to dial. It tells me what to do if I want to call out of the city, if I want to call out of the country, if I want to use my AT&T calling card to phone the States direct.

'Long time no hear!' says Tommi. 'We were gettin' a little worried about you. I really wish you'd call more often.'

Ahead of us at the end of the broad, dusty road lined with garbage, small houses and old American cars is the boardwalk, far enough away to seem almost attractive, and beyond it the ocean, neither glass-blue nor green as jade but the colour of lightly milked tea.

But there's an upside to most things.

'At least we're not in Lima,' says Victor.

We're in Pisco. The largest port between Callao and Matarani, once the site of San Martín's headquarters, now a holiday town where you can sit at a café on the main square eating seafood and drinking Pisco sours, or catch a tour to see the sea lions, the flamingos and the Ballestas Islands. Pisco, where the patriots were defeated in 1822.

'No,' I agree. 'We're in Hastings.' Or at the Jersey shore, or at any one of a thousand other shabby seaside resorts where salt and squawking and sadness all mingle in the air.

But nothing will dent Victor's optimism. 'At least the youth hostel has a kitchen.' He stops at the corner, checks in the guidebook and looks to the left, down a deserted beach road that leads back to the ocean. 'Now all we have to do is find it.'

'I don't really worry about the cops,' the Swedish girl is saying. 'They're really only interested in drugs, aren't they?' She pauses long enough to take another bite of her pink and yellow ice-cream, which isn't quite long enough for anyone in the kitchen to answer her. 'And I don't touch drugs.' The Swedish girl is called Chris.

The French girl sprinkles some salt and pepper into the sauce the German guy is stirring. 'Me neither.'

'Um,' says the German guy.

The English bloke, taking a quick look into the pot he's got simmering on the back burner, and the American woman, watching him take a quick look into the pot on the back burner, are noncommittal.

'I mean, really,' the Swedish girl continues, shaking a few Pringles potato chips from their container into her hand. 'Besides leading to crime and everything, all drugs really do is wreck your health, ruin your skin and age you prematurely.' She'd probably get along quite well with Mrs Thatcher and my mother. 'Why risk getting thrown in prison for that?'

The German guy is comparing his recipe for spaghetti sauce with the recipe of the French girl and finding them strikingly similar. The French girl is too. The English bloke is mumbling to the onions as he tosses them into the pot. It's up to the American to answer.

'No one would do drugs if all they did was give you acne,' I suggest.

The suggestion evaporates around the Swedish girl. 'I have a very sensitive body,' she explains, crunching. 'I'm allergic to wheat, and red meat, and mint, and sometimes chicken.' She finishes the ice-cream and drops the stick on the table. 'It's made me very aware.'

The French girl glances over, not quite managing not to smile. The German guy changes the subject. 'So you two came from Lima,' he says to the English bloke. 'How was it? You have any trouble?' He takes a taste from the spoon the French girl is holding out to him.

The English bloke says that despite Lima's reputation we didn't really have what you could call trouble.

'You're lucky,' says the German guy. He knows people who went through worse, but he himself lost his camera and was held up at knifepoint going back to his hotel one night. 'Scared the shit out of me,' he says.

The French girl murmurs sympathetically.

'It wouldn't really bother me,' says the Swedish girl, temporarily forgetting the sensitivity of her body, 'because all they could really do is cut me.' She shakes the last crumbs of potato chips into her hand. 'And anyway, you can always tell by their eyes what the situation is.'

The German guy looks at the French girl. The English bloke looks at me. If the Swedish girl can't tell by looking at the eyes of the men in the kitchen that they would both like to stuff something other than potato chips and ice-cream into her mouth it seems unlikely that she could judge what's going on in the mind of a Peruvian chap with a knife.

Victor takes the plate of chopped carrots from me and tosses them in with the onions. 'They could do more than cut you,' he says.

Beside him at the stove, the German guy tastes his spaghetti sauce. 'They could kill you.' He glances at Victor.

But I haven't travelled all these months with Victor Sanchez for nothing. I start chopping the tomatoes. 'Or they could rape you,' I offer.

'I don't really worry about that kind of thing,' says the Swedish girl. 'I lived in the Bronx for two months. I can handle anything.' Finished with her Pringles, she opens a packet of corn chips. 'God, I'm so hungry,' she goes on above the sound of tearing cellophane. 'My friends back home won't recognise me. I've wasted away to nothing. You can't believe how much weight I've lost on this trip.'

Now everyone – the German guy, the French girl, the English bloke and I – look at the Swedish girl. She's right, we can't believe it.

The corn chips opened, and the possibility of starvation

forestalled for the moment, she returns to her previous line of conversation. 'I know how to handle myself,' says the Swedish girl. 'I know how to judge people.'

The French girl and the German guy confer over how much pasta to use. The French girl and the Swedish girl are sharing the room next to ours. They met the German guy on the bus.

'Corinne and I aren't worried about Lima,' says the Swedish girl. 'Are we, Corinne?'

Corinne, in the act of wresting the pasta from the German with a playful slap, doesn't answer.

Victor dumps the tomatoes into the pan with the onions. 'I'm going to take a shower,' he says, in much the way another man might say, I have to have a drink. He gives me a look. 'Keep an eye on everything.'

I keep an eye on everything while the German guy and the French girl take their meal out on to the terrace to eat it under the grapevines by candlelight and the Swedish girl fills me in on other aspects of her personal philosophy while she obliterates the corn chips.

Victor returns as the Swedish girl is saying, 'You really wouldn't believe it, but I used to be shy. Living in New York cured me of that. Living in New York made me wild.'

Victor goes straight to the stove. 'Have you been checking this?' He lifts the lid on the pot on the back burner. 'Can you remember when we put it on?'

I'm surprised I can still speak. 'Four.'

The Swedish girl is surprised I can still speak, too. Plus, something's finally caught her attention. 'Four?' she repeats. 'What have you been cooking since four o'clock?'

Victor slams the lid back down. 'Nothing,' he says. 'We're just making some tea.'

There's a rough wooden cross at the entrance to the beach. It stands on a base of blue concrete, tall and thin, decorated with a ladder and a staff, a horn and a hammer, a skull and crossbones, the sacred heart and the holy Eucharist, a tin can of flowers at its foot and the sky behind it like a slab of pale slate. It's the most beautiful crucifix I've ever seen, better than anything in gold or silver encrusted with jewels, better than anything, I'd wager, that we would have seen had we ever gotten any further into any of the churches and cathedrals we've come upon than the signs in the basilica that say Keep

Your Basilica Clean and Have You Put Enough in the Collection Plate? I make Victor stop while I take a picture.

Beyond the cross the beach is deserted. It's too early for the sun-bathers with their folding chairs and umbrellas, too early for the sellers of soda and ice-cream. The beach is ours, and the murky ocean, and the clouds that look like other things – like faces and flowers and dancing dinosaurs.

We glide across the sand like ground jewels, the day all ours, heading downwards, away from the restaurants and stalls at the other end. We want to keep the day ours, to sit in the sand and look out towards an unknown horizon, imagining not blood on the beach and the patriots slaughtered on the shore but galleons materialising like ghosts, reed boats bobbing on the water like birds. Imagining . . .

Victor takes a picture of me in my bandanna and my mirrored sunglasses with my back to the ocean as though I'm standing on the edge of the world. I take a picture of him in his red bandanna and the white silk shirt he had made in India, his back to the ocean as though he's just walked ashore.

The waves are speaking, a gabble of low voices telling sad stories, telling terrifying tales, whispering secrets that everything else on the planet forgot centuries ago. The sky sings along.

We climb over the first quay, past the man pushing his boat out and the dog chasing waves. We're talking about something – about something that made us laugh or the drummer and the guy in drag who came into the Chinese restaurant on our last night in Lima or an album we wish we could hear now; something – and I'm thinking about unicorns, envisioning a unicorn with black and silver ribbons in its mane. We come to a small inlet, a pool of water the only way across.

'Go on or go back?' asks Victor.

The way I'm feeling I could almost jump it, or just float over it, or just walk through, enjoying the feel of the water seeping through my sneakers and the sand shifting between my toes. 'Go on.'

But we don't go on.

Victor is a few feet ahead of me, about to cross the inlet, but he is no longer alone. There is a man on either side of him, men in jeans with their shirts wrapped around their heads – which might in other circumstances make them look like construction workers on an August day in Alabama, but which here makes them look like warriors. I don't see the knife till Victor falls to the ground. I can't see their eyes, but I have no trouble assessing the situation. He's about to be killed. Ahead of us, on the next quay, four boys sit watching, their legs dangling over the edge.

So now I know the real reason you should never take drugs. Victor's about to be killed by two yobs with a dirty fishing knife and there's a man with a shirt wrapped around his head and his arm wrapped around my neck.

'*Tranquilo*,' he says.

I am not feeling *tranquilo*. I have always wondered, as one does, what I would do if my life or the life of someone else were being threatened, and now I know. I'm really mad. I'm furious that I'm powerless to help Victor. I'm furious that I was thinking about unicorns and didn't even hear them coming. I'm angry that there's not anything I can do to even help myself.

'*Tranquilo*,' says the man, tightening his grip.

Go for the balls. That's the advice men give you in those late-night discussions in the back rooms of bars when the conversation turns to rape and beating. Go for the balls.

Experience has shown that most of the advice men give you in your life is wrong. But not this piece. I know it works because I hit the ground with such force that I feel the sand break beneath me. The man falls beside me, his arms around me, '*Tranquilo, tranquilo*,' he pants.

I lie still. We have nothing to steal. Our passports and travellers' cheques are under our bunks at the youth hostel. The thought makes me *tranquilo*. One of the men has the knife to Victor's throat, the other is going through our bag. Victor's eyes are on the knife, which trembles near him like an hysterical wasp. 'Don't touch me with that,' he says, trying to keep from being accidentally stabbed. 'Get away from me with that bleedin' knife.' My eyes are on the few things we brought with us as they hit the sand: the packet of biscuits, the backgammon set, the cheap plastic camera. The searcher stands up, waving the empty bag. '*Nada!*' he shouts to the guy holding me. '*No hay nada.*' Victor pulls his own knife from his pocket. 'Use this!' he says, throwing it on the sand. 'Just get away from me with that bleedin' thing.' Reminded, the searcher starts digging at Victor's pockets. A few coins, a wadge of toilet paper, a small spiral notebook and the stub of a pencil. '*Nada!*' he screams. '*Nada!*' Even I, counting my heartbeats and waiting for my life if not to flash at least to lope past my eyes in a quick shuffle – the disasters and catastrophes, the missed opportunities, the mistakes, of which this moment could be counted as one of the worst – can tell that these are not professional thieves, cool and practised and sure of themselves. They're as frightened as we are. More frightened. They're even less sure about what they're doing, which makes me almost as frightened as they are. The knife quivers near Victor's skin and he pulls back his neck.

'Stop! Stop, I have money,' I scream, as Victor shouts out, 'She's got the money!'

Suddenly everyone's interested in me. 'She's got it!' shrieks the searcher. The knife dances around Victor's throat. My new companion makes a go for my jeans. I push his hand away. 'I'll get it,' I say. 'Just wait a minute.' He pulls back his hand.

The first man picks up the camera from the sand. 'If you're taking that,' says Victor, 'let us have the film.' The man opens the back of the camera and tosses the film cartridge into the sand as the man holding me snatches the money from my hand and drops me back down.

And then they are gone. Not like ghosts, or memories, or the good times that will never come again, but like thieves, strutting across the beach, twirling the camera over their heads, counting our bills and laughing, slapping each other on the back.

'You all right?' calls Victor.

Except for my ribs and my back and my pride. I nod. 'You?'

'Christ,' says Victor. 'Did you see that knife?'

We walk back the way we came. All Victor can talk about is the knife. 'Did you see that knife?' he keeps asking me. Just the thought of it makes him shudder. 'It was filthy. All he had to do was touch me with it and I'd be dead of something.' He shudders again. 'Whatever happened to the glint of cold steel?' he demands. 'It was more like the shimmer of fish guts.' He holds up his head. 'You're sure he didn't nick me?'

'I'm not telling you again,' I say, nimbly stepping over a pool of seaweed studded with used syringes and condoms. 'Though I do think it's pretty endearing that if you were going to mug people at knifepoint on a beach you'd make sure you used a clean knife.'

'Of course I would,' says Victor, steering me clear of the dead puppy and the dirty tampons. 'I'm considerate of other people.'

At last we come to a church on a plaza, shops and vendors around the square. Victor has enough change still in one pocket to buy us two warm bottles of Coke. We sit on the kerb, surrounded by three barefoot boys who watch each sip we take as though we're all lost in the desert and we've got the water.

'What a morning,' says Victor. He hands the smallest boy his half-finished soda and they pass it between them, you first, no, you first, no you.

'Maybe next time we travel,' I say, 'we should bring an adult along.'

'What?' says Victor. 'And spoil all the fun?'

26

I HAVE SEEN THIS MOVIE BEFORE

Everything around and behind the station is obscure and slipping away – the trees and buildings, the roads jammed with traffic, the climbing streets of the town – as though the barn-like building, the glinting statue of the Virgin, the platform and the slatted gates, the old train wrapped in clouds, its lights a dusky yellow behind the dusty panes, have all been carved from the night. The cab stops a few feet into the drive, unable to move on. Carved from the night and dropped into a human moat. 'Be careful,' says the cab driver, nodding to the bodies oozing around us. 'They're all thieves.'

Comforted by these helpful words, Victor forces the back door open a few inches into the undulating mass. 'Just stick close to me,' he orders, and thrusts himself through the doorway. His momentum carries me with him. I stick close behind, my face in his backpack, my toes on his heels. He moves a few inches forward into the shouting and grabbing hands and I move with him, dodging the vendors and beggars and pickpockets.

'Cigarettes, señor . . .'
'Candy, señorita . . .'
'*Frutas* . . .'
'*Bebidas* . . .'
'*Arepas* . . .'
'*Un regalo*, señor . . .'
'*Un propio, señorita* . . .'
'Gringo, I'm hungry . . .'
'Gringita, I'm poor . . .'

'I'll clean your shoes, señorita. I'll do them really cheap . . .'

This the Third World of song and legend, teeming with colour and romance and adventure, making your heart kick into overdrive and your blood impersonate stampeding wildebeest; life on the edge. Take a picture that you will later show to your friends as you sit around the living room, drinking wine and eating Spanish olives and French cheese and Italian bread, music on the stereo and a fire in the grate. Look at that, isn't that something? Jesus Christ, it must have been incredible . . . I bet it really stank. It's the scene from dozens of films you've forgotten ever watching – adventures, thrillers, romantic comedies – an Arab market, an Eastern port, a street celebration in Africa, a railway station in Peru. This is the place where the hero loses the heroine in a ragged, churning sea of humanity, his shouts unheard in the deafening din. The place where the heroine has the map nicked from her bag while she's frantically trying to get the monkey in the fez off her head. Where, while he searches for the heroine like a man looking for a tree in a forest, someone slides a dirty blade into the hero's back and he staggers on, held up by the benignly hostile crowd, not even realising how badly he's bleeding till he notices the blood dripping on to his boots. 'Shit,' mutters the hero as he collapses into a kid selling bananas who automatically removes his wallet as he sets him on the ground. 'I knew I should've stayed in bed this morning.' The bad guys kick his legs out of their way as they pass with the heroine rolled up in a carpet. 'Get out of our way, Yanqui dog.' 'Umphumphumph,' grunts the gagged heroine, catching sight of the hero's hat. The hero doesn't hear her. He's just passed out.

'Christ,' mutters Victor as we reach the kerb. 'Which way next?'

There's a knob of people at the barred main entrance. There's a knob of people at the barred side entrance. There's a knob of people pressing against the railing at the far end, behind which the train itself can be seen, filling up fast. The only person missing from this scene is the calm, unflappable, uniformed train agent with a seasoned air of authority and a whistle around his neck, collecting the tickets, directing the confused and panicking passengers to the right car.

We make for the railing. Victor surges forward, his size alone making room for him, till he is just a blob of purple bobbing above everyone else's head. Step by step, clutching my pack, I battle after him, pretending to be deaf.

'Señorita! Señorita!'

The blob of purple is near the gate. I shove a little harder, step a little faster.

'Señorita! Señorita!'

The blob of purple ducks out of sight.

'Señorita!

It doesn't reappear.

'Señorita!' A thin hand touches my shoulder. 'Señorita, stop!'

I turn around. My blue mirrored sunglasses are hanging in the air.

'Señorita, you dropped these.'

When I turn back, sunglasses in hand, Victor is five shouting heads in front of me, eyebrows raised. 'Now what are you doing?' he demands.

The man in the seat in front of us, who, as we have, has chained his luggage to the rack above his head, comes from Nebraska. His wife is working in Bolivia with single mothers, teaching them about hygiene and health and nutrition. 'It's not an easy job,' says the man from Nebraska. 'Not in a country where they sell kids for spare parts.' He's just bumming around, his clothes and his camping equipment in an oversized backpack, a cowboy hat on his head. 'I know what you mean,' he says, sympathising with Victor's complaints about the fishing knife held to his throat in Pisco. 'Nearly got stabbed once myself, in La Paz. It was just like you, if he'd touched me with the damn thing I would've had to have every injection they had.' While his wife tries to educate the poor single mothers of Bolivia, the man from Nebraska has been seeing the sights – 'Never had but that one bit of trouble' – and now he's wandering around Peru. 'Can't say much for the food,' says the man from Nebraska. 'Anything worth having gets exported.' His daughter and her husband used to be vegetarians, but after six months in South America they admitted defeat. 'It's bad enough if you do eat meat,' said the man from Nebraska. 'The diet has less variety than your average American dog's. But if you don't eat meat . . .' He has never been to Puno, but he's heard a lot of good things about the Peruvian side of Lake Titicaca, the floating islands, the fishermen weavers. 'I think you two are in for a treat,' he says.

The train rolls and sways through the night. The man in the seat in front of us, like nearly everyone else in the car, is sleeping now, his snoring a rhythmic melange of snorts and grunts in the dark.

I remember now. It's not totally true that I never dreamed of travelling. Or at least thought about it wistfully from time to time. I used, in fact, when I was young and vulnerable to the idea of romance, to imagine that train travel would be interesting, and even fun. More interesting than a weekend spent at the local mall; more fun than watching the midnight movie with a can of beer and a bowl of potato chips. I can still see the image I had of a long, black dragon of a train, snuffling and belching, winding over fields soft in the sunshine, past tiny villages sleepy in the rain, over mountains disappeared in snow, myself at the window, pulling back the red velvet curtain, wiping clear the glass, leaning back against a soft plush seat as we forged our way through the hushed, expectant night, the whistle calling like a coyote, the rails singing, the wheels as certain as the heartbeat in the womb. This, I now realise, was partially the result of reading too many novels set in England and Europe at a formative age, though part of the blame can also be placed on that peculiar American nostalgia for a forgotten, continental past.

The train shudders to a stop. In the unlit car someone coughs, a child moans, the man from Nebraska goes off like a broken car alarm. I look out of the window at the train man hurrying along the side of the track with a lantern in his hand. There is nothing to see but the barren dunes, slightly silvery in the moonlight, and, miles away, the front of the train bent towards us on a curve. Victor shifts in his sleep. The train man shouts something to his comrade in the last car.

I can't sleep.

In my childish imaginings, sleep was easy. You pulled down the blinds of your compartment, climbed into your couchette like a toy put back on the shelf for the night, and were rocked to sleep by the gentle motion of the train and the song of the tracks.

But not on the train to Puno. There are no couchettes on the train to Puno, and the seats are straight and narrow and hard. There are no blinds to shut; the train doesn't rock so much as pitch; the song of the tracks is a lonesome one that hums in your bones. Instead of drifting off into the kindly arms of sleep, I lean my head against the window and watch the moon follow the train like a hunting god, hearing old stories in the clacking of the wheels, reading older stories in the black and silver sky.

Besides which, I have to go to the bathroom.

In my childish imaginings, going to the bathroom on the train steaming through a somnolent world was not a problem. To go to the bathroom you left your cosy compartment, where the blinds were drawn and the tiny lights on, and bumped down the carpeted corridor, toilet bag and towel in hand, aimlessly glancing through the glass doors of other compartments at people drinking tea or nibbling on sandwiches or reading a book or playing cards, feeling as though you were part of a town on wheels. At the end of the quiet, sashaying corridor, you came to the toilet. You turned the long brass handle of the door, you pressed against the ceramic sink to brush your teeth as the train swayed and someone down the car sang a song about love, you sat on the wooden toilet and gazed out at the shadowy moon and the distant lights, idly wondering where you were.

But on the train to Puno there are no snug and private compartments, no carpeted corridor where you can stop for a smoke or to watch the passing scenery or walk unimpeded to the end of the car. On the train to Puno we're lucky enough to have a seat. Those who weren't quick enough getting on – or clever enough to shove their travelling companion through the nearest window to the first vacant seats they saw when they finally staggered on to the platform – are sleeping in the aisle. To go to the toilet, which is somewhere beyond the door that may or may not be locked for safety, you have to climb over the less fortunate and their luggage in the vibrating dark.

The train man screams again, the man in front of us honks and grunts, the train grinds back into motion.

I don't want to go to the bathroom. I'm worried about stepping on children. I'm worried that I won't get the carriage door opened. I'm worried that the bathroom will be occupied and I'll have to stand between cars, waiting to be jumped by some bandit of the rails; or that I'll think the bathroom is occupied and will end up standing outside like a stupid gringa until someone else turns up to use the loo. I'm worried that I'll lock myself in. I'm worried that I won't find my seat again in the dark.

Like shadows in the blackness, the woman across the aisle gets up and goes to the bathroom, comes back and falls to sleep again, a man several rows forward shuffles to the front and returns, two small children march hand in hand and vanish out the door, rematerialising minutes later, giggling in whispers.

I sigh, trying not to think about how badly I have to go, how likely it is that I can last until Puno. I rearrange myself and watch the engine, so far away that it might be part of a different train, twisting and bending through the moon-pale hills, carrying me and Victor and the man from Nebraska and hundreds of Peruvians and their chickens through the night like a needle drawing thread, suddenly imagining Franz and his mother and his sister circling the remains of Germany with no place to go, round and round and round and round. It would have been a long wait to the last stop if I'd been with them.

You're an adult, I tell myself sternly. You're a wild woman. Wild women don't balk at using the loo.

Squinting hard, I carefully step over Victor, over the bags in the aisle next to him, and over the first sleeping child. The second sleeping child, looking like a sack of potatoes in the shadows, trips me up and I land on the lap of a man who has dozed off with a bottle in his hand. The bottle, more gifted at finding clear space than I am, clanks to the floor. Several people start awake. Guided by the movement of bodies and heads, I march on. At last I reach the end of the car. I was right, I can't open the door. The man whose foot I'm standing on can, however, open the door. 'Thank you,' I whisper. 'For what?' he whispers back. There is no one in the loo, though there is evidence that several hundred people have been here recently. Different coloured bits of used tissue and toilet paper bob on the liquid that covers the floor. Someone's been sick in the sink. The window won't shut. Though those are not the real problem. Now I know why the floor is so wet. The real problem is trying to perch on a rimless toilet seat in a moving train. I brace my arms against the walls, but this doesn't actually give all the stability you might imagine. My shoulders aren't going to slip off but my feet aren't quite so sure. You would think that the sound of the train itself would make it difficult to hear a body crashing off the toilet seat at the front of the car, but you'd be wrong. Within seconds someone is pounding at the door. 'Señorita, what happened? Señorita, are you all right?'

'For Christ's sake,' Victor mutters as I finally climb back over him. 'What were you doing in there? Why didn't you take the torch? It's right at the top of my bag.'

'I thought you were sleeping,' I accuse him, collapsing into my seat.

'Who can sleep?' asks Victor, pointing out of the window at the front of the train snaking ahead of us in the dark and the upside-down moon reflected in the frozen puddles at the side of the track. 'This is better than travelling through space.'

Inflexibility is the enemy of progress, learning, experience and growth. This is not something my mother taught me at her knee when she was giving out information about taking drugs on deserted

beaches and travelling in dangerous countries with men to whom
you aren't married and who, therefore, are not legally bound to bring
you back again. My mother is less flexible than Jehovah. She should
have travelled more. Travel encourages, not to say forces, flexibility.
The traveller learns not to be too wedded to time, means or destination. The bus that should leave at 6.30 leaves at 7.45, goes three
blocks and stops for dinner. The bus that should leave at 6.30 never
comes and you have to hitch a ride in a truck. The bus that should
go to Arequipa isn't going to Arequipa today so you go to Nazco
instead. The traveller learns that the thing she swore she would
never do yesterday is going to be the thing she ends up doing today –
eating another plate of cold rice, riding at the back of the bus, getting
into a jeep in the middle of nowhere with a bunch of guys who
laugh a lot together, taking a tour.

There are several tour agencies on the same street as our hotel,
but the one recommended by Mario at the front desk is Floating
Island Tours. 'They're very good,' he assures us, flashing a brochure.
'Very reasonable. Very reliable.' But, as with any temptation to veer
from your best resolutions – no more wine, no more cigarettes, no
more chocolate, no more nacho-flavoured tortilla chips – availability
makes all the difference. Not only are Floating Island Tours next
door, they're also the only ones open on this sluggish afternoon.

The office is decorated with reed matting and colourful posters of
magical, mystical, exotic Peru. Reed baskets of plants hang from
woven bands around the room. There are several miniature reed
boats drifting across the walls. Two women sit behind the counter at
the back, brighter than the single desk lamp in pink ruffles and
metallic sequins and make-up that shines.

'Buenas tardes,' they beam, immediately reaching for forms and
brochures. 'What can we do for you?'

They can show us the beauty and wonder and traditional lifestyles
of Lake Titicaca. We confess that Mario next door has recommended
them.

'Ah, Mario!' they exclaim happily. 'Un buen hombre.' The one in
the ruffles gestures to the formica kitchen chairs in front of the
counter. 'Please sit down.'

The representatives of Floating Island Tours talk rapidly and
enthusiastically, making it sound as though Indiana Jones himself
would find it difficult to get anywhere on the lake without their
help. 'What?' Indiana would mutter, slapping his hat on his head.
'Go on my own and risk missing the really good bits when I can go

with Floating Island Tours, see everything, and be sure there'll be somewhere to get lunch?' The tour representatives argue their case eloquently. They offer to show us the real life of the floating islands, they offer us a visit to the remote and fascinating island of Taquile, they offer us a legendary lake to tool around on with men who know it as well as they know their own names. We can go for the day or we can stay overnight with an indigenous family, the price is the same. It would take hours to get to the dock on our own. When we got to the dock, if we got to the dock, and if we got to the dock on time, we would have trouble getting a reliable boat and guide. If we got a reliable boat and guide we would be at their mercy – what if the boat was needed for some other task at noon? What if the guide couldn't be bothered to take us where we wanted to go? What if the guide, reliable as he was, missed out the most interesting bit? What if the boat, as reliable as it was, sprung a leak?

'Don't laugh,' chides the lady in pink. 'It's been known to happen.'

Victor looks at me. The package is wildly expensive. 'What do you think?'

I think that though we never actually found the jungle, there's a good possibility that we could probably find the harbour. Puno is not that big a town.

He returns the agents' encouraging smiles. 'I'm not sure,' he hesitates. 'We have to get our train tickets tomorrow, too.'

Let it not be said that anything is easy in Peru. You can't just go to the station and buy a ticket for the next train to Cuzco. You can only buy it between certain hours on a certain day. Tomorrow: between eight and ten.

'We'll get the tickets for you,' says the one in gold glitter. For a nominal charge. 'You don't have to worry about queueing.'

'And you don't have all the inconvenience of having to get to us,' says her work-mate. 'We'll pick you up at your hotel, seven o'clock sharp.'

'Our hotel's next door,' I remind her.

'Sí, sí,' they laugh together. 'Seven o'clock sharp.'

'What do you think?' I ask Victor.

Victor thinks we don't have the time to fart around – Machu Picchu calls. We're only staying one day in Puno. If we stay any longer we won't have enough time to walk the Inca Trail. The Inca Trail may not be our reason for living, but it is our reason for being in Peru. If we buy the tickets to Cuzco ourselves, we won't have time to see Lake Titicaca.

I think so too. 'We might as well simplify things,' I say. Give in.

'*Bueno*,' says the one that glimmers. She takes a form out of the top drawer. 'Now, where are you staying?'

'No,' says Victor, his voice full of regret, his head shaking sadly, 'we really don't want any.'

The woman smiles, not regretfully, not sadly, but a smile full of that demon hope, and continues to pull out jumpers from her bundle. 'Look!' she cries gleefully. 'Look at the colours!'

We both nod. Lovely colours, really lovely colours, but we don't want a jumper. Victor points to his arm. I have a jumper. I would point to my own, but I refuse to take my hands out from under my armpits. If the tour guide doesn't show up soon I'll be too stiff with cold to get into the jeep.

Discouraged, but not daunted, the seller of sweaters keeps pulling. Her smile snaps back on. 'Llamas!' she shouts, stretching out a jumper decorated with blue and green llamas out in front of us. 'You don't have one with llamas.'

'And we don't want one with bloody llamas,' mutters my companion.

But the woman has already dumped the llamas back in the pile and is rummaging in her blanket for something else. She yanks it out, smiling now much in the way you'd imagine the serpent smiled when he was showing the apple to poor Eve. 'Gloves!' She waves the bunch of gloves in our faces. 'Gloves!'

'All right,' says Victor. 'Let's look at the gloves.'

If you venture out for a newspaper or a carton of milk at seven in the morning in my neighbourhood in London you'll find yourself wandering the streets with the early-rising homeless and the local cats, gazing as wistfully as they into the caged storefronts like the Little Match Girl. Nobody sells anything before eight in my area. But not so Puno. By seven o'clock in Puno you just have to stand still for a few minutes to be offered cigarettes, sweets, shoeshines, model reed boats, soft drinks, a full range of woollen goods, mostly with llamas, and several rides to the harbour.

We put on our new gloves and look up and down the road again. The clock in the hotel lobby – a portrait of Jesus that makes him look less like the Messiah than a chap who's been on thorazine too long – says 7.30. An awned tricycle teeters to a stop inches from our toes. The driver leans towards us. 'Lake Titicaca!' he shouts. 'You want to see the lake?'

'Maybe we should just get a cab.'

'And then what?' asks Victor. 'We don't know what boat we're on.'

'Lake Titicaca!' screams the driver of the tricycle. 'Very cheap. Only two soles.'

'Maybe we could take another boat.'

It is Victor, however, who has the clinching argument. 'We've already paid.' He waves the driver away. 'Christ,' says Victor as the tricycle disappears at the corner. 'Who takes a tour with people who can't even remember that you're staying next door? We should've known they'd never show up on time.'

I rub my hands in my hand-knitted gloves, making the llamas move. It looks like we do.

Another small, rounded woman with black braids and a sackful of jumpers stops beside us. 'Hand-made sweaters,' she says, smiling so confidently you'd think we'd flagged her down. Though our reactions are quick, she starts pulling out jumpers before we can stop her.

'No, no,' says Victor. 'We don't want to buy anything now. We're going to the islands.'

He hopes.

The woman nods, her confidence undented. 'That's all right,' she says. 'I'll come back later.'

While we stand on the dock beside *Mi Amor*, waiting to board, one of the Germans tells Victor that they aren't with the tour company, they came on their own. 'It's much much cheaper. The tours are a rip-off.'

'I told you we shouldn't go with a tour,' hisses Victor as he pulls me into the boat.

With the composure of a person who can no longer be surprised by anything, I remove my foot from a bucket that looks as though it once contained blood. 'What? And risk not getting to the dock on time? Risk not getting a reliable boat?'

Mi Amor, though possessing a certain homely charm, is not a luxury craft. She's a fishing boat, by the smell of her, has seen better years by the look of her, and has either recently been bathed or sunk, judging by the state of the deck.

'Hurry them up,' the captain shouts to the first mate, who, like him, is wearing a traditional shirt and waistcoat, to reassure us, I assume, that they are the genuine article. He glances at Victor and me. 'We have time to make up.'

The first mate hurries us up. 'Señores, señoritas, please take your seats.'

We wade across to the peeling benches, shove a net out of the way, and gingerly take our seats as instructed. The captain takes his seat among the cargo and the solitary chicken in a plastic bag at the front of the boat. The first mate and his son take theirs on either side of the rudder. The Italian girl turns up her personal stereo. Her mother takes out her compact and lipstick. Her boyfriend puts on his sunglasses. The Americans start pulling sunblock and water from their bags. The Germans bring out a flask of hot tea. The engine rumbles, gags, and dies. The engine rumbles, gags, and dies. The first mate lifts the hatch on the wooden box in the centre of the deck and looks at the engine. He picks a dripping length of pipe up from the floor and whacks it around inside the box.

'*Bueno!*' shouts the captain as the engine catches in a quivering roar.

'I hope I don't get seasick,' says one of the Americans. 'Remember how seasick I was in Bolivia?'

The Italian girl bobs her head to the music. Her mother starts doing her nails. One of the Germans takes a pair of binoculars out of his pack and begins to polish the lenses. We pull away from the dock, slowly and purposefully, as befits a reliable boat with a reliable crew. Another sound surfaces above the noise of the engine: it's the sound of wood being wrenched apart very close by. The American girl who is prone to seasickness jumps and screams as part of the dock – the part still attached to *Mi Amor* by a rope – crashes into the water behind her. Her scream turns into words. 'I can't swim! I can't swim!'

'Thank God we didn't listen to you and not take the tour,' says Victor. 'This is going to be fun.'

The lake spreads out in all directions, still and blue, dotted with clumps of reeds and distant islands, high and green. It reminds me of butter.

'Butter?' repeats Victor, ducking back as another boat passes and sprays us with water. 'Lake Titicaca reminds you of butter?'

You can see Victor's point. Lake Titicaca, according to the first mate, who from time to time shouts some detail above the engine's growl about the lake and its history that he clearly knows as well as he knows his own name, having said it so much more often, is the highest navigable lake in the world, the largest lake in South America, and the home of the ingenious Uros, who took to the water centuries ago in order to get away from less mind-your-own-business tribes like the Collas and the Incas. It is the Uros who live on the floating islands – a phrase which conjures images of gently drifting hills covered in trees and dusted with flowers, trailing clouds, drawing fish that shine like stars in their wake, not of slabs of butter.

'It's because of Land o' Lakes butter,' I explain. Land o' Lakes butter has a picture of an Indian maiden sitting cross-legged by a blue lake beneath a yellow sun. The maiden with the pound of butter on her lap always made me think of that dire poem about the shores of Wikiwachi. 'Titicaca sounds just like Wikiwachi.'

'Not to me, it doesn't,' says Victor.

The first mate shouts out something else that no one catches, something about altitude and hotels, though the Italians smile and nod politely and the Americans turn from smearing sunblock on each other as though listening to every word.

We pass a man in a rowing boat with an outboard motor and a sheep beside him. Our boat veers left.

'We're going to stop at a floating island now,' screams the first mate.

The Americans put away their sunblock. The Italian girl takes off her headset. I turn in the direction he's pointing, half-expecting to see a miniature Bali Hi bobbing towards us over the blue water, calling, but what I see is an over-populated raft of reeds.

'We'll stop for twenty minutes,' he continues. 'You can take pictures.'

The islanders are waiting for us. Small children encircle us as we carefully pick our way across the soggy raft, hands out and voices childishly loud and clear, give me some money, give me a sweet. The Germans check their light-meters. The Americans and the Italians start taking pictures. A group of boys runs towards us, waving their model reed boats, buy one, buy one, very cheap. One of the Americans takes a picture of her boyfriend buying a boat. A group of women have spread out their displays of their own traditional crafts to one side of the central clearing, reed baskets and woven bands, buy a souvenir to take home with you, buy a memory. The Italian girl's mother takes her picture buying a memory.

'I hate this,' mutters Victor as we follow the others across the clearing to where several men and women are roasting potatoes and fish on an open fire. 'It's like walking through someone's kitchen while they're eating.'

'No it's not. It's like walking across their dining-room table.'

The Americans, the Italians and the Germans beetle around snapping photos of the reed huts and the fishing nets, the cooks, the begging children and themselves standing up to their ankles in water. Victor goes off to talk to a fisherman. I stand in the town square, thinking about buying a memory. There's no electricity here, no running water, no much of anything. It's a precarious existence, repairing the boats, repairing the nets, repairing the island, waiting for tourists to come with their oohs and wows and cameras, their money and pockets full of sweets and toys.

'You see,' I say to Victor as we all troop back on to the boat. 'It is like Land o' Lakes.' There you are, the descendants of people who successfully avoided being taken over by the Incas, still floating on your island of rotting reeds while you watch the white men march all over your home in their hiking boots and trainers. It's not that different from ending up on a box of butter. 'It makes you seriously reconsider the phrase "He who laughs last laughs longest."'

'It makes you realise you're in the movie where the white man always wins,' says Victor.

'Smoke,' shouts one of the Germans. 'How do you say "smoke" in Spanish?'

This one I know. I asked Juan Mario when we were being asphyxiated by his fire in the hut in Quilotoa. 'H·umo,' I say, turning around.

Victor turns around, too. 'Shit,' he says.

'Humo! Humo!' shout the Germans.

'Jesus H. Christ,' says the American who hasn't dozed off. 'The engine's on fire.'

Which does, in fact, seem to be true. Dark smoke, not a lot, perhaps, but enough to be noticeable, is squirming out of the cracks in the hatch.

Only the first mate doesn't seem to take this as a bad sign. 'Es nada,' he says, giving his small son the rudder and coming over to take a closer look.

The Italians look up from their game of cards. 'Is something wrong?'

The first mate shakes his head. 'No, no, there is nothing wrong.' He smiles at all of us. 'Just a little smoke.' He shouts something to the captain in Quechua that might, of course, be, 'there's nothing really wrong, but there is a little smoke here that wasn't here before', or might be something else. Without turning around, the captain cuts the engine.

The sudden silence wakes the other Americans.

'Are we there already?' asks the girl who can't swim.

One of the Germans hands the first mate a small fire-extinguisher.

By the time we reach Taquile, the Americans are looking a little red around the noses, the Italians are pantomiming to the first mate the question, 'Can we buy film on the island?', and Victor and I are in a better mood. The three-hour journey has left the dirty streets and scavenging dogs, the tour agencies and cigarette boys of Puno, the bay Indians on their beds of reeds, and the bitterness that has been building since 7 am far behind. We're happy again. The tour isn't so bad. Overpriced, yes. Under-toured, considering the fact that, as it turns out, we are the only ones on board who are with Floating Island, definitely. And we could have done without the invasion of the islanders. But not so bad. Not so bad when you see Taquile, a small but perfect mountain island, serenely green and shining against a sunny sky.

'Jeez,' says one of the Americans. 'We don't have to climb those steps, do we?'

The captain looks at me and Victor. 'If you're not staying the night, be back here by two.'

Victor looks at the watch of the nearest American. It's 12.33.

'Two?' repeats Victor. 'Back here by two?'

The captain nods. '*Dos en punto.*'

'But that's not enough time,' argues Victor as the others and their backpacks struggle out of *Mi Amor*. 'What about seeing the island?' The Inca and pre-Inca ruins? The Inca terracing? The tranquil scenery? The farmers and fishermen going about their traditional lives?

'Two,' says the captain. 'After lunch. There's a restaurant in the square.'

Victor mutters about money-grabbing tour operators and the imbeciles who pay a fortune to travel three hours each way to get to a place where all they can do is have lunch all the way up the ancient stone stairway that leads to the top, but it is all I can do just to breathe. We stagger upwards, past the Germans constantly stopping to check the scenery in their glasses, the Italians resting on a stone seat, the Americans rearranging their backpacks and putting on more sunblock, and finally reach the welcoming committee from town, three men wearing colourful traditional clothes and knitting around a small wooden table. We pay our fee and sign the register.

'Where are the ruins?' asks Victor.

The men all smile. 'Just follow the path,' says one of them. 'The restaurant's straight ahead.'

Later that night, cold, tired and hungry, we are standing in a doorway out of the rain, checking the address of the vegetarian restaurant in the guidebook with the street we're on, when a small, round woman with a large bundle slung over her shoulder comes up beside us.

'There you are!' she cries in delight, dropping the blanket of jumpers at our feet. 'Do you want to buy that sweater now?'

27

INTO THE LAND
OF DREAMS

The train to Cuzco is full. Six, even seven, in seats made for four in first class, mobs in second, blocked aisles. It's what my mother would describe as like 'riding in a cattle car', a not totally inaccurate simile if you allow for the fact that there are seats and windows, and that cattle don't usually travel with half their possessions and aren't likely to walk off with yours if you forget to chain them to the rack or wedge them under your seat.

Fritz taps his hard-boiled egg on the table between us. So long as you have a couple of hard-boiled eggs with you, Fritz maintains, you will never starve. 'At least this is better than travelling in India,' he says.

The baby behind Fritz and Gemma is wearing pink Dr Denton's and a red headband with a large red flower in the front, making her look like a sleepy flapper. The baby behind Fritz and Gemma is being held out of the window so that she doesn't throw up on the seat.

Gemma rolls her eyes. 'India!'

Victor smiles. 'India!'

The crowds, the chaos, the soot. The queues, the bureaucracy, the meaninglessness of time. Fighting to get your seat back every time you left it for a few minutes. Children pissing on your shoes. The feeling that you could drown in people, suffocate in the simple act of trying to get on a train.

With Victor, I am the non-traveller, the ingenue in the group. Victor has gone on his own to India and Morocco. I've been to

France, Spain, Italy and Milton Keynes, but always under heavy escort. Victor has walked through the Himalyas, crashed in monasteries, ridden elephants, lived in a tree-house surrounded by monkeys. The most exciting things that have happened to me in my previous journeys to foreign ports and strange places were getting thrown off the bus to Pisa for not paying my fare and being knocked into a fountain in a shopping mall by a fleeing thief.

When it comes to trekking through the Third World, however, Fritz and Gemma make even Victor seem like a greenhorn. Fritz and Gemma feel about reckless adventure the way most of us feel about a cup of tea. They shy away from any trail too beaten, any path too smooth. Like us, they surreptitiously do all their laundry in sinks and showers, unlike us they always carry a stove and a sleeping bag, just in case. Fritz and Gemma are old pros. Fritz can fix anything from a truck to a broken zip with minimum equipment, travels prepared for any impossible emergency, once repaired a broken crankshaft on the Sahara because he had with him, of course, just the right tool. Fritz and Gemma have crossed the globe in boats, cars, trains, buses and planes, drawn to places that attract few visitors and fewer tourists, taking chances that anyone with a choice would rather not take. Even when their children were small and you would have expected them to restrict their travels to package tours in Greece, they buggered off to India and Africa every chance they got. Fritz has driven a bus up a mountain in Africa, the driver singing beside him, too drunk to argue about being deposed; he and Gemma have danced in whorehouses, and broken down on deserts, and been chased by pirates. South America is a doddle to Fritz and Gemma. They know the ropes. They're experienced.

'Or Mozambique,' Fritz continues. 'Mozambique had its difficult moments.'

Gemma nods. Or Mozambique.

'You should try the commuter train to Long Island on a Friday night,' I say, trying to hold up my end of the conversation. 'Now, that's real hell.'

'Oh, America!' says Fritz. American Customs wouldn't let them cross the border till they'd searched their car. After American Customs searched their car, they wouldn't let them cross the border till they'd confiscated the seeds they'd brought from Mexico to plant in their garden in Holland. Seeds! Did they think seeds couldn't cross the border on their own? 'Americans think they can control everything. They want it all wrapped in clingfilm.'

The rest of the world wraps nothing in clingfilm. It doesn't worry about germs, or boiling the water, or anarchy, or unpasteurised milk, or unpeeled fruit. The rest of the world gave up on control long ago. They've seen it all before – too often and too many times – to worry about what might happen next; to believe you can hold death at bay with bright lights and plastic and antiseptic cleaners. The rest of the world knows it's doom alone that counts.

'Americans are afraid of the air,' laughs Fritz.

'They should be afraid of the air,' says Victor. 'Considering all they've done to destroy it.'

The terraces of beans and cocoa, the roaming sheep across the swampland, the herds of grazing llamas give way suddenly to a scattering of thatched mud huts. Several women dressed in high-crowned brown hats, full dark skirts, sweaters and cardigans in uncomplementary colours, their hair in long plaits, sit by the side of the tracks, carrier bags and bulging bundles, small children in knitted caps with rubbed-raw cheeks hanging off their shoulders. We're approaching a station. The train starts slowing down.

Fifteen minutes ago, we were alone in the Andes, or, more exactly, alone in the Andes with several hundred other passengers, but now we're surrounded by people crowding against the sides of the train selling food and souvenirs, fresh juice in a green plastic jug. In fact, many of them are the same people who surrounded the train at the last station. The same smiling young musicians still playing 'Strawberry Fields' on guitars and pan pipes, the same woman with juice in a green plastic jug, the same *empanada* and biscuit vendors.

'The cookie man!' shouts Fritz, jumping suddenly to his feet. 'I have to find the cookie man!' Fritz bought four coconut cookies at the last stop on credit because of a lack of change.

The band starts playing 'El Condor Pasa' as Fritz hurls himself into the mob on the platform.

A young man appears beside Victor, sticking a fistful of clay huts and placid Indians into his face. Ten soles.

'No, *gracias*,' says Victor.

Six soles.

'No, no.'

Four.

'No.'

Two.

'No, really . . .'

One native hut for a ballpoint pen.

Passengers are getting back on board, the sellers step back, quiet but still watchful. The man who sits across the aisle from Victor races past the window with a naked round of cheese in his arms.

Gemma raises herself in her seat. 'I wonder what happened to Fritz,' she says.

Someone starts banging on the window. It's the coconut cookie man. 'Where is he?' he's screaming. 'He owes me four soles.'

'He's looking for you,' I shout back. 'He's out on the platform.'

The train jolts and creaks.

'My money!' screams the cookie man. 'I want my money.'

Gemma is craning her neck. 'Now where's he got to?'

The train jolts again. I hand 4 soles through the open window.

'Maybe I should go and look for him,' suggests Victor. The train starts to move.

Something akin to panic but less noble overcomes me. I don't want Victor to get out of the train to look for Fritz. I don't want Fritz to be left behind, but I'd prefer that to Victor being left behind. I am, after all, the greenhorn here. I have not been left alone with a tyre iron while my companion walked off across the desert in search of petrol. I have not stood at my hotel window and watched my companion being bundled into an old car by men I'd never seen before. I haven't lain ill in a brothel for ten hours waiting for my companion to return with a bottle of Coke. And nor do I want to experience any of these things. I'm American. I don't like getting too close to doom.

'No, it's all right,' says Gemma. 'He'll turn up. He always does.'

As though he heard her, Fritz turns up in that instant, a tall, thin, bearded, white-haired gringo surrounded by a two-deep circle of small, stocky, clean-shaven, black-haired Peruvians, carrying him with them as they experiment with time and space and all push their way into the train at once.

We all look at him expectantly as he collapses into his seat. His hands and face are smeared with grease.

'Well?' says Gemma.

'I couldn't find him,' says Fritz.

The eleventh and last Inca to rule the entire empire was Huayana Capac, son of the great unifier and builder Pachacutec. Dying in one of the European epidemics that moved across the continent a lot more surely and quickly than the conquistadors themselves, he divided the empire between his two sons, Atahualpa and Huascar. Which, with hindsight, can be seen as the wrong move. A fateful move. A jumping into the open arms of doom. Huayana might as well have been working for the Spaniards. Civil war ensued. Atahualpa, hoping to buy his freedom from Pizarro, promised the invader a roomful of gold and two of silver if he'd let him go. A roomful of gold and two of silver? Pizarro lost no sleep over this decision. The Spaniards were on their way to Cuzco.

After all the months of marching and fighting, the hunger and cold and lonely deaths in a hostile environment, Pizarro's men must have felt a certain amount of scepticism and disappointment as they approached the capital, sprawled across the valley like a sleeping puma, hazy with the smoke of hundreds of cooking fires. They marched past the reminiscently mediaeval thatched mud huts of the city's outskirts. This was it? They trudged on in single file as the streets, divided by channels, became paved and narrow and the houses turned to stone. Cuzco was orderly, clean and notable for its excellent sanitation, but it was nothing, really, to write home about. Nothing, really, to interest a foot soldier, never mind a king. But then they reached the heart of the capital, the great central ceremonial square of Aucaypata, surrounded by the palaces of the Incas. They discovered Coricancha, the Gold Courtyard, covered with gold. This was more like it.

'The city is the greatest and finest ever seen in this country or anywhere in the Indies,' they informed the King. 'We can assure Your Majesty that it is so beautiful and has such fine buildings that it would be remarkable even in Spain.'

And then they proceeded to destroy it.

The Incas hadn't anticipated the Spaniards. Secure in their power over their empire and accustomed to a certain amount of honesty from their citizens, their palaces had been kept as their builders had left them, their mummified bodies resting nearby. What a gift.

The Spanish stripped Coricancha, they took over the palaces, they demolished the great hall of Casana to build arcades and shops, they turned the house of the Acclahuasi, the Chosen Women, into a convent. Where Huayana Capac's palace once stood they built a church. Once Cuzco had been captured, looted and settled, its importance declined as quickly as the city itself. Fifteen years after Pizarro's arrival, the riverbanks were heaped with rubbish and there were no more gold trinkets left behind by bathing Incas and their women in the once-clear water, only filth and shit. Cuzco was no longer the capital of anything.

'But it's not all bad news,' says Victor, his eyes on the guidebook and not on the pack of young men and boys who run along beside us, shouting at the windows. 'Part of the walls of Pachacutec's palace can still be seen in the Roma restaurant in what is now the western corner of the Plaza de Armas. '

'Oh, it sounds good,' says Fritz, 'but it just won't be the same.'

We've been feeling a certain amount of scepticism and disappointment ourselves in our approach to the capital, starting with the hot springs of Aguas Calientes, described in the guide as 'steaming pools . . . in the middle of the green grass; a startling sight', which turned out to be small smoking puddles in muddy mountain grass, less startling than simply puzzling. The feeling continues now as the train, crawling slowly through the crowded, shabby outskirts of the city, finally nears the splash of lights that mark its core.

Gemma looks out of the window. 'We're going backwards,' she announces.

The rest of us look out too. The train is retracing its tracks.

'Is this right?' I ask. 'Are we supposed to go backwards?'

Fritz shrugs. Gemma shrugs.

'Maybe the driver forgot something,' says Victor.

By the time we reach the station it's too late to eat or shop or even contemplate walking to the hotel.

Fritz looks at his watch. 'Three hours off schedule, that's not too bad.'

Not too bad for them. Fritz and Gemma, equipped with the foresight that Huayana Capac could have used, booked a hotel by phone in Puno through one of the tour agencies.

We start getting our things together.

'Why don't you come with us?' asks Fritz. They're being met at the station; they'll have a room with a private hot shower; they've been given an excellent price. 'It's very popular, but it may have a vacancy.'

We, however, have made our choice, a cheap hotel that allows washing and cooking and will store your luggage while you walk the Inca Trail.

'At least we know where we're going,' says Victor, keeping the guidebook out in case it turns out that the cab driver doesn't.

The cab driver, however, does know where we're going. He just doesn't want to take us there. 'It's not a good neighbourhood,' he argues. 'It's dangerous at night.'

We don't trust policemen or cab drivers. There's too much tempting them to scams. Even cab drivers who are really jazz drummers and university students and agreeable to stopping quickly at the corner to pick up a litre of bottled water. And besides, the guide-book, usually thorough about this sort of thing, says nothing about danger. The guidebook says the hotel is friendly.

The hotel may or may not be friendly, but it is definitely full. The driver, who's been tense and watchful as he chatted about jazz drum-mers whose names I wouldn't have recognised in English while we waited for Victor to find out about a room, is visibly relieved.

'Pick another one from your book,' he says. 'But hurry. We want to get there before the tour buses.'

We pick another – also full – and then another – overpriced. 'Maybe we should've gone with Fritz and Gemma,' says Victor as he gets back in the cab for the third time. 'Everybody else is using our guidebook.'

This time the cab driver picks. 'It's a good hotel,' he says, speed-ing past buildings that rest on the remains of Inca walls. 'I take a lot of gringos there.'

There is a tour bus dead ahead of us on Calle Tiecseccocha, its brake lights flashing on as we come around the corner.

The cab rocks to a halt, its front wheel up on the kerb. 'Come on!' the driver shouts to Victor. 'I'll help you.' He opens his door and jumps onto the sidewalk. 'You mind the cab!' he shouts at me.

I sit in the cab, waiting for someone to ask me to move it or jump in the front and move it for me, wishing that for once we'd decided not to go off on our own, when suddenly a face appears at my win-dow.

I'm about to scream when I realise it's Fritz.

'Bloody tour agent!' he screams. 'He booked us into a more expen-sive hotel!'

'You don't think we might need a guide?' asks Anna.

Victor leans across the wooden table so that his chin is in the tiny vase of wild flowers, trying to hear. We are at that part in the Hare Krishna tape loop where the chanting becomes a little feverish. 'What?'

'A guide!' shouts Anna. 'Don't you think we need a guide?'

Victor still looks puzzled. The journey to Machu Picchu isn't like going round a church with someone pointing out the age of the windows, the style of the altar. It isn't like visiting the islands of Lake Titicaca. This journey is a private one. As far as he's concerned, it is enough of a concession to the warnings about the Inca Trail that we are willing to walk it with strangers. 'What for?'

Warnings aside, it's a good question. Anna does not seem like a woman in any particular need of a guide. Unlike us – unlike at least one of us – she is solid and athletic-looking, the sort of person who skis and jogs and hangs off cliff faces at the end of a rope. She started out in Nicaragua four months ago, with a friend who left her two weeks later after an argument over mosquito coils, and has been on her own ever since. Her obsession with having a guide makes me a little uneasy. Is there something we don't know; some detail of doom and destruction that we've managed to miss?

'The guides carry all the equipment,' says Anna. 'They cook—' She breaks off, distracted as the door beside her flies open and two serious young Krishnas carrying enormous plastic buckets stagger in. For visitors from countries where microwaves are as common as kettles, this is a rare and interesting sight, a bit of local colour the like of which they may never see again. Lunch has arrived at the Cuzco Govinda.

Victor, who has seen lunch arrive here before, continues the conversation. He refused a guide even the first time we rented horses in Colombia and is not about to drag one along with him on the Inca Trail. 'We can carry our own equipment and cook our own food,' he says shortly. 'It'll save a lot of money.'

Anna isn't from the frugal north of England, and she isn't convinced. 'But I've heard of trouble on the trail,' she argues, assuming that we haven't. 'Robberies . . . the Shining Path . . .'

Victor's smile is the smile of a man of infinite patience and reasonableness. 'That's why Dyan and I are looking for other people to go with us,' he says. 'There's safety in numbers.'

Anna looks from Victor to me and back again. 'Not always in the number three,' says Anna.

The buildings of Cuzco are built on Inca ruins, walls of stones as perfectly fitted and strong as they were when new; the markets are filled with souvenirs of what was: antique blankets, replica pipes and statues, replica beads and ornaments, waistcoats and purses, bags and jackets made from scraps of old textiles.

I've bought a small tin pin in the shape of a turkey perched on a spray of either flowers or feathers, a clear blue stone in its centre; a bowl, an arrowhead and what looks remarkably like a butter dish dangling beneath it on tiny chains, an ancient Inca design. Victor has bought a jaguar pipe just like one once smoked by an Inca priest. We've both bought silver pins of gods and animals that are just like the ones that once held closed the robes of the Incas and their wives. Even if we never find it, we're taking the past back home.

'*Mira*,' says Antonia, spreading out the blanket with one hand and hefting her son on her hip with the other. '*Es esquisito, no?*'

'Witches,' says Victor, pointing to the faces woven in the cloth.

'*El Inca*,' corrects Antonia, shaking her head. '*Es muy vieja.* You won't find this anywhere else.' Antonia is impressed that we are walking to Machu Picchu. She's never been there, but she hears that it's beautiful. She's seen pictures; there are postcards for sale in the shops around the plaza. She says that if we see a condor it will bring us luck.

I look at Victor. 'What do you reckon?' I ask, thinking of Incas. 'Should we go for a guide?'

'These are very hard to find,' says Antonia, re-entering the conversation. 'No one sells them cheaper.'

'It's nice,' Victor assures Antonia, running his finger over the hat of the Inca and his spreading hair. 'It's very nice.' To me he says, 'Anna will come round. We'll get another person and she'll come round.'

I touch the old blanket, made by someone with a special purpose. Every picture with a meaning; every stitch carefully planned. The machine-made ones that sell everywhere for a fraction of the price are bold and bright, their stripes uniform, their designs slightly Mexican – fishes or diamonds, or sometimes both. The colours of the Inca blanket are dull and faded; there are tears in the weave; the stripes twist and wobble. No two pictures are the same. I don't want a blanket I can buy in Camden, I want one I can only buy here. On the other hand, though I don't want a guide, I don't want to die on the way to Machu Picchu either. 'What if she doesn't?'

'There are plenty of other gringos around,' says Victor. 'We'll put up a notice in the hotel.'

'We will?' This sounds hopeful.

'Of course we will,' says Victor. 'If there's time.'

This sounds less hopeful. I've read Joseph Heller, I should have known there'd be a catch. We will if we have time, but we won't have time because we're waiting for Anna to make up her mind.

Victor takes a small woven bag, faded and stained, from the hook on the stall. 'How much is this one?' he asks Antonia. To me he says, 'Don't worry. She'll come round.'

'*Was hat er gesagt?*' asks Günther. Unlike Anna, Günther is German, not Austrian. Like Anna, he is solid and sturdy, and looks like a young man who plays tennis and squash.

Anna leans across the table. 'He said they have a list of prices from one of the camping stores,' she tells him.

Günther nods, his smile tense and thin as a tissue. He was out late last night in one of the discos with some other Germans and is not, perhaps, at his brightest or best, but even in the unreliable lighting of the Cuzco Govinda it is possible to see that he is unimpressed by the imaginative blending of East and West in the decor – pictures of Krishna in the many stages of his life, the crucified Christ, and magazine photos of flowers and kittens – by the Collected Krishna Chants playing on the tape deck, the copy of the *Bagharad Gita* in German on the shelf above Anna's head, or the incense wafting through the small, cramped room.

Victor pulls out the list and puts it down in front of Günther. 'See,' he says. 'This is everything.' His finger runs down the line: tent, stove, sleeping bags, groundsheet, backpacks, galoshes . . . 'Ninety-six dollars for the lot.'

Günther nods and looks at Anna as the front door opens and the Krishnas arrive with their plastic bins. I can see in his eyes that he was about to say, '*Was hat er gesagt?*' but has changed his mind. '*Was ist das?*' he wants to know.

Anna raises her voice above George Harrison's. 'It's lunch.'

Günther nods, his eyes still on the buckets of curried vegetables, lentil soup and rice, cloudy with steam, being lugged past him down the narrow aisle between our table and the serving counter. Then he looks at Victor and me. He isn't too impressed with us, either.

Günther is Anna's choice for number four.

'Ninety-six dollars for everything is a good price,' Victor is saying. 'And that's for five and a half days.'

'Ninety-six dollars,' says Anna loudly without having to be asked. 'It's a good price.'

'But that's just equipment,' says Günther. 'That doesn't include the admission fee. That doesn't include the train.' His eyes wander to the serving counter, where the contents of the buckets are being dished out. 'That doesn't include food.'

'It's still cheap,' says Victor.

'I think it is not much more costly with a guide,' says Günther. 'And it's more safe.'

'I doubt that,' says Victor. 'You could always be ripped off by your guides.'

'But they carry the equipment. They supply the food.' He gives the two of us another see-through smile. 'It's a hard walk, you know. Not everyone makes it. You have to be fit.'

Victor returns the smile. 'You and Anna look fit enough to me.'

Günther turns to Anna. '*Was hat er gesagt?*'

'He says we look fit enough to him,' she answers.

Günther picks up his menu. 'I wasn't meaning us,' he says. 'I was meaning you.'

'Galoshes?' Señora Muñoz raises her eyebrows and gazes at Victor over the rims of her glasses. 'No, no, no,' she says firmly. 'You don't want galoshes. Not for climbing to Machu Picchu. You want good hiking boots.'

'No, I don't,' says Victor. 'I want galoshes.'

Señora Muñoz has been patient and tolerant with us for the hour and a half it has taken us to select our equipment according to our budget. She didn't flinch when we chose the smallest, least attractive of her tents. She didn't baulk at our minimum requirements for dinnerware and cutlery. She accepted without a single 'but' our decision on the sleeping bags and backpacks. We didn't feel we needed a lantern? We didn't require air mattresses? *Bueno*. It was no skin off Señora Muñoz's nose. But she is showing signs of breaking now. She shakes her head and makes a grab for the black rubber wellies.

Victor holds firm. 'I don't want hiking boots,' he says again. 'I want dry feet.'

'But no one walks the trail in galoshes.' She gives us a smile we have seen before – and one which we are seeing more and more often of late. It's not a cold smile exactly, but it is restrained, the smile of a mother listening to a small child explaining the way to achieve world peace. 'You need strong, sturdy, comfortable boots for that.' She doesn't think we're going to make it, either.

If I were doing this trip with someone else, I wouldn't lose sleep over what might or might not happen in the next few days. Someone like Hamlet, for instance. If I were travelling with some bloke like Hamlet, we might never leave the room.

The alarm rings. It's 5 am, time for independent travellers to get up, stagger out into the pre-dawn gloom, and try to figure out how to get to the train. I sit up in my bed. Hamlet sits up in his. He turns off the alarm. I'm about to hurl myself into the chilly arms of the pre-dawn when Hamlet speaks. 'Let's think about this,' he says. 'Let's consider all the possible outcomes of our actions.'

'The possible outcome of our actions is that we'll miss the first train in nearly a week if we don't get up now,' I say.

'No,' says Hamlet. I can tell that he is shaking his head in a cautious, thoughtful manner. 'That's not what I meant. I meant what might happen if we go.'

I lie back down. We've been through this before.

He lies down himself, arms folded under his head. 'If we do go,' he continues, forgetting that we've been through this before, 'we still might not make the train.' We might get out in the street and not find a *colectivo* to take us to the station. We might find a *colectivo* to take us to the station but it might already be full. If it isn't full it might be slow, might puncture a tyre or detour to pick up someone else and we'd miss the train anyway. Which means we'd be worse off, stranded in some three-huts-and-a-gas-station town, having to come all the way back to Cuzco, where, there is every likelihood, our room would already have been let. If, on the other hand, we did find a *colectivo* to take us to the station and it managed to arrive before the train left for Machu Picchu, there's still a good chance that it would already be full. And then what? Was it worth it to have to stand all the way, squashed and jostled and risking infection from all the germs carried by the children who scrabble on at every stop, selling food made by their mothers? What if the train broke down? What if another sudden storm washed out the tracks a second time?

'So you're saying you don't want to go after all?' I ask.

Hamlet props himself up on one elbow. 'No,' says Hamlet in that laconic, slightly superior way he has. 'No, I'm not saying we shouldn't go after all. I'm just asking you to think.' Really think about what we're about to do. The Inca Trail is forty-four kilometres long. What if it is as difficult as everyone says? Sure, he's young and strong, but what about me? I'm not young. I'm strong enough, but I weigh less than your average twelve-year-old. I have no subcutaneous fat, no reserves to call on. My mother is convinced I have a heart condition. What if it turns out that I really can't make it? What if I collapse after only a few hours; only a day? Once we've started we can't just call a cab to go back. And what if I don't collapse? What if – somehow, some way – I am able, if not to keep up, to at least stagger on? Have I forgotten how I tripped and sprained my ankle seeing the ruins in Tierradentro? Have I forgotten how long that took to heal? What if this time I broke it? If I didn't fall and break a leg, I might still get altitude sickness and be unable to go on. I might cut myself badly, or burn myself badly, or, 700 metres up a mountain in a place un-inhabited for several hundred years, one of us might come down with the worse case of the shits ever seen this side of Thailand.

I pull the blanket over my head. 'Okay,' I mutter, 'so let's not go.'

'On the other hand,' Hamlet rumbles on, 'it's unlikely you'd injure your ankle again. The odds are against it.' And I was fine scaling Quito, fine climbing to Quilotoa, had no trouble scrambling around the mountains of Cajamarca. Our bowels have been steady since reaching Cuzco.

I pull the blanket down. 'So let's go.'

'There's still the chance of robbery or murder,' counters Hamlet, a man with more hands than a battleship. Alone, there would be nothing we could do to help ourselves. We might end up at the mercy of thugs like the ones who mugged us in Pisco. We might end up at the mercy of the Sendero Luminoso, guys not given to return-ing your used film.

'You're right,' I finally admit. I retreat under the covers once more. 'It's not worth the risk. There's too much that could go wrong.'

The bed creaks. 'Not so fast,' says Hamlet. 'Sure there's danger, sure there are things against it, but let's not forget that there are other things to take into consideration.' He pauses for a few minutes, taking other things into consideration. When he speaks again his voice is soft and far away. 'If we don't go,' he says, 'we might be miss-ing the experience of a lifetime.' What about all our talk, all our fantasies and days lost to dreams? Hacking our way through the jungle much like Dr Bingham, sitting side by side on an Inca wall gazing up at the stars and the impassive smile of the moon, shiver-ing together, our breath like clouds, as we watch the sun rise over the Lost City of the Incas, immortal in the warm and comforting embrace of the past?

I sit up again. 'You're right,' I say. 'We can't afford to miss it. We'd better hurry.'

'But . . .' says Hamlet.

I fall back with a groan. 'But what?'

He sighs. Dreams and fantasies are not reality. Dreams are full of magic and hope and a mythic perfection that never really was. Reality is full of dirt and blood and old rocks. 'But we might be dis-appointed.'

The café on the corner of the square is all bamboo and plants, come-and-see-this posters and traditional native crafts. There are piles of magazines and papers in Spanish, English and German, there's a cappuccino-maker and chocolate cake, and for that authentic touch there is cocoa-leaf tea. It's always packed with sophisticated Cuzcoans and more sophisticated gringos, easy to distinguish because the Cuzcoans are dressed like Westerners and the Westerners are dressed like citizens of the world in Nepalese hats made in Guatemala, antique waistcoats, llama jumpers and Ecuadorian shirts. Victor and I come here every evening to play a few games and have a couple of beers while we wait for the Govinda to open for supper. And, tonight, to discuss our next move.

I pick up the dice. Nothing is ever as you imagine it will be. In travel as in life. Aside from the danger – which, realistically can't be much greater than walking home from Euston Station at one in the morning – I'm beginning to worry that walking the Inca Trail is going to turn out to be like Christmas: weeks of feverish preparation and hysterical anticipation, and in the end it's all over in an hour and you're left sitting in a mound of used wrapping paper wondering what all the fuss was about. 'Well . . .'

Although neither of us is looking, we see the small boy with a tray of cigarettes and middle-aged eyes stop in front of our table. If it is true that in Peru they sell children to the West for spare parts, this is a child who might have been sold. Victor, who has already turned down four boys tonight whose kidneys also might easily have wound up in California or Milan, has been waiting for this one. He picks up his coffee and raises his eyes.

I don't look up, but stir the leaves in my glass of hot water while I decide what to do, hoping that the movement will create some chemical reaction. Cocoa-leaf tea is the sort of drink the intrepid traveller feels she needs to try at least once, but it isn't quite as interesting as she thought it would be. I take another sip. Stirring did nothing for it, it still tastes like hot water clogged with dead leaves. And Machu Picchu will turn out to be a pile of old stones.

Juan puts his tray on the table. 'Who's the champion this time?' he asks Victor.

'She's lucky tonight,' says Victor. 'I'm letting her win.'

Juan laughs. His missing teeth make him look almost as old as his eyes, though we have seen him look like a child, batting the white balloon covered with stars that we'd given him around the plaza with his friends this morning, just like a regular nine-year-old.

Juan is Victor's favourite among the cigarette-sellers. We run into him every morning on our way to breakfast. Victor asks for two cigarettes and Juan says, 'Then two this afternoon, and two tonight . . . Why not buy a whole pack?' We run into him every afternoon on our way to the train station to see whether there are any trains running to Machu Picchu. Victor asks for two cigarettes and Juan laughs. 'And two tonight, and two tomorrow morning . . . Why not buy a pack?' And every night we meet him in here.

Juan is bright and cheerful, full of talk and questions. He has picked up the rudiments of backgammon watching us play, but he prefers chess. He thinks that Victor must be a good basketball player because of his height. He doesn't understand why gringos – having razed the past – are so interested in everything old. 'Es loco,' said Juan. 'If I had the money, I'd buy only new things.' Juan's proudest possessions are his Chicago Bears baseball cap and a postcard of London, a picture of two fluorescent-haired punks in front of an old-fashioned call box. He was interested to learn that though there are many people in our country who don't have jobs or even homes there are no boys like him, working seven days a week from morning to night to earn a few pennies for food. 'Really?' asked Juan. 'What do the poor boys do to make money?'

'They sell drugs,' said Victor.

'Qué?' asked Juan.

'Forget it, said Victor.

Victor rolls the dice while he talks to Juan about the lost city of the Incas, occasionally glancing at me to gauge my reactions.

Juan has never been to Machu Picchu, but he hears that it's very beautiful. He's seen the posters in the stores around town. He has a friend who has been there. 'You're going to walk the whole way?' he says to Victor, but he's looking at me.

Victor moves six and three and doesn't look at me. 'Sure,' he says. 'No hay problema.'

Juan considers this for a few seconds, then he smiles in understanding. 'Ah,' he says. 'You're going with a tour.' Es mejor, he decides, going with a tour.

'You see,' I say to Victor. 'Even Juan thinks we shouldn't go alone.'

'If you'd been with him, Castenedas would've gone to Mexico with Thomson's,' mutters Victor.

I find this a little unfair. 'Even Castenedas had a guide,' I say a trifle sharply.

'Spirit guide,' says Victor. 'Not some guy who's hoping you'll give him a big tip.'

I move four and two. 'But what if it turns out to be like the meteor-crater in New Mexico . . .' A hole in the ground with an entrance fee and a souvenir shop. 'Or the petrified forest . . .' Pieces of fossilised trees scattered over the desert and a souvenir shop. 'Or the floating islands . . .'

Both Juan and Victor look at me curiously.

'Why didn't you move that one?' points Juan. 'Then you'd be safe.'

'Now what are you talking about?' asks Victor. 'Are you saying you don't want to go? Are you saying that we've come all this way to see Machu Picchu and now you don't want to see it?'

I answer Juan first. 'I don't know.' I shrug. The problem with dreams is that they can't be caught, they never really come true. 'Of course I want to see it,' I say to Victor. 'I'm just a little concerned that—'

'If we go with a tour it will be like the floating islands,' says Victor. 'It'll only be worth it if we go by ourselves.'

But maybe they aren't supposed to.

'And anyway,' continues Victor, knocking out my vulnerable chip, 'it's the journey that matters, not the destination.'

'You see?' says Juan. 'I told you you moved the wrong one.'

The woman at the cappuccino-maker hisses at Juan. 'What are you doing? You can't hang out here.'

Juan picks up his tray. '*Dos cigarillos?*' he smiles at Victor.

I take another sip of my tea. 'Tomorrow he'll buy a pack,' I promise.

Both Victor and Juan look at me curiously.

'He will?' asks Juan.

'I will?' asks Victor.

I make a face. Cold now, the tea tastes as if it might have been used to wash the dishes. But at least I can say I tried it. 'Well, you can't buy cigarettes on the Inca trail.'

The railway station is across the street from the more or less indoor market – indoors when it's sunny, not quite so indoors when it rains – which even the most resigned and weary traveller has to recognise as a considerate location. During the long, sluggish and tedious hours spent waiting to buy your tickets you at least can wander through the stalls of fruits and vegetables, knitted socks and ponchos, woven blankets and pan pipes, plasticware and kitchen goods that snake out of the market building and into the surrounding streets, haggling over prices to relieve the boredom, buying nuts and roast corn to stave off starvation, getting in the supplies of food and cocoa leaves you'll need should you ever get as far as the Inca Trail. And when you're not killing time by shopping, you still have something to watch. The Cuzconeans going about their daily lives. The cabbies and street sellers hustling for custom. The pickpockets slipping through the crowds like phantoms. The tourists who come and leave and come again, trying to find out what the hell is going on.

Right now, I am watching the two Australian sisters who were here earlier, battling their way through the sea of shoppers and vendors, shaking off offers of fresh fruit and warm soda and taxis as they determinedly move towards the stairs.

The Australians march past us up the broad stone steps of the railway station. The elder of the two checks her watch. 'Hurry up,' she says, 'it's already one,' and steps over my bag of groceries.

Victor lights a cigarette and leans back on the stairs. 'We'll let them deal with it this time,' he says.

Which is fine with me. This is our third day waiting at the station for some news of the train to Machu Picchu. Three days of come back at ten, come back at one, come back at three, come back at five, come back in the morning. Three days of waiting outside the locked doors of the station, ducking from the rain and fighting off the beggars and the vendors and the shoeshine boys while trying to overhear the rumours of accidents and washed-out tracks that rumble through the weary would-be passengers whenever another hour passes and there is still no sign of anything happening. Three days of grabbing any man who looks as though he might work for the railway – men with official hats, men with official brooms – and trying to scare some information out of them. By now it doesn't really matter if the news is good or bad, so long as it is.

'See?' the Australian girl says to her sister, her voice rising loudly and clearly above the hum of the surrounding mob. 'I told you the guard said to come back at one.' She points through the window, opaque with dirt. 'There's someone coming.' Several gringo heads turn. Like dry grass picking up fire, her words move through the foreigners, spreading down and across the broad stone steps. Someone's coming . . . someone's coming . . . they're about to open the office . . . they're starting to sell the tickets . . .

Neither Victor nor I look around as the several Germans, Israelis and Italians climb by us.

No one comes. This in itself is not significant. One and two and three and four, this afternoon and tomorrow morning are all the same. Either the trains are running or they aren't. Either someone will start selling tickets – some time – or they won't. Zen and the art of travel in Peru.

The Germans, the Israelis and the Italians, however, do think it's significant and go off again.

The Australians come over and sit down beside us. They aren't walking the trail, the elder one informs us. They don't have the time. They've been suffering from altitude. The younger sister has the green-apple splatters. They've heard of robberies and worse. The younger sister smiles at everything and says nothing. The elder smiles at nothing and does all the talking. 'You're going on your own?' she asks, her eyes moving between us. It isn't too obvious which of us she thinks is the more improbable trekker. 'Wouldn't it be better to go with someone else?'

Not if the people you find to go with you decide to go with someone else, someone who will cook their meals and carry the tents.

'The only thing we need to go with us is a train,' says Victor.

Getting to the station on time – which, as Hamlet worried, we almost didn't do – was difficult. Getting on to the hopelessly over-booked train – which also caused the young prince some concern – was difficult. Enduring the slow, rough ride sitting on our packs, buffeted by women and children – all of them, undoubtedly, riddled with germs – selling everything from lunch to toy llamas was difficult as well.

But the first quarter of a mile is harder.

I can't really tell if I'm disappointed or not yet as we come out of the woods into a stretch of huts, farmland and sketchy Inca ruins. I'm too tired. Too tired, and too out of breath. Hamlet was right, I'm not young. Everybody else who got off with us is young – the Germans, the Israelis, the Italians and the Dutch – but I'm not. I'm almost old enough to be the mother of any one of them. They must wonder what I'm doing out here, tramping through the jungle with a twenty-five-pound pack on my back, when I should be home watching TV and worrying about what my children are up to. I'm thinking of beginning to worry, too.

'Rest,' I gasp, finally reaching the rock on which Victor is waiting for me. 'I have to rest.'

'Up there,' says Victor, striding on. 'At the bend.'

To tell the truth, not only am I not young, I'm not even that strong any more, not after four months without falafels or kombu or smoked tofu. The pack that seemed quite reasonable to carry when I tried it on in our room has already gained considerable weight. I can carry a load of shopping from Camden up to Tufnell Park, but I'm not so sure about carrying this all the way to Machu Picchu. Looking forward to stopping for lunch, I stumble up the path after Victor.

The two German couples who started out with us at the entrance are sitting on the rocks at the bend in the trail, catching their breath.

'It is going to be pretty strenuous, I think,' says Wolfgang, wiping sweat from behind his glasses and looking at his map.

'It isn't so bad,' says Dieter, so large and strapping that he's carrying everything except the day bag. Dieter's gear is all serious and new. He's probably the only person on this narrow, rocky curve ever to have climbed anything higher than the Eiffel Tower. 'You only must know how to pace yourself.'

Sylkie, Wolfgang's girlfriend, smiles wanly.

Dieter's girlfriend doesn't smile.

Victor hands me half an orange. And smiles.

Wolfgang and Sylkie finish their water, heft their packs and continue on. We pick up ours and prepare to move. Dieter looks at his girlfriend. She isn't ready yet.

At the half-mile point we are passed by the guides and horses of the Israeli ex-soldiers. 'Don't you want a guide?' they shout. 'Don't you want a horse? It's a very long walk.'

We smile and stagger on behind them.

The Israelis themselves pass us a few metres later, strolling.

'You'd think they'd carry their own stuff,' Victor mumbles.

At the three-quarters-of-a-mile point we are passed by Anna and Günther's group.

'You could still join us,' shouts the lead guide. 'It's not too late.'

We smile and stagger on, watching them vanish behind another bend.

At the mile point, we collapse on a ledge covered with horse shit to have our lunch. Our rolls have been flattened, the hard-boiled eggs I bought aren't cooked, the horse whose shit we're sitting in would prefer that we ate somewhere else.

The Italians and Dutch come around the turning, determinedly forging ahead. They smile at us as though we're children playing.

'Christ,' mutters Victor. 'And we were worried about being alone.'

At a mile and a half we start on the cocoa leaves. The leaves have to be chewed to a pulp with a little ash. Lord knows what it does for your breathing, but it makes your teeth and lips green and your mouth dentist-numb. The first effect is less than attractive, the second rather pleasant. We forget not to smile when Anna's group overtakes us again.

The Italians and the Dutch are setting up camp at the first site as we near the river, talking and laughing and making coffee. I watch, for a few seconds, the steam rising from the pot of water, thinking not of the cooking fires of an ancient civilisation, safe in the clouds, but of Tennessee. We're going to be pitching our tent in the dark as usual. I can tell.

'It won't be dark for hours yet,' says Victor, reading my mind, and strides on, doing some forging of his own.

The Israelis are resting in the clearing on the other side of the bridge. It's too steep and rocky for packhorses now. Their guides have gone back.

We stop to look at the map we bought at the South American Explorers' Club in Quito. An Inca runner, hurrying to Machu Picchu with a message from Atahualpa – Don't let them find you! Or Stay away from Cuzco for a while! – would have no trouble reading it, but for anyone who hasn't done the journey several times before the map is a little vague. Left or right? It's a question of interpretation. Left dissolves into a wall of wilderness. Right goes straight up a cliff.

One of the ex-soldiers looks up from the guidebook he's studying for clues. 'Can I look at your map?'

He looks at our map. He is not an Inca runner, either, not in this life or one in the past. 'What do you think?' he asks.

It looks like left to him. It looks like left to Victor. It looks like left to me. We go left.

Half an hour later, clinging to branches to keep ourselves upright, mud up to our ankles and brambles pulling at our clothes, we decide to turn around and go right.

The Israelis have gone from the clearing by the river. In their place, Anna's group has pitched its camp. The tents are up and the fire is going. The guides are beginning to cook. Two of the party are sitting to one side playing cards, the rest are either checking out the neighbourhood or checking their feet. Anna is sitting in the doorway of her tent, looking a little pale and weary. She waves a sock.

Onwards we go, onwards and up the deep and narrow rut of road that moves along the mountains like a snake. You have to hand it to the Incas, they might have been short but they could climb like bloody goats. Twenty feet and rest. Ten feet and rest. Thirty and throw yourself on a rock. 'How much cocoa do you think they chewed?' gasps Victor. One of the straps on his backpack is threatening to break. My Dr Marten's, soaked through now, are starting to hurt my feet. Victor checks the map included in our entrance fee, vaguer even than the one we bought in Quito. Not much farther, he decides. There's a campsite just up from the river. He gives me an encouraging pat on the shoulder. *You can make it to the river, can't you?*

I look around. To our left there is jungle. To our right is open space and below it jungle. 'What river?' I ask.

Victor points to the dark line on the map. 'That river.'

By the time we reach the river dusk is beginning to settle over the forest. It's getting cold. The path ends abruptly in rocks and trees, passable, perhaps, to an agile Inca who isn't lugging a pack half his size with him, but trickier for your average white person.

Victor stares at the map like an old-time seer staring into the still-warm intestines of a sacrificial lamb for clues to the future. Is that a plague? a famine? part of the trail? 'It's definitely on this side of the river,' he says, managing to make it sound like a question. He raises his head and gazes upstream. 'It must pick up again further along.' He jabs a finger at the map. 'See?' he says. 'There should be a campsite right about there,' maybe half a mile on and back up the bank. He waves his hand towards the water. 'We just have to get past that.'

I gaze upstream, too. That is a small but interesting falls. 'Oh, is that all?' I lean my pack against a rock, easing the weight for a few minutes while I wonder in the casual way one does if it will pull me under and cause me to drown should I slip.

We jump rocks and walk logs to get to the other side so that we can then jump more rocks and walk more logs to get back again. Almost as much fun as it sounds.

There are two tents, one large and yellow, one small and blue and green, already pitched in the clearing above the river. The Israelis are stretched out in front of the yellow tent, finishing their supper; Wolfgang and Sylkie are hunched around their stove, cups of coffee in their hands. Cutlery clatters, steam rises from the cups, easy, relaxed voices drift among the trees as the daylight fades. It's a homey and inviting scene, like a full-colour holiday ad – this year why not try camping in the Andes?

We pick a spot off to one side and struggle with the tent. There are pegs missing. There's a rip in the roof we didn't see before. The zip is tricky. The Israelis light their lantern and start playing cards as Dieter and his girlfriend shuffle into the clearing. She still isn't smiling. Dieter snaps their bright green tent up in one and a half minutes while his girlfriend sits on a stump and watches.

Victor goes off for water while I start the stove. This one, Señora Muñoz assured us, is easy. We won't have any problems with this stove. I decide to take it as a good sign that she's right. This is not like our Whisper Lite: it starts first time; it burns blue and clean; it doesn't go out. My feet will stop aching. My boots will dry out. My breathing will return to normal. After a meal and a good night's sleep I will be able to face tomorrow not with the enthusiasm of a galley slave, which is all I can muster at the moment, but with that of a bold adventurer.

Victor returns from the opposite direction. 'When you have to go to the loo,' he says, pointing just beyond our clearing to where the trail picks up again, 'it's right around that bend.' He holds the torch on the pot while I add the soup mix to the vegetables. 'Remember to cover your shit with a rock.'

Sometime in the night it starts to rain.

But isn't it beautiful, the mountains magical, the sky within reach? As you climb ever further into the clouds and look down at the dense, verdant valley so full of secrets and memories, don't you feel that you've lost your hold on time? Isn't the overwhelming silence full of voices and music, ghosts whispering in the trees, skitting through the ruins of storehouses and way stations, nimbly slipping ahead of you up the steep, narrow steps that were already worn when the first Spanish foot touched Inca soil? Isn't it worth the hardship and pain just to sit on a stone stair and watch the sunlight falling across your hand, imagining the men who might have sat on this same stair centuries ago, at peace with the planet, certain of their destinies, gazing towards Machu Picchu, thinking of home?

Probably.

But none of us are paying that much attention to the immutable beauty of the landscape or the cracks everywhere in the moment of now. One of the Italians is ill. Dieter and his girlfriend have turned back. Anna is miles back, still struggling towards the highest point, after which, we used to believe, the trek would become immeasurably easier. Even the Israelis and Wolfgang and Sylkie have fallen behind us, slowing down.

'No,' says the blonde in her sharp, perfect English. 'I think we go this way.'

Coming down, we are discovering, is no easier than going up. Your muscles still strain, your breath still stumbles, your pack still gets heavier and heavier – and slips suddenly on its faulty strap, threatening to break or at least to roll you down a rocky slope, if you're Victor. If you're me, you've started to hobble. The rain still falls.

'No,' says Victor, pointing left and behind us. 'I think we go that way.'

The blonde shakes her head. Insecurity is not a problem of hers. 'No, this way,' she repeats, smiling at us thinly. She isn't going to be talked out of anything by Englishmen dressed in dark green plastic and rubber boots.

Günther nods, giving an I-don't-like-them-much-either look to his new companion. 'She is right,' he says. 'We go down here.'

'All right,' says Victor. 'You go down there. We're going left.'

Left takes us back down to the river, miraculously enough where we wanted to go. Victor looks at the sky. 'I wonder if we should risk taking off the wets?'

'Not me,' I say quickly. To get off the wets I'll have to take off my Docs. If I take off my Docs I may never get them back on again.

At least the land is level here. We pick up speed, though not so you'd notice – all it means is that we have to stop only to readjust Victor's damaged strap and give me, limping seriously now, a chance to catch up; not to breathe. We beat our way through the thick vegetation, a little more like Professor Bingham hacking his way through the underbrush than Buggs and Daffy.

At the first campsite in a quiet clearing before the trail heads uphill once more – the campsite we, of course, don't want – we stop for lunch. We're just cutting the cheese when Günther and the blonde come tromping through the bushes. '

'It wasn't that way,' she says to Victor as though he misled her. 'Obviously, we wanted the left.'

We're just biting into our sandwiches when Wolfgang and Sylkie turn up, dry and human-looking in their lightweight raingear. 'It's going to rain,' says Wolfgang, nodding skywards. 'You'd better eat fast.'

We're eating fast when it starts to pour.

The ex-soldiers, too accustomed to physical hardship to worry about wets, slodge through our dining room, smiling amongst themselves.

Victor stuffs the last bit of soggy sandwich into his mouth. 'I hate it when they get ahead of us,' he says.

So much does Victor hate the Israelis overtaking us that we spend the next few hours staggering past each other up the high, slender steps that wind up the mountain to the next campsite, the one we do want. The Incas may have been short, I decide as I lead the way up yet another peak, but they had to have long legs. Or they hopped. Or the whole thing is a hoax: they never built this road, it was made by aliens trying to confuse us.

'I'm going to have to stop,' I gasp as we reach a narrow bend. 'Just for a minute.'

Victor is right behind me. 'Keep going,' he hisses. 'We're almost at the top.'

I keep going, despite the stake being driven through my feet and the hoover working on my lungs. We're almost at the top, we're almost at the top.

At what should be the top, another peak appears, twisted round with more impossible steps.

Desperation allows me to speak even though I can't actually breathe any more. 'I'm begging you. Just one minute.'

He glances behind us. The Israelis aren't exactly running up the path, but they are gaining. 'Just to that next curve.'

At the next curve Victor says, 'We're almost there. Look, there's the top. We'll rest there.'

There is no top, that's the answer. This is the road that really does go on forever.

'One minute,' says Victor.

I collapse on a rock. Thank God he doesn't have a watch.

Pissing down one minute, blue skies the next. That might be a description of the Andean weather, or it might be a description of my changes in mood. Now that we've reached the campsite in the valley, green trees and a stream beside the clearing, the shell of an Inca building just a few metres away, I am happy again. This isn't so bad after all. It's still daylight and, first at the site, we've pitched our tent, we've unloaded our bags, we've made an afternoon cup of tea. I sit log next to Victor, gazing in new appreciation at the stairway of ca on the opposite peak, climbing into the clouds.

'This is great,' I say. 'Maybe we can have a leisurely meal tonight, play a game of backgammon.' Maybe even take off my socks for the first time and see what's happening to my feet.

'They're coming,' says Victor.

I look to the left. Just passing the hut that was here before Pizarro are Wolfgang and Sylkie. They wave. We wave back.

'And the tent will have a chance to dry out.' I pass him the chocolate and raisins and start to pour out the rest of the tea. 'Maybe my boots will even have a chance to dry,' I continue, still hope's sucker after all these months.

Victor says, 'They're not stopping.'

I look up. Wolfgang and Sylkie aren't stopping, stooped and lagging, they're heading towards the stairway.

'It's too soon to stop, I think,' calls Wolfgang. 'There are better ruins further on.'

'It'll be dark soon,' I say to Victor. 'I hope they make it in time.' I'm delighted we're not them, that we run no risk of trooping through the night.

Victor says, 'Here comes the army.'

The army marches past us, too, also stooped and also lagging. One of them is carrying two packs now, and one is following the other two well behind. They don't smile or wave.

The guides from Anna's group turn up next. They start setting up camp between us and the ruins.

'They would be the ones who stay here,' mutters Victor, his eyes on the last Israeli as he crawls up the mountain on his own.

My happiness has started to fade. The stairway that was so eerily beautiful twenty minutes ago is beginning to look considerably less alluring.

Victor puts down his cup and glances up at the sky.

What it's beginning to look like is a threat.

Victor stands up. 'Come on,' he says. 'Let's go.'

I look at our tent, perched near the river, and our sleeping bags drying on a tree. 'Go?'

He doesn't hear me. He's already walking away.

'But what about supper?' I shout, limping after him. 'What about backgammon? What about drying out the tent?'

'There'll be time for all that,' says Victor, handing me my sleeping bag. 'It isn't far.'

Not if you're an Inca, maybe, but by my standards it's far. By my standards, just making it to the next peak is far. Every foot up the too-deep but still nearly perfect steps is as good as a mile on Camden High Street. I climb and stop, climb and stop, unmoved by the skill that built this staircase, built the huts into the rocks, built the arch that leads down to the valley; unmoved by the little lake that shimmers near the summit. I don't so much stagger up those last few feet as force myself up them with the last few grams of strength I have. My sister and my mother and my friends were right. I'm never going to return to tranquil, safe and civilised London. I'm going to die out here where I have no more business being than the conquistadors, and like them my last thoughts won't be of home but of what a fool I was ever to leave it.

Victor is below me, looking out at the grey strip of road that continues downwards along the side of the mountain; the dark strip of river that cuts through the hidden valley, dense and green. Not speaking, we stand together beneath the arch at the next plateau.

'Look!' whispers Victor, his finger to the clouds.

I look. Gliding graceful, certain circles in the enormity of space above our heads is a large, lean bird, black against the watery paleness of the twilight sky. Still dumb, we pass through the arch, unhurried, undesperate now, safe with the long, steady centuries of ghosts. Ahead of us on the thin grey road are the sure grey walls of an Inca outpost sprawled across a ragged hill, hidden away like a wizard's castle. We stop breathing together. The remoteness is total, the stillness absolute. The moment holds. This time, it seems, we've found the entrance back.

Tomorrow night we will set up our tent in the Doorway to the Sun, looking down on Machu Picchu in all its tattered beauty as the low clouds drift by. The next day we will reach Machu Picchu itself – and in some ways it will be as disappointing as I'd feared, a sprawl of ruined buildings and an expensive restaurant and hotel; tourists snapping pictures of each other looking out of windows, waving from staircases, mugging on the sacrificial stone where Che and Granados once discussed the revolution. And in less than a week we'll arrive at Heathrow in the middle of a bomb scare – welcome back – but tonight we are here.

It doesn't matter that it is dusk before we make our camp. Doesn't matter that we cook in the dark and the stove runs out of gas before the pasta's done. The little grey tent is pitched in what was once someone's room, doorways and steps to other rooms and niches in the mossy walls. Victor and I light candles and sit in the night, side by side on the highest staircase, looking out over the ruined town, magical and mysterious in the shine from a billion stars, watching the night from long ago.

At the other end of the enclave, Wolfgang signals good night with his torch.

'You know,' says Victor. 'I think that really was a condor.'

We watch a star fall freely through the universe.

I think so too.